Children's Britannica

CHILDREN'S BRITANNICA

Volume 14

PONY—RHYME

17 68

ENCYCLOPAEDIA BRITANNICA INTERNATIONAL, LTD
LONDON

First edition 1960

Second edition 1969

Third edition 1973

Revised 1975, 1976, 1978, 1981, 1985

ISBN 0 85229 190 6

Printed and bound in Great Britain by
Hazell Watson & Viney Limited,
Member of the BPCC Group,
Aylesbury, Bucks

PONY. There is not much difference in appearance between horses and ponies, except in their size, for ponies are smaller than horses. In some countries a full-grown pony is counted as a horse if it is more than 14·2 hands high. (A hand is 10 centimetres.) Elsewhere, 15 hands is the limit for a full-grown pony. The breed of horse known as the Arab is always known as a horse, whatever its height, and the pony used in the game of polo is always a pony whether it is tall or short.

Apart from their size, ponies must have certain qualities. These are hardiness, sure-footedness, ability to live on small amounts of poor food and rather more intelligence than horses —except those of the Arab breed—possess. All true breeds of ponies, wherever they are found, have these qualities, but many modern show ponies are simply small versions of the thoroughbred breed of horses.

It is doubtful whether any true pony breeds exist outside Europe, Asia and Africa. The "cow" pony of the western parts of the United States and the Criollo of South America, which are unbeatable for endurance and the power to live on little, are really horses.

European Ponies

Probably the best known and most important ponies of Europe are those belonging to the mountain and moorland group found in England, Scotland and Wales. There are nine distinct breeds, and each is quite different in appearance from the others.

The New Forest. It is not known what the ancestors of this pony were, but it was known as far back as the days of King Canute in the 10th century. It is a handy, sturdy pony, which is good to ride and a useful animal for drawing traps (which are light carts) and it is the most

W. Suschitzky

A pony with her young foal. A foal can walk soon after it is born.

Jonathan III, a prizewinning New Forest stallion. The New Forest is a sturdy breed which is found in Hampshire. It is one of the mountain and moorland group.

Heatherman, a champion Exmoor stallion. The rather prominent eyes which are typical of the Exmoor pony can just be seen in this photograph.

Photographs by John Nestle

Coed Coch Madog, a champion Welsh Mountain stallion. White is an unusual colour for this breed, for the ponies are generally grey, brown or chestnut.

easily managed pony of the mountain and moorland group. It is up to 14 hands tall, and is found in the New Forest in Hampshire.

The Dartmoor is a charming and very tough pony which takes its name from Dartmoor in Devonshire, where it roams in an almost wild state. It is an ideal riding pony for children, and it is also very popular in the show ring because it is so handsome. Officially it must not stand higher than 12·2 hands, and it may be any colour except piebald (white with black markings) or skewbald (white with brown, the reddish-brown colour called bay, or chestnut).

The Exmoor. The next-door neighbour of the Dartmoor is the Exmoor pony, which resembles it only in size and hardiness. Its muzzle is mealy, or spotty, and it has the same mealy colouring all round the eyes (which are known as "toad" eyes) and on the upper parts of the legs, often running up into the underside of the body. The colour is bay or brown. The mane is very thick and often falls on each side of the neck, which is unusual. The eyes are very large and stick out, rather like the eyes of Arab horses.

The Welsh Mountain is generally said to be the most beautiful of the mountain and moorland group. It is hardy and tough but very gay and dainty, with a lovely Arab-like head. Officially it must not be taller than 12 hands, and it is therefore the smallest pony except for the Shetland. Greys, browns and chestnut are the main colours. Like the Dartmoor, it is a popular pony for children.

The Fell. This pony is nearly always black, though it is sometimes dark brown or other colours. It belongs to the English Lake District of Westmorland and Cumberland. Before the days of trains it was chiefly used to carry lead in panniers (baskets) from the mines to the coast, for it is good at carrying heavy loads. It is a very hardy, sure-footed pony, with a thick tail and mane of coarse, curly black hair.

The Dales. Though now a very different pony from the Fell, owing to crossing with other breeds, the Dales were originally the same. Fells live on the west of the Pennine Range and Dales on the east.

The Highland. From Scotland come both the largest and strongest of the European group of ponies—the Highland—and the smallest—the Shetland. There are three types of Highland pony : the Barra, up to to 13·2 hands, the riding pony, 13·2 to 14·2 hands, and the stronger and heavier Mainland, which stands at round about 14·2 hands. This pony is very strong and easily managed, and it is beautiful as well, for it has large, wide-open and expressive eyes and a rather Arab-like head. It will climb steep hills and carry heavy weights.

The Shetland. Although it is the smallest pony, the Shetland is almost the strongest. At one time it was much used as a pit pony to draw trucks underground in coal mines, because of its small size. Today it is mainly a family pet and is used to carry young children. When in its wild state on the Shetland Islands it is the toughest of all ponies. The average height is 9·3 hands.

The Connemara is the only Irish pony. It comes from Connaught, on the west coast, and until recent years it lived in a wild state under very hard conditions. It is a pony of wonderful strength and health and able to endure a good deal. It is also gentle and intelligent. It stands at 13 to 14 hands, and may be almost any colour, though greys and duns (dull grey-browns) seem to be the main ones.

The Iceland. More than 1,000 years ago some Norwegians went to settle in Iceland and took some animals with them, including some ponies. They are very hardy animals and are ridden, driven and used for pack carrying. Many of them are dun in colour, and they have very thick manes and tails.

The Norwegian pony is between cream and dun in colour, with a dark stripe down the back, running from the forelock just above the fore-head, through the mane to the tail. The legs are dark and occasionally striped. Norwegian ponies stand from 14 to 14·2 hands high. They are strongly built animals with thick necks and broad chests. It is thought that they may be descended from the wild horse of Mongolia.

Asian Ponies

There are several groups of ponies in Asia as well. The following are some of them.

The Russian Steppe. Among the toughest of all ponies, the Russian Steppes stand 13 to 14

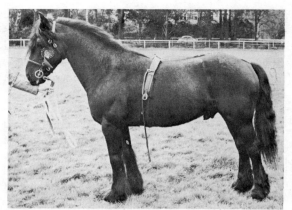

Roundthwaite Lucky Jim, a prizewinning Fell pony stallion. This hardy, surefooted pony gets its name from the fells (hills) of the Lake District from where it comes.

Harviestoun Rusko, a champion Shetland pony. The Shetland is the smallest kind of pony but is very strong, as can be seen from its thick, powerful neck.

Photographs by John Nestle

Golden Treasure of the Glen, a prizewinning Connemara mare. The Connemara is the only Irish pony and is very strong and enduring.

□ Read about PONY TREKKING in the blue pages of this volume

hands, and are immensely strong. They are rather heavy and have ugly heads. Their legs are very short and muscular, with small, hard hooves, and the bitter climate in which they live causes them to grow coarse, protective hair. They belong to the Mongolian group.

Shan or Burmese. These ponies are also descended from the Mongolian breed and are bred in Burma, the Malay peninsula and in much of China. They are slower than the Steppe pony.

The Spiti is the native pony of Kashmir and the borders of Nepal (both north of India). It moves with a short, quick step, and long strings of Spiti ponies can be seen with their heads close to the ground, apparently half asleep. They enjoy walking on the edge of frightening precipices among the mountains. Spiti ponies, too, are Mongolian in origin.

The Manipur pony was named from a state in Assam, India, where it had been bred for thousands of years. Although it may be counted as a distinct breed, it would seem that both the Mongolian and the Arab breeds have influenced it. Carrying packs, riding, polo and racing can all be done by the Manipuris.

The China pony is not really a breed at all, but a mixture of Mongolian and Turkestan breeds. It is small and tough, with a heavy head and shoulders, small eyes, thick neck, deep chest and iron-hard hooves. The coarse mane and tail are long enough to sweep the ground.

POOR LAWS.

Although the Christian Church had always taught that poor or ill people should be helped, it was not until the 16th century that laws were passed to set up funds of money for such people. These were known as the poor laws, and at first their main purpose was to keep law and order.

In Tudor times there were swarms of beggars wandering around England without homes or jobs. They were able to work but had been turned adrift because of the enclosing of land; that is, the taking of land for sheep farming. (See ENCLOSURES.) At the same time the prices of everything was very high, and this increased the poverty. The number of beggars alarmed the rich people, for many were strong and sturdy and quite capable of causing trouble.

The first poor law was passed in 1536, but the most important of the early ones was that of 1601, now known as the Old Poor Law. Under this law each parish (see PARISH) collected money for the poor from every owner of a house. With this money old people were to be provided for, poor children taught a trade and beggars given work. However, in country parishes it was often difficult to get these laws carried out.

The coming and spread of the industrial revolution, when factories began to be built and machinery to be used (see INDUSTRIAL REVOLUTION), brought new difficulties. In 1834 the New Poor Law was passed and life became much harder for poor people. It was argued that providing poor people with money helped to make them lazy and troublesome, so more institutions known as workhouses were built and all the poor, young and old, men, women and children alike, were sent to them and treated with great harshness to compel them to do all they could to find work. Charles Dickens had much to say about workhouses in his novel *Oliver Twist*.

In the 20th century, however, when people were beginning to understand the causes of poverty, methods of treating people who could not help themselves were improved. Old people were paid a weekly pension. The government introduced insurance schemes for the sick and unemployed, and the Poor Law of 1834 was broken up. The modern "welfare state" took its place. You can read more about this in the separate articles INSURANCE; NATIONAL HEALTH SERVICE; PENSIONS; SOCIAL SERVICES.)

POP,

from "popular", is a term used to describe a style of art which became fashionable in Britain and the United States in the 1960s. In one way Pop artists set out to poke fun at "serious" art, which often seemed to have little to do with ordinary people's lives. They chose for their subjects themes from popular culture, such as films, television, comics and advertisements, which people saw all around them every day, often repeating the same image many times.

Among the best known Pop artists are the American painters Roy Lichtenstein, whose paintings look like comic strip pictures, and Andy Warhol, who has painted soap cartons,

Andy Warhol's soup can was painted in 1965.

soft drink bottles and soup tin labels. In Britain Peter Blake and David Hockney are painters who have done work in the Pop style.

POPE, Alexander (1688–1744).

One of the greatest poets of the 18th-century "age of satire" was Alexander Pope. Born in London, of Roman Catholic parents, he suffered from ill health throughout his life. He was short and stooped, and was very sensitive about his appearance. But he had a brilliant wit, and at his home beside the River Thames at Twickenham he entertained many famous writers and politicians who became his friends.

Pope became successful for his verse translations of the writings of the Greek poet Homer. He also edited the plays of Shakespeare. In the *Essay on Criticism* he set down his views on the art of writing. But he is enjoyed today mostly for his satirical poetry, in which he made fun of fashionable society and also attacked his own enemies and critics. A good example is *The Rape of the Lock*, written in mock-serious style, which is about a young lady of fashion who is robbed of a lock of her hair. *The Dunciad* contains clever portraits in verse of his enemies and makes fun of their dull, fussy opinions.

Pope made great use of the rhyming couplet: this has two lines rhyming together and containing a complete thought. This is an example.

"True wit is nature to advantage dressed,
What oft was thought, but ne'er so well expressed."

Pope's poetry was admired abroad and translated into French and Italian. He was particularly skilful at putting his ideas into epigrams (see EPIGRAM). Two often-heard examples are "Fools rush in where angels fear to tread" and "To err is human; to forgive, divine."

POPE, THE.

The Pope is both a spiritual ruler and the ruler of a state : he is the head of the Roman Catholic Church and is recognized by Roman Catholics as the representative of Jesus Christ on earth. At the same time he remains sovereign of the tiny Vatican City State which has diplomatic relations with many countries and observer status at the United Nations. It is important to distinguish between the Pope's spiritual authority and his power as state ruler. (See ROMAN CATHOLIC CHURCH; VATICAN CITY.)

There have been Popes for 1,900 years—since the time of St. Peter who was the first bishop of Rome. The word "pope" means "father", and it was a name given generally to bishops, the fathers of their flocks. However, from the 4th century onward the title has been reserved for St. Peter's successors, the bishops of Rome. When Jesus Christ died, Peter took charge of the infant Christian Church and after many missionary journeys went to Rome. He was put to death there, probably in A.D. 64, and from the earliest times Christians believed that he was buried there. Early in the 4th century the Emperor Constantine built a church over what was believed to be his tomb. The present Basilica of St. Peter's is on the site of Constantine's church. Archaeologists, working in the foundations in the 1950s, claimed to have found the position of St. Peter's grave.

For 300 years after St. Peter's death the Roman emperors persecuted the Christians, and many of the first Popes were put to death. The places of their tombs can still be seen in the catacombs (see CATACOMBS) under the city. Although the Christians of different cities could not easily communicate with one another there are records which prove that the early churches in other cities recognized the bishops of Rome as their leaders.

In A.D. 313 the Emperor Constantine gave the Christians the right to practise their religion publicly. Churches were built in Rome and the Popes were everywhere acknowledged as having authority in the church.

In 330 Constantine left Rome and made Constantinople (in what is now Turkey) the capital of the Empire. For centuries Rome was at the mercy of barbarian invaders from the north. The Popes remained in Rome and though they were powerless to stop the invaders they converted many of them to Christianity. St. Leo the Great (reigned 440–461) is the best remembered Pope of this time, and he did much to develop the feeling of unity in the church. But political disagreement and difference of language (Greek in the east, Latin in the west) led to continual rivalry between Rome and Constantinople, and the Christians in eastern Europe and Asia grew farther and farther apart from those in western Europe.

At the end of the 6th century Pope Gregory the Great (590–604) began a great period of missionary work. He sent St. Augustine to England (see AUGUSTINE OF CANTERBURY; GREGORY, SAINT), and other priests to Germany, France and Spain, thus bringing more people to a knowledge of the message of Christ.

In the 8th century the kings of the Franks conquered most of western Europe. When they were converted to Christianity they strengthened the spiritual authority of the Popes by recognizing them as the spiritual rulers of all the Christians of the Frankish dominions.

It was also in the 8th century that the Popes began to have territory of their own and thus became earthly rulers as well as spiritual rulers. In 756 King Pepin of the Franks gave the territories of Ravenna, Bologna and Ferrara (all in Italy) to Pope Stephen III. The idea behind this was to provide the Popes with money and thus make them independent of earthly rulers, and to give them extra dignity. However, it brought great disadvantages, for as soon as the Popes had territories to rule over they became involved in political rivalries. During the 9th and 10th centuries the Papal States (as the Popes' territories were called) were brought near to ruin by internal strife. In the 11th century the disputes between the eastern Christians and the western Christians came to a head, and in 1054 those in the east broke away and set up their own church. (See ORTHODOX EASTERN CHURCH.)

Even before this last blow fell, Pope Leo IX (1049–1054) had already seen that reform was needed, and with the help of his great adviser Hildebrand he began to carry out reforms. The Papal States were freed from the interference of the Roman nobles, the arrangements for electing new Popes were improved and church discipline was restored. In 1073 Hildebrand was elected Pope and under the title Gregory VII continued the reforms. The Popes who succeeded him, especially Urban II, Alexander III and Innocent III, were men of great ability. They played an important part in English history by supporting the bishops against the kings. Adrian IV was himself an Englishman (see BREAKSPEAR, NICHOLAS).

The Popes at this time were called upon to settle disputes between kings, they gave the lead in the Crusades, founded universities and did much to build modern Europe by their efforts to make people obey the law—both the law of the church and the laws of states.

However, the Popes became entangled in national rivalries. As yet nobody questioned their spiritual authority but all the kings wanted to gain their support in the political sphere. The French kings, who were rapidly becoming the most powerful in Europe, had the greatest influence over the Popes and from 1305 to 1377 the Popes (who were mostly Frenchmen) lived in France. Pope Benedict XII built the papal palace at Avignon in southeast France, and Rome was abandoned for more than half a century.

The return of the Popes to Rome did not end the trouble, for national rivalries led to disputed elections. When Urban VI was elected Pope his violent conduct led to the election of a rival, Clement VII, who was known as an anti-Pope. From 1378 to 1417 there were rival claimants, each backed by different states. Unity was not restored until the election of Pope Martin V in 1417. This schism, or series of disputes, was political rather than spiritual, but it damaged the reputation of the church in many countries.

However, the Papacy was restored to full vigour in the 16th century by a long line of most remarkable Popes. The first of these. Paul III, was faced with many problems. European countries were at war, Martin Luther was leading Germany to revolt against the church in what was known as the Reformation, and the discipline of priests was very slack. (See LUTHER, MARTIN; REFORMATION.) Paul's reforms were successful and the Council of Trent (which he summoned in 1545) condemned the errors of many heretics, stated clearly what the correct beliefs were in cases where there was uncertainty, and inspired new enthusiasm. He authorized the foundation of the Society of Jesus (see JESUITS) which sent missionaries to such far countries as America, India, China and Japan. The Popes Paul IV and Pius V put the reforms of the Council of Trent into practice.

This Counter Reformation, as it is called, greatly increased the spiritual power of the Popes, although their earthly, political power was growing less. Two centuries later their political power was threatened again—by the French Revolution and the Napoleonic Wars that followed it. (See FRENCH REVOLUTION; NAPOLEONIC WARS.) Napoleon captured Rome and Pope Pius VI was made a prisoner in France. His successor Pope Pius VII was also taken prisoner and kept in custody at Fontainebleau in France. Finally by 1870 the Italian government had seized all the Papal States and made them part of Italy.

Pope Pius IX was one of the youngest Popes elected in modern times (he was 54) and he had one of the longest reigns (1846–1878). To begin with he was very popular : he freed political prisoners, started gas-lighting in the streets of Rome, began a railway system and reformed education and the prison service. But after 1848—the year of revolution in Italy—the Pope began to denounce the errors of the contemporary world. His successor, Leo XIII (1878–1903), had a very different temperament. He tried to come to terms with the modern world. He set out the rights of factory workers to decent conditions and a living wage. He also gave great encouragement to missionary work.

The Popes at this time would have nothing to do with the new Italian state which had taken control of the Papal States in 1870. This quarrel was ended in 1929, with the signing of the Lateran Treaty. The Pope recognized that the Papal States were now definitely part of Italy ; and in return the Pope was recognized as the sovereign of the Vatican City State.

Pius XII (1939–1958) became Pope just before the outbreak of World War II. His constant pleas for peace were ignored. He denounced Nazism, Fascism and Communism as harmful doctrines which led to crimes against God and man. His successor, John XXIII (1958–1963) was born a peasant. He quickly won people's hearts by his goodness and simplicity. His most lasting achievement was to summon the Second Vatican Council in 1962. (The First Vatican Council was held in 1869.) Nearly 3,000 bishops from all over the world gathered at this meeting to discuss relations with other Christians and with Jews. They tried to bring Christian doctrine up to date. The Council lasted for four years and was concluded by his successor, Paul VI.

Paul VI (1963–1978) became the first modern Pope to travel widely outside Italy. While he was Pope the Mass began to be said in modern languages instead of in Latin, and good relations with other Churches were encouraged. He died in 1978 at the age of 81. His successor, John Paul I, died after being Pope for only 33 days. But in that short time he did much to get rid of papal pomp.

The college of cardinals then elected Karol Wojtyla, Archbishop of Cracow in Poland. He took the name John Paul II to show that he intended to continue the simpler style of his predecessor. His command of language and his easy way in public quickly made him popular.

There are separate articles on some of the Popes. The article ROMAN CATHOLIC CHURCH describes how a new pope is elected.

POPLAR. The word poplar comes from the Latin name for the tree's genus, or group, *Populus*, because it was the *arbor populi* or "people's tree" of the Romans. Poplars belong to the family Salicaceae and are related to the willows. They are found in all northern temperate, or mild, countries.

There are many varieties of poplars, among

them being the black, grey and Lombardy poplars, and the aspen with its quivering leaves. The best known is the tall and beautiful Lombardy poplar, which is shaped rather like a church spire. It is a favourite tree for planting along straight roads in Europe. All the Lombardy poplars in England are said to be male and to have been raised from suckers and shoots.

The black poplar has pointed, sticky buds and its leaves have jagged edges and are shiny and green on both sides. In the grey poplar the buds and undersides of the leaves are covered with white cottony stuff. The black and grey poplars are not as slender as the Lombardy poplar. They have male flowers hanging in long thick catkins and female flowers growing on separate trees.

The aspen is also known as the trembling poplar because its leaves, which are very pale underneath, quiver in the slightest breeze. It is the only kind of poplar that has not been brought to Britain from another country. (See ASPEN.)

A very tall poplar is the western balsam poplar, so named because of its scent in spring, which is like that of the gummy substance called balsam. Another scented poplar is known as balm of Gilead.

The timber of poplars is used for matches and

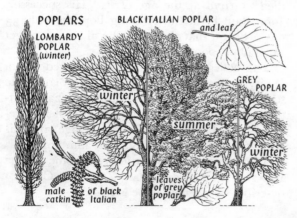

POPLARS

LOMBARDY POPLAR (winter)

BLACK ITALIAN POPLAR and leaf

GREY POPLAR

winter

summer

winter

male catkin of black Italian

leaves of grey poplar

packing cases and sometimes for floors. Poplars have very long and spreading roots and are therefore not suitable for growing near houses because they may harm the foundations.

POPOCATEPETL MOUNTAIN. Southeast of the Mexican capital, Mexico City, rise two majestic snowclad mountains, Popocatepetl

Ewing Galloway
Smoke drifting from the snowy crown of Popocatepetl.

and Ixtacihuatl. The higher of the two is Popocatepetl, 5,452 metres high, which is a dormant (sleeping) volcano. Its name comes from the Aztec language and means "the smoking mountain". (See AZTECS.) Popocatepetl has not had a serious eruption since 1540 but smoke still rises from its crater, which is about 450 metres wide and 300 metres deep. Sulphur is dug from it.

Firs and oaks grow on the lower slopes and higher up there are pine trees and many alpine plants. Higher still, the sun beats fiercely on the slopes of loose lava and ashes and the glare from the snow-covered summit cone is blinding.

Ixtacihuatl (5,286 metres), whose name is Aztec for "the white woman", has three summits and seen from Mexico City looks like a shrouded human figure. For this reason most of the people call it *la mujer gorda*, or "the fat woman".

POPPY. One of the brightest of all flowers is the poppy. In gardens it is grown in many different sizes and shades of red, pink and mauve; in cornfields wild poppies with small scarlet flowers can be seen growing among the ripe corn. The Iceland poppy, which is found in the Arctic

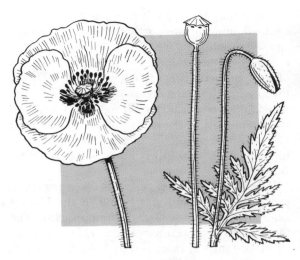

A poppy flower, seed-box, opening bud and leaf.

and Antarctic, is red and orange, and a wild poppy with blue, purple or yellow flowers grows in western Europe, including the west of England, Yorkshire, Wales and Ireland, although the blue poppy grown in gardens comes from central Asia and China.

Poppies belong to the genus, or group, *Papaver* and their family is called Papaveraceae. They open in June and July; the buds lift their heads, the two enclosing sepals fall off, and four or six petals, sometimes with a round black mark at the base, unfold. These petals, as soft as silk and as fine as gossamer, are neatly folded and refolded in the bud so that when they first open they are all creased. In the centre are rings of purple stamens.

A poppy bud hangs down because one side of the flower stalk grows more quickly than the other. When the flower is ready to open, however, the stalk is quite straight and firm. Insects visit the flowers for their pollen. The seed case, which acts rather like a pepperpot, has firm, smooth walls and little holes protected by a cap. Out of these holes the seeds are shaken when the plant sways in a strong wind.

When the stems of some poppies are snapped, a milky liquid oozes out. This is called latex, and is carried by a network of vessels over the whole plant. The drug opium is made from the latex extracted from the unripe seed cases of the opium poppy. (See OPIUM.)

In many gardens grow the gay Shirley poppies, which are not only scarlet but crimson, orange, salmon, smoky-blue and other colours, although without the black mark. They were grown by W. Wilkes of Shirley in Surrey in 1880. He found in his garden a corn poppy which had a white lining to the edges of its petals. He took seeds from this plant and after some years he bred the Shirley poppy.

Poppy Day

World War I ended on November 11, 1918, and after that Britain and many other countries kept November 11 as a day of remembrance in honour of the men and women who had been killed during the war. Since World War II Remembrance Sunday (the Sunday nearest to November 11) has been kept in memory of men and women in the services killed in both wars: the Saturday before is called Poppy Day.

Artificial poppies, made by people who were disabled in the wars, are sold on or just before that day. The money is used by the Royal British Legion to help ex-servicemen and women in need. The poppy was chosen because it grows in the fields of Flanders where so much fighting took place in World War I.

POPULAR MUSIC. The songs and tunes which teenagers enjoy are usually different from those which their parents, or even their elder sisters and brothers, enjoyed when they were teenagers. Generally, popular music is music which is popular at the time it is written: in ten years' time another style of music may be popular. Very few popular songs are written down in musical notation in the way that, say, a Beethoven symphony was when it was composed. Instead, they are often fairly short and repetitive, so that people will recognize them after hearing them only a few times.

Every age has had its favourite songs. But how did people in the past get to hear them? In ancient Rome, street musicians sang the songs which were popular in the theatres. Throughout the Middle Ages minstrels (see MINSTREL) travelled across Europe earning their living by singing contemporary songs at court and in fairgrounds and market places. (See BALLAD.)

Later, when people lived in the new industrial towns, theatres and music-halls (see MUSIC-HALL) provided the popular songs of the day.

The invention of the radio and the gramophone brought popular songs to a much wider audience. Gramophone records were popular in the 1920s but it was not until the 1950s that pop records became the big business they are today. Rock and roll, which had its roots in American Negro blues, became popular among young people. This special popularity with one particular age group made it different from other kinds of music. Also, young fans could see their favourite singers on films and on television. As a result, some performers—Elvis Presley and the Beatles, for example—became famous throughout the world.

At different times, popular music has been influenced by many types of music. See the articles JAZZ; FOLK DANCE AND SONG.

POPULATION. The word "population" comes from the Latin word *populus*, "the people", and means the number of people who live in a certain place, whether it be town, village or country. There are altogether about 4,260,000,000 people in the world. (The population is increasing by about 70,000,000 every year.) The total area of the world's land surface is about 150,000,000 square kilometres, if the frozen wastes of the Antarctic continent are included. Thus, if the whole population of the world were spread evenly over its land area, the number of people occupying each square kilometre would be 4,260 ÷ 150, or about 28. This figure is called the world's density of population. The density of population for any country or region shows how thickly it is peopled. It is obtained by dividing its population by its area.

The population of a country can be accurately found only by counting it. This counting is generally done by the government and is called taking a census. Censuses of one kind or another have been taken ever since rulers have had to raise taxes or collect men to fight in their armies. The Bible tells how King David had a census taken of the fighting men of Israel, and how a terrible pestilence broke out shortly afterwards. Many people believed that this was sent by God

to show that He did not like His people being counted, and this was partly the reason why censuses were unpopular right up to the 19th century. The Romans took a census of citizens and of their property every five years, in order to fix the amount that each person should pay in taxes. The famous census taken in England by William the Conqueror in the years 1085–1086 counted not only the people but also their oxen, pigs, mills, pastures and fish ponds. (See DOMESDAY BOOK.)

The modern kind of census is taken regularly every few years and was begun in the United States in 1790 and in Great Britain in 1801. The interval between censuses is generally ten years so in Britain the most recent have been 1961, 1971 and 1981. (There was no census in 1941 because of World War II.) The questions asked at a census include not only those about the number of people in each house and whether they are male or female, but also about age, marriage, children, language, education and housing. The answers provide many facts valuable to the government and to social workers. A partial census, in which facts are collected from (for example) one household in ten, may be used to obtain more detailed information. Partial censuses are taken in Britain.

The figures for world population are estimates, for in many parts of the world census figures are rather inaccurate. Where no census figures exist, the population has to be estimated. The Earth's population has not only increased, but has increased at an ever-growing rate. In 1650 it was 545 millions; in 1750 it was 728 millions; by 1800 it had increased to 906 millions and by 1850 to 1,171 millions; rising to 1,608 millions in 1900 and to 2,389 millions in 1950. By 1980 the figure was well over 4,000 millions and scientists forecast that by the year 2000 the population is likely to be over 6,400 millions.

In advanced industrial countries the rate of population growth is slow. For example, it will take almost 700 years for the population of Britain to double, but those of Libya and Kuwait will double in only 18 years at their present rates of growth. The countries with the largest populations are China and India.

For a number of reasons the density of population varies from one region to another. Deserts, high mountain ranges and places with a harsh climate or a poor soil are generally thinly populated either because people are unable to live there or because they do not want to. If a map of the world is shaded according to the population densities of the different regions, with darker shading for the higher densities, the darkest patches show in western Europe, the eastern United States, the Nile Valley in Egypt, India, Java, China and Japan. In western Europe and the United States the dense populations have been encouraged by a temperate climate, fertile soils and rich supplies of coal and other minerals. In Egypt, India and China most of the people live in the basins of the great rivers, where the soil is extremely fertile. Java has fertile soil and a hot, damp climate in which crops grow rapidly.

In other areas of the world, however, the density of population is very low. Northern Canada, the mountainous parts of the western United States and much of South America except the coastal regions, have a density of less than 4 people to the square kilometre. The same is true of huge areas in Africa, Arabia, central and northern Asia and Australia. The Antarctic continent, having no permanent population, has a zero density. One of the illustrations in the article GRAPH shows the density of population in Great Britain.

A country is over-populated when it contains more people than it can support. Countries which cannot grow enough food for their populations must buy food abroad, paying for it with money earned either from selling oil, coal, timber or other products, or by carrying goods for other nations or from the tourist trade.

The populations of many poorer, less developed nations of the world are growing at a faster rate than the richer, more industrialized countries. For example, countries in South America, Africa and Asia have the fastest growing populations whereas those in Europe are increasing only slowly. The less developed nations are therefore held back in their efforts to produce enough food and a higher standard of living for their peoples. Any advance made is countered by the continual additions to the number of people who have to be fed, housed and educated. Although in some of these countries there is also a high death rate, and many children die in infancy, this does not compensate for the numbers of children being born.

Programmes to help keep populations steady, by encouraging people to have fewer children, are being carried out by governments in many parts of the world. Improved methods of food production are also being sought.

If these population programmes are not successful, the world's resources, especially of food, will become increasingly strained as countries try to cope with an ever growing demand.

PORCUPINE. Like a hedgehog the porcupine is covered with sharp prickles, but unlike the hedgehog it is a rodent, or gnawing animal, and has strong teeth. Porcupines are slow moving and tend to be solitary. There are many

The crested porcupine is about 1 metre long.

kinds of porcupines and they are divided into two quite distinct groups, the Old World porcupines of Africa, Asia and Europe and the New World porcupines of North and South America.

Some porcupines have more dark, coarse hairs

and brown-black fur than quills. Both hair and quills are erect. It is sometimes said that porcupines can shoot their quills like arrows at an enemy, but this is not true. However, when an enemy attacks a porcupine it is likely to get sharp quills stuck into both face and paws. If attacked, the porcupine drives its powerful tail against its attacker. The quills are easily detached from the skin and bed themselves in the enemy. The spines of baby porcupines are soft when they are born.

Porcupines mostly eat plant food such as bark and leaves. In the tropics some kinds do damage by eating root crops such as yams, and in Canada they often kill trees by eating their bark. They live in burrows, hollow logs and caves.

The largest is the crested porcupine, which is about 1 metre in length and lives in southeast Europe, much of Africa and southern Asia. Its dark brown and white quills are long and sharp.

American porcupines, of which the biggest is the Canadian porcupine, spend quite a lot of time climbing trees. Their short, sharp quills are usually barbed and they are mixed in among ordinary hairs. The spiny anteaters of Australia, although sometimes called native porcupines, belong to another family. (See ANTEATER.)

PO RIVER. The longest river in Italy is the Po, which rises near the French border and flows east across northern Italy. It is 652 kilometres long. Its basin includes the low, flat Lombardy Plain which is the most fertile part of the country. To the north and west of the plain rise the Alps and to the south are the Apennines. On the east, the plain ends in the marshy delta where the Po and Adige rivers enter the Adriatic Sea.

The tributaries of the Po that flow from the Alps are bigger and more numerous than those flowing from the Apennines. Many of them rise in the glaciers and snowfields of the high Alps and are particularly full when the summer sun melts much of the snow and ice. They also drain the beautiful Italian lakes. Some of their valleys are followed by the roads and railways coming from France and Switzerland. These tributaries also provide water power to make electricity for factory towns such as Milan and Turin. On the plain, ditches have been dug to carry water from

the Po to fields where rice is grown. Tugs and barges can use the river below its junction with the Mincio River near the city of Mantua.

PORPOISE. Among the smaller members of the whale family is the porpoise. It looks like a fish and (except when it leaps out for a few seconds) spends all its life in water—yet it is a mammal. It is warm-blooded, the female feeds her young on milk and it has lungs instead of gills with which to breathe.

There are several different kinds of porpoises, including one that lives only in the Black Sea. The common porpoise, which is more often seen round the coasts of Great Britain than any other member of the whale family, is up to 2 metres long with a rounded, streamlined body. It has a black back and a triangular back fin, which appears above the surface of the water as the porpoise rolls along. It can be distinguished from its relative the dolphin by the fact that its head is rounded, whereas the dolphin possesses a beak-like structure in front. (See DOLPHIN.) The porpoise has about 100 sharp teeth and lives on fish, especially herring and mackerel.

Porpoises go about in small groups known as schools and come into bays and the estuaries, or mouths, of rivers.

The porpoise's back fin breaks the surface of the sea.

PORTSMOUTH is an English city on the Hampshire coast. Old Portsmouth lay in the southwest corner of Portsea Island, but the city today stretches to the mainland beyond. With such a fine, sheltered harbour facing the English Channel, it is easy to see why the Royal Navy has made its home here. There are sailors every-where, countless memorials to seamen, Nelson's famous ship "Victory" in dry dock and all manner of modern warships in the harbour.

Today Portsmouth is the greatest naval port in the United Kingdom. Its vast dockyard is a giant workshop for naval ships and near by there are barracks, training schools and supply depots. There are other industries as well, such as brush and corset making, but the navy is the life-blood of this city of about 197,000 people. East of the dockyard area lies Southsea, a residential district and popular holiday resort.

Until the 12th century Portchester, three miles to the north, was the chief port on Portsmouth Harbour. There the remains of a Roman fort and a mediaeval castle still stand. As Port-chester declined, Portsmouth grew. An import-ant mediaeval base and dockyard, it has been of outstanding national importance since the 17th and 18th centuries.

Portsmouth suffered severely in air raids dur-ing World War II. The main shopping centres have been rebuilt and the Guildhall restored. St. Thomas's Church, since 1927 a cathedral, is the oldest of the few ancient buildings. The house where the Duke of Buckingham was murdered in 1628 can still be seen.

Famous men born in the city include Charles Dickens, the novelist; Isambard Brunel, the engineer; and John Pounds, who started schools for poor children.

Crown copyright

Frigates of the Royal Navy in Portsmouth Harbour

PORTUGAL is the most westerly country of the mainland of Europe and is the oldest ally of Great Britain. Together with the Atlantic islands of the Madeira and Azores groups, the Portu-guese Republic covers an area somewhat larger than Ireland. Spain borders Portugal to the north and east and the two countries make up what is known as the Iberian Peninsula. How-ever, there are wide differences between them.

In most places the Portuguese coast is low and sandy and has a fairly wide coastal plain behind it. The main ports are near the mouths of the larger rivers, all of which rise in Spain and form part of the boundaries between the two countries. The Minho River, forming part of the northern boundary, runs through a mountainous district that stretches south to the Douro River (see DOURO RIVER). South of the Douro the country inland rises to 1,991 metres in the Serra da Estrêla, the highest mountain range in Portugal. Farther south the land falls away to the fertile plains of the Tagus River (see TAGUS RIVER). South of the Tagus the country changes greatly, most of the inland regions being flat or gently

Courtesy, Portuguese National Tourist Office

Lisbon, the capital of Portugal, stands on the bank of the River Tagus. Shown here is Edward VII Park, which was given its name after King Edward VII of Britain visited the city in 1903.

rolling tablelands. The chief river in southern Portugal is the Guadiana.

The climate is generally mild and pleasant and cool winds from the Atlantic bring enough rain to most parts except in the extreme south. The vegetation is rich and tropical plants grow beside those common in northern Europe. Pines, chestnuts, limes, elms, oaks and cork-oaks are common, as also are olives, palms, cactuses and mimosas. However, there are also wide areas of heath, scrub and barren mountain slopes. There are few large wild animals.

The Portuguese are people of rather mixed ancestry but most of them are short, dark and sturdy. Every Portuguese province has its own national costumes, those of the northern districts being the most colourful. The women wear very wide skirts of brilliant greens and reds, richly embroidered, or black skirts covered with glittering sequins. Over their long-sleeved white blouses they have little sleeveless jackets of the same colour as their skirts, and their head scarves also match the rest of their costumes. The men's clothes are mostly dark colours except the "campinos" (cowboys), who often have bright red sashes and green stocking-caps. Red and green are favourite colours because they are the colours of the national flag.

The Portuguese eat a lot of fish. They are very fond of dried cod which they call *bacalhau*. .Other foods **are** rice, maize, beans and fruits, especially grapes. Most cooking is done in olive

FACTS ABOUT PORTUGAL

AREA (including the Azores and Madeira): 91,641 square kilometres.

POPULATION: 10,056,000.

KIND OF COUNTRY: Independent republic.

CAPITAL: Lisbon.

GEOGRAPHICAL FEATURES: In the north are mountainous plateaus, or tablelands, between 900 and 1,500 metres high. The central region is crossed by mountain ranges rising to over 1,500 metres in places. In the south are lowlands with gentle hills and marshy plains. The two main rivers are the Tagus and the Douro.

CHIEF PRODUCTS: Wheat, maize, rice, rye, potatoes, wine, olives, cork, sardines and tunny fish; wolfram, iron ore, tin; textiles, fabrics.

IMPORTANT TOWNS: Lisbon, Oporto, Coimbra, Setubal, Funchal (on Madeira).

EDUCATION: Children must attend school between the ages of 6 and 14.

MONEY UNIT: Escudo.

oil. Besides football, the favourite sports are hockey on roller-skates and bull-fighting, but it is forbidden to kill the bull. The country people love singing and dancing.

The Portuguese language, which is also spoken in Brazil, sounds rather harsh and "twangy". Among the greatest of Portuguese writers was Luis de Camoes (1524–1580), one of the best poets of the 16th century. His most famous work is *Os Lusiadas*, which means "the heroic story of the Portuguese". He was also a soldier and he visited many parts of the world with the Portuguese discoverers, writing his great poem while he travelled. As a boy he studied at Coimbra, whose university is still one of Portugal's two chief seats of learning. The other one is Lisbon University. Children must attend school between 6 and 14, but there are still a good many of the older men and women who cannot read or write, although their numbers are dwindling rapidly. Most of the people are Roman Catholics.

Portugal has many beautiful buildings, including the monastery and church in Belem, Lisbon, and the Abbey of Santa Maria at Batalha, which is said to be the loveliest building in the Iberian Peninsula except perhaps the Alhambra in Spain. The castles at Evora and Sintra are fine examples of Moorish-style architecture. Near Braga is a shrine which every pious Portuguese tries to visit at least once in his life. A more modern but very popular place of pilgrimage is Fatima, where the Virgin Mary appeared in a vision to some children in 1917.

The only large cities are Lisbon (see LISBON) and Oporto, which with its seaport Leixoes lies near the mouth of the Douro River and which has a thriving trade in wine and fish.

About a third of the people of Portugal are employed in agriculture. The chief food crops are wheat (grown in the south), maize and potatoes (grown in the north) and rice (grown in the river valleys). Fruit is abundant. Setubal is famous for oranges and Elvas for plums. Olives grow in most districts, and oranges, lemons, figs, locust beans and almonds in the south. Central Portugal is a garden of vineyards from whose red-purple grapes the wine called port is made. This wine takes its names from Oporto, and

much of it is sent to Britain. Another important product is cork, which is made from the bark of the cork-oak tree. Coastal fisherman catch sardines and tunny (tuna) fish and every summer a fleet sails to fish for cod on the Grand Banks off Newfoundland.

Portugal has little good coal but there are minerals such as tin, tungsten, copper, iron and manganese. They were not mined very much in the past because of a shortage of power. This shortage has been made up by very large hydro-electric power schemes, in which the rivers are dammed to provide electric power (see WATER POWER). The chief of these schemes are at Picote on the Douro River, at Castelo do Bode on the Zezere River and at Paradela on the Cavado River. Apart from the factories preparing cork and canning sardines and tunny fish, most of the manufacturers produce goods for sale within Portugal and for export to other parts of Europe. These goods include woollen

Courtesy, Portuguese National Tourist Office
Oporto, also called Porto, is the country's second largest city and the centre of the port wine trade.

Courtesy, Portuguese State Office; Portuguese National Tourist Office
Above: The Museum of coaches at Lisbon. Right: A Portuguese woman makes sausage skins.

and cotton cloths, and also cement and paper.

Most of the Portuguese railways, like those of Spain with which they connect, have a broad gauge (distance between the rails) of 1·65 metres (5 feet 6 inches). The roads are generally good and there are bus services between most towns. The peasants still occasionally use oxen for pulling ploughs and carts, and donkeys for carrying their goods.

Besides the Azores and Madeira, the only Portuguese territory overseas is Macao, which lies between Hong Kong and Canton in China. Portugal's African possessions (Angola, Mozambique, Portuguese Guinea and the Cape Verde Islands) became independent after the change of government in Portugal in 1974. (See An-GOLA; AZORES; CAPE VERDE ISLANDS; GUINEA-BISSAU; MADEIRA ISLANDS; MOZAMBIQUE.)

History

Portugal was once the Roman province of Lusitania. For many years after the fall of the Roman Empire the history of Portugal was the same as that of Spain. In 1143 Portugal became an independent kingdom and the reign of John I (1385–1433) saw the beginnings of a great overseas empire. Much of this was the work of his son, Prince Henry, who helped in training the explorers and in planning their voyages. (See HENRY THE NAVIGATOR.) Thanks to explorers such as Bartholomew Diaz and Vasco da Gama, Portugal became the master of the southern and eastern seas. (See DIAS, BARTHOLOMEU; GAMA, VASCO DA.)

After that there was a steady decline in Portugal's power. Weakened by extravagance and a disastrous war in Morocco, the country fell into the hands of King Philip of Spain in 1580, and the Portuguese Empire was fiercely attacked by Spain's great enemies the Dutch and the English. In the year 1640 Portugal regained her independence under King John IV, but her eastern empire was never the same again. Her most important colony, Brazil, remained until 1822 when it became independent. (See BRAZIL.)

In 1910, King Manoel II was overthrown and Portugal became a republic with a president. For more than 15 years there were continual changes of government and political squabbles while the country remained poor and troubled. In 1926 some military leaders seized power and restored order. Dr. Antonio de Oliveira Salazar, a professor of Coimbra University, had the task of saving the country from bankruptcy and succeeded. He became Prime Minister in 1932 and gave the country a new

The Castelo dos Mouros is a Moorish castle on a mountain peak near Sintra.

constitution, with a national assembly elected by the people. Salazar, a virtual dictator, was prime minister until 1968.

The Anglo-Portuguese alliance, many times renewed, dates from 1373. Portugal fought on the side of the Allies in World War I. In World War II it remained neutral but helped the Allies by allowing Britain to use the Azores as a base.

The conservative regime of Salazar (who died in 1970) was followed by a government led by Marcello Caetano. In 1974 the army overthrew the government. A new coalition government, which included opponents of the Salazar regime, was formed and political prisoners were freed. One of the first actions of the new government was to withdraw from the Portuguese territories in Africa where Portuguese troops had fought against nationalists. The former colonies (Angola, Mozambique, Guinea-Bissau and the Cape Verde Islands) became independent. Many Portuguese settlers returned to Portugal.

The return of democratic government after so many years was not easy. Portugal faced many problems. To improve its trade and to play a more active part in European affairs, Portugal applied in 1978 for full membership of the E.E.C. or Common Market.

POSEIDON was the Greek god of water and of earthquakes. He was the son of Cronus. The Romans called their water-god Neptune, and the article NEPTUNE tells some stories about him.

POSTER. At one time or another everyone has probably seen a man with a paste-brush sticking a poster on to a wall or a hoarding. It may have been just one piece of paper or several which fitted together to make a picture or design with lettering. The purpose of this kind of poster is to advertise, or give a message. (See ADVERTISING.)

The first thing a poster has to do is to attract attention. It does this by its design and colour, or perhaps by the unusual way in which the designer conveys his message. A poster has to give its message much more quickly than a colour-page in a magazine, for example, because it must be seen from a wall or hoarding by people in a hurry, whereas the magazine page is seen by people sitting in a comfortable chair at home. Lettering on the poster has to be easily read.

For this reason a poster is drawn in strong, bold lines to present a clear picture which will catch people's attention.

Although you will sometimes see hand-

An 1890s lithograph poster by Toulouse-Lautrec for the Ambassadeurs cabaret in Paris.

This farm safety poster, by a 12-year-old boy, won a competition. It is a collage made from pieces of felt.

painted posters in shop windows or on church notice-boards, most posters are printed copies of an original design. Before a poster is printed, the people who want it to advertise their goods have to decide what kind of message they want to get across. They then consult a designer who makes a rough sketch. He may decide to use a photograph, a painting or some other form of artwork as the basis for the design. What he must do is make his design memorable; it must catch the eye and sell the goods. But it must also be easy to copy and print. To make sure, the designer consults the printer about the colours to be used and so on.

Posters are not only used in advertising. Posters designed by famous artists, such as Toulouse-Lautrec, are collected as works of art. Cheap posters (whether of a well-known painting, a pop singer or an amusing animal) are popular as wall decorations.

POST OFFICE. The familiar postman who delivers our letters is a messenger, and many years ago people who carried mail were called messengers or couriers. (The word "mail" comes from an old word for a pack or bag.) Today, much of the Post Office's work goes on at night. Trains and planes carry the mail across the country, and vans collect it from the railway station or airport and bring it to the sorting office. There the letters are sorted into the correct order of the streets and houses which the postman visits on his "walk" or delivery route. As well as delivering the mail, the Post Office also collects letters from post boxes (in Britain

these are called "pillar" boxes because of their shape).

This kind of postal service is common throughout most of the world. But the idea of sending letters by messenger is a very old one. It was long ago discovered that the fastest way to send a message was to use a chain of messengers, stationed at posts along the road with fresh horses. The posts were often roadside inns. This was how the modern postal system began. The Bible mentions posts—the Old Testament tells how "the posts went with the letters from the king and his princes throughout all Israel and Judah". Generally, these services were reserved for the king or ruler and his officers, although as time went by noblemen, bishops and large trading companies had their own postal systems.

The growth of knowledge and prosperity in the 17th century made people dissatisfied with the postal system in England. They needed a faster and more reliable system for exchanging news and information. Important changes were made by Thomas Witherings, who was postmaster in 1635. He arranged posts travelling night and day on the main roads, with branch services working to and from the post towns on the way. A single letter could be sent

Courtesy, Post Office

Commemorative stamps are particularly popular with stamp collectors. Here artist Gordon Beningfield finishes the design for one of a special set of butterfly stamps.

18

from London to Edinburgh but the charge was fairly high—8*d*. each way. An act of parliament in 1657 set up a government monopoly of the postal services; that is, no one else was allowed to conduct a postal system. In 1680 the London merchant William Dockwra started a penny post within the capital, but as soon as it became profitable it was taken over by the government.

The great improvements made to the roads towards the end of the 18th century led in 1784 to the introduction of regular mail coaches for the posts. Examples of the times taken were: London to Edinburgh 60 hours, to Falmouth (Cornwall) 29 hours; but it cost 1*s*. 1½*d*. to send a letter of a single sheet from London to Edinburgh in 1812.

An enormous improvement was made by Sir Rowland Hill (1795–1879). He realized that the real cost of conveying letters lay not in carrying them from one town to another but in collection and delivery, and saw that if people could be encouraged to exchange more letters the postal charges could be greatly reduced. Hill was a former school teacher and it took him some time to persuade the government that his ideas were sound, but at last it was agreed that the postage should be the same over any distance within the kingdom. On January 10, 1840, it became possible to send a letter weighing not more than half an ounce anywhere in the British Isles for a penny. Hill also introduced postage stamps which had to be bought at the post office and stuck on the letter by the sender to pay for the postage. This replaced the practice of collecting postage when the letter was delivered.

Hill's scheme, which was much assisted by the spread of railways, was a great success. In the period 1839 to 1864 the number of letters rose from 76,000,000 to 679,000,000 a year. It is now about 9,800,000,000 a year, and in addition some 183,000,000 parcels are carried and more than 5,000,000,000 stamps are printed for Britain alone.

Before the introduction of steamships, overseas mail was carried in small, fast sailing vessels called packets, which were owned or hired by the post office. Their place was taken by steam vessels early in the 19th century and the years from 1840 saw the growth of a service of fast mail-carrying steamers on important routes.

After World War I a regular airmail service between London and Paris was started in November 1919. Nowadays nearly all letters and postcards for Europe are carried by air without extra charge. Air-mail letters from Britain can reach some countries outside Europe such as Canada, the United States, South Africa, Australia and New Zealand in two or three days, and almost any other part of the world within a week.

Postage stamps were introduced in 1840, but nowadays a good deal of mail is paid for in another way. Many business firms obtain a Post Office licence to use their own postal franking machines. These print impressions of the various postage charges directly on to envelopes, wrappers and labels, the impressions taking the place of postage stamps. The total postage paid is recorded by the machine. These machines, of which over 130,000 are used in Britain, were introduced in 1922.

The Work of the Post Office

Postal services are nearly always managed by the state, usually under the control of a minister. In Britain the Postmaster-General headed a government department run by civil servants until 1969, when the Post Office became a public corporation under a chairman and a board of control. In 1981 the postal and banking services of the Post Office were separated from the telephone and other communications operations of British Telecommunications (British Telecom). Day to day running of the postal services is controlled by four board members responsible for mail services and property; personnel; finance and counter services; and marketing. The United Kingdom is split into ten regions or postal boards. Sub post offices are usually part of a shop in places where the amount of postal work is not enough to call for a separate post office. Altogether, there are over 22,000 post offices in the United Kingdom. This makes it convenient for the post office to be used also for business connected with the government.

The letter post handles postcards, newspapers and small packages as well as letters, while the parcel post deals with packages up to a weight of 22.5 kilograms. Letters, unless intended for registration or recorded delivery, are usually posted in street pillar boxes or at post offices. Parcels and registered letters are handed in at the post office, though parcels can be collected from business customers. Registered letters often contain documents or objects of value which require special care. The poster pays an extra charge so that, if the letter is lost or damaged, more compensation is payable than would be for an ordinary letter. The compensation fee service is available to customers wishing to post parcels containing items of reasonable value. The recorded delivery service provides customers with proof of posting and delivery, but does not provide special handling. Every year about 30 million compensation fee parcels and registered letters and 27 million recorded delivery items are carried.

In 1968 the Post Office introduced what is called the "two tier" system for letter post within the United Kingdom. Anyone who posts a letter can choose between the first-class service, which ordinarily delivers the letter the day after posting, or the second-class service which usually takes one or two days longer and is cheaper. Other services have since been introduced. *Datapost* is a fast, reliable delivery service for urgent packages. *Expresspost* is a same-day messenger service which delivers locally and nationally. *Intelpost* is a high-speed facsimile transmission service (see FACSIMILE) which operates nationally and internationally, while *Electronic Post* uses computer technology to speed up and simplify large mailings.

Each post office has a counter at which business with the public is done. A head post office has offices away from the counter for the head postmaster and the clerks. On the ground floor is the sorting office and a large yard for the mail vans. The posted letters and packets are taken to the sorting office where their stamps are cancelled, or postmarked, before being sorted and placed in sealed mail-bags for distribution by rail, road, sea or air.

Many of the sorting operations formerly done by hand are now done by machines. Some sorting offices have machines that automatically "face" the letters—that is, arrange them so that they are all facing the same way—and cancel the stamps. These machines work by detecting phosphor lines printed on the stamps and turn the letter so that the stamp is in the right-hand top corner. The phosphor lines also enable the machines to separate first-class from second-class letter mail.

In nearly all sorting offices letters are sorted into boxes which are generally arranged in nests of 48. The size is limited by the reach of a worker's arms. At many post offices sorting is done by machines which sort 16,000 letters an hour into 150 boxes. The address must first be put into machine language, which is done by an operator who by using a keyboard imprints a pattern of phosphorescent dots on the envelope. The pattern imprinted corresponds to the Postcode written on the envelope by the sender. Every address in Britain now has a Postcode, which people are asked to show on their writing paper so that their correspondents can copy it when replying. The Postcode should always be the last item of the address, for example:

Miss R Black
46 Kings Road
Kempston
BEDFORD
MK4Z 8LA

Once the keyboard operator in the sorting office has transcribed the Postcode into the corresponding dot pattern, the letter can be rapidly sorted at high speed at all stages of its journey to the postman who delivers it.

Most mail is posted in the afternoons and evenings and the main burden of carrying it falls on the railways. In London, the Post Office has its own underground railway linking the chief sorting offices with Liverpool Street and Paddington stations. It has 10 kilometres of tunnels 20 metres below ground level and its electric trains, which have no drivers, are automatically controlled. They travel at 55 kilometres an hour between stations and carry about 45,000 bags of mail a day.

In Britain travelling post offices are attached to some trains. These consist of one or more coaches specially built as sorting offices. Some-

Courtesy, Post Office

Above: Mail is loaded on to one of the Post Office's underground trains. Top right: Workers sort letters into first and second class and stack them the right way up ready to be postmarked. Lower right: Letters are delivered to any address, no matter how remote it might be. Below: Today a lot of first-class mail is transported for part of its journey within Britain by plane. Work goes on through the night at East Midlands airport as mail planes arrive. Some mail bags continue their journey by road and others by rail.

times the entire train consists of postal coaches. In these travelling post offices, which were established in 1838, the letters for the various towns along the journey are sorted. Night flights carry mail out of the London airports to link up with chartered flights from Liverpool and East Midlands airports. Luton airport is used for the Datapost services.

Most post offices deal with all types of business and in the course of a few minutes may sell stamps, sell or cash postal orders, saving certificates or premium bonds, or accept a deposit or withdrawal from a National Girobank savings account. Clerks may also issue one-year passports, pay family allowances and retirement pensions, issue a television, dog or motor car licence, or accept a parcel through the hatch at the end of the counter.

Post office clerks must also answer questions about all kinds of post office business, ranging from customs declarations on parcels to the best way of sending valuables through the post. All these questions, however, are answered in the *Post Office Guide* which can be bought or consulted at any post office counter.

The idea that the postal services of the different countries should work together was first thought of in the 1860s and in 1874 the first Universal Postal Convention was signed. This international agreement provided for broadly comparable rates of postage and standard methods in the exchange of mail between states. The headquarters of the Universal Postal Union are at Berne in Switzerland.

POTASSIUM is a metal that most people never see. It is very soft, so light that it floats on water, and melts at about the same temperature as beeswax. Potassium combines readily with other substances. Its brilliant silvery shine is soon dulled by a film of tarnish formed by combination with the oxygen of the air. When thrown on water, potassium sets free the hydrogen in the water and the hydrogen burns with a violet flame. The metal must therefore be protected from air and water and is normally kept covered with oil in bottles.

As potassium combines so readily with other substances it cannot exist in the pure state in nature, but many of the compounds formed by its combination with other elements are very stable—that is, they do not easily break down into their separate parts. It exists in many kinds of rocks and clays but cannot be extracted from them. Most of the potassium used is obtained in the form of potassium salts from minerals such as carnallite and sylvite. These are mined at Stassfurt in Germany and in France, Poland, Spain, the U.S.S.R. and the United States. Potassium salts are also extracted from the briny waters of the Dead Sea (Palestine) and from the beds of dried-up lakes such as Searles Lake in California (United States).

All land plants contain potassium, which they obtain from the soil. Potassium carbonate was first prepared by dissolving the ashes of plants in water and then boiling away the liquid in iron pots. For this reason an early name for it was potash ("pot-ashes"). The ash from a wood fire is rich in potash and helps growth when spread on the soil. By far the greatest use of potassium is in fertilizers such as potassium chloride and potassium sulphate. These replace the potassium taken from the soil by the crops (see FERTILIZER). When combined with other substances, potassium forms compounds which are used for making soap, glass, match-heads, gunpowder, fireworks, disinfectants, drugs, paints and photographic chemicals. Potassium cyanide is a deadly poison.

Pure potassium was first prepared in 1807 by the English chemist Sir Humphry Davy, who obtained it by the electrolysis of caustic potash, or potassium hydroxide. (See ELECTROLYSIS.) Davy was so delighted with his success that he danced with joy around his laboratory.

POTATO. The common potato is now one of the chief foodstuffs of the western part of the world, but it was not known in Europe and North America until the middle of the 16th century, and it was not generally grown on English farms until the end of the 18th century.

The home of the potato is the highlands of the Andes mountains in South America, and it has been cultivated by the American Indians for many hundreds of years. It was brought to Europe by the Spaniards who conquered South

America in the 16th century. The crop was taken to England after it reached Ireland, but it is not known for certain who introduced it.

At first the potato was a luxury, eaten on important occasions, and was grown only in the gardens of the rich. In Ireland, however, large crops were produced from the 17th century onward, and the potato quickly became the main food of the Irish people. The importance of potatoes increased greatly at the coming of what is known as the Industrial Revolution, when large numbers of people began to work at machines in factories and much cheap food had to be grown on farms for them. By the middle of the 18th century, potatoes rather than bread were the main food of many people.

In the winter of 1846 and 1847 blight attacked the potato crops, and there was famine in Ireland and the Scottish Highlands. (You can read more about this in BLACK FORTY SEVEN or POTATO FAMINE.) During the second half of the 19th century food from America and Australasia began to reach Europe. Bread, meat and dairy products became more plentiful, and potatoes were not such an important food.

Today the principal countries that produce potatoes are the U.S.S.R., Germany, Poland, the United States, France, the United Kingdom, Czechoslovakia, the Netherlands and Ireland.

Potatoes are part of the plant's underground stems.

In England the largest crops come from Lincolnshire, the Isle of Ely, Norfolk and Yorkshire, and in Scotland from the Lothians, Angus and Perthshire.

By far the greater part of the world's potato crop is used for human food. "New" or "early" potatoes are the first to be dug up and they appear in the shops in the late spring; they are delicious but they cannot be cooked in as many ways as "old" potatoes, the usual method being to serve them boiled, with mint or parsley. In factories, "old" potatoes are made into potato crisps, dried and riced potato and mashed potato powder. On the continent of Europe and in Ireland, large quantities of cooked potatoes are fed to animals. Potatoes can be used to produce pure starch, distilled alcohol and other chemicals. They contain starch, calcium and vitamin C.

Potato Growing and Pests

The potato is related to the tomato and to the tobacco plant. All belong to the Solanaceae family. About 100 varieties of the potato grow wild in South America, and fourteen are cultivated by the Indians.

The potato plant cultivated nowadays is between 25 and 75 centimetres high. It has green or purple stems and large leaves growing in pairs. The flowers are white, yellow, purple or striped, and the fruit is a small green berry, like a green tomato, containing tiny kidney-shaped seeds.

The potatoes themselves are tubers, or short, thick parts of underground stems and in them is stored the starch manufactured by the plant. The "eyes" correspond to the buds on an ordinary stem and from them new shoots arise. Normally potatoes are grown from small tubers called seed potatoes.

Potatoes grow best in light, deep, loamy (rich) soils, but heavy crops can be grown on peaty and sandy soils. They are planted in furrows about 70 centimetres apart. The potatoes are planted 40 centimetres apart for an ordinary crop and 30 centimetres for an early crop, and even closer together for a crop of seed potatoes. Fertilizers are also spread in the furrows and the potatoes are covered with 6 centimetres of soil.

Early potatoes are lifted (dug up) in the late spring and summer, but the main crop is left until the tops are withered. The potatoes grown on farms are dug by machines called potato spinners, or potato diggers.

Unfortunately, potato crops are liable to be infected with fungus diseases, such as blight, dry rot and mosaic disease, and catch virus (germ) diseases spread by green-fly (aphids). Other insect pests are the dreaded Colorado beetle and the eelworm. The larva, or young, of the striped black and yellow Colorado beetle causes great destruction in the potato fields. Eelworms are tiny, worm-like pests which destroy potato stems near the ground.

Sweet Potatoes

The sweet potato, although very like the ordinary potato except for its sweet taste, belongs to the Convolvulus family and so is quite a different plant from the ordinary potato. Its home is America, and it was not taken to Africa and Asia until after the days of Christopher Columbus. Sweet potatoes are usually planted from leafy slips set in ridges or mounds. The trailing tops make a close cover over the ground, and the sweet potatoes are ready to gather in from 4 to 12 months' time, according to the kind.

POT-HOLING AND CAVING is the sport

of underground exploration. Caves which have deep vertical openings or which contain pitches (that is, steep drops) are called pot-holes. These are commonest in Yorkshire, so the sport is there called pot-holing.

Apart from seaside caves almost all caves are found in limestone. This rock is slowly dissolved by the weak acid in the rain-water which trickles through the natural cracks in it. The cracks may be further enlarged by water flowing through them after it has sunk underground through openings called sinks, swallow-holes or swallets, some of which may be open caves. Some caves, like Wookey Hole in Somerset, act as outlets for underground streams, while many are now dry.

The caver or pot-holer enters a world of darkness and carries an electric or acetylene lamp, usually fixed to a miner's helmet, with a candle for emergencies. He has to scramble over rough piles of rock, wade through water, slide down mud banks and crawl through narrow openings. For this he wears strong nailed boots and old but warm clothing covered by a boiler suit. It is unwise to enter caves alone and help is needed when descending pitches. These require portable rope ladders which are carried coiled up and are unwound and tied together when wanted. For descents of more than 7 metres a lifeline is tied round the chest and held by a man at the top to prevent accidents. Pitches approached from below need special equipment.

Deep, open pot-holes like Gaping Gill Hole (103 metres) in Yorkshire are sometimes descended on wooden seats attached to a wire rope wound on to a winch. Deep pools must be swum or crossed on inflatable boats, which are pumped up with air rather like a motor-car tyre. Short flooded passages can be got through by ducking right under the water, but longer ones can be explored only by specially trained cave-divers wearing breathing apparatus.

Most pot-holers belong to clubs which arrange visits to known caves or search for new ones. The members usually make their own ladders and tackle and in many caving districts have built huts or repaired old buildings where they can stay. There are more than 60 caving clubs in Great Britain, for the most part in Durham, Yorkshire, Derbyshire, Somerset, Devon and Wales. There are also active caving clubs in Australia, New Zealand and South Africa. Ireland has many fine caves, especially in the counties of Clare, Fermanagh and Sligo, but not many cavers or pot-holers.

Caves and their Exploration

Some of the finest caves are found in Austria, France, Switzerland, Spain, Yugoslavia and the United States. The world's deepest pot-hole is Gouffre Berger (1,097 metres), near Grenoble in France. The longest cave system is the Mammoth Cave in Kentucky, United States, whose known passages are more than 240 kilometres long. Those of the Hoelloch in Switzerland are more than 58 kilometres long and those at Postojna in Yugoslavia can be visited by electric train and are about 22 kilometres long.

In Great Britain all the known caves and potholes have been explored and much effort is needed to find new ones. Occasionally, huge caves may be found. For example, in 1946 two men cleared away some rock and stones and discovered the entrance to Ogof Ffynnon Ddu in Brecknockshire. It was found to be a maze of passages more than 6 kilometres long. The cautious exploration of such a cave is a thrilling experience, for the caver enters a world previously unknown to man. He may find the way blocked by a roof fall, or he may be halted by a steep pitch. Again, he may find beautiful groups of stalactites and stalagmites, surrounded by draperies formed by mineral substances left by the water (see STALACTITE AND STALAGMITE). After the discovery comes the slower work of making a map of the cave, photographing its more striking sections and searching for the small animals—often blind—which spend their whole lives underground. This kind of work is more scientific than ordinary caving and is called speleology, but all speleologists must learn pot-holing and caving to begin with.

United Press International Photo

A pot-holer lowering himself into a cave in Kentucky.

POTS AND PANS. The containers and vessels used for cooking and serving meals are usually called hollow-ware by the makers and ironmongers, but most people think of them as pots and pans. They have a long history. Prehistoric man invented pottery vessels for cooking and the first metal pots and pans were made of bronze. Later, when men had learned how to refine (purify) metals, copper and iron were used.

For centuries cooking pots changed little. In the middle ages the most important was the great iron cauldron hung over a fire from a tripod, or three-legged support, or even by a kind of crane. It was used for boiling clothes, stewing food (for which an earthenware pot was placed inside) and even for bathing the baby! There were also bronze skillets, which stood on long legs, brass pots, iron saucepans, frying pans, gridirons, spits and flesh-hooks for roasting, mortars and pestles for mixing, and wooden or leather buckets.

In 1700 most housewives were still using iron vessels, although these were heavy and liable to rust, for as long as the open fire remained the chief method of cooking strong pots were necessary. They also had a collection of brass kettles and copper saucepans and pots which, although lighter, needed constant cleaning.

Modern pots and pans began to be developed in the 18th century when various processes were made use of to prevent rusting. The first of these was the use of tin for coating thin sheets of iron, and the tinman making kitchen goods was to be found in most towns. The production of this "tin-plate" grew rapidly in the 19th century and the manufacture of kitchen utensils became especially important in the Birmingham area. At the same time a process was introduced for coating the inside of the heavier pots with tin. Also, a new alloy (mixture) called Britannia metal, which was made of copper, tin and antimony, came into use for making tea and coffee pots. Later, these were made of an alloy called "German silver" containing copper, zinc and nickel (but no silver). This alloy is now called nickel silver and is often given a thin coating of silver by electroplating it (see ELECTROPLATING).

A method of coating iron articles with a hard,

fireproof and glossy enamel was adopted in England in 1839 and by 1850 this enamelled ware had become very popular. Later, enamelled pots and pans stamped out of mild steel largely took the place of iron and tin-plated ones.

Aluminium cooking pots were made in Germany in the 1890s but were not much used in Britain until the 1920s. They are popular because of their light weight and because aluminium conducts heat well and does not develop "hot spots" which burn the food.

Vessels of heat-resisting glass and stainless steel are also used in modern cookers. Stainless steel is not a good conductor of heat, so pans made of it usually have copper-clad bottoms. Non-stick pans are usually made by coating the metal thinly with a varnish containing silicone (a compound of the elements silicon, carbon, hydrogen and oxygen).

POTTER, Beatrix (1866–1943).

Once upon a time there were four little Rabbits, and their names were—Flopsy, Mopsy, Cotton-tail and Peter. They lived with their mother in a sand-bank, underneath the root of a very big fir-tree.

This is the opening of *The Tale of Peter Rabbit*, the first of a series of pocket-sized picture books which have been loved by two generations of children all over the world. Yet when Beatrix Potter wrote *Peter Rabbit* she had to pay for it to be printed herself. No publisher would take the risk. It is now the best loved of all her books.

Mr McGregor was quite sure that Peter was somewhere in the tool-shed, perhaps hidden underneath a flower-pot. He began to turn them over carefully, looking under each. Presently Peter sneezed— "Kertyshoo!" Mr McGregor was after him in no time.

That is a single page of the book, and opposite is a picture of Mr. McGregor turning up the flower-pots, while in the foreground Peter's ears stick out of the green watering-can where he is hiding.

It would be difficult to say which are the best of Beatrix Potter's books, apart from *Peter Rabbit*. Some say *Jemima Puddle-Duck*, some *The Tale of Two Bad Mice*, others *The Tailor of Gloucester*. This is longer and for slightly older children. It is a Christmas story of a poor tailor, his cat Simpkin and the little mice that ran through the old houses, and it reads like a fairy tale. Other popular tales are *The Flopsy Bunnies, Squirrel Nutkin, Timmy Tiptoes, Johnny Townmouse* and *Mrs. Tiggy-Winkle*.

One reason why Beatrix Potter's books are so popular is that every animal and bird in her stories seems completely real. It seems to the reader that if animals could really talk they would speak exactly as she makes them do.

Beatrix Potter was a very shy person. As a child she lived a solitary life with her parents in London, and even when she grew up her life was very quiet. She amused herself by writing stories and illustrating them for children she knew— Peter Rabbit first appeared in a letter sent to a little boy belonging to a former governess—and later she made some of the stories into books.

Beatrix Potter loved the country and in 1905 she bought a farm in the Lake District, though at first she could only live there part of the time. In 1913 she married a solicitor called William Heelis and settled down on her farm to spend the rest of a happy and uneventful life.

Courtesy, Frederick Warne and Co.
Beatrix Potter and some of the characters she created.

Courtesy, Wedgwood

In pottery factories, cups are manufactured on a machine called a jolley. The process is called jolleying. Clay is measured out into equal portions, each of which is just the right amount for one cup. One ball of clay at a time is thrown into a plaster of paris mould which will shape the outside of the cup. While the mould rotates at high speed, a metal arm—called the profile—is lowered into it. This will shape the inside of the cup. The profile causes the clay to open out and be drawn up the mould, thus forming the complete cup shape. The pottery then has to be dried, fired and decorated.

POTTERY AND PORCELAIN.

Things that are made from clay and then dried and baked hard—"fired"—in a hot oven called a kiln are known as *ceramic* materials. They include bricks and tiles as well as pottery. Many pieces of pottery are useful everyday objects like plates, cups and saucers, but pottery also includes all kinds of beautiful and ornamental articles, such as figures and vases. The pottery industry also makes many other things from clay, including tiles for walls and floors, wash-basins and electrical insulators. The usual type of pottery is called *earthenware*; two special kinds of fine pottery are *porcelain* and *bone china*.

Human beings were making and using pottery long before the times we know anything about in history. Early peoples could find clay on the surface of the ground, or by some river bed, and gradually they learned to shape it into pots and bowls which could be dried in the sun. The next step was to put the shaped clay in an open fire to harden it, instead of leaving it to dry naturally. If a clay vessel is only dried, it will become soft again if it is filled with water. If the dried vessel is fired at a bright red heat, it will become hard and will then never again become soft, even if left in water for hundreds of years.

The first potters moulded the clay into shape with their hands, or coiled long "snakes" of clay round and round to build up the sides of bowls and jugs. These methods often made the pots slightly uneven in shape. Decorations could be added by scratching patterns or by pressing cord or matting on the wet clay. Patterns were also painted on with different coloured clays.

There was a great improvement in pottery when the potter's wheel was invented. At first this was probably a round flat stone, balanced in the middle, which spun round when the potter pushed it with his hand. The clay rested on the top of the wheel, and as the wheel was kept spinning the potter shaped the clay. He was then able to make objects perfectly round and also to make them much more quickly. Later on, wheels were invented which could be worked by the potter's foot, leaving both his hands free. Today potters' wheels are often worked by electricity.

The process of firing, which was at first carried out in an open fire, later came to be done in a kiln. In early times wood was used as the fuel.

Clay that has been fired has a rough surface. In order to make it smooth and shiny a *glaze* is used. The glaze is a film of glass formed by covering the piece of ware with a mixture of materials that, when the ware is fired for a second time, melt together. One of the first materials used for glazing pottery was *galena*, or lead sulphide. A colour can be added to the glaze mixture and often the beauty of pottery comes from the shine and colouring of its glaze. A pattern or picture can also be painted or printed on the ware, which is then fired once more, but this time not so hot.

Pottery down the Ages

Greek Pottery. The pottery made by the ancient Greeks was beautifully decorated. They did not use a glaze but made their pottery shiny by covering it with a thin wash of very fine clay, sometimes mixed with other substances. They also knew that iron oxide is red if heated in a clear fire but turns black if heated in a smoky fire. By using this knowledge they were able to decorate their vases in red and black.

The Beginnings of Pottery in Europe. A thousand years later, potters in the Middle East discovered that if tin oxide is added to a glaze it makes it white and non-transparent. They also found that, if copper or silver is added to the glaze and it is fired in a certain way, pottery can be made to look like metal. The Moors later brought this knowledge to Europe, by way of Spain. The Spanish tin glazed pottery was taken in ships to Italy, but the Italian merchants thought it was from the island of Majorca and called the ware *majolica* or *maiolica*. In Italy, ware of the same type began to be made at Faenza and when it was imported by the French they called it *faience*. In Holland it was made at Delft, and it was from there that this kind of pottery came to England in about 1700 under the name *delft-ware*.

Chinese Porcelain. While all these developments had been going on in Europe, the potters of China, as yet unknown to the Western world, had been making some of the most beautiful pottery of any age. They had discovered *kaolin*, a pure form of clay that turned a pure white colour when fired, and another material, *petunse*, that helped the clay to become hard and glass-like at a lower temperature. The pottery that they made from kaolin and petunse was *porcelain*. The styles of Chinese pottery are known by the names of the Chinese dynasties ruling at the time : the most important styles are therefore called Tang, Sung and Ming. (See CHINA.)

Meissen (Dresden), Sèvres and Chelsea.—The beauty of Chinese porcelain fascinated people in Europe and many potters tried to discover how it was made. In about 1675, French potters succeeded in making a kind of porcelain called "soft-paste". The name that became best known for such porcelain was Sèvres, a place near Paris where the French royal porcelain factory was established. In 1710 a factory was founded at Meissen, near Dresden, in Germany, where craftsmen had discovered the secret of how to make porcelain of the kind known as "hard-paste", which was more nearly like the Chinese ware. Later, the French potters at Sèvres also began to make this kind of porcelain. Gradually the process became known in other countries, and during the 18th century English as well as French porcelain factories were using the new discovery. However, most English porcelain was still "soft-paste". The most important English factories that made it were at Chelsea and Bow (both in London), and at Derby, Worcester, Coalport (Shropshire) and Lowestoft.

The Staffordshire Potters. During all these years while skilful craftsmen were producing such fine porcelain and pottery for the houses of rich people, plain pottery was still being made in every country for ordinary household use. The jugs and bowls and mugs were covered with glaze in plain colours such as green, brown and grey. German potters discovered that they could glaze their ware by shovelling common salt into the kiln while the pots were being fired. This pottery came to be known as "salt-glazed" ware, and in the 17th century it began to be made in English potteries in Staffordshire. In this district there was clay that was suitable for making not only salt-glazed ware but also other kinds of pottery; in addition there was plenty of coal in the area for the firing of the kilns.

In the 18th century Staffordshire craftsmen, like those in other European countries, tried to copy Chinese porcelain, but they did not fully succeed until kaolin, or *china clay*, had been discovered in Cornwall, and also *Cornish stone*—a material similar to petunse.

Staffordshire is now one of the world's biggest centres of the pottery industry. The man who did more than anyone to transform the simple craft of potting into a great industry was Josiah Wedgwood. (See WEDGWOOD, JOSIAH.)

The following pictures show step by step the procedures used in making ceramic objects in a pottery workshop.

(1) The variety of colour and texture of the pottery shown here is caused by using different materials in the glaze combined with various intricate firing processes. (2) The shaping of a bowl starts by placing a lump of clay on the fast-spinning potter's wheel. The potter presses with one hand on the outside. At the same time, he uses the other hand to shape the top. (3) The finishing touches of the shaping of the bowl are made while the clay is still soft and can be moulded. The potter's wheel is turned slowly and the potter delicately shapes the upper rim of the bowl.

Photos, Dalzell Hatfield Galleries

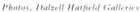

1

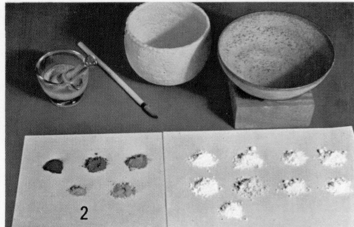

2

(1) After the bowl is shaped on the potter's wheel, it it allowed to dry until it is practically "leather-hard". Then it is put upside down on the potter's wheel and carefully centred. The wheel is set in motion. The base of the bowl is shaped by cutting off any excess clay with turning tools, as shown here. After the turning, all pieces are carefully cleaned and allowed to dry completely. They are then fired for the first time (bisque). (2) Fourteen different chemicals and minerals went into the making of the glaze for the Pompeian green bowl to the right. The separate chemicals and minerals are shown in the foreground. The prepared glaze is seen in the mortar to the left. Before the green bowl went through the glaze fire, it looked pink and rough like the bowl in the middle. The pink bowl has gone through the first firing. This changed its clay chemically, gave strength to the clay, and made it impervious to treatment with water. (3) The glazing process is started with the careful weighing of all glaze materials. The materials are then thoroughly mixed and prepared with water to which some gum has been added as an adhesive.

Photos, Dalzell Hatfield Galleries

3

(1) The potter applies the prepared glaze with a brush. Several coats are applied to each piece. After glazing, the pieces are allowed to dry completely before being fired for the second time (glaze fire). (2) The glaze kiln is ready for firing. The pieces have been carefully set on stilts to prevent their sticking to the kiln shelves. Care is taken in placing the pieces to avoid their touching each other.

Photos, Dalzell Hatfield Galleries

The completed objects. (1) The glaze kiln is opened after the firing. The pieces show their final colour and texture which was developed during the glaze fire. (2) The colour of the glaze of the bottle-shaped vase comes from the use of iron oxide. This bottle, in addition to its regular glaze fire, has undergone a second firing which produced the vase's particular shade of colour. (3) Two semi-rough textured bowls. (4) The bowl on the left, with its rough and pitted texture, is a green lavastone bowl. The two smaller bowls have been glaze fired a second time.

Photos, Dalzell Hatfield Galleries

The Pottery Industry Today

At Stoke-on-Trent in Staffordshire more than 60,000 people are busy every day making pottery, but by no means all these people are making plates and cups and saucers. Many of them are making tiles for walls and floors, wash-basins for bathrooms, sinks for kitchens, w.c.'s, porcelain insulators for telephone lines and electric power lines, sparking-plug cores for cars and aeroplanes, and great jars for storing chemicals. It has been found that if other materials are mixed with clay (or sometimes even used without any clay at all) and then shaped and fired at a high temperature, ceramic ware can be made which has special properties.

Before we say more about these special ceramics, we will look at what goes on in a modern factory making ordinary cups and saucers. First, the raw materials all have to be transported to the factory. For making earthenware, *china clay* is brought from Cornwall, *ball clay* from Devon and Dorset, *flint pebbles*, usually from Kent, and *Cornish stone* from Cornwall. The china clay is very pure and white but it is not very plastic (when mixed with water it cannot be moulded very easily). Ball clay is much more plastic but is not so pure and when fired is not so white. China clay and ball clay are therefore mixed in equal parts to try to get a "body" that is as white as possible and that, at the same time, can be easily moulded. However, a body made all of clay would crack when it was dried and fired because it would shrink so much. Something that is white, does not melt and does not shrink must therefore be added. The powder formed when flint pebbles are heated and then finely ground has just these properties. Lastly, something is needed that will make the body harden at a temperature that is not too high for the kilns normally used. Cornish stone, which contains *felspar*, does this.

These four materials have next to be thoroughly mixed. This is done by *blunging* each of them in water in a big tank to make a creamy liquid called a *slip*. The slips themselves are then mixed in another big tank and this "body slip" is then pumped into a filter-press in which most of the water is squeezed out through nylon filter-cloths. The moist cakes from the filter-press are then passed through a *pug* (which is like a big sausage-machine) and a nice column of the body is thus produced. All is then ready to make the ware. This is done either by feeding pieces of the moist body to a machine which presses the body against a revolving plaster mould, or by pouring the slip itself into plaster moulds. If the latter method, known as *slip casting*, is used, the body is not first passed through the pug.

The shaped ware is dried, usually on conveyors that carry it through hot drying chambers, and is then ready to be fired. Nowadays, most pottery is fired in *tunnel kilns* which, as the name shows, are long tunnels, with gas burning in the centre, through which the ware passes on special trucks. This is the *biscuit firing* and the ware coming from the kiln is *biscuit ware*. It still has a rough surface and is therefore dipped in a creamy mixture of glaze; this may be a mixture of materials containing lead or borax with some clay. The ware is then fired again, this time in another tunnel kiln at a lower temperature.

All that remains to be done now is to put on the decoration (sometimes this is done before glazing). Special colours are used. They are put on by painting the ware by hand, or by using a transfer. Sometimes a machine is used which stamps the pattern on the ware. The decorated ware is then fired once more, usually in a smaller electric kiln, to fuse the decoration into the glaze.

Wash-basins, w.c.'s and many wall-tiles are made from the same materials as earthenware, but *bone china*, the best type of British tableware, is made from a mixture of 2 parts of calcined bones, 1 part of china clay and 1 part of Cornish stone. The ware is shaped and glazed in the same way as earthenware, but it is fired at a higher temperature. If bone china is held against a strong light, some of the light can be seen through the ware.

Electrical porcelain of the kind that carries telephone wires is made from china clay, ball clay, felspar (a special kind of rock) and pure sand. This porcelain is not good enough to resist the very high voltages of some electrical equipment. Therefore other materials, such as talc (another kind of rock) have to be added. Even

Above left: Japanese white porcelain bottle, decorated with enamel at Delft in the Netherlands about 1730. Above right: Harlequin modelled by Johann Joachim Kändler at Meissen, Germany, about 1738. Below left: Staffordshire figure of a dragoon by John Astbury, about 1740. Below right: Japanese dish with a chrysanthemum design, made around 1700.

Courtesy, (top right) Hastings Museum; (others)
Victoria and Albert Museum

Top left: An incense jar from China, dating from the Han dynasty (206 B.C.–A.D. 221). Top right: A large Italian *maiolica* dish decorated with hunting scenes; it was made at Modena in 1594. Centre left: A covered jug painted in enamel colours and mounted in ormolu (imitation gold) made in Mennecy, France, about 1760. Centre: An English slipware dish by Thomas Toft, about 1685. Centre right: A Delft tile decorated with a landscape, about 1700. Right: A bottle of Medici porcelain made in Florence about 1580. Far right: English porcelain figure of a carpenter, made at Chelsea about 1752.

more unusual materials have to be used in some of the ceramic parts of radio and radar instruments. Yet all these things are made in the same way as pottery. The different materials are all mixed together, shaped under pressure or by casting in a mould, and then fired to harden them. They are all "ceramics": some ceramics are among the oldest things made by man, others are being made today to play their part in his newest inventions.

POULTRY. The general name given to birds kept to supply food for man either as eggs or as meat is poultry. The fowl, usually called the hen, is the commonest. Other poultry include turkeys, ducks, geese, guinea-fowl and quail but this article is only about fowls.

The fowl is believed to have originated from the jungle fowl still found in Malaysia and Java. This is about the size of a bantam. In captivity it lays only about 30 small eggs a year. The domesticated jungle fowl spread over the world and many distinct breeds developed. Pure breeds no longer kept mainly for eggs or meat but for interest include the White Leghorn, Brown Leghorn, Rhode Island Red, Buff Orpington, Cochin, Wyandotte, Light Sussex, New Hampshire and Old English Game. Bantams are dwarf fowls. They do not provide many eggs or much meat.

Nowadays fowls are bred either for egg production or for meat. Farmers do not buy pure breeds but "crosses" between different breeds (hybrids) which produce more eggs or meat.

Reproduction

A hen starts to lay at about 18 weeks old. The yolk of the egg is the female germ cell and grows in the ovary. Formation of the egg takes just over a day and it is usually laid in the morning.

After laying a number of eggs a hen may go broody. She stops laying eggs and tries to incubate them; that is, to keep them warm by sitting on them. If the egg is kept at about 38 degrees Centigrade for three weeks the embryo develops into a fully formed chick. Broodiness reduces the time available for laying; moreover it is easier to incubate eggs artificially. Farmers have done this for centuries and even the ancient Egyptians built incubators. Modern hatcheries can incubate 100,000 eggs at a time. During incubation the eggs must be kept warm and airy, and must be turned several times a day so that the embryo develops properly. On the 21st day of incubation the chick makes a small hole in the shell (called pipping) and then breaks out. When newly hatched it is damp, but in the incubator it soon becomes a golden, fluffy chick.

As egg producers usually require only the females—called pullets until they have been laying for a year—it is wasteful to keep all the young males (called cockerels). It is possible to distinguish the sexes but it requires skill, and expert chick sexers usually travel from one hatchery to another.

The day-old chick cannot stand the cold and

(1) A. Rice. (2) Sport and General. (3) Horace Hall.

(1) Young Rhode Island Red hen. (2) Cochin hen, with thickly feathered legs and feet. (3) Silkie hen.

Picturepoint

Two-day-old chicks. In the background is a water dispenser. At this age the chicks need to be kept warm and well fed.

for the first three or four weeks must be kept warm. Different methods are employed for this, but central heating of the poultry house is increasingly used. Chicks may be kept on the ground on a litter of dry wood shavings or in cages. They can be let outside, but are more likely to catch disease. At about five weeks old they no longer require extra heating and can be reared on fields with shelters for the night, but in Britain it is usual to keep them indoors. At about 17 weeks they are transferred to laying quarters which may be battery cages, on litter or sometimes houses with slatted floors. Battery cages have sloping floors so that the eggs roll to the front where they are easily collected. Food and water are provided automatically through continuous troughs and pipes. The droppings are automatically removed from underneath the cages and the air is kept fresh and cool by ventilating fans.

When eggs are required for hatching the pullets are kept on litter or on free range (out in the fields) so that they can mate with the cocks and lay fertile eggs.

Egg Production

The fowls developed for egg production lay about 250 eggs by the time they are 70 weeks old, or within about a year after they start laying. The eggs laid are small at first but after about a year three-quarters of them weigh two ounces or more. They are collected and sent in boxes to an egg packing station. There they are placed on a moving belt and inspected, those with thin shells or other faults being removed. The eggs are then separated by weight into grades and delivered to shops within a day or two of laying, but may be kept fresh in cool stores.

A fowl continues laying for more than a year but the number of eggs decreases and the quality of shell and white falls off. Eventually laying ceases and the bird moults. When new feathers have grown she will lay again but this takes several weeks and poultry farmers do not usually consider it worth while to keep the bird so long without getting any eggs. The fowl, now correctly called a hen, lays fewer eggs in its second year and fewer still each year after, but its life span may be from 5 to 7 years and in that time it can produce 1,000 eggs.

Meat Production

In the old days poultry meat came either from birds specially grown and fattened for 16 to 18 weeks or from hens which had finished laying.

A. Rice

(1) Black Leghorn cockerel. (2) White Leghorn hen. (3) Young Brown Leghorn hen.

It is now possible to breed fowls with extremely fast growth rates—for example, four pounds at eight weeks old, requiring only ten pounds of food during this time. This kind of bird, called a "broiler" or roasting chicken, may be either a cockerel or pullet. The day-old chicks bred for broilers are reared thousands together on litter in buildings in which automatic controls provide food, water, the correct temperature, light and ventilation. When they are the right age or weight, the broilers are sent to a processing factory where, under hygienic conditions, they are killed, plucked, cleaned and packed for delivery to shops or into cold storage. Cockerels grow rather faster than pullets but it is seldom thought worth sexing them and raising them separately.

Feeding and Care

Fowls cannot get much nourishment from grass and they are fed mainly upon cereals, of which maize, wheat and barley are the most important. Protein-rich materials (see PROTEIN) which are added to the milled grain are usually the by-products of other industries, such as the remains of soya beans and ground-nuts after they have been crushed to give up their oil, and waste fish and meat scraps when specially treated. Some minerals are also needed, particularly calcium for egg-shell formation, and also additional vitamins.

A laying bird eats about four ounces a day and needs about four pounds of food for every

A. Rice

(1) Croad Langshan cock. (2) Light Sussex hen. (3) Young Buff Rock hen.

dozen eggs it lays. A broiler needs a more concentrated type of food if it is to show its fastest growth rate.

In modern poultry farming particular attention is paid to the prevention of disease. It is seldom possible to pick out individual sickly birds, so an outbreak of disease can spread rapidly through the flock. All poultry buildings, including incubators, are carefully cleaned and disinfected before fresh stock is put in them and eggs for hatching are fumigated before being placed in the incubator.

Diseases caused by parasites such as worms can be prevented by special chemicals added to the food. Some diseases can be treated by adding antibiotics (see ANTIBIOTICS) to the food or drinking water. Other diseases, such as fowl pest and infectious bronchitis, can be prevented by vaccination but for some diseases such as fowl paralysis there is no known prevention or cure.

See also DUCK; GOOSE; GUINEA-FOWL; TURKEY.

POWYS is a county in eastern central Wales which was created in 1974 by the reorganization of local government in Wales. It consists of the former counties of Montgomeryshire, Radnorshire and most of Brecknockshire. (The Brynmawr region of Brecknockshire became part of Gwent.) Powys is a long county running from north to south and is bordered by Clwyd to the north, to the west by Gwynedd and Dyfed and to the south by West and Mid Glamorgan and Gwent. To the east lie the English counties of Hereford and Worcester and Salop. The county is divided into three administrative districts which coincide with the former county areas. For more about the history and places of interest see the separate articles BRECKNOCKSHIRE, MONTGOMERYSHIRE and RADNORSHIRE.

Much of Powys is hilly and in the north the Berwyn Mountains rise to 825 metres. The Plynlimon range (750 metres), Brecon Beacons (885 metres) and Black Mountains (800 metres) are all in the county. The main rivers include the Vyrnwy and Dovey in the north, the Teme, Elan, Arrowe, Lugg and Ithon. The River Usk flows in a broad valley between the Brecon Beacons and a group of smaller hills called Mynydd

Epynt and then southeast towards the sea at Newport in Gwent. The Wye and the Severn both rise in the Plynlimon hills. The river valleys are fertile with rich grass for cattle while on the hills many sheep are grazed.

Reservoirs such as those at Vyrnwy and Cwm Elan supply water for the English cities of Liverpool and Birmingham. The Forestry Commission owns a large number of forests.

The county is mainly agricultural and the towns are small. Beef and dairy cattle are raised and there is some arable farming. Some quarrying for granite and limestone takes place and there is open cast mining at Ystradgynlais. Small light industries have been established in towns such as Newtown, Welshpool, Montgomery, Brecon, Builth Wells, Hay on Wye and Talgarth. Tourism is an important industry. The county includes the Brecon Beacons National Park and many tourists visit the area for fishing, pony trekking, boating and other pastimes. Mineral springs have led to the development of spas at Llandrindod Wells, as well as at Wantwrtyd, Llangammarch and Builth.

Powys is the least densely populated of the Welsh counties. Its largest town, Welshpool, has a population of less than 7,000.

PRAGUE is the capital of Czechoslovakia. It lies on the Vltava River and its newer parts are like those of any industrial city. The chief beauties of Prague are the many older buildings in the baroque style. (See ARCHITECTURE.)

The 16th-century Hradcany Palace, once the dwelling of the Bohemian kings, is now that of the President of the Republic. In its inner yard is the Cathedral of St. Vitus, begun in 1344 and completed in 1929. Below the Hradcany lies the *Mala Strana*, or "little quarter", a district of narrow winding streets and old palaces, many of which are used as government offices. The Charles Bridge, dating from 1357, leads across the river to the *Staré Mesto*, or "old town", on the east bank. Here too there are many fine baroque churches, whose gilded roofs gave the city the name of *zlata Praha* ("golden Prague"). The gothic-style Tyn Church was the centre of the religious movement started by John Huss (see MORAVIANS) and contains the tomb of the Danish astronomer Tycho Brahe (see BRAHE, TYCHO). Close by are the remains of the old Jewish quarter with a synagogue and 13th-century cemetery. East of the old town is the modern city with its centre at Wenceslas Square, where there is a statue of the good king.

Prague is an important industrial centre. Its factories, most of which are in the east, make engineering products such as railway engines, buses, motor cars and machinery, as well as chemicals, clothes and leather goods. The city is the meeting place between eastern and western Europe. It is the centre of the Czech railway

Paul Popper
Hradcany Palace, with St. Vitus Cathedral rising above it, is in the background. In front is the Charles Bridge.

system and has a large airport at Ruzyné, 12 kilometres distant. The river is fairly shallow and freezes in winter, but at other seasons barge traffic uses the inland harbour of Holesovice.

The history of Prague is the history first of the ancient kingdom of Bohemia and then of modern Czechoslovakia, but many incidents are especially connected with the city. The Thirty Years' War (1618–1648) started with the "defenestration of Prague", when the Czech leaders began a rebellion against Ferdinand of Austria by throwing his officials out of the Hradcany windows. The Battle of Prague, one of the most savage in history, was a Prussian victory over the Austrians on May 6, 1757, during the Seven Years' War. Prague has often been besieged but suffered little damage in World War II, seeing only a few days' fighting when in May 1945 the

citizens helped the Russian forces to drive out the Germans, who had occupied it for six years. In 1968 Russian troops and their allies entered Prague in order to end Czechoslovakia's increasing independence from the policies of the U.S.S.R.

The population of Prague is about 1,083,000.

PRAIRIE. The French word *prairie* means meadow or grassland. The early French explorers gave the name to the wide plains which they found in the Mississippi valley and in Canada west of the Great Lakes. The name is now also given to similar grasslands elsewhere.

Prairies are found in those middle latitudes (that is, roughly half way between the equator and the poles) where the winters are cold and the summers hot. Their rainfall is moderate and comes mainly in summer. Trees are rare except along the rivers. Grass grows quickly in the spring and in the autumn changes to hay as it stands. Great herds of bison ("buffalo") used to feed on the North American prairies and were hunted by the American Indians. The European settlers used the prairies first as cattle ranches and then as wheat farms. In South America the prairies are called pampas (see PAMPAS).

PRAYER is really conversation with God. When the Christian prays he both listens to what God has to say to him and he also talks to God.

The "listening" part of prayer is done mostly by meditation; this means thinking quietly about what God has to say through the reading of the Bible. The "talking" part of prayer is made up of a number of different parts. You will remember them more easily if you think of the word ACTION. The different parts of talking prayer are A—adoration, or praising God; C—confession, owning up to what one has done wrong in thought, word and deed, and expressing sorrow for it; T—thanksgiving; I—intercession, or praying for other people; O—oblation, offering oneself in the service of God; N—needs, asking God for things one needs oneself, especially the Christian needs, such as more faith and love.

As well as private prayer there is also corporate, or public, prayer. Even in his private prayers the Christian prays as a member of the

Dan Morrill

Grasslands have a finely balanced ecology, and human activities (farming, cattle-grazing, hunting, fencing) can damage this. Short grass prairie (seen here) occurs in North America, the U.S.S.R. and parts of Europe and is used mostly for cultivation and ranchland.

family of God into which he has been baptized. That is why he says "Our Father" and not "My Father". But there are other occasions when he prays with the rest of the family of God in church. This is corporate prayer, sometimes known as public worship. The greatest act of worship, in most denominations, is Holy Communion (see SACRAMENTS).

Prayer plays an important part in most of the great religions of the world. Whatever religion people follow, they need to feel themselves in touch with the Supreme Being, and getting into touch with Him is the heart of the idea of prayer.

PRAYER BOOK. All Christian churches have prayers, and many churches collect their prayers together in a book. What is often called simply The Prayer Book belongs to the Church of England, and its correct title is the Book of Common Prayer. It is more than a collection of prayers, for it also sets out the services to be held and the form they shall take.

In its original form it was produced by Archbishop Cranmer and was issued for use in all English churches in 1549. Until that time services were held in Latin, and the Book of Common Prayer was partly a translation of these Latin services into English and partly a simplification of them. It did away with some of the services and fixed the number of ordinary daily services at two—morning prayer and evening prayer. This prayer book was known as the *First Prayer Book of Edward VI*. At that time some people wished to cling to the old Catholic beliefs while others were following the new beliefs known as Protestantism. King Edward VI favoured the Protestants and in 1552 had a *Second Prayer Book* issued. It carried the reforming work of the Protestants a little further. The reformers were guided by the idea that, in all the services of the Church of England, worship should be as similar as possible to that of the church in New Testament times. For example, the word "Mass" was dropped from the *Second Prayer Book* and the service was called simply the Lord's Supper or Holy Communion. To the reformers the ideas lying behind the word Mass were different from the ideas lying behind the Lord's Supper as given to the disciples by Jesus.

The *Second Prayer Book* was banned during the reign of Edward's half-sister Mary, who was a Catholic, and Latin services were reintroduced. Elizabeth I, who was a Protestant, restored it with slight changes. It was prohibited by Oliver Cromwell because the Puritans (see PURITANS) disapproved of it, but Charles II brought it back in 1662 after slight changes had been made. Since then it has remained almost the same.

In the 20th century some people wanted to modernize the prayer book. In 1927 and 1928 the government refused to allow changes, though parts of the book suggested in 1928 are used in some churches by permission of the bishop. In the 1970s the government gave the Church power to alter services, and an Alternative Service Book (containing all the modern services) was prepared. However, the traditional prayer book, though not used so much now, remains protected by law so it will never be lost or forgotten. The Book of Common Prayer has been adapted for use in the Protestant Episcopal Church of the United States and in churches of the Anglican Communion throughout the world.

PRAYER WHEEL. The simplest form of prayer wheel consists of a small cylinder that is mounted on a handle and revolves when moved

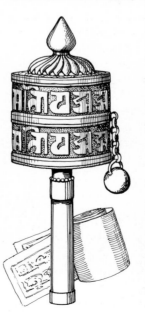

by hand. The Buddhists (see BUDDHA AND BUDDHISM) of Tibet carry such prayer wheels about with them. Inside the cylinder are pieces of paper that have prayers and extracts from sacred books written on them. The object of the prayer wheel is to send out as many prayers as possible, the idea being that the more prayers that are said the more likely they are to be heard and answered. Nevertheless, turning the wheel is not thought to be of any use unless the person who

Prayer wheel and scroll. turns it is thinking good

thoughts. Some prayer wheels are as big as drums and worked by machinery driven by water or wind.

PRAYING MANTIS.

The insect called the praying mantis gets its name from the way it holds up its forelegs in front of its head, as though it were praying. It is, however, very fierce, and uses its legs to catch insects. To understand how each leg works, imagine a pen-knife in which the blade has a row of teeth like a saw and the handle is armed with a row of teeth into which those of the blade lock with a snap when closed. The front leg of the mantis has two parts that work like this. When an insect comes within reach, these two parts, which are called the tibia and the femur, are opened out and the insect is seized with lightning speed, held tight between the two rows of teeth and afterwards slowly eaten up.

No mantis is to be found in Great Britain, but it lives in southern Europe, and in the warmer parts of the world there are a great many different kinds. It is said that some of the very large kinds found in the tropics will even catch small lizards and frogs. Most of them are green and for this reason are not easily seen as they wait among the leaves of a plant for their prey. Other kinds are brightly coloured and look so much like flowers that insects are deceived and come to them, only to be caught and devoured.

The female lays her eggs on anything suitable, such as a twig, and covers them with a mass of froth which soon hardens. The young are just like their parents except that they do not have wings until they are full grown. The insects most like the praying mantis are the grasshoppers and stick insects.

PRECISION INSTRUMENTS.

The word "precise" means exact or accurate, and precision instruments are those which are used to make accurate measurements of size, weight or other qualities. Not all instruments need to be very accurate. The spring balance used in the kitchen for weighing flour and sugar is much less accurate than the weights and scales used in a

Courtesy, Cook, Troughton and Simms Ltd.

A theodolite, used to map or measure land.

laboratory. An error of one degree in a wall thermometer used for measuring the temperature of a room does not matter, but the same error in a clinical thermometer measuring the temperature of a sick person may be serious. An error of one minute in a clock is usually of small consequence, but to a ship out of sight of land it may mean an error of 25 kilometres in calculating the position. Many years ago errors of that kind were common. Then in 1714 the British government offered a reward of £20,000 for an accurate timekeeper. Some years later this was won by John Harrison, who invented the chronometer, a very accurate clock.

The development of precision instruments has made it possible to produce large quantities of high-grade, smoothly running machines and appliances. Unless the parts of a machine fit together closely it does not work well or smoothly.

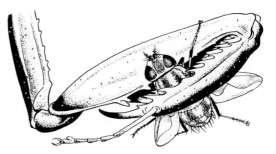

Left: The mantis holds up its forelegs as though it were praying. Right: A foreleg snaps shut on a fly.

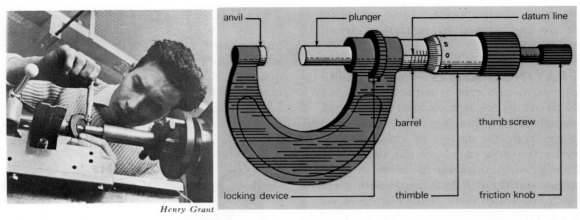

Henry Grant

This micrometer can be read in hundredths of a millimetre.

In order to fit, the parts must be produced exactly to size, and this requires the use of precision methods. The various qualities that may have to be measured include not only size, weight, temperature and time, but also pressure, rate of flow, and electrical measurements such as voltage and resistance.

The Micrometer

The precision instrument commonly used for measuring lengths (such as diameters of parts in engineering workshops) is the micrometer. Its working can be understood by comparing it with an ordinary nut and bolt. The nut travels along the bolt as it revolves. The distance it travels along the bolt for each complete turn is called the *pitch* of the screw. The micrometer has a bow-shaped steel frame, the gap between the ends of which can be altered by screwing a plunger in or out. The micrometer is held in the right hand and the object to be measured is placed in the gap between the plunger and the anvil. Fixed to the plunger is a thimble which, as it turns, travels along the barrel of the micrometer. With forefinger and thumb the thimble is turned until the plunger grips the object lightly.

The metric micrometer illustrated above can be read in hundredths of a millimetre. The screw in the micrometer has a pitch of 0·5 mm, which means that one complete turn of the thimble moves the plunger 0·5 mm and moves the thimble 0·5 mm along the barrel. There are marks on the barrel at intervals of 0·5 mm but to

make them easy to read they are arranged in two rows. The upper row shows whole millimetres, with figures marked at 5 mm, 10 mm and so on. The lower row shows the half millimetre sub-divisions. Hundredths of a millimetre are read from the thimble, whose edge is divided into 50 equal divisions. Since a complete turn of the thimble moves the plunger 0·5 mm, a fiftieth of a turn moves it 0·01 mm. The reading is taken from the line on the thimble which lies opposite the datum line running along the barrel. This thimble reading is added to the barrel reading.

Some micrometers can be read in thousandths of a millimetre with the help of a vernier scale. The markings of a vernier micrometer are shown below. The thimble reading on the datum line is between 0·16 mm and 0·17 mm. At a guess it might by 0·165 mm, but the vernier lines make it possible to read the thousandths. Only one of the vernier lines lies exactly opposite any line on the thimble, and this vernier line is marked 6. That is the number of thousandths of a millimetre to be added—so the reading of the measurement is 10·666 mm. If

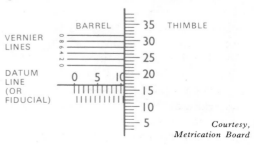

Courtesy,
Metrication Board

none of the vernier lines was opposite a line on the thimble, the reading would be taken between the two vernier lines nearest to being opposite lines on the thimble.

The vernier scale is named after Pierre Vernier, the Frenchman who invented it in 1631. It is used also on vernier callipers, in which the object to be measured is lightly gripped between the fixed jaw of the instrument and its sliding jaw. A vernier scale has divisions of slightly different length from the divisions of the scale against which it is read. If you have number rods you can work out the principle by making a main scale of a line of tens, and putting beside it a sliding vernier scale made of a line of nines.

Comparators

For making accurate measurements in industry, comparators are widely used. As their name suggests, they compare rather than measure. The standard for comparison is usually built up from *slip gauges*, which are polished bars of hard steel made in sets, each bar marked with its exact thickness. These slip gauges can be piled on top of one another like building bricks to make up any measurement required.

This pile of slip gauges can be used with a dial indicator for comparing the thickness of other objects. The dial indicator, which looks rather like a watch with one hand, is fixed to a stand. On the underside of the indicator is a plunger which, when lifted against the pressure of a spring, turns the pointer around the dial. The movement of the plunger is magnified (multiplied) by gearing in the indicator so that a vertical movement of 0·001 mm by the plunger moves the pointer one division on the dial.

The dial indicator and the pile of slip gauges are stood on a flat smooth steel plate and the plunger is allowed to rest on top of the pile. The dial of the indicator is then turned so that its pointer is at zero. The divisions in one direction from the zero are marked + (plus) and those in the other direction − (minus). The object to be measured is then put in the place of the pile of slip gauges and the difference of height is read from the dial.

In some comparators, the pointer is moved electrically by movement of the plunger. In optical comparators, movement of the plunger changes the direction of a beam of light which moves along a marked scale.

Gauges

The micrometer, vernier callipers and the comparator used with slip gauges all require skill and in actual practice the measurement of parts which are produced in large quantities is done either automatically or by means of gauges applied by hand. An inspection machine, which does the work automatically, is a complicated device, often of comparator type. It may make several measurements at once and may have indicator lamps that light up to show errors.

When using gauges by hand the system of limit gauging, sometimes called "go and no-go gauging", is generally used. As an example, suppose it is required to inspect a number of steel balls each of which must have a diameter (width) of 25 mm. If the inspector is given two ring gauges of hard steel, one having a hole 24·99 mm wide and the other a hole 25·01 mm wide, he can reject, or throw away, all the balls that pass through the smaller gauge and all those that fail to pass through the larger gauge.

Other Precision Instruments

The shape of a part such as a toothed wheel or a screw may be checked by means of a projector. This is an optical instrument which throws a much enlarged shadow of the part on to a screen. The outline of the shadow is compared with the outline of an accurate enlarged drawing of the part, the drawing being marked on or fixed to the screen. Microscopes are also used for inspecting the accuracy of small parts (see MICROSCOPE).

Another precision instrument, which is used by surveyors when mapping or measuring land, is the theodolite. It measures angles both in the vertical and horizontal planes and is usually set up so that it stands exactly vertical, this being checked by means of a very accurate spirit level whose bubble must remain at the same position in the tube as the instrument is rotated about its vertical axis. This spirit level is made by part filling with fluid a glass tube whose inside bore is barrel shaped, being very slightly larger in the

Courtesy, Kelvin and Hughes Ltd.
A sextant, used to find the position of a ship in mid-ocean. In front are eye-pieces and telescopes.

middle than at its ends. When this tube is level the bubble of air contained in it will be half way along it.

The sextant is used by sailors when finding their position when out of sight of land. It measures the angle above the horizon of the Sun or stars. It has a vernier adjustment so that the angle can be read to within one-tenth of a minute (a minute is one-sixtieth of a degree). (See Navigation.)

PREFABRICATION is a method of constructing buildings, ships and machines. In this method the various parts are shaped and, as far as possible, finished before they are brought to the building site or shipyard to be put together. As an example, a modern motor car consists of a number of units (parts or groups of parts) such as the body, engine and gearbox. These are made and finished separately, often in different factories, and brought together for assembly, or putting together.

It has long been the practice for the parts of a ship such as the boilers, engines and electrical machinery to be made separately and assembled in the ship at a "fitting-out berth" after the hull, or outer body, has been launched. In World War II, however, the hull itself was sometimes prefabricated and the huge sections joined together by welding on the building berth (see Welding). This method was widely used in the United States for building merchant ships, and towards the end of the war was adopted by Germany for the rapid construction of large submarines. In this way, each ship occupied the building berth for only a few weeks instead of for several months.

Some builders have long believed that buildings could be put up more cheaply and quickly if large parts of them could be put together and finished before being brought to the building site.

The disadvantages of prefabrication are, first, that it is expensive to transport and erect large sections of buildings. Special vehicles and cranes may have to be provided and there is a risk that the sections may be damaged before they are safely in place. Secondly, the joints between the sections have to be carefully finished off if the building is to look well and keep out the damp.

Prefabrication is easiest with wooden sections

Courtesy, Brockhouse Steel Structures Ltd.
Two prefabricated schools in Nottinghamshire. Left: An infant school being built. The roof has been put on but the steel framework of the walls is still visible. Right: Three storeys of a rural secondary school.

since, as timber is light and fairly strong, quite large sections can be transported without risk of damage. Most garden sheds are made in this way, their walls being complete with windows and doors so that the whole shed can be quickly put together. The same method has been used for wooden houses. Besides the main sections of the house itself, fittings such as doors, windows, cupboards and staircases are prefabricated and merely have to be lifted into place on the site.

Concrete and steel have also been used for pre-fabricated buildings (see CONCRETE). Usually a framework of large pieces is built and wall and roof coverings attached in large sections, often called cladding. The areas of cladding have an outside skin that keeps out the weather and an inside skin that provides a suitable indoor finish. The air space between the two skins helps to keep the building warm. Aluminium has sometimes been used for the outer skin, and its lightness allows the prefabricated sections to be very large.

After World War II the great shortage of houses in Great Britain was partly made up by the rapid erection in many places of prefabricated bungalows usually called "prefabs". Later, however, prefabrication was used less for houses than for factories, offices and schools.

PREFECTS AND MONITORS.

The practice of choosing outstanding boys as leaders is very old. In ancient Greece the Spartans trained their boys in this way, and in England at the founding of Winchester College in 1382 "scholars of good repute" were chosen to super-vise their fellow pupils. Dr. Thomas Arnold, the 19th-century headmaster who introduced reforms at Rugby School, achieved his success largely because of the prefect system which he established. (See ARNOLD, THOMAS AND MAT-THEW; PUBLIC SCHOOL.) Appointing carefully chosen senior boys as prefects, he put great trust in them : and they helped him and the staff to put an end to rowdyism. With his support they changed the spirit of the school, and in a few years the lawlessness that Arnold found at Rugby had disappeared and it had become a point of honour to behave like "a Christian gentleman". This victory made the prefect system famous and many boys' and girls' schools adopted it.

Monitors have a different history. In days when the state did nothing for education, the money for schools had to be raised by private subscriptions or from fees, "the children's pence" as they were called. Many schools had to be run cheaply and one of the methods was to have very large classes of 100 or more. With a class of this size the teacher needed assistance, so the older pupils were employed as "monitors" to help him. At one end of a big room the teacher sat at his desk with his cane handy, and the chil-dren worked in groups under the direction of monitors. The word "monitor" is still used, but today it has another meaning ; for monitors are now usually pupils responsible for some special duty in school or classroom.

PREFIXES AND SUFFIXES.

Look at the following words : *report, import, export, deport, support, portable, portly, portliness*. You can see at once that in each word there is a part that is the same—*port*—yet all the words have dif-ferent meanings. The differences come from the parts of the words that are joined on to *port*, either in front of it or after it. These parts are called prefixes and suffixes—prefix means "fixed in front of" and suffix means "fixed after".

The main part of a word that has a prefix or suffix attached to it is called the "root" of the word and gives the main meaning. In these words the root *port*, which came into English from a Latin verb, means "to carry", and the prefixes and suffixes add something to or alter that meaning. *Report* means to carry *back* news or information about something; *import* means to bring something *in* to a country; *export* means to send something *out* of a country; *deport* means to send a person away *from* a country ; *support* means to carry something from *beneath*—that is, to uphold it or bear its weight ; *portable* means *able* to be carried. *Portly* and *portliness* have meanings a little different : when we speak of a person's way of standing, walking or moving generally, we speak of his "carriage" or "the way he carries himself", and it is this sort of carrying that the *port* in these two words means. *Portly* means stately or dignified (having a good *carriage*) and also nowadays large or stout in a dignified way ; *portliness* is the noun made out of the adjective "portly" and means the quality of being stately or stout.

It is obvious from these examples that prefixes and suffixes are a useful and economical way of making one root word express many different meanings. Adding prefixes or suffixes to root words is in fact one of the main ways in which our language grows and finds new words for new things and ideas.

PREHISTORIC ANIMALS.

The animals now living on the Earth are only the latest in a long series of different types. These evolved over the enormous periods of time which have passed since life first evolved on the Earth. (The article EVOLUTION describes the way in which these changes took place, and GEOLOGY describes how these great stretches of time in the Earth's history are divided up into Periods.) The earlier types of animals are known to us today only through their buried remains (usually only of

such hard parts as shells, bones and teeth) preserved in the rocks as fossils, or by such traces as their footprints. (See FOSSIL.) It is possible to trace how some earlier types gradually evolved into present-day animals such as horses or elephants. Other types, such as the dinosaurs, died out altogether, leaving no living descendants.

Early Life in the Seas

Animal life probably began in the sea over 600,000,000 years ago and many different types of sea creature had appeared by about 570,000,000 years ago. Descendants of most of these can still be found in the sea today, but a few died out or became "extinct". For example, about 600,000,000 years ago, during the Cambrian Period, a group of sea creatures known as trilobites were very numerous in the sea. Like the insects, their bodies were divided into a series of portions or "segments" to most of which a pair of legs was attached. Trilobites lived on

Illustrations reproduced by kind permission of Brooke Bond Oxo Limited

Eusthenopteron had primitive lungs.

Stenaulorhynchus, an early reptile.

Ichthyostega, the earliest amphibian.

Dimetrodon, a mammal-like reptile.

Eryops, a large amphibian.

Cryptoclidus, one of the plesiosaurs.

Ichthyosaurus.

Pteranodon.

Archaeopteryx.

Iguanodon.   Corythosaurus.

Cetiosaurus, a huge land dinosaur.

Stegosaurus.

Brachiosaurus.   Tyrannosaurus.

Triceratops.

Illustrations reproduced by kind permission of Brooke Bond Oxo Limited

sandy or muddy sea beds and were between 2 and 60 centimetres long. Many could roll up into a ball for protection, like woodlice.

Much later, two groups were important for a long span of time but then became extinct. Known as the ammonites and belemnites, these were both related to the squid and octopus of today. They lived in the Jurassic and Cretaceous Periods, from about 200,000,000 to 60,000,000 years ago. Ammonites had shells which were coiled up into a flat spiral (like a watch spring) up to 2 metres across. The shell was formed of a series of chambers, a new chamber being formed each year. The old chambers were full of gas, so that the shell floated in the sea, and the animal lived in the last chamber, looking very like the nautilus of today (see NAUTILUS). The most common remains of belemnites are their pointed cylindrical skeletons, up to 22 centimetres long, but traces of their soft parts have also been found. These show that they were very like squids, with a parrot-like beak and long flexible arms, on which were hooked suckers for catching their prey.

Giant Amphibians

Not until the end of the Devonian Period, nearly 350,000,000 years ago, did a type of fish evolve that possessed both limbs and lungs, and could therefore walk on land and breathe air. They became amphibians that, like the frogs, toads and newts of today, still spent their early lives in water. But they were much bigger than our living amphibians and, unlike them, had dry or scaly skins. Though they could live on land, most still lived in the water and fed on fish. The skeletons of some have been preserved in coal, which is formed from the compressed remains of the dense vegetation of hot swampy forests. These covered parts of Europe and North America in the Upper Carboniferous Period, about 300,000,000 years ago. Some of the amphibians that lived in lakes and streams were up to 4·5 metres long. Others of the early amphibians went back to live in the sea and preyed on the fish that lived there. A few came out of the water permanently to spend all their adult life on land, and the amphibians of today probably evolved from these.

The First Reptiles

Reptiles evolved from amphibians about 300,000,000 years ago, by developing a shelled egg inside which the baby reptile developed until it was old enough to hatch. When they think of fossil reptiles, most people think first of the dinosaurs. But in fact another group of fossil

reptiles, called the mammal-like reptiles, were the only common land reptiles for over 100,000,000 years, from the beginning of the Permian Period. They evolved into a great variety of types including both herbivorous (plant-eating) forms and the carnivorous (flesh-eating) forms which preyed on them. Their remains are most common in Texas (United States), the U.S.S.R. and South Africa. Some of the early mammal-like reptiles, such as *Dimetrodon*, had a sail-like crest down their back, which may have helped them to absorb heat from the sunshine if they were feeling cold. The commonest herbivores, known as dicynodonts, had lost most of their teeth and evolved a horny beak like that of tortoises and turtles. Some of the carnivorous forms which preyed on them, called cynodonts, may have developed a warm coat of hair. These were the ancestors of the mammals.

Reptiles in the Sea and Air

Although they first evolved for life on land, some reptiles found that they could return to the sea and feed on the animals that lived there. Two main types are known, both of which evolved about 200,000,000 years ago, near the end of the Triassic Period. One type, called the ichthyosaurs, had small limbs and swam by threshing their rather shark-like tails from side to side. Ichthyosaurs were about 10 metres long. The other type, called the plesiosaurs, paddled themselves along, like the turtles of today. Some plesiosaurs had very long necks. In *Elasmosaurus*, which was 13 metres long, the neck was twice as long as the body. Some ichthyosaurs and plesiosaurs fed on fish, others on the ammonites and belemnites mentioned earlier in the article. Both groups became extinct at the end of the Cretaceous Period, 60,000,000 years ago, and their fossils are often found in rocks on the south coast and in the midlands of England.

Other reptiles developed wings and took to the air. One group, the pterosaurs, had bat-like leathery wings. Some were as small as sparrows but the largest, *Pteranodon*, had a wing span of over 8 metres and had a long crest on its head. Pterosaurs probably fed on fish swimming near the surface, by swooping down to stab them with their sharp beaks, without themselves entering the water.

The other group of flying reptiles evolved into the birds. The earliest known bird, called *Archaeopteryx*, lived about 147,000,000 years ago and was about the size of a crow. It had already developed feathers, but still had teeth and a long, reptile-like tail.

The Dinosaurs

The first dinosaurs appeared about 200,000,000 years ago, and it was not long before they had replaced the mammal-like reptiles as the most important group of land animals. Over the next 140,000,000 years a great many different kinds of dinosaur evolved, some herbivorous and some carnivorous, some quadrupedal (walking on all four legs) and others bipedal (walking on their hind legs). Though a few were as small as chickens, most were large and many were enormous. Their remains have been found in many parts of the world, especially in England, North America, Mongolia and East Africa.

The biggest dinosaurs of all were great herbivores such as *Diplodocus* and *Apatosaurus* (or *Brontosaurus*) which were 30 metres long—although most of this length was made up by a long neck and tail. *Brachiosaurus*, which belonged to the same group, must have weighed about 50 tonnes and is the largest land animal ever known. It had unusually long front legs which, together with the long neck, would have allowed it to raise its head to a height of about 13 metres—the height of a three-storey building. These long-neck dinosaurs probably fed on the higher branches of trees, as do giraffes.

These big herbivores provided food for great carnivores such as *Tyrannosaurus*, 16 metres long and 6 metres high, with teeth 15 centimetres long. These dinosaurs could run on two legs because the heavy tail balanced the weight of the rest of the body, and the front legs were very tiny.

Some herbivorous dinosaurs were protected from the attacks of the great carnivores by bony armour. *Stegosaurus*, about 7 metres long, had a double row of triangular plates down its back and spikes on its tail. *Ankylosaurus* had bony plates and spikes on its body and a heavy club-like tail, which it probably swung to break the legs of attackers. *Triceratops*, about 8 metres long, had great horns on its head and a big bony frill over its neck. A relative of *Triceratops*, called *Protoceratops*, lived in Mongolia. Scientists have found nests of its fossilized eggs.

Not all the herbivorous dinosaurs were quadrupedal. Some, like *Iguanodon*, used only its hind legs for walking and probably used its front limbs to pull down the branches of trees so as to eat the leaves. The front of the jaws was armed with a sharp horny beak, but there were sharp teeth further back in the jaws. *Iguanodon* was about 10 metres long and 5 metres high. There was a bony spike on each thumb, which they may have used for defence. Remains have been found in Britain and Belgium.

Another herbivorous type of dinosaur, the duck-billed dinosaurs, were similar to *Iguanodon* in their size and in having a horny beak and teeth. They probably used only their hind limbs when running, but they may have walked on all fours. They had a strange bony crest on the top of the head; scientists are still uncertain what this was used for.

Perhaps the biggest mystery is why the dinosaurs suddenly became extinct at the end of the Cretaceous Period, about 60,000,000 years ago. All sorts of explanations have been suggested. One is that they grew too large to survive—but even the smaller dinosaurs became extinct at the same time as the large ones. Possibly the dinosaurs starved to death as the plants on which many of them fed died out. Unable to adapt to a new diet, the plant-eaters quickly became extinct, and so the carnivorous dinosaurs which preyed on them died out as well. However, changes in the Earth's plant life known to have occurred during the Cretaceous Period took place long before the disappearance of the dinosaurs. Climatic change could have been fatal, even though it has been suggested that the dinosaurs may have been warm-blooded (and so less likely to suffer if the climate became colder). No-one knows for sure what happened. But we do know that the dinosaurs were succeeded by a hitherto insignificant group of animals—the mammals.

Hyracotherium, the first "horse".

Baluchitherium, almost 6 metres high.

Smilodon, the sabre-toothed tiger.

Glyptodon.

Aepyornis, over 3 metres tall.

Megatherium, the giant ground sloth.

Coelodonta, the woolly rhinoceros.

Mammuthus, the woolly mammoth.

Illustrations reproduced by kind permission of Brooke Bond Oxo Limited

Sivatherium, a hoofed mammal.

Extinct Mammals

Though the first mammals evolved at the same time as the first dinosaurs, it was not until the dinosaurs became extinct that the mammals took over as the most important group of land animals. Most of these groups of mammals are still alive today, but a few groups have already died out. These include several South American types, such as the glyptodonts and ground sloths. Glyptodonts, about 3 metres long, were rather like enormous armadillos, with a bony armour over the body, and a tail with rings of armour and a number of spikes on its end. The ground sloths were massive herbivores, 6 metres long, which probably reared up on their hind legs and pulled down the branches of trees so as to feed on the leaves. They were hunted by sabre-toothed tigers which used daggerlike stabbing teeth to pierce their thick hide.

Many mammals, and especially the larger ones, died out in the series of Ice Ages which have taken place in the last 2,000,000 years. (See ICE AGE.) During each Ice Age glaciers extended southwards over the northern parts of North America, Europe and Asia. Some new types of animal evolved, such as the woolly elephant (or mammoth) and woolly rhinoceros, adapted to living in the colder climate. The bodies of some of these, with flesh and hair still preserved, have been found in the permanently frozen soil of Siberia. Early man (see MAN) was familiar with some of these mammals. He kept ground sloths penned in caves, perhaps for food, and hunted both the mammoth and the woolly rhinoceros. Just as today man's activities are causing the gradual extinction of some animals, prehistoric man's hunting may have contributed to the disappearance of some of these Ice Age mammals.

PRELUDE is a word which comes from the Latin *prae* meaning "before" and *ludere* meaning "to play". In music, a prelude is a piece which is usually played before another piece in order to introduce it. It may be composed for any instrument or combination of instruments and has no fixed form. J. S. Bach placed a prelude before each of his 48 fugues. Frédéric Chopin and Claude Debussy each wrote 24 beautiful piano preludes which are complete pieces in themselves. A prelude to an opera is generally shorter than an overture, as in the case of the preludes to Richard Wagner's *Lohengrin* and *Tristan und Isolde*. Many preludes have been written for the organ. Certain of these, called chorale preludes, are based on hymn tunes.

PREPOSITION. Look at these two sentences —"He went *up*", and "He went *up the river*". In both of them the little word *up* shows the direction of an action. In the first sentence *up* is an adverb, a word that describes or modifies a verb—the verb *went*, in this case. (There is a

separate article ADVERB.) In the second sentence, however, *up* is what is called a preposition. Preposition means "something that is put before", and here *up* is put before the noun *river*. The three words *up the river* make the kind of word group called a phrase. Notice that *up the river* does the same work as the adverb in the first sentence.

From this it can be seen that a preposition is a word which stands before, or introduces, a phrase describing another word or words in the sentence. Prepositions also do another job, that of linking together various words in a sentence. In Latin, and in English at the time of King Alfred, many of the links or relationships between words in a sentence were shown by endings joined on to the words themselves. As these endings ceased to be used in later English, the use of prepositions increased. In English today we still say "the man's hat", in which the *'s* ending shows that the hat belongs to the man, but we can also say "the hat of the man" where the preposition *of* shows the link relationship between "hat" and "man".

Many words which are used as prepositions can also be used as adverbs: *in, up, down, across, behind, along, over, after.* When they are prepositions, they always introduce a phrase, beginning with the preposition and ending with a noun or pronoun. Examples of prepositional phrases, as they are called, are *after him, up the hill, across the deep river, under his best hat.*

In the examples given so far, all the prepositions have been single words. There are also prepositions made up of two or three words which work like a single preposition. Examples of these compound prepositions are : *in spite of, because of, on account of, in place of, according to.*

PRESBYTERIANS. At the time of the Reformation in the 16th century (see REFORMATION), many people believed that the Roman Catholic Church had ceased to be the church as the New Testament showed it. They therefore re-formed the church, as they believed, according to the New Testament pattern. One body of such people was that which followed the teachings of the reformer John Calvin (see CALVIN, JOHN). On the continent of Europe churches reformed on this pattern are usually called Reformed churches and there are large churches of this kind in Switzerland, Germany, France, Hungary, the Netherlands and Czechoslovakia. In English-speaking countries churches of this kind are usually called Presbyterian. The national Church of Scotland is Presbyterian (see CHURCH OF SCOTLAND) and there are Presbyterian churches in England, Ireland and Wales. There are also large Presbyterian churches in the United States, Canada, Australia, New Zealand and South Africa; and through missionary work Presbyterian churches have been formed in Asia, Africa and South America.

Except in Hungary, the Presbyterian churches have no bishops. Instead they are governed by *presbyters*. (In the early church this title was given to leaders in each local church.) There are two kinds of presbyters—ministers and elders. A minister is ordained (set apart) for life to preach the Word (the Bible) and administer (carry out) the Sacraments (see SACRAMENTS). His duties are like those of a clergyman of the Church of England. Elders, who are chosen by the congregation, are also ordained for life, but earn their living in ordinary jobs besides undertaking their special church duties.

The presbyters govern the church through a system of church courts. In the *local congregation* the minister and elders form the "session", which looks after the spiritual well-being of the members of the church; that is, those who have been baptized and have declared their faith in Jesus Christ before the congregation, and been admitted to Holy Communion. Also, the session must see that the children are cared for and attention given to the service of the church to the community and the wider mission of the church.

In the *district*, the ministers and one or more elders from each congregation form the "presbytery". While the local congregation chooses its own minister, that choice has to be confirmed by the presbytery which is, like a bishop in his diocese, responsible for the care of all congregations in its area. Ministers are ordained by the presbyters, elders usually by the minister and session.

In some large Presbyterian churches groups of presbyteries are formed into *synods*, but the supreme court for the Presbyterian Church of a whole country is usually called the General Assembly, and controls all the work of that church at home and overseas. The minister presiding over each of these courts is called the Moderator. The one chosen as Moderator of the General Assembly is usually regarded as that church's public representative for his year of office.

The Presbyterian form of worship is usually simple but follows a careful order. It consists of prayer, Bible readings, hymns and psalms (usually "metrical"; that is, in verse) and preaching. Presbyterian churches use the two Sacraments that Christ specially commanded, Baptism and the Lord's Supper (Communion). The former is given to children of believing parents. The Lord's Supper is usually observed rather rarely but made a very special time. Elders visit members' homes to bid them to be present. The minister, standing behind the holy table, presides, and the elders take the bread and wine to the people.

See also UNITED REFORMED CHURCH.

PRESIDENT is a title that is given to somebody who *presides over*, or is the head of, an organization of one kind or another. The organization may be a small club or society or it may be a great nation like the United States.

At the meetings of a society there must be someone to guide the discussion, to decide who shall speak at any particular time and, if a vote is taken, to state clearly what the members are to vote on. The man who does this duty is generally known as the chairman or president. Sometimes the head of a college is called a president and in the United States it is the title for the head of a university or business firm.

President is the usual title of the ruler or head of state of a republic. Unlike kings, who hold their office by birth or for life, presidents are elected for a limited period. The word was first used in this sense as the title of the ruler of the United States, whose people elected George Washington as their first president in 1789. The president of the United States is today the most famous and the most powerful president in the world. (His responsibilities are explained in the article UNITED STATES OF AMERICA.) Other states that have presidents include France, the Federal Republic of Germany and the U.S.S.R.

PRESS GANGS were naval parties who went round England compelling civilians to join the navy. Although fishermen and the sailors from merchant ships were, at the end of the 16th century, freed from having to serve in the army, they were still liable to be "pressed" for service in the navy, for which there were never enough volunteers. The press gangs were composed of tough naval petty officers and seamen who, in time of war, scoured the seaports for men. Real sailors hid or fled from them and rather than return empty-handed the press gangs sometimes seized landsmen. In the 18th century some exceptions were made, and apprentices (lads learning a trade) and some fishermen and seamen were spared from being impressed, as it was called. The sheriffs and mayors of towns often supplied the press gangs with the men they demanded by clearing out the prisons. The introduction of bad characters into the navy in this way was one of the causes of the mutiny of 1797 (see MUTINY).

The press gangs have not been used since the end of the Napoleonic Wars in 1815, although it is lawful to this day to impress men for service in the navy.

PRESTER JOHN. In the middle ages, when the people of Europe imagined the Far East as a land of riches, splendour and enchantment, stories were told of a mighty Christian king in Asia called Prester John, or John the Priest. He was said to rule over regions beyond Persia and to make war against the heathens with jewelled crosses carried before him. Later the legend changed a little and Prester John was called the king of Ethiopia in Africa.

It is almost certain that Prester John never existed and that his story grew up because people confused some of the real facts about eastern rulers. Thus the king of Ethiopia was a Christian and Jenghiz Khan was a great conqueror

A press gang seizing men to force them into the navy. This was done because the navy was always short of men.

55

The Republic of South Africa government building overlooking Pretoria. In front of it are terraced gardens.

in the East (see JENGHIZ KHAN). However, probably in 1165, a letter came to the Emperor Manuel of Byzantium from someone calling himself Presbyter Joannes ("presbyter" is another word for priest). This gave a full account of Prester John's realms.

The priest king described the enormous size of his empire, which was divided into 72 kingdoms, each with a king who was Prester John's subject. Strange races of people and animals lived in these kingdoms and great ants dug up gold. In front of Prester John's palace there was a mirror on a towering stand, and in this mirror he could see everything that went on in his empire.

A king of Ethiopia, said to have been Prester John, set up a chapel and altar in the Church of the Holy Sepulchre in Jerusalem. Even in the 16th century the Portuguese explorer Vasco da Gama heard tales of Prester John reigning in the interior of Africa.

The book called *Prester John*, by John Buchan, is about an African who hoped to establish a kingdom in Africa like that of Prester John.

PRETORIA is the capital of the Transvaal province of South Africa. It is also the headquarters of government of the Republic itself, although the South African parliament meets at Cape Town.

Pretoria lies in a valley and its central part is arranged in rectangular blocks. In the middle is Church Square, where stand the Palace of Justice and other official buildings. East and west from the square runs the main street, Church Street. Here the house of the great South African leader, President Kruger, has been restored and made into a museum. (See KRUGER, STEPHANUS JOHANNES PAULUS.)

The chief pride of Pretoria is the government building overlooking the city from the hill known as Meintjes' Kop. It was completed in 1913 and contains most of the government departments and ministers' offices. The slopes below it are laid out in terraced gardens and along the same hillside are the houses of the prime minister and other ministers.

On the opposite side of the valley, the Voortrekker Monument overlooks the city from the south. It was built to honour the memory of the *voortrekkers*, or pioneers. (See SOUTH AFRICAN PIONEERS.) The city is famous for its streets lined with jacaranda trees, whose mauve flowers bloom in October and November. Pretoria has a large university, two cathedrals and numerous churches and schools. It has an important iron and steel industry, which produces $2\frac{1}{2}$ million tons of steel a year.

Pretoria was founded in 1855 and named after Andries Pretorius (1799–1853) who was one of the Boer military leaders. The population of Pretoria is about 561,000.

PRICES. In very early times people exchanged goods with each other, rather as children swop things with each other at school. This was called the barter system. The amount of one thing which a person would ask in exchange for another was its price, and, roughly speaking, this price depended on how long it had taken to make the object. If it took a man five hours to make an earthenware pot and only one hour to catch a rabbit, he expected to get five rabbits for one pot. Later on people began to use a precious metal like silver for money and then all prices were worked out in amounts of silver.

As soon as a child begins to have pocket money, he is affected by the cost of living ; that is, the prices of the things he wants to buy. If the cost of a model aircraft goes up, the child has to go without something else, unless perhaps the price of chocolate comes down or he can persuade his father to give him more pocket money. Parents are affected too when the price of food rises in the shops (or when their children's pocket money goes up, for that matter), unless they can earn more in some way. It is important to remember, also, that the cost of living depends on the *kind* of things people buy, as well as on the prices in the shops.

Just as in the early days, the prices of goods still depend in the long run on what the goods cost to produce. Suppose a man's business is making kettles. Before he knows what price to charge for his kettles he must do several things. He must work out the cost of the aluminium or tin plate for making them, the wages he has to pay his workpeople, the cost of the fuel and light they will use, the rent for the factory and all the wear and tear on the machines. He must also allow for the cost of taking the kettles to the shops from his factory. Finally, he must allow something for his own profit, because it is on this profit that he relies to earn his own living.

Supply and Demand

The price of a thing also depends on how much it is wanted and how much of it there is for sale. In other words it depends on the *demand* for it and the *supply* of it. This does not apply to kettles much, because most people need a kettle or two in the house and there are usually enough in the shops. However, the price of other goods is affected a good deal by supply and demand. The price of food, for example, often depends on the supply. Suppose, for example, the shoals of cod desert the Dogger Bank in the North Sea, and the fishing vessels come home half empty. Then the fishmongers start putting up "sold out" notices and the price of cod begins to rise. Again, there might be a glut of plums one year and their price might drop a few pence or more.

However, although the *supply* of certain goods is often affected by things people can do nothing about, the *demand* depends more on how much money they have and on charges in the kind of things they want to buy, as well as on prices. The demand for necessities like bread does not change much but some items, such as cameras or records, may not always sell. In this case the shopkeeper may reduce their price to encourage more people to buy. He might also reduce the price of one or two items to attract customers into his shop. Once inside he hopes they will buy more of his range of goods.

PRIEST is the word used today, in all except the Free Churches, for a man set apart by the church to care for the souls of people. It is one of three orders in the church. When a man first enters the Christian ministry he becomes a deacon; then after about 12 months he is made a priest ; and some priests are later consecrated as bishops.

A priest has two kinds of duties. First he preaches the word of God and teaches people about the Christian faith, both in church and in everyday life. Secondly he administers certain sacraments (see SACRAMENTS) of the church. For example, he baptizes children, celebrates Holy Communion and, in the name of God, forgives people their sins in the Sacrament of Penance (sometimes called Confession). A deacon is allowed to administer only the sacraments of Baptism and, sometimes, Marriage. Only bishops can administer the sacraments of Confirmation and Ordination.

Most priests are appointed to work in particular districts known as parishes. However, some work as missionaries to spread Christianity in countries where it is not the main religion, and others are chaplains to prisons, hospitals, schools and the armed forces.

In the early days of the Christian church they were called presbyters more often than priests. Indeed, the title "priest" does not appear to have been generally used in the church until 200 or 300 years after it was founded.

In the Free Churches clergymen are known by such titles as minister and pastor. They are not divided into the three grades of deacon, priest and bishop, and all of them are allowed to baptize and celebrate Holy Communion.

PRIESTLEY, Joseph (1733–1804). Joseph

Priestley was one of the pioneers of experimental chemistry and was also a man of wide interests. He was the son of a Yorkshire cloth-maker and during his education and training for the Nonconformist ministry he learned a number of ancient and modern languages. After some years as a minister and teacher he became librarian to Lord Shelburne at Calne, Wiltshire. Later he moved to Birmingham.

Priestley is remembered chiefly for his work in discovering the common gases and showing their importance. He had no scientific training but was able to think of brilliant experiments. By collecting what he called the "fixed air" given off when brewing beer he was able to force it into water and thus invented soda water. (Actually the "fixed air" was the gas carbon dioxide, on which there is a separate article.) In August 1774 he discovered oxygen (see OXYGEN) and was able to show that this gas is necessary in breathing and in burning. Among other gases discovered by Priestley were sulphur dioxide and ammonia.

Priestley had strong opinions about politics and expressed them freely. He was in favour of democracy, or rule by the people, and is supposed to have been the author of the phrase "the greatest happiness of the greatest number". He sympathized with the Americans in their War of Independence and with the revolutionaries in the French Revolution. In 1791 a society to which he belonged gave a dinner to celebrate the success of the French Revolution. Thereupon the Birmingham mob set fire to Priestley's chapel and wrecked his house. In 1794 he went to the United States and lived in Northumberland, Pennsylvania, for the rest of his life.

PRIME MINISTER. In Great Britain, the

Commonwealth and many other countries, the leader of the government is the Prime Minister, or Premier as he is sometimes called. He is the government's chief spokesman in parliament, he controls the meetings of the Cabinet and since 1902 in Great Britain he has always sat in the House of Commons. Before that he was often a member of the House of Lords.

In Great Britain the sovereign (that is, the king or the queen on the throne) chooses the Prime Minister. Usually the sovereign sends for the leader of the biggest political party in the House of Commons and asks him to form a government, but sometimes the sovereign has to choose from among two or three men and when this happens the sovereign consults his or her advisers. When Sir Anthony Eden resigned in 1957, for example, the Queen talked to her

Priestley used the apparatus shown below in his experiments. The gases were collected in glass jars inverted over water. The mice in the jar at the front were used to test whether the gases were poisonous.

Left: Courtesy, National Portrait Gallery. Right: Mansell Collection

advisers and then chose Harold Macmillan as Prime Minister rather than R. A. Butler. In Australia, Canada and New Zealand the Governor-General chooses the Prime Minister for the sovereign.

The British Prime Minister lives at Number 10 Downing Street, in London, and holds his official meetings there. The Prime Minister also has the use of a country mansion in Buckinghamshire called Chequers. (See CHEQUERS; DOWNING STREET.)

There has not always been a Prime Minister. Until the time of Queen Anne the sovereign used to control the meetings of the Cabinet, and for some years after that the sovereign went on attending the meetings of cabinet ministers. However, George I was a German and could not understand his English ministers when they spoke fast, so in 1717 he gave up going to their meetings. In 1721 Sir Robert Walpole took over the leadership of the Cabinet and he was really the first Prime Minister. The English people did not like the idea of one minister having so much power, however, and it was a long while before the name Prime Minister was used.

Little by little the Prime Minister, who has usually held the office of First Lord of the Treasury, began to choose the other ministers, although he still had to get his sovereign to agree. He acts as the chairman of the Cabinet when the chief ministers meet. He has to tell the sovereign what happens at these meetings and in parliament, although today it is the Prime Minister and the Cabinet who take the blame for mistakes in governing the country, and not the sovereign. Also, it is the Prime Minister who now advises the sovereign when parliament should be brought to an end (dissolved) and a general election held.

Some Famous Prime Ministers

There is a list below of all the British Prime Ministers and the dates of their governments. They include William Pitt the Younger, who was actually the youngest Prime Minister at 24. He saw Britain through the worst perils of the Napoleonic Wars. He also did a great deal to make the Prime Minister an important person. Sir Robert Peel is best remembered for repealing

(abolishing) the Corn Laws and so reducing the price of bread when there was a famine in Ireland. Lord Palmerston was the Prime Minister who greatly increased British power abroad in the middle of the 19th century. Benjamin Disraeli is remembered because he did so much to modernize the Conservative party; his great opponent was W. E. Gladstone who was a Liberal and was Prime Minister four times during Queen Victoria's reign.

Among modern Prime Ministers, David Lloyd George was notable for his rise from poverty and for his energetic leadership during World War I. Winston Churchill was a great war leader during World War II, leading Britain to victory in 1945. The youngest Prime Minister of the 20th century was Harold Wilson, 48 when he took office in 1964. In 1979 Margaret Thatcher became Britain's first woman Prime Minister.

LIST OF BRITISH PRIME MINISTERS

Prime Minister	Party	Date
Sir Robert Walpole	Whig	1721
Earl of Wilmington	Whig	1742
Henry Pelham	Whig	1743
Duke of Newcastle	Whig	1754
Duke of Devonshire	Whig	1756
Duke of Newcastle	Whig	1757
Earl of Bute	Tory	1762
George Grenville	Whig	1763
Marquess of Rockingham	Whig	1765
Earl of Chatham	Whig	1766
Duke of Grafton	Whig	1768
Lord North	Tory	1770
M. of Rockingham	Whig	1782
Earl of Shelburne	Whig	1782
Duke of Portland	Coalition	1783
William Pitt	Tory	1783
Henry Addington	Tory	1801
William Pitt	Tory	1804
Lord Grenville	Whig	1806
Duke of Portland	Tory	1807
Spencer Perceval	Tory	1809
Earl of Liverpool	Tory	1812
George Canning	Tory	1827
Viscount Goderich	Tory	1827
Duke of Wellington	Tory	1828
Earl Grey	Whig	1830
Viscount Melbourne	Whig	1834
Sir Robert Peel	Tory	1834
Viscount Melbourne	Whig	1835
Sir Robert Peel	Tory	1841
Lord John Russell	Whig	1846

Prime Minister	Party	Date	Prime Minister	Party	Date
Earl of Derby	Tory	1852	J. R. MacDonald	Labour	1929
Earl of Aberdeen	Peelite	1852	J. R. MacDonald	National (Labour prime minister)	1931
Viscount Palmerston	Liberal	1855			
Earl of Derby	Conservative	1858	S. Baldwin	National (Conservative prime minister)	1935
Viscount Palmerston	Liberal	1859	S. Baldwin		1935
Earl Russell	Liberal	1865	A. N. Chamberlain	National (Conservative	1937
Earl of Derby	Conservative	1866	A. N. Chamberlain	prime minister)	1939
Benjamin Disraeli	Conservative	1868	W. S. Churchill	Coalition	1940
W. E. Gladstone	Liberal	1868	W. S. Churchill	Conservative	1945
Benjamin Disraeli	Conservative	1874	C. R. Attlee	Labour	1945
W. E. Gladstone	Liberal	1880	C. R. Attlee	Labour	1950
Marquess of Salisbury	Conservative	1885	W. S. Churchill	Conservative	1951
W. E. Gladstone	Liberal	1886	Sir A. Eden	Conservative	1955
Marquess of Salisbury	Conservative	1886	H. Macmillan	Conservative	1957
W. E. Gladstone	Liberal	1892	H. Macmillan	Conservative	1959
Earl of Rosebery	Liberal	1894	Earl of Home	Conservative	1963
Marquess of Salisbury	Conservative	1895	H. Wilson	Labour	1964
A. J. Balfour	Conservative	1902	E. Heath	Conservative	1970
Sir H. Campbell-Bannerman	Liberal	1905	H. Wilson	Labour	1974
H. H. Asquith	Liberal	1908	J. Callaghan	Labour	1976
H. H. Asquith	Coalition	1915	M. Thatcher	Conservative	1979
D. Lloyd George	Coalition	1916			
D. Lloyd George	Coalition	1918			
A. Bonar Law	Conservative	1922			
S. Baldwin	Conservative	1923			
J. R. MacDonald	Labour	1924			
S. Baldwin	Conservative	1924			

PRIMITIVE ART. Early men, living in caves during the Stone Age, made beautiful drawings on the rock walls. (See Cave Art.) They were primitive in the sense that they had no writing or machines, and only the simplest tools. Yet they were skilful artists. By "primitive art" we mean those forms of art produced by people before they came into contact with the great world civilizations, and in particular with the modern world as we know it. However, artists may also be described as "primitives" if they are untrained and paint in an almost childlike style. A good example is the French painter Henri Rousseau (1844–1910).

Primitive artists are usually craftsmen. Just as some members of a tribe are better hunters, others are more expert at making things such as tools, ornaments, household goods, and objects with religious and magical uses. Primitive artists usually work in their spare time and hardly ever make objects to sell (until tourists begin to arrive). They use whatever local materials are available.

Some of the finest primitive art comes from West Africa, the Pacific and North America, although there are good examples of local work to be found in South America, Asia and elsewhere in Africa. Common materials are wood, stone, clay, metals, bone, ivory, shell, beads, reeds, fibres and feathers. Often colours

Keystone

Three British Prime Ministers. Anthony Eden, Winston Churchill and C. R. Attlee on the day World War II ended.

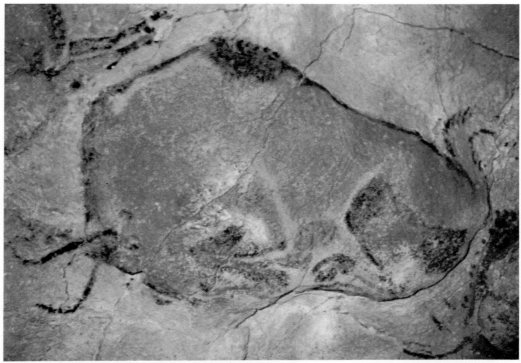

Top: Courtesy, Spring Books Ltd. Left: Courtesy, Museum of Primitive Art, New York; photo Elizabeth Little. Above: Courtesy, Trustees of the British Museum

Top: A bison painted on the roof of a cave in Altamira, Spain, between 10,000 and 30,000 years ago. Left: Painted clay vessel from Mexico. Above: A rattan basket, ornamented with beads, from Borneo.

(1, 5) From "Arts of the African Native", by M. Griaule; courtesy Thames & Hudson Ltd. (2, 6, 7) Courtesy, American Museum of Natural History. (3) Courtesy, Nat. Museum of Natural Sciences, Madrid. (4) R. H. Bomback.

(1) Bronze slab from Benin. (2) American Indian "X-ray" drawing. (3) Prehistoric cave-painting. (4) Decorated paddle from Solomon Islands. (5) Pot made by the Mangbetu of the Congo Republic. (6) Eskimo mask representing an evil spirit. (7) Alaskan chest with a design of the jumbled parts of an animal.

are painted on these materials. Tools are usually adzes (a type of axe) for carving and knives for whittling and detailed carving, and many peoples also use needles and tools for boring. Colours may be made from natural dyes.

Carving in the Pacific islands is done by stone adzes, since there is no metal in the area, and many parts of Africa have no stone that is suitable for people to carve on. In the Arctic region antlers, tusks and teeth provide the best material for carving. In the Kalahari desert of southern Africa the Bushmen use only rock-surfaces and ostrich eggshells for their delicate engraving. In the Amazon valley the only art is that found in basketry, pottery and featherwork, since there are no other materials available.

The primitive artist may be a maker of household objects such as stools, pots, axes and baskets. He sets out to make a thing like a stool, but at the same time he makes it in a pleasant form and will decorate it. He does not make some things only beautiful and others only useful as Western people tend to do. Paintings upon a flat surface, for use purely as decoration to be looked at, are not common in primitive societies, although decoration for its own sake is sometimes found, such as the Eskimo bone figurines (small statues) made to while away the long winter nights or the ornaments of shell, elaborately carved and decorated, from much of the Pacific. Things like pots and canoe paddles may be highly decorated with paint, shells and beads.

What is usually thought of as primitive art, however, is more likely to be an object to be used in religious or magical ceremonies. It may represent a god, an ancestor or a legendary person who is supposed to enter it while rites (religious ceremonies) are performed. The primitive artist therefore tries to show the *nature* of the god in the work of art. He may show a war god as menacing and snarling, or a god of sickness as a face or person suffering from the sickness. This kind of representation, as it is called, can be seen especially in the masks that are found in almost every part of the world and which are worn by human beings who act the part of gods, spirits or ancestors in rituals, dances and other ceremonies. (See MASK.)

In Indian religious art the god Shiva may be shown not as a man but as a bull and in much of the religious art of ancient Egypt the artists used animals to show gods in their drawings. It was believed that the gods descended to their worshippers in the shape of these animals, and also showed some of the qualities of the animals, rather as a king may be compared to a lion, which has courage and majesty. In African art a king may be shown to be a king because he carries a special axe, or his attendants hold an umbrella over him. Often he may be shown far larger than other men, as in the bronze from Benin shown in the illustration. This means that he is more important than other people. The same idea is found in many European pictures painted during the middle ages.

Many peoples think that a picture of an animal should show not only its head, legs and body but also the heart, liver and other internal organs. An example of such an "X-ray" drawing, in which an artist of an American Indian tribe has shown the internal parts of a snake, a wolf, a bird and a whale, is shown in the illustrations. This does not mean that he thought the animals look like this to the eye, but that he was trying to show in a picture what for him were the most important things about them; in other words, the parts that can be eaten and can be used in magic.

It is clear that these kinds of drawings are important, but it is sometimes very difficult to know what they mean. A black cloud in a picture might be a sign of rain to us. For the Australian Aborigines, however, a sign of rain is a serpent, and many of the Australian drawings show the rainbow serpent which not only represents rain but also, in a more general way, the richness of the land and the prosperity of man and nature. It is not a picture of a real serpent at all and may in fact be hardly recognizable as such, but be shown merely by a few wavy lines.

Portraits of actual people or pictures of actual plants and landscapes are very rare in primitive art. Most of those that do exist seem to be portraits of dead kings.

Primitive art has told experts much about primitive societies and how they worked. This knowledge is all the more valuable because many of these societies have vanished for ever. Rapid

Top: These finely modelled Japanese clay figures, known as *haniwa*, were placed around tombs, apparently to protect the dead from harm. They date from around A.D. 300. Left: Part of an embroidered mantle made by the Paracas people of ancient Peru. Centre right: A clay urn, associated with funerals, from China. It was made about 2500–2000 B.C., and at the time this pottery had few equals anywhere in the world. Bottom right: A protective idol from the Solomon Islands in the Pacific. Made of blackened wood inlaid with mother-of-pearl, this small figure was placed in the prow of a war canoe.

Courtesy, (top) Tokyo National Museum; (left) National Archaeological Museum, Lima; (centre right) Royal Ontario Museum, Toronto; (bottom right) Museum für Volkerkunde, Basle social changes in many parts of the world have meant the end of primitive art.

PRIMROSE. The name primrose means "first rose", but of course the primrose is not a rose, although in shape it is rather like the wild rose, being round with five petals. Groups of the pale yellow flowers grow in woods, hedgerows, railway embankments and other sheltered places in the spring. Primroses are found in most parts of Europe, growing where the soil is fairly rich and damp and the sun is not too strong.

The name of the primrose's genus, or group, is *Primula* and it belongs to the Primulaceae family. Among its relations are the cowslip, polyanthus, cyclamen and pimpernel. Garden primroses can be red, pink and purple as well as yellow.

There are two kinds of primroses, pin-eyed and thrum-eyed. In the pin-eyed primroses the

John Markham

The common primrose, *primula vulgaris*.

style, or little stem on top of which is the stigma, is long, coming to the top of the tube-shaped calyx, while the five stamens are attached halfway down the tube. In the thrum-eyed primroses the style is short and the stamens are at the top of the tube.

The evening primrose is a tall plant which belongs to a different family, the Onagraceae.

PRINCE EDWARD ISLAND is Canada's smallest province but is also the most thickly populated. It is somewhat larger than the English county of Norfolk. The island lies in a sheltered bay at the south end of the Gulf of St.

Lawrence, being separated from the mainland province of New Brunswick and Nova Scotia by Northumberland Strait, which is about 30 kilometres across.

Prince Edward Island is crescent-shaped with a very irregular coastline, deep inlets dividing the land into three almost equal parts. A ridge of low hills runs from north to south across the middle part but none of the island rises above 150 metres. The island was once thickly wooded but most of the trees have been cut down so that the land can be cultivated. The summers are mild and the winters cold with much snow, but the warming effect of the sea prevents the weather from becoming too cold.

A few American Indians of the Micmac tribe live in reservations, or areas set apart for them, but most of the people are Canadians of British descent and about half are Roman Catholics. The primary schools are free and children have to attend them. The only city in Prince Edward Island is the capital, Charlottetown, which is on Hillsborough Bay on the south coast. It is a pleasant town with tree-lined streets.

The soil of Prince Edward Island is a rich, sandy loam, deep red in colour, often fertilized with mud dredged (scooped) from the bays and tidal rivers. The chief crops are hay, clover and oats for feeding the animals. Prince Edward Island is particularly noted for its potatoes, and barley, wheat and fruits are also grown. Large numbers of dairy cattle, pigs and poultry are kept and the island is famous for its bacon, canned chicken and seed potatoes.

The breeding of silver foxes in captivity for their fur was begun on Prince Edward Island in 1887. Mink are also bred but fur-farming is less important than it used to be. There are valuable fisheries, the most important catch being lobsters, and the oysters from Malpeque Bay are famous for their flavour and quality. There are a number of sawmills but there are few factories except for those producing butter and cheese or packing meat and fish.

The chief port of Prince Edward Island is Charlottetown, which is closed by ice for a few weeks in the spring. The island's railways are linked with those of the mainland by ice-breaking ferries which carry trains all the year round

The Legislative Building, Charlottetown, the headquarters of the government of Prince Edward Island.

between Port Borden and Cape Tormentine in New Brunswick. These ferries also carry motor cars and lorries. Another car-ferry service runs between Prince Edward Island and Nova Scotia. The island has good roads and an air service connects Charlottetown and Summerside with Moncton in New Brunswick.

Prince Edward Island is a popular holiday resort. The wide sandy beaches and mild climate are ideal for swimming and the streams abound in trout. Some visitors come to shoot wild geese and ducks in the late summer and autumn.

History

The Canadian Indians called the island Abegweit, meaning "the home cradled on the waves". It was discovered in 1534 by the French explorer Jacques Cartier but few Frenchmen came to settle there until the 18th century. The explorer Samuel de Champlain named the island "Isle St. John".

In 1758 British forces occupied the island and drove out some of the French settlers. The island became a British possession in 1763, at first as a part of Nova Scotia and then in 1769 as a separate colony. It was renamed Prince Edward Island in 1798, in honour of Prince Edward, Duke of Kent, the father of Queen Victoria.

In 1864 representatives of the Canadian provinces met at Charlottetown to discuss a plan of federation, or union. This led to the creation of the Dominion of Canada in 1867, and therefore Charlottetown is sometimes called "the cradle of confederation". Prince Edward Island itself was not one of the original members of confederation but joined in 1873. It manages its own local affairs and sends representatives to the Canadian federal parliament at Ottawa.

The population of Prince Edward Island is about 111,600.

PRINCES IN THE TOWER.

When Edward IV died in 1483 he left his two young sons—the boy king Edward V, who was 12, and his brother Richard, Duke of York, aged 9—in the care of their uncle Richard, Duke of Gloucester. To keep the princes' mother and her relatives from gaining power through the children Gloucester took charge of them and housed them in the Tower of London. Several times the princes were seen playing in the Tower garden but soon they disappeared for ever. Gloucester meanwhile had been declared the rightful king as Richard III. It is possible that the princes were murdered on Richard's orders. In Shakespeare's play *Richard III* the children are

The princes, Edward and Richard, as shown in the glass in Canterbury Cathedral.

smothered by two murderers acting on Richard's instructions. However there is no positive proof that Richard did order their deaths and two other men have been suggested as being responsible. One is the Duke of Buckingham and the other is Henry VII, Richard's successor. The princes would have been rivals for his throne.

In 1674 a wooden chest was found in the Tower containing some bones which were probably those of the princes. They were buried in Henry VII's Chapel in Westminster Abbey.

PRINTING is the means of reproducing, usually on paper, identical copies of words or pictures. Some of the things that are printed include books, magazines, newspapers, business forms, labels, packages and tickets. The list is almost endless, for printing is one of the most important ways in which we get information. (Just try to count the number of times during the day you look at a piece of printing!)

Several different printing methods, or pro-

cesses, are used. This article deals with the three main ones : they are called *Offset* (or *Litho Offset*), *Letterpress*, and *Roto* (or *Rotogravure*). Whichever process is to be used, the "type" must first be "set". If it is a book that is to be made, then the type matter, when set, will make up the words of the text and the captions for the illustrations. This is known as composition.

Composing

Printing from movable type (there is a separate piece of type for each letter or "character") was invented in Europe by Johannes Gutenberg in about 1438, and introduced to England by William Caxton. (See CAXTON and GUTENBERG.) For many years, the most important printing process was letterpress. In letterpress printing, ink is transferred under pressure from the type onto the paper. For centuries, the letters of type were assembled by hand. From about 1900 this was done mechanically, using Monotype or Linotype machines. The early type was made of wood but later a lead alloy was used.

A monotype machine has a keyboard similar to a typewriter, and produces the type in metal either as single letters (Monotype) or line by line in a strip or "slug" of type metal (Linotype).

Today, typesetting is mostly done by computerized filmsetting systems. It is called "filmsetting" because type is produced not as metal pieces but on photographic film. The characters or letters making up each word are transferred

Courtesy, Trustees of the British Library
The earliest illustration of a European printing press, made in France in 1499. It shows printers and a bookseller, bothered by demons.

A reproduction of the first page of Genesis from the Bible printed in Latin by Johann Gutenberg about 1455. The decorations were added to the printed page by hand.

photographically on to a metal plate, which is then used to print the book or magazine.

Filmsetting machines were first used in the 1950s. It is cheaper to use computerized film-setting than the old "hot metal" methods. The main parts of a filmsetter system are usually a keyboard, a computer with disc drives, a printer, visual display units and finally the filmsetter itself (which is driven by the computer).

How Filmsetting Works

Before the operator starts "keying" the text, he or she "encodes" the instructions to the computer. This tells the computer which type style, or "face", is to be used, the size of the type, and the width and number of lines required on each page.

Before the computer passes this information to the filmsetter, it displays the type matter that has been prepared on a screen or visual display unit (VDU). This has its own mini computer and its operator (the compositor) can make corrections by using the VDU keyboard. The author too can make corrections on a proof, a "rough copy" produced on a printer driven by the computer. When printer and author are satisfied, the computer is told to "output" the information to the filmsetter. It exposes photographic film or paper to images of the required characters and, when processed, this provides complete pages on film. If the pages are to contain illustrations, these too can be put in, on the film, before plate-making takes place.

Offset

This is the method used for most printing today. The transfer of the image from the plate to paper depends on the principle that water and grease will not mix. This process was originally known as lithography and was invented by the Bohemian Alois Senelfelder who, in about 1798, applied the "water-grease" principle to printing. He used a stone on which the image was drawn with a greasy substance. Offset today uses metal plates, often made of zinc. They are coated with a light-sensitive chemical and then exposed to the films of the pages to be printed in a vacuum using a powerful light. When the plate is "developed", the coating remains only in those areas which

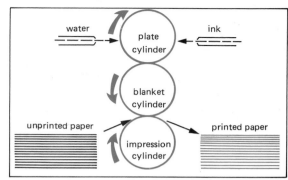

In sheet-fed offset, there are three cylinders. The image (words or pictures) are "offset" from the plate to the blanket, and then from the blanket to the paper.

are required to print and which will repel water.

The offset printing press needs a method of applying a thin film of water to the plate, and an inking system, plus a system of rollers or cylinders to transfer the image from the printing plate to the paper.

The plate is clamped round a cylinder which, as it rotates, receives first an application of water which sticks to the "non-image" areas, followed by contact with the ink, which sticks only to the "image" areas. The plate cylinder touches another cylinder which is covered with a rubber blanket. The inked image on the plate cylinder is transferred ("offset") to the rubber blanket, which, in turn, is pressed against the paper. And so the paper is printed.

There are two kinds of offset printing machines: those which print *sheets* of paper, and those which print on a continuous *web* of paper fed from a large roll. Sheet-fed machines range in size from very small for office printing, to large presses, such as are used to print Children's Britannica. These print 32 pages of the encyclopaedia at one time, on one side of the sheet, which is then passed through a second time to print on the other side—making a total of 64 pages. These sheets are then folded by machine, sewn, trimmed and bound to make the book.

Web-fed rotary machines run much faster than sheet-fed machines, and print both sides of the paper in one go. The printed web passes through a drier, then into the folder which cuts and folds the paper, to produce folded sections ready to be bound together to make a book. Many newspapers are printed by web-offset.

Letterpress

This is the oldest method of printing. It is based on taking an impression from a raised printing surface which has previously been inked. Letterpress presses also fall into two groups: sheet-fed and web-fed. In a sheet-fed press, the metal type, held in a steel frame called a chase, is placed on a flat bed which passes to and fro and presses on to the sheet of paper on the impression cylinder. In the small letterpress machines known as platens, the chase is positioned vertically and the paper is presented to the inked type on a "platen" or flat plate. This opens and closes for the sheet of paper to be fed in and withdrawn after printing.

Letterpress is simpler than offset but the presses are usually slower and need more preparation or "make-ready". Letterpress is also less suitable for computerized filmsetting. For these reasons, letterpress is no longer the main printing process, having been overtaken by offset.

Rotogravure

Printing by rotogravure depends on translating the matter to be printed into cells or pits etched with acid into a copper cylinder. Each different-sized cell prints a greater or lesser amount of ink when brought into contact with the paper.

To produce the etched cylinder, the matter to be printed is first photographed and a film positive made. (See PHOTOGRAPHY.) This is photographically printed on to a sheet of light-sensitive pigmented gelatine which has been exposed to a gravure screen. The gravure screen appears as a network of opaque squares formed by transparent lines which, when printed on to the pigment paper, produce a lined grid in the gelatine. The pigmented gelatine is applied to the copper cylinder and "developed" in hot water. The image is then represented by "cells" of varying thickness of gelatine. The gelatine "resist", as it is called, protects the plate from the acid, allowing a pattern of cells (of the same size but different depths) to be etched on to the metal. When acid (ferric chloride) is poured over the cylinder, cells of varying depths are left on it.

On the rotogravure press the cylinder surface is sprayed with an ink containing a spirit solvent. Immediately before the cylinder comes into contact with the paper, its surface is wiped by means of a moving steel blade, called a doctor blade. This leaves the surface clean but the ink remains in the etched cell pattern.

Most gravure printing is now done on web-fed or rotary presses. Rotogravure can print good full-colour pictures on cheap paper. But because making the gravure cylinders is relatively expensive, the process is generally used only for magazines and mail-order catalogues printed in very large quantities. Small fast-running gravure presses are also used in the packaging industry.

Illustrations

Illustrations may be divided into two main types: *line* and *half-tone*. Line illustrations are usually drawings in which only lines are used, and in which there is no range of tone (from shadows to high-lights) such as you see in a photograph.

The printing of line illustrations is relatively simple, but to achieve the effect of a full tone range in letterpress and offset, the printer uses an illusion. The original picture is turned by photography into dots of different sizes. A "screen" (like a fine mesh) is used to break up the picture into dots. There are usually 52 dots to each centimetre. If you examine a newspaper illustration under a magnifying glass, you will see the dots clearly. Although when printed all the dots are as black as each other, your eye sees something very like the original photograph.

For offset printing, the original picture is recorded in dots on film in a similar way, and then transferred to the litho plate from which the actual printing is done. For letterpress, the "screened" dot image must be engraved on to a metal plate so that the dots are effectively raised *above* the surrounding white areas. The metal plate (usually copper) is mounted on wood or other suitable material so that the tops of the dots are at the same height as the metal type-matter.

In rotogravure the cell structure makes it possible for different amounts of ink to be transferred by cells of different size. So reproduction of illustrations by gravure is in theory more

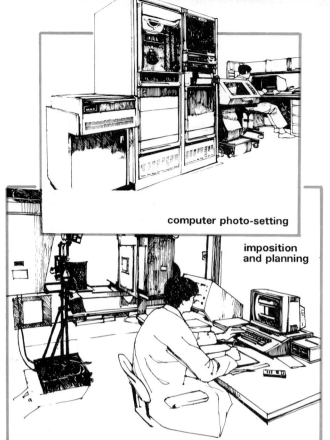

computer photo-setting

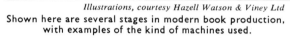

imposition
and planning

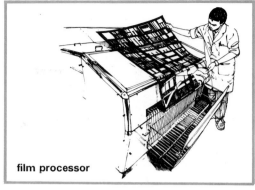

film processor

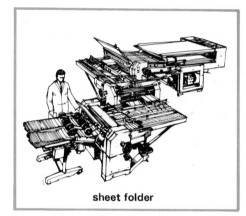

sheet folder

Illustrations, courtesy Hazell Watson & Viney Ltd

Shown here are several stages in modern book production, with examples of the kind of machines used.

First, the words (known as "copy") are set in type, and then pages made up with the help of computers. The planned pages, with illustrations correctly positioned, are turned into large sheets of film, ready for platemaking and printing. A large web-fed rotary press (shown below) can print paperbacks which are then bound on another machine at the rate of up to 15,000 books an hour. A sheet-fed press prints large sheets which are folded and cut to make the right number of pages, folded into sections. The sections are gathered in the correct order, and glued and sewn together. If the book is to be a hardback, it is cased inside board covers on a case-binding machine (right).

case binding

web-fed rotary press

Printing brought about a great change in art and learning. During the middle ages the monks of the Christian monasteries of Europe spent tedious hours copying books by hand. Their work was very beautiful, but the slow process meant that books were few and precious. Printing by machine made books much more plentiful.

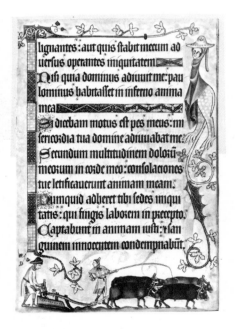

An example of a handwritten manuscript. The pages were often richly decorated, as in this English book from the 1300s.

accurate than by offset or letterpress. However, control of the process is more difficult, and the cost is usually higher.

Colour

Full-colour illustrations are made by analysing the original art-work or colour photograph into its colour components (yellow, red, blue and black), and then making a printing plate or cylinder for each colour. (See COLOUR.) This analysis is done photographically using colour filters, or by electronic "colour-scanning" of the original. It is possible to separate the four colours, and at the same time make colour "corrections" to take account of the shortcomings of the colour printing inks. The scanner also performs the screening operation, and out come four films of the picture ready for printing down on a litho plate. (See diagram.)

Page Assembly

Before the offset printing plates or rotogravure cylinders can be made, the printer must assemble or "plan" the films of the pages together with the films of the illustrations. For colour work, the films must be planned in "register" so that when printing takes place, the four images (yellow, red, blue and black) fall precisely on top of each other "in register". Otherwise, the result will look blurred and "out-of-focus". This can be done by computer: electronic page make-up saves time and money, but is useful only with offset and rotogravure printing. Letterpress uses half-tone blocks and type-matter which cannot be planned electronically.

Printing Tomorrow

Until the 1970s almost all printing was done by one of the three methods described above. Electronics have not only changed printing processes but have also, to some extent, provided alternatives to the printed book or magazine. News and other data is now available in word form as "teletext" on television screens. (See COMMUNICATION and TELEVISION.) Home printers, connected to word processors, may replace large printing presses in some cases. However, the printing processes in use today will probably continue to produce our books and newspapers

To print a colour picture, the original (in this case a photograph of a butterfly) is first broken down into its colour "parts" — yellow, red, blue and black. This can be done either by photographing the picture four times, using special filters to shut out all but one colour, or by "scanning" it electronically. Four pieces of film are produced in this way, each piece bearing just its own colour "part" of the original. Here you see the picture gradually building up. First, yellow (left); then yellow plus red; then yellow plus red plus blue; and finally, with the black film added, the complete colour picture.

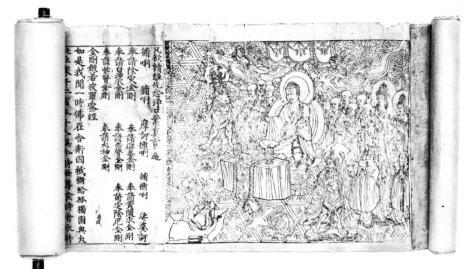

The Chinese were the first to use printing, by wood-cuts (see WOODCUTS). The oldest printed book in the world is the Buddhist Diamond Sutra, printed in China in A.D. 868. It consists of six sheets of printed text and a woodcut picture of Buddha.

Courtesy, Trustees of the British Library

with the increasing aid of electronics, particularly in setting type and making up pages.

For more about the printed word, see the articles BOOKS, JOURNALISM and NEWSPAPERS.

PRISONS. Imprisonment is a method of dealing with people who commit crimes. The length of time in prison may be for any period up to life, according to the seriousness of the crime. Other ways of dealing with offenders are the paying of fines; and being placed on probation, which means that the offender agrees to obey certain conditions and to be supervised by a probation officer. (See PROBATION.) People who are to be tried for a crime may also be kept in prison until their trial.

In Great Britain a prison sentence may be suspended or deferred, and only imposed if another offence is committed. Young people under 17 are not normally sentenced to imprisonment. Young offenders may be sent to attendance centres, where they have to work for some hours each week in their spare time; detention centres to which young male offenders may be sent for short periods; and day training centres. There is also community service, where offenders do unpaid work, usually at weekends.

Prisons in the Old Days

Before the middle of the 19th century the penalty for a great number of offences, even for stealing a few shillings, was death. In fact, however, most British offenders, instead of being hanged, were transported to the colonies, the best known place being Botany Bay in Australia. Prisons were used only to hold offenders awaiting trial, transportation or death.

Criminals in those days were herded together in prisons, women and children as well as men, in conditions so dreadful that each year thousands died of disease, particularly a kind of typhus fever known as jail fever.

In the 18th century John Howard tried to reform prisons, declaring that they should be made healthy, that prisoners should have separate cells (small rooms) to sleep in and be given work and religious instruction. Later, Elizabeth Fry (see FRY, ELIZABETH) worked to improve conditions for women in Newgate prison in London. For a long time, however, prisoners continued to be treated more like animals than human beings. Some prisoners were shut up in cells in solitary confinement (that is, entirely by themselves) and had to do "hard labour" on treadmills and similar machines. The treadmill was a series of steps on a revolving cylinder, on which the prisoner was made to tread. In Victorian times in London the Marshalsea prison was used for people who could not pay their debts, and debtors were also sent to the dreadful Fleet prison.

Today prisons try to "contain" their prisoners in decent conditions and, if possible, to prepare them for honest lives outside. Unfortunately prison often fails to prevent a prisoner returning to a life of crime after release, even though loss of freedom is always a serious punishment.

Prisons Today

There are different types of prisons, so that prisoners can be occupied in ways suited to them and their sentences. People who have already committed several serious crimes and against whom the public must be protected may be given long sentences and sent to maximum security prisons.

Offenders whose mental condition is such that they are unfit to be tried or who, after being sentenced, are found to need special treatment, are sent either to a psychiatric hospital or to a special hospital with security arrangements.

Those sentenced to imprisonment may be released (if they behave well) when they have served two-thirds of the time. This is called remission of sentence. In addition, people serving sentences of over 18 months may be freed on parole after they have served one third of the sentence or 12 months (whichever is longer). If they break the conditions of the parole, such prisoners can be returned to prison.

All prisoners go first to the local prison. Those serving short sentences or who are not suitable for long term prisons remain there. Those who have not been in prison before, and others who are not very dangerous are kept separate from the rest. Some are sent to "open" prisons, which are camps or large houses with nothing to stop the prisoners running away.

In prisons for long-term prisoners and in some other prisons there are modern industrial workshops, and the prisoners can undertake educational courses, even to a university degree. But some of the work done remains monotonous, and there are prisoners who must be taught to read and write.

Inside prison the prisoners are allowed the use of the prison library, to have newspapers, to listen to the radio and watch television. Volunteers called prison visitors or associates may come and talk to them as friends and listen to their problems. Home leave towards the end of a long sentence is given to suitable prisoners who can be trusted. This is done to help them adjust to life outside, to find a job in advance of their release and to renew their ties with friends and relations before they return home for good.

Male prisoners wear grey suits, but most women prisoners may wear their own clothes, and may use make-up.

Prison officers are selected and trained for the difficult job of containing and sometimes controlling people who may be violent. Yet they must also show concern for the lonely prisoner. Where conflicts occur, they must be handled with skill. In addition to governors and assistant governors, prison staffs also include chaplains, teachers, physical education instructors and trade instructors.

The prison welfare officer has an important job to do, for he helps prisoners with troubles outside. Families can all too easily break up while a father is in prison. The welfare officer helps to prepare prisoners for life after their release, when they will be offered help by the probation and after-care service and by voluntary organizations. Many ex-prisoners have no homes to go to, and they are normally offered a place in a hostel.

Mansell Collection

Prisons in the 18th century often consisted of large gloomy chambers in which many prisoners were crowded together under the watch of the gaolers.

PRIVET. The name privet is used for over 40 kinds of shrub and small tree. Most privets make good hedges, for they grow quickly and are hardy.

Maurice Nimmo

The wild privet has pretty white flowers.

The common privet seen widely in Britain and northern Europe also grows in North America. It reaches a height of over 4 metres, but is usually cut back as a hedge. Because it is clipped by gardeners, the privet's creamy-white flowers are not often seen. The privet has black berries, which are poisonous to eat.

PRIVY COUNCIL. Every so often the Queen holds a council of her ministers and advisers and approves a proclamation or an "order in council". The privy council has a long history. Throughout the centuries the sovereign has been helped in governing the country by various councils. Their names and their duties have changed, but there have always been at least two : a big council and a small council. Originally the big council was a body that was called together from time to time to settle big questions. It started with the Witan (see WITAN) in Saxon times and changed in Norman times into a council made up of persons in royal service and persons who held their lands from the Crown. In the end the place of this big council was taken by parliament.

The smaller body, sometimes called the "privy (or private) council" and sometimes the "continual council", had some judicial duties and also carried on the day to to day business of government. However, as parliament became more powerful it expected the sovereign to choose ministers from among the members of parliament, so the cabinet finally took the place of the privy council in the government of the country. (See CABINET, THE.)

But the privy council has continued to exist

and there is a link between it and the cabinet, for all cabinet ministers have to be members of the privy council. Today it has about 300 members. Appointments to the council are made by the sovereign and are for life. Most of the members are politicians—cabinet ministers and ex-cabinet ministers, including some from the dominions—but the archbishops of Canterbury and York are also members and so are a few other persons distinguished in public life. There are a few judicial members—the Lords of Appeal in Ordinary, the Lord Chief Justice and the Lords Justices of Appeal—who are there for a special reason that will be explained later. The privy council as a whole never meets.

Although it has lost most of its power to the cabinet, it still has power to make what are called orders in council, to issue proclamations and to carry out certain formalities on behalf of the state. These orders in council deal with much the same sort of things as acts of parliament, but they deal with minor questions which do not need an act of parliament. Then a meeting of four or five privy councillors is held under the chairmanship of the Lord President of the Council (a member of the cabinet) and various orders are given formal authority by the Queen in council.

The privy council still has certain judicial

Radio Times Hulton Picture Library

Richard II presiding at a meeting of his Privy Council.

duties. This is why it has judicial members, and they make up what is called the judicial committee of the privy council. Its members sit as a court of law.

PROFITS. When a business decides to make and sell something—chairs, for example—it has to buy such things as wood, cloth and springs to make the chairs, to take on workpeople to manufacture them, an office staff to do the necessary clerical work, and a manager for the factory. The business has to pay money to those who supply the wood and other raw materials and also its own staff. It may also have to pay money to the bank or whoever lent the money to build the factory.

In order to be able to pay all these people, the business must sell the chairs for a certain amount of money. The difference between what the business earns by selling the chairs and what it pays out to suppliers, workpeople, and so on, is called *profit*. It is, in fact, the money that is left over.

Since they represent the difference between what a business pays out for products and what it gets for them, the size of profits depends on how many articles are sold and how much they are sold for. If, for example, it costs a chair-maker £20 to make a chair, and she sells her chairs for £25 each, then she makes £5 profit for every chair she sells, and the more chairs she sells the bigger are her profits. If, however, business becomes bad, the chair-maker may find that nobody will buy the chairs for £25. She may have to lower their price to £22.50 to sell them, and if she does this her profits will be only £2.50 a chair. However, if she is forced to lower the price of each chair as much as this, she will have to sell many more chairs in order to make enough money to pay for the running of the business. A business may do this for a time in the hope that trade will improve.

PROKOFIEV, Sergey (1891–1953). The Russian composer Sergey Prokofiev was born in the Ukraine. He was first taught music by his mother, and later studied at the conservatory in St. Petersburg (now Leningrad). He gave his first public performance as a pianist in 1908.

Prokofiev's music is often grand and stirring. He wrote piano concertos, symphonies, chamber music and opera. After time spent in the United States, France and Germany following the 1917 Revolution, he returned to live in Russia.

Among his best-known works are the music for the ballet *Romeo and Juliet*, the film *Alexander Nevsky*, and the children's tale *Peter and the Wolf*.

PROMETHEUS. According to ancient Greek beliefs, Prometheus was one of the Titans, a group of gods even older than the gods of Olympus led by Zeus. Some stories told how Prometheus created man, first making images in the likeness of gods and then giving these images life. After he had put them on the earth he gave them a torch which he had lighted at the chariot of the sun, and in this way men first got fire.

The younger god Zeus later took away this gift of fire when he quarrelled with the people on the earth, but Prometheus discovered where he had hidden it and brought it back again. In revenge Zeus chained Prometheus to a rock in the Caucasus Mountains and sent an eagle to eat his liver. Because Prometheus was immortal the liver grew again at night, so day after day the eagle came back and ate it again. At one

Prometheus lighting his torch at the chariot of the sun.

time Zeus offered to release him if he would reveal a secret which threatened the rule of the gods, but Prometheus refused to be freed in this way. He bore his torture unflinchingly, for he knew that in the 13th generation a son of Zeus would save him. And so it came to pass, for the hero Hercules, who was one of Zeus's sons, killed the eagle and set Prometheus free.

PRONOUN. "John took *his* books out of *his* case. *He* then put *them* in *their* places on *his* shelf." In these two sentences the words *he, his, them* and *their* are all pronouns. If there were no such words as pronouns, the nouns *John* and *books* would have to be repeated several times: "John took John's books out of John's case. John then put the books in the books' places on John's shelf." That example clearly shows what a pronoun is : a word which is used in place of a noun and which stands for a noun. *Pro-noun* in fact means "*for* a noun". By means of pronouns we can refer to ourselves and to other people and to things without having to repeat their names all the time.

Personal pronouns. All the pronouns in the example at the beginning of the article are personal pronouns. When a personal pronoun refers to the person who is speaking, it is described as being in the first person : *I* and *we* are in the first person. A pronoun is in the second person when it refers to a person or persons spoken to: *you* and the old-fashioned *thou* are in the second person. Pronouns in the third person are used for persons or things that are being spoken about: *he, she, it* and *they* are in the third person.

Pronouns change their form or spelling according to the work they are doing in a sentence. When a pronoun is the subject of a verb, or when it comes after the verb "to be", it is in what is called the *nominative case*. Examples are *"I saw John", "He did this", "It was I"*. When a pronoun is the object of a verb, or comes after the part of speech known as a preposition (see PREPOSITION), it is in the *objective* or *accusative* case ; and to show this it usually changes its spelling and appearance. Thus we say "John saw *us*" (not "John saw we") and "Play with *me*" (not "Play with I"). The *possessive* case shows "belonging" or possession : *my* room,

your friends, *their* plans, *his* books, *her* doll, *its* weight. (Note that the possessive case of *it* has no apostrophe.)

Personal pronouns show two other facts about themselves by their form or spelling. One is their *number* : pronouns like *I, me, he, it,* which refer to one person or thing, are described as being in the singular number, whereas *we, us, they, them* refer to more than one person or thing and are in the plural number. The other fact shown by the form of a pronoun is its *gender* ; that is, whether it is masculine, feminine or neuter (neuter means "neither"). This only happens with pronouns that are in the third person singular : *he* stands for a male person or animal, *she* for a female person or animal and *it* for a thing, which is neither masculine nor feminine.

Relative pronouns. The relative pronouns are *who, which, that* and *what.* They are rather more complicated to understand than other kinds because they do two kinds of work in a sentence at the same time. As well as standing in place of a noun, which all pronouns do, they join together, or relate, two parts of a sentence. An example is, "He is the man *who* came to dinner", in which the word *who* stands for "the man" and also begins the new part of the sentence about coming to dinner. (See SENTENCE.)

Who is used about persons, and like the personal pronouns has different forms to show what case it is in : *Who* for the nominative, *whom* for the objective and *whose* for the possessive. *Which* is used about things; it does not have a different form for the objective case, but it can have *whose* for the possessive case, although *of which* is sometimes used instead. *That* can be used about persons or things. *What* is only a relative pronoun when it means "that which", in a sentence like "He knew *what* he wanted." Here are some other sentences containing relative pronouns : "This is the house *that* Jack built", "The tap *which* had been dripping was now mended", "She is the woman *whom* you insulted".

Demonstrative pronouns. These are pronouns that point out or show certain persons or things. They are *this* and *that* (singular), *these* and *those* (plural). *This* and *these* point out persons or things that are close at hand, *that* and *those* persons or things that are farther away.

Interrogative pronouns. Pronouns used in asking questions are called interrogative pronouns. They are *who, which* and *what.* Examples are "*Who* is coming?" "*Which* of you has done this?" "*What* did he say?"

Who changes to *whom* when it is in the objective case even in a question, so that we should correctly write "*Whom* did you see?" and not "*Who* did you see?"

Indefinite pronouns. Words such as *one, each, anybody, none, someone, everyone* are called indefinite pronouns because they do not refer to a definite person or thing. Most of them are singular in number and so need singular verbs and pronouns after them, as in "*Each* of them *has* blamed the others", "*None* of them has brought *his* book." *None* is really *no one,* or *not one,* which shows clearly why it is singular.

PRONUNCIATION.
The pronunciation of words—that is, the way they are made to sound when they are spoken—is very important in any language, for if there were no accepted rules and habits of pronunciation people would all say words differently and it would be difficult to understand another person's speech at all. Every individual language, however, has its own system of pronunciation and nearly always this is different from that of other languages.

Although it is essential that any one language should have general rules of pronunciation, pronunciation does vary in different parts of a country. Thus the *a* sound in *class* is pronounced as a short sound in the north of England, rather like the *a* in *bat*; in the south of England the *a* in *class* is a longer sound, to rhyme with the sound in *heart.* A Cornishman pronounces words very differently from a man from Northumberland, and one may find it difficult at first to understand the other if he is talking at all fast. In languages where this sort of variation does occur it is usual for one form of pronunciation to be regarded as more "correct" than the others, and called the standard pronunciation. In English it is the kind of southern English spoken by educated people. Nevertheless, each individual person has slight differences in pronunciation even if he is speaking standard English and this gives variety and character to his speech. There are differences too in the forms of English spoken in the United States and in the Commonwealth countries.

Pronunciation of course has something to do with spelling but it is not always possible to tell how a word is pronounced by looking at its spelling. Only what is called a *phonetic* alphabet can properly show the pronunciation of all words. (See PHONETICS; SPELLING.)

PROPAGANDA.
It is natural that the government of a country should wish to make its people and those of other countries think well of it. To achieve that purpose it generally makes use of propaganda, which means that it does everything it can to spread information about itself. The means which it uses are the newspapers, sound radio and television, and books and pamphlets.

People often make the mistake of thinking that propaganda is a bad thing, whereas in fact every country uses it to some extent and it is only bad when a government spreads lies and twists the facts in order to mislead its own people and those of other countries.

The first use of the word "propaganda" was by the Roman Catholic Church. In 1622 Pope Gregory XV set up the *Congregatio de Propaganda Fide*—the College for spreading the Faith. This was a group of cardinals who were given the job of persuading as many people as possible to become Roman Catholics.

PROPERTY.
The word property means either something that belongs to somebody, or else the right that somebody has to own something. In other words, it can mean the thing owned or the fact of ownership.

You may perhaps have read an advertisement of a property, such as a house with a garage and a garden, that is to be sold. Or you may read that one man, Mr. X, has parted with his property in a certain house to another, Mr. Y. That does not necessarily mean that Mr. X lived in the house before and that now Mr. Y lives in it. It may mean that the man who lived in the house used to pay rent to Mr. X, and now has to pay it to Mr. Y. There are several different kinds of property, and the thing that is owned need not be something solid, which can be touched. It may be the right to fish in water on somebody else's land, or a debt, which is a sum of money that one man owes to another.

The law divides property into two main classes, *real property* and *personal property*. Real property means land, including buildings on land and the trees and crops that grow on it, and rights over land; for example, the right to cut trees on it or simply to walk over it. All other rights, whether to occupy a house for a certain number of years, or to own a house or a watch, or a claim to be paid a sum of money at a particular time, are classed as personal property.

PROPHETS are especially linked with the Old Testament. Today we use the word "prophet" to describe someone who foretells the future. But in the Old Testament it meant someone who explained the ways of God to man—someone who brought a message from God to His children. He was only foretelling the future in the sense that he "prophesied" disaster to those who ignored that message. The prophets were men of unusual powers and gifts who were able to reveal God's will to men. "Thus saith the Lord" is the way in which they often introduced their messages from God.

Moses is the first of these great figures who shaped the religious faith of the ancient Jews.

The prophets explained the ways of God to man.

With God's help he led them out of slavery in Egypt and he never let them forget that their escape was due to God's help. The Ten Commandments and other laws of the Old Testament came to be known as the laws of Moses.

Samuel and Elijah are other outstanding prophets of the early history of the Jews. Samuel lived at a time when the Israelites were in great danger from the Philistines (see PHILISTINES), and he was guided by God to choose a king (Saul) who could unite the tribes against their enemies. Elijah lived slightly later, in the 9th century B.C., when the people of Israel had begun to worship a false god, Baal. Elijah brought them back to the worship of the true God.

In the 8th century four great prophets appeared whose teaching can still be read in the Bible. They are Amos, Hosea, Isaiah and Micah. By this time the Jews had split up into two kingdoms—Judah and Israel—and both had fallen into bad habits. Some of their people had become very rich whereas others had become extremely poor, and the poor were cruelly oppressed. Men thought it was enough if they offered sacrifices to God, and they failed to pray to Him. Each of these four prophets had his own particular message but they all warned their people that nothing but disaster would come to nations that ignored the laws of God. It was not the sacrifice of animals that God wanted. "What doth the Lord require of thee but to do justly and to have mercy and to walk humbly with thy God?" asked Micah.

In spite of the stern warnings some of them gave, there was always a note of hope in the teachings of the prophets. They all believed that God's purpose was being worked out on earth, and they were sure that God had chosen to work it out through the Jews. Isaiah believed that even if God allowed the Jews to be punished (by the invasion of the Assyrians) He would never allow them to be destroyed completely, and that a small number—whom Isaiah called "the remnant"—would always remain. He also spoke of an ideal ruler (Messiah) who would arise, through whom the purposes of God would be accomplished.

When Jerusalem lay in ruins and the leaders of the Jews were in exile, one of the greatest of the Hebrew prophets appeared whose teaching is contained in the Book of Isaiah, chapters 40–45. (It is generally agreed today that this book contains the writings of more than one author and these chapters are of later date than the early part of the book.) He sounded again the note of hope. The Jews would go back to their own land and "the glory of the Lord" would be revealed. In describing the mission which awaited his people, this prophet painted a portrait of "the servant of the Lord" (see especially chapter 53) whose sufferings would bring healing to men. Christians see this expectation fulfilled in Jesus.

There are separate articles Amos; Elijah and Elisha; Ezekiel; Ezra; Isaiah; Jeremiah; Jonah; Moses; Samuel.

Other religions besides Christianity have had their prophets. For example, the founder of Islam was the Prophet Mohammed (see Mohammed).

PROSE. Most people can recognize a piece of verse when they see it in a book, but sometimes they think there must be something more difficult and complicated to understand about prose. On the contrary, it is much simpler, for prose is the name for all writing, or speaking, that is not in verse. That means that nearly everything we write ourselves—letters, school work, stories—is in prose, nearly everything we read in books, newspapers and magazines, and nearly everything we say as well. A character in a play by Molière was once very surprised to hear this:

Mr. Jourdain. What? When I say, "Nicole, bring me my slippers and give me my nightcap", is that prose?
Professor of Philosophy. Yes, sir.
Mr. Jourdain. Good heavens! For more than 40 years I have been speaking prose without knowing it!

Sometimes, however, the name prose is given to writing that is deliberately intended to be a work of art in the same way that a poem is. Prose of this sort is a part of literature, the kind of writing that lasts for centuries and can be read and loved by generations of people. (See Literature.) A great deal of prose is in novels, which are described in a separate article, but many other great writers besides novelists have pre-

ferred to use prose rather than poetry, for it expresses things in quite a different way. Where poetry gives us *feelings* about things, prose gives us *thoughts* about them. Prose is best for telling stories clearly, for explaining things and for arguing and persuading.

This does not mean that prose is dull, for the prose writer uses his imagination as much as the poet and he can make his prose plain or full of flourishes, beautiful or mocking, solemn or funny just as he pleases.

One of the first people to realize how important good prose in English was going to be was King Alfred, in the 9th century. He encouraged people to write in English, instead of the Latin which was usual then, and wrote simple, clear prose himself. Many great and famous writers have come after him, and prose has been changing all the time. One author of beautiful and sad prose was Sir Thomas Malory, in the 15th century, who wrote the story of King Arthur's Knights of the Round Table in a book called the *Morte d'Arthur*. Some writers of the 17th century such as Sir Thomas Browne preferred to make their prose complicated and flowery instead of plain and simple, and often it is rather hard to understand; but the best known of all books in English prose, the Authorized Version of the Bible, was also made at this time, and this is both simple and beautiful.

John Milton, the most famous of English poets after Shakespeare, also wrote prose, expressing his belief in liberty in fine and thrilling language. Another poet of the 17th century, John Dryden, who was a playwright and a critic as well, wrote plainer and more modern-sounding prose than Milton. Since then, although there have been exceptions, plain clear writing has been the rule. Joseph Addison and Sir Richard Steele, who wrote a magazine called *The Spectator* in the 18th century, followed it, but another writer of their time, Dr. Samuel Johnson, was famous more for his dignity and solemnity in prose. Charles Lamb, an author of essays in the 19th century, wrote prose in such a natural and pleasant way that he almost seemed to be just having a friendly chat with his reader. It would take too long to mention all the interesting and skilful writers of prose since

Lamb's day, but among them have been Matthew Arnold, Lytton Strachey, Max Beerbohm, G. K. Chesterton, Rudyard Kipling, Kenneth Grahame, Virginia Woolf, Sir Compton Mackenzie, James Joyce, D. H. Lawrence and Sir Winston Churchill.

PROSECUTION.

When a man or woman is to be charged with having committed a crime, such as burglary or dangerous driving, the reasons for supposing that he or she is the person guilty have to be given to the court, and the witnesses whose evidence may prove it have to be examined in court. Before this happens, it has to be decided whether the person can be charged with the offence. In Britain, arrangements have to be made for calling the necessary witnesses before the examining magistrates—who decide, if it is a serious offence that is charged, whether the accused person ought to stand trial before a jury or not—and then to the trial before a judge and jury if the case goes to the Crown Court.

All those people who are concerned with this work, whether in preparing the case or in presenting it in court, are generally referred to as "the prosecution". (See COURTS.) In many countries, the chief prosecutor is a government official, who may be elected to office. The prosecutor may also be in charge of the police investigation.

In Britain, the police bring most prosecutions themselves. In England and Wales, it is the chief constable of the area where the offence was committed. In very serious or difficult cases the decision whether to prosecute is made by the director of public prosecutions, whose duties extend to the whole country. There are certain classes of case where only the attorney-general (see ATTORNEY-GENERAL) can decide. Chief constables frequently refer difficult points to the director of public prosecutions, and, if this happens, the director of public prosecutions sometimes takes charge of the case.

In Scotland the decision to prosecute is taken not by the police but by the procurator fiscal, who is not a police officer but a lawyer. Certain classes of case have to be referred to the office of the lord advocate, who has much the same duties and position in Scotland as the attorney-general in England. In both countries prosecutions in the higher courts are conducted by barristers. In the lower courts the prosecution is often conducted by solicitors, and sometimes, in England, by police officers.

PROSERPINA.

This was the name by which the Romans called the goddess Persephone, wife of Pluto, the king of the underworld. Her story is told in the article CERES.

PROTEA

is the name given to a group of plants belonging to the order known as Proteales. These are shrubs and trees found in Australia, South Africa, Madagascar, Malaysia and in parts of Central and South America.

The Proteales include several trees grown for their colourful flowers and attractive leaves. Examples are the silver-tree, which has leaves covered in silky hairs, the Australian honeysuckles, the fire-tree, and various members of the Hakea and Grevillea families. Two other Australian trees belonging to this group are the silky oak and the Queensland nut.

Most of these plants grow in countries with long, hot dry seasons. The thick hairy leaves reduce the amount of moisture lost by the plant, and so give it a better chance of surviving until the rains come.

PROTECTIVE COLORATION.

Some animals are coloured in such a way that they match the background against which they live and so cannot easily be seen by their enemies. Such colouring is known as protective coloration. Leaf-eating caterpillars and the tree frogs of the tropics are generally green. Lions, which live in open, sandy areas, are tawny or golden coloured. The polar bear, which lives among the Arctic snows, is white.

Animals that live on the ground in the woods of countries such as Great Britain are often brown, in order to blend with the earth and the dead leaves that have fallen on it. Brown animals are better protected when they are several shades of brown, darker here and lighter there, like the ground itself. Examples of this among British birds are the nightjar and the

Eric Hosking

Against a background of twigs and bark, this nightjar would be even harder to see if it were not yawning!

woodcock, which seem to melt into the dead leaves among which they sit.

In countries where the ground is white with snow in winter, animals with brown coats would show up against the snow if their coats remained the same colour. The arctic fox and arctic hare therefore become white in winter. The fur of stoats and the plumage of ptarmigans also turns white in northerly countries, including Scotland.

Some animals can change their colour a few minutes after they have moved into new surroundings. The best known example of this is the chameleon, a reptile which can become green, gold, brown or blackish as it moves from one background to another. Flatfishes, which include the plaice, flounder and sole, lie on one side at the bottom of the sea and only the upper side is coloured, as only that can be seen. Most

*Photographs: Satour (top), Tony Morrison
(above left), M. C. Wilkes—Aquila (left),
B. and C. Alexander (above)*

Four examples of protective coloration: sleepy leopard
(top), cautious bush cricket (above left), motionless frog
(left), and watchful Arctic fox (above). The trick is to
look as much a part of the surroundings as possible.

of them are able to change the colours of their upper sides to match the sea bed.

Some large tropical animals seem to be very brilliantly and strikingly coloured when they are seen against the dark bars of a zoo cage, but in their own surroundings they are very hard to see. The spotted coat of a leopard, for instance, resembles the light and shadows of sunlight falling through leaves as the animal lies on a branch. Another camouflaged cat is the tiger, which, with its orange and black stripes, can prowl unseen through the tall grasses, dried by the hot sun of India, where it lives. The leopard and tiger are coloured in these ways so that it is easy for them to creep up on their prey without being seen. They themselves have few enemies.

Birds that spend much time on the wing are generally lighter in colour underneath than above, so that enemies from below cannot see them easily against the sky. Fish also tend to have dark backs and light undersides. You can see for yourself that it is very difficult to distinguish the dark back of a fish against the water and the weedy, pebbly bed of a river.

Insects are sometimes hidden from their enemies by their shape as well as their colours. In tropical countries there are stick insects, which look exactly like pieces of twig. In Britain there are tortoiseshell butterflies which, when they close their wings together, look like brown leaves.

Other insects have quite a different kind of protective coloration. Instead of disguising them, it acts as a warning. Certain butterflies and moths that taste unpleasant to birds are brightly coloured so that birds will recognize them and leave them alone. The black and yellow stripes of wasps warn their enemies that they sting. The same method of protection is found among reptiles and amphibians. Many that are poisonous have bright markings.

Yet another kind of protective coloration is the one that acts as a warning to other animals of the same kind. The best example of this is the white on a rabbit's tail. If a group of rabbits are outside their burrows and one sees or hears an enemy, it will pop down its burrow and the other rabbits, seeing the white flash of the tail, will follow its example.

Some animals have what is called disruptive (breaking-up) patterns. The outline of the animal is disguised by rather unexpected lines, and this principle was used in wartime to camouflage ships, lorries and buildings. The giant vipers of West Africa are very striking examples of this kind of camouflage.

PROTEIN comes from a Greek word meaning "first" and proteins are of the first importance in life of any kind. They are complicated chemi-

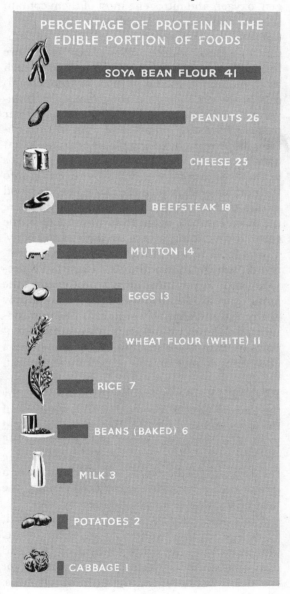

PERCENTAGE OF PROTEIN IN THE EDIBLE PORTION OF FOODS

SOYA BEAN FLOUR 41
PEANUTS 26
CHEESE 25
BEEFSTEAK 18
MUTTON 14
EGGS 13
WHEAT FLOUR (WHITE) 11
RICE 7
BEANS (BAKED) 6
MILK 3
POTATOES 2
CABBAGE 1

cal substances which are found in all living cells and in many things made by live creatures. For instance, white of egg, horn, hair, finger-nails and silk all contain proteins. A supply of proteins in food is important for the health of the body. Probably life could not exist at all without proteins. (See DIET.)

There are certain chemical elements (pure substances) contained in all proteins, but the various types of protein contain them in different amounts. All proteins contain carbon, hydro-gen, oxygen and nitrogen ; most of them contain sulphur and some contain phosphorus.

Proteins are formed by the union of sub-stances called amino acids. These acids are formed by plants from chemicals in the soil such as ammonium salts and nitrates, or from chemi-cals in the air such as carbon dioxide. Herbi-vorous (plant-eating) animals like cows get their proteins by eating plants, and man in turn ob-tains his proteins by eating plants or animals that have taken in protein from plants. The proteins in the body are broken down by digestion into their amino acids, which are carried by the blood stream to the different parts of the body. There the acids combine again to form proteins in the cells, thus building up the strength of the body.

The foods rich in proteins are eggs, lean meat, cheese, fish, gelatine and milk. These foods pro-vide proteins for building up protoplasm (the living part of the body-cells) and also supply energy. Generally, the proteins in plants con-tain the different amino acids in less suitable pro-portions than those in animals, so it is quite a good thing to include animal protein in the diet.

PROTEUS. According to the stories told by the ancient Greeks, Proteus was the shepherd of the fishes and sea animals. He was very wise and knew all things past, present and future, but did not like telling what he knew. He could change his shape at will, becoming a lion or a snake or a tree or even a fire. He used to sleep through the heat of the day in a cave guarded by seals.

Gods and mortals used to try to consult Proteus when they wanted to know the future. One was Aristaeus, whose swarm of bees had died because he had been partly responsible for the death of Eurydice, the wife of Orpheus.

Proteus, chained by Aristaeus, tries to avoid his questions by becoming a lion. In the distance are Proteus' seals.

Aristaeus decided to ask Proteus what to do, and accordingly hid in the cave until Proteus was fast asleep and then bound him with chains. Proteus, angry at finding himself captured, turned himself into every imaginable shape but could not escape. Finally he asked Aristaeus what he wanted. Aristaeus told him about the bees and Proteus said that he must sacrifice four bulls and four cows and pay funeral honours to Eurydice. Aristaeus followed his instructions, and was rewarded when new swarms of bees sprang from the rotten carcasses.

PROTON. One of the kinds of particles of which atoms are composed is the proton. It occurs in the nucleus, or central core, of the atom. Each proton carries a positive charge of electricity which balances the opposite negative charge carried by an electron, so that when an atom is in its normal condition the number of protons in the nucleus is equal to the number of electrons surrounding it. The proton is about 1,800 times heavier than an electron.

The nucleus of a hydrogen atom is a single proton. The nuclei of other atoms contain both protons and uncharged particles called neutrons (see NEUTRON).

PROVERBS have been called "potted wis-dom", and "the wit of one man, the wisdom of many". Here are some examples : "Waste not,

want not", "Look before you leap", "More haste, less speed". Sayings like these are often repeated, partly because they are short and easy to remember, but also because they say something which most people think true or wise. Usually the wisdom is in the form of a warning, like "Safety first", but sometimes a proverb tells us to be bold or carefree : "Nothing venture, nothing win", "It's no use crying over spilt milk".

Many proverbs are like this last one and mean more than they actually say, rather like a parable or a little fable with its moral. "Too many cooks spoil the broth" is true not only of cooks and broth but of any task in which several people might get in each other's way. When we say "A rolling stone gathers no moss" we are usually thinking not of a stone and moss but of a person who does not stay long enough in one place to get any benefit from it. Other examples of this kind of story or picture proverb are : "A bird in the hand is worth two in the bush", "Still waters run deep", "The proof of the pudding is in the eating", "Those who live in glass houses should not throw stones".

Some proverbs go back hundreds, or even thousands, of years, and no one knows who first invented them ; but occasionally a short wise remark by a famous author becomes a new proverb, like one of Shakespeare's sayings,

"Brevity is the soul of wit". This one, which means that a witty saying should be short, applies very well to all good proverbs.

PRUNING is the name given to the practice of cutting away growths or branches from trees and bushes. There are various reasons for doing this. Sometimes it is to improve the shape of the plant by stopping it from spreading widely or growing very tall. Sometimes it is in order to remove useless shoots so that the plant has more energy to produce flowers and fruit. Later, when the plants get old and weak and begin to decay, branches may have to be cut away or else they may fall suddenly and be dangerous. Poplars, elms and willows have sometimes to be pollarded, or have their top branches removed, to make them safe or to prevent them from shutting off light from houses near them.

The most usual reason for pruning a plant is to limit its growth, and this is particularly the case with hedges. They may be pruned once or twice a year, and most of the season's young shoots must be cut back. The pruning of fruit trees needs much more skill. They are pruned twice a year, in summer and winter. Summer pruning, done in July and early August, shortens the shoots. This encourages the tree to put its strength into the growth of the fruits forming at the base of the shoots.

Winter pruning is done after the leaves have fallen, when the remaining part of the season's growth is cut back so that only two or three buds (according to the type of fruit tree) are left. All fruit trees are not treated in the same way, and some only have their branches trimmed and any dead wood removed.

Bushes, such as blackcurrant bushes, are pruned as soon as the fruit is gathered. The growth should be fairly drastically reduced, so that the shoots that will grow during the remaining summer months are able to bear the fruit for the following season.

Flowering shrubs vary in their need for pruning. Some only require thinning, and others have to be pruned thoroughly immediately they have finished flowering. Forsythia, the Japanese golden bell, is one of the best examples of the kind that needs severe pruning.

Some plants, such as roses, are pruned severely each year, so that as much growth as possible is produced each season. Shoots with ornamental and coloured barks will be brighter if pruned than if they are left to grow normally. The purple-leaved hazel nut is a good tree for severe pruning, and so are all the willows and some of the dogwoods.

Roots as well as shoots can be pruned, and this checks the rapid growth made by many trees, particularly fruit trees. More fruit is also borne by the tree. It develops slowly and becomes much closer and neater in shape than if left unpruned.

Although pruning is so important to many plants, some, such as the magnolias, suffer from it, and any wounds made will not heal at all easily. If the leading shoot is removed from a pine tree, the tree will be stunted, that is, it will not grow properly for the rest of its life.

PRUNUS is the Latin for plum tree, and the word is used to mean a genus, or group, of about 200 different plants in the Rosaceae family. With the exception of a few South American species, or kinds, all *Prunus* plants grow in mild regions of the northern hemisphere. Some are evergreen, some have copper-coloured leaves, some are trees, some shrubs, but nearly all have beautiful white or pink flowers which usually come out before the leaves. Many of the blossoming trees seen growing in gardens, along the sides of roads and in parks are *Prunus* trees. Among the fruits included in the *Prunus* group are plums, peaches and cherries.

Prunus plants are divided into four main kinds. There are the plums, blackthorn and apricot; the almonds (which grow wild in central Asia), peaches and nectarines; the cherries (which probably first grew in the Balkans and Asia Minor); and the bird cherry and cherry laurel.

The bronze-leaved flowering plum has lovely pale rose blossoms with leaves that at first are bright red and later turn to purple. The fruit is also purple.

The large-fruited almond blossoms in the early spring, before the peaches and cherries and just after the common pink almond. Its flowers are larger than those of the ordinary almond, being usually two to three inches across. Inside they are pink, becoming white at the edges of the petals, and with pink stamens. The leaves come out after the blossoms. Another variety, which is closely related to the large-fruited almond, produces bitter almonds.

One of the loveliest of the cherry types of *Prunus* is the double gean or mazzard, which has long-stalked double blossoms, pure white in colour, hanging in clusters of from three to six. Each blossom has about 30 or 40 petals and they are long-lasting. This graceful tree, which flowers in England in May, has been cultivated for at least 200 years.

From Japan, where flowering trees are much cultivated, comes the Yoshino cherry, which is one of the best early flowering kinds. Its flowers, which are an inch across with a faint scent, are pink when they first open and later become white. The fruits are round, black and bitter.

The common or cherry laurel is an evergreen shrub with pale green shoots and dark green, leathery older leaves. The white flowers blossom in April and the berries are black-purple. There are many varieties of this plant, which is good for making hedges. The leaves of cherry laurel are often used for making wreaths.

There are separate articles on the main kinds of prunus plants mentioned in this article, and each one has an illustration.

PRUSSIA. Until the end of World War II, Prussia was the most important province of Germany. It included nearly the whole of northern Germany, stretching from the Dutch and Belgian frontiers in the west to those of Poland and Lithuania in the east. In population and in area it made up about two-thirds of the whole country. For some 300 years it had played the leading part among the German states and finally it had formed them into a united country.

The history of Prussia began in the 13th century when a band of German knights called the Teutonic Order conquered the lands on the Baltic Sea east of the Vistula River belonging to a heathen tribe known as the Pruteni (Prussians). In 1525 the Grand Master of the Teutonic Order, Albert of Hohenzollern, made himself Duke of Prussia. In 1618 his title descended to another Hohenzollern who was ruler of Brandenburg, which was the land between the Elbe and Oder rivers.

In 1701 the ruler of Brandenburg and Prussia took the title of King of Prussia. It was, however, a kingdom in two parts, with Poland in between. The idea of partitioning (dividing up) Poland in order to make Prussia a single land was born in Berlin. It was achieved, with the help of Russia and Austria, by Frederick the Great (1740–1786). Prussia was remarkable for three things: the Protestant religion, an aristocracy consisting of harsh landowners called Junkers and a very powerful army. A French statesman said: "Prussia is not a country with an army; it is an army with a country."

Although the power of Prussia was for a time reduced by its defeat at the hands of Napoleon at Jena in 1806, it soon recovered. Its troops helped in the final defeat of Napoleon at Waterloo in 1815 and later it began to join in closer relations with some of the smaller German states. Prussia's great aim was reached when William I, its king, was crowned German Emperor at the end of the Franco-Prussian War in 1871 and became the ruler of all Germany.

After that, the state of Prussia was really no more than a large province of Germany, although it was by far the most important one. After World War II the part of Prussia lying to the east of the Oder and Neisse rivers was re-gained by Poland, while a small area around Königsberg (renamed Kaliningrad) was given to the U.S.S.R. The state of Prussia was dissolved, or abolished, on March 1, 1947.

PSALMS. The word "psalm" comes from a Greek word meaning "a song, accompanied by a string instrument". The Book of Psalms in the Old Testament contains 150 psalms of various lengths. They have been used both in Jewish and Christian worship, some of them for nearly 3,000 years. Millions of people have found their words an inspiration when they have wanted to approach Almighty God in praise or thanksgiving, in sorrow for sin, in joy or sadness and in health and sickness.

For many centuries most people thought that David wrote the Psalms, but it is now known that only a few of them go back as far as David's time. They were probably written by many different poets from the time of David onwards for a period of some 800 years, and were finally put together in book form.

In the public worship of churches the Psalms are usually sung. In their private prayers the clergy of the Roman Catholic, Orthodox and Anglican churches recite portions of the Psalms daily.

It is clear from the New Testament that Jesus Himself had been brought up on the Psalms, for He constantly quoted from them. On the Cross He used words from two of them: "Father, into thy hands I commend my spirit" (Psalm 31), and "My God, my God, why hast thou forsaken me?" (Psalm 22).

PSYCHE. In Greek stories the beautiful maiden Psyche stood for the human soul. The story of Psyche and Cupid is told in the article CUPID AND PSYCHE.

PSYCHOLOGY. The word psychology comes from the Greek *Psyche,* which means "mind" or "soul", and it is the name given to the study of the soul or mind.

Unlike other living things, animals (including human beings) have minds. They spend part of their time conscious and part of it unconscious. A person who is asleep is unconscious. When he is asleep, his mind continues its activity. Dreaming is a part of this activity (see DREAMS). When he wakes, he is fully aware of his actions and thoughts, for consciousness really includes three things : knowing, feeling and willing.

(1) *Knowing* covers all the ways in which people know things. The first way is by using the senses—eyes, ears, nose, tongue and skin. Sensation, as this is called, is the simplest form of consciousness. When the eyes are closed, things can still be seen as pictures in the "mind's eye", as it is generally called. When lessons have been properly learnt, they are remembered. Imagination and memory are also forms of knowing.

Human beings can think of things that are neither seen nor heard—"abstract ideas", as they are called. They can argue about such questions as "What is goodness?", and work out the answers to sums. This is called reasoning and is the highest form of knowledge. Most of human thinking and reasoning is done by means of words. People vary in the way they think and reason, and often their ways of doing so can be measured by means of tests known as intelligence tests. (See INTELLIGENCE.)

(2) *Feeling.* Nearly all sensations and thoughts are accompanied by feeling or emotion. The warmth from a fire and the taste of ice cream are pleasant; a burn on the skin and the taste of quinine are unpleasant. Pleasure and unpleasantness are not sensations, but feelings.

(3) *Willing.* Finally, whatever is seen, thought of or felt tends to make us do something. A person swallows ice cream when he tastes it and cries out when he feels a burn. The most important movements are those which are deliberately *willed*. Yet, even when it is not actually willed, each movement requires some effort, some striving or trying. In every conscious process there are always these three things —knowing, feeling and willing or striving.

The psychologist is a scientist who studies these processes of the mind, and the methods he uses are much the same as those of other scientists. He observes both himself and other people, and he makes experiments on them. Psychologists have discovered that much of human conscious life depends on the body and its various parts— the brain, the nerves, the sense organs and the glands. For instance, when a player sees a cricket ball, currents run up the nerves from his eyes to his brain ; when he rushes to catch it, currents run down again and make the muscles of his legs and hands contract.

Psychology has many uses. It has helped doctors to understand and treat crime and mental illness, and has led to better understanding of people's reactions to education, industry and war as well as of their everyday behaviour.

PTOLEMY (CLAUDIUS PTOLEMAEUS) was a famous Greek astronomer.

It is likely that he was born at Ptolemais Hermii, a city on the River Nile in Egypt, and that he was 78 when he died. His observatory was on top of a temple near the Egyptian city of Alexandria, and he was at the height of his fame between A.D. 127 and either 141 or 151.

In spite of its inaccuracies, Ptolemy's map of the world was used as a model by many later cartographers.
Royal Geographical Society

Ptolemy wrote a book containing everything that was then known about astronomy and trigonometry. He called it *The Mathematical Collection,* but it is now always called *The Almagest,* from an Arabic and a Greek word which together mean "the greatest". Many of the ideas in this book were worked out so completely by Ptolemy that nobody was able to carry them any further during the next 1,400 years. He got many of his ideas from another Greek astronomer called Hipparchus (see HIPPARCHUS). Ptolemy thought that the Earth was at the centre of the universe, with the Sun, Moon and planets going round it, and this idea is called the "Ptolemaic system". Nearly everyone believed it until it was replaced by the Copernican system—the idea put forward in the 16th century by the Polish astronomer Copernicus. He said that the planets, including the Earth, all go round the Sun. (See ASTRONOMY ; COPERNICUS, NICOLAUS.)

Ptolemy was the first man of ancient times to study geography scientifically. His maps of Asia and Africa and his notes on latitude and longitude were collected in his *Guide to Geography*. These maps led Columbus to believe he could reach India by sailing west across the Atlantic.

PUBLIC HEALTH, or environmental health,

are terms which describe the methods by which serious infectious diseases are kept under control in a country, the occurrence and spread of ill-health is avoided, and conditions of living and working are good enough for people to be thoroughly healthy.

Certain diseases which are still widespread in poor or tropical countries may be carried by sailors or air travellers from abroad. One of these diseases is cholera. It is very dangerous and spreads rapidly, so even a single case is a serious matter. (See CHOLERA.)

If a ship arrives in port with a person on board who is suspected of having a dangerous infectious disease, the captain must report to the port health authorities. They will send the port medical officer and his staff on board before anyone has been allowed to go ashore, and the crew and passengers will be examined. Anyone who has the disease or shows signs of having it will be

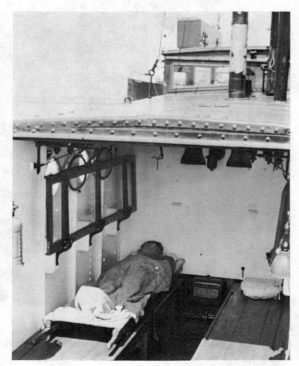

Radio Times Hulton Picture Library

A man suffering from an infectious disease being taken ashore from his ship in a Port of London Authority launch.

taken to an isolation hospital, the rest of the crew and passengers will be vaccinated and the affected accommodation and bedding is fumigated (to kill any germs). (See VACCINATION AND INOCULATION.)

Every medical officer for environmental health in the country will be given the names of persons from the ship who are going to the area for which he is responsible. He will arrange for an eye to be kept on them until the risk of their getting the disease has passed. In this way serious epidemics are prevented. Air passengers from countries where serious infectious diseases are common must give the airport authorities their address in Britain, and each receives a card which he must hand to his local doctor if he falls ill. Should his disease be serious, his card is sent to the airport medical officer, who writes to the passengers who were on that flight and tells them to be medically examined.

Disease can also be carried by animals, and so they are kept in quarantine if they are brought from abroad. (See QUARANTINE.) Plague, once

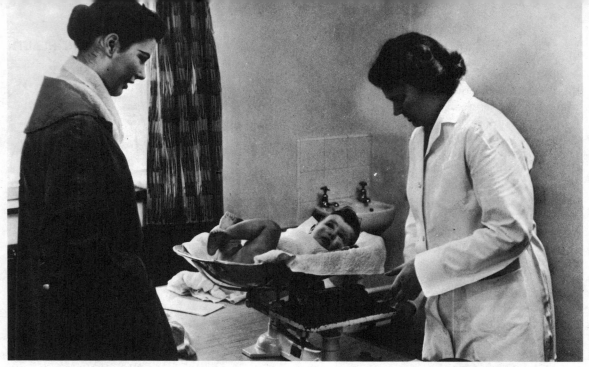

Photos, Henry Grant (top); Barnet Saidman

Above: A mother watches as her baby is weighed by a health visitor in the local clinic. Below: Pregnant women attend an ante-natal class. The course helps them get ready for the birth of their baby.

one of the most terrible diseases in Europe, can be carried by rats, and so precautions are taken to prevent rats from leaving ships and coming on shore.

Another danger to public health which may be brought by ships is unsound food, and the port authority therefore has the power to examine and destroy food which is not fit for human beings to eat.

Local councils are responsible for environmental health. They are advised by doctors, who in their turn are helped by environmental health officers and health visitors (nurses). All these officials work to see that the people of their area breathe pure air, eat clean food and live and work under the best possible conditions.

In big industrial towns one of the most serious problems is polluted air, for factory chimneys send smoke, dust and poisonous fumes into the atmosphere. People breathe in dirt, which irritates their lungs, and the health-giving rays of the sun cannot easily get through such impure air. (See POLLUTION.) To improve the quality of the air we breathe, "smokeless zones" have been set up in certain areas. Householders in these zones have to burn smokeless fuels.

Local authorities have to deal with the removal of refuse and sewage in order to prevent flies from collecting and carrying disease. Food and water can also be polluted and cause such diseases as typhoid.

The environmental health officer and his staff have the right to examine food which is on sale and to destroy it if it is not fit for people to eat. Every day thousands of tons of food are examined to make sure that there will not be an outbreak of food poisoning among the public and also that the standard and purity of food is high. There are standards for many foods and it is an offence to sell a food below these standards.

Milk too must be kept safe. It should come from cows which have no trace of tuberculosis and must also be free from other harmful germs. It is an offence to add water to milk intended for sale.

It is the job of the environmental health officers to visit homes and make sure that there are no "sanitary defects"—which include leaking roofs, broken drains, dirty rooms or the presence of rats or insect pests such as cockroaches. If any of these are found, the landlord or owner of the house must put things right.

The conditions under which people work are as important as those in which they live. In particular, there are strict laws about factories for the sake of the workers in them. Factories must be properly lighted and ventilated and kept as clean as possible. There must be as little noise as can be managed, dangerous machinery must be guarded, the hands and eyes of workers protected from anything that may harm them, and the workers must not be allowed to breathe in dusts and fumes. (See FACTORY ACTS.)

The first medical officer of health in England was appointed in the middle of the 19th century, after there had been a public outcry for better water supplies and means to remove filth and refuse which had caused severe outbreaks of cholera. Environmental health is still concerned with getting rid of anything which causes harm, but its motto is "prevention is better than cure".

People needing Special Care

Expectant mothers (women who are going to have babies) are among these people. They need to live on a healthy diet and to be seen regularly by doctors to make sure they remain healthy so that they will have strong, healthy children.

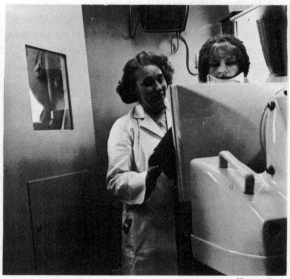

Henry Grant

A radiographer puts the patient in the right position for the X-ray at a mass radiography centre.

Young babies, too, must be looked after carefully, for nothing is more helpless than a new-born child, and if it does not get the proper treatment it may not grow properly and may die. There are thousands of health clinics in Britain to which mothers can bring their babies every week to be weighed and examined. The babies are vaccinated against smallpox and immunized against diphtheria so that they will not catch those dangerous diseases. They are also vaccinated against poliomyelitis, tetanus (lockjaw) and measles.

Special foods for babies are sold cheaply and advice given. Mothers are also visited by health visitors who can if necessary teach them how to look after their babies and young children.

All counties and big towns must make these arrangements for the care of children under five years of age. Later, when they start going to school, they still need attention because they are growing taller and heavier week by week, and if they are to thrive they need body-building food and must be able to exercise both their muscles and their minds. Therefore the schools in which they spend much of their time must be clean, well-ventilated and have plenty of light. Schools have health services and in Britain and many other countries school children are regularly examined.

Children who need even more attention are those who have something wrong with them, such as poor sight or poor hearing. As soon as their trouble is discovered, they are sent to what are known as "special schools" which will teach them in a way suited to their needs.

PUBLIC SCHOOL. Rather confusingly, a public school in Britain is actually a private school, for its pupils are fee-paying. (Education in state schools is free.) The term "public school" was used as long ago as the 12th century, and later was used to distinguish education given in a school from that given privately at home. In time a few grammar schools became famous, and well-to-do parents began to send their children to those schools. This led to their being called " the great schools" and in 1861, it was decided to have a special inquiry into the way they were conducted. It was reckoned that there

were nine of them, and the group of people who carried out the inquiry was known as the Public Schools Commission. The famous nine were Eton, Winchester, Westminster, Charterhouse, St. Paul's, Merchant Taylor's, Harrow, Rugby and Shrewsbury. Although this list includes one (St. Paul's) which is still mainly a day school, and two (Westminster and Merchant Taylor's) which have more day boys than boarders, a public school is usually thought of as a boarding school, with high fees.

As boarders get no home life during the term, a public school has to provide plenty of out-of-school activities, and through its prefects (see PREFECTS AND MONITORS) and in other ways it has to ensure a happy and orderly social life. In the 18th century this side of school life was badly neglected. Rowdyism, bullying and brutal discipline were common and earned the public schools a bad name.

As a result, people in the 19th century demanded that these schools should be improved, and a few great headmasters succeeded in making enormous changes. Dr. Thomas Arnold, who was headmaster of Rugby from 1828 to 1841, was the most famous of them. *Tom Brown's Schooldays* gives some idea of what he was up against and how he dealt with it. He sought out good masters, established the system of prefects and made them largely responsible for discipline, and treated bullies very severely. (See ARNOLD.)

Girls' schools had to fight against the 19th-century idea that girls did not need to be educated. Miss Frances Buss helped to establish the North London Collegiate School and in 1858 Miss Dorothea Beale became principal of the Ladies' College at Cheltenham in its very early days and made it famous as a girls' public school.

The improvement of public schools took place at a time when Britain was very prosperous and some people were making money quickly. These people wanted their children to have the best possible education, and the new railways made it easier for children to travel to schools away from their homes. So not only were the existing schools improved and expanded, but many new ones were founded or developed out of small local grammar schools. Independent fee-paying schools are still a feature of the British education system, although the great majority of children attend state schools. (See SCHOOL.)

PUCCINI, Giacomo (1858–1924).

The most popular of the Italian composers after Giuseppe Verdi is Giacomo Puccini. His operas *La Bohème, Tosca* and *Madam Butterfly* are heard in opera houses all over the world.

Puccini was born at Lucca, Italy, of a family long distinguished in music. He intended to follow the family tradition as an organist, but a great moment came when he heard a performance of Verdi's *Aida*. He knew then that he should write music for the theatre. He studied music at the Milan Conservatoire and soon after leaving wrote his first opera, *Le Villi*, which was successfully produced in 1884. It was followed in 1889 by *Edgar*, which was less successful because of its poor libretto (words), and in 1893 by *Manon Lescaut*, which is performed today.

The most popular of Puccini's operas was *La Bohème*, first produced in 1896 and based on a book by Henri Murger about the lives of art students in Paris. In 1900 came *La Tosca*, which was based on a blood-curdling tragedy by Victorien Sardou and contains some of Puccini's strongest and most effective music. *Madam Butterfly*, which is the story of an unhappy romance between a Japanese girl and an American naval officer, was a failure when first produced in 1904, but Puccini altered it and divided it into three acts instead of two and it became a great success. Both the words and music of his next opera, *The Girl of the Golden West* (first performed in New York in 1910), were rather inferior, and Puccini afterwards wrote three one-act operas, *The Cloak, Sister Angelica* and *Gianni Schicchi*. They were first performed in 1918. His last work, *Turandot*, an opera set in China and full of colour and eastern splendour, was unfinished when he died in Brussels on November 29, 1924.

Puccini's operas succeeded because of his keen theatrical sense and his love of warm Italian melody. They have fast-moving scenes full of action and suspense.

PUDDING.

Some dishes made with meat or vegetables are called puddings, but most puddings are sweet, not savoury, and are served after the main course of a meal. They are often referred to as sweets.

Ways of preparing some kinds of puddings are described in the article RECIPES. This article simply gives a list of the main kinds of puddings and what they are made of.

Hot Sweets. Pastry is the basis of many puddings, some of which can be eaten hot and some cold. Suet crust pastry can be used to make good nourishing puddings, especially for cold weather. Short crust pastry can be used for fruit pies, turnovers, flans and tarts, all of which can be served hot or cold. Flaky pastry and puff pastry are sometimes used for mince pies, cream horns, jam puffs and pastry slices. Pies, which are generally covered with pastry, are often served in place of puddings. (See PIE.)

Custard is poured over many hot puddings to serve as a sauce. There are also custard dishes, such as baked custard and caramel custard, and custard may be used as the basis for bread-and-butter pudding.

Batter can be made with milk, eggs and flour and cooked in several ways to produce sweets

Radio Times Hulton Picture Library
A singer playing Madam Butterfly, Puccini's best known heroine. The opera is a sad love story.

PUDDING

TO MAKE APPLE SNOW

You need: 3 apples, 3 tablespoonfuls of sugar, 1 tablespoonful of water, the white of an egg, a ½ lemon and 2 squares of dark chocolate.

1 peel, core and cut up the apples

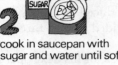
2 cook in saucepan with sugar and water until soft

3 beat with fork until smooth

4 squeeze the juice from the ½ lemon

5 whisk the egg-white until it is stiff

6 grate the chocolate

7 add lemon juice and beaten egg-white to apples

8 serve in little dishes, sprinkled with grated chocolate

such as pancakes, waffles and fritters, and baked fruit batter. Other fruit dishes include baked apples, apple Charlotte and fruit crumble. Certain cake mixtures can be baked in a shallow dish with jam or fruit and served hot with custard and sauce.

Steamed puddings can be made from suet pastry or from cake or sponge mixtures, such as canary pudding and sponge pudding.

Soufflés are very light sweets which are made from a sauce foundation to which several eggs and a flavouring have been added; this makes them very light and nourishing. *Soufflés* can be baked or steamed.

Cold Sweets are generally served during the summer or at parties. They include jellies, creams, cold *soufflés* and ice creams. Gelatine is used for setting jellies and creams. They are usually made from fruit juice with the addition of sugar, water or milk.

Fruit salad is a combination of different fruits, tinned, fresh or bottled. It is especially good with sponge fingers and whipped cream.

Cold *soufflés* are very rich sweets often used for parties. They contain beaten egg whites which are added to a foundation of jelly, flavouring, egg yolk and sugar. Finally whipped cream is added to the mixture and it is all put to set. It is delicious to eat, and can be made to look very attractive with cream and fruits.

Ices can be made at home with milk, eggs, sugar and cream, or using custard or evaporated milk. (See ICE CREAM.)

PUERTO RICO is an island in the West Indies and is a self-governing territory of the United States. It is the easternmost of a chain of large islands called the Greater Antilles and is about the size of the English counties Norfolk and Suffolk put together.

Puerto Rico has coastal plains but most of its area is covered by mountain ranges running east and west, rising to a height of about 1,300 metres. Between the ranges are fertile valleys of great beauty. Most of the swift rivers and streams flow northwards and some are useful for making electricity from water power and for irrigating (artificially watering) the plains. Although it is in the tropics, Puerto Rico has a warm, even climate with a cool breeze from the northeast for most of the year. It has many beautiful beaches, with luxury hotels for tourists from the United States. Hurricanes, which are great

FACTS ABOUT PUERTO RICO

AREA: 8,897 square kilometres.
POPULATION: 2,712,000.
KIND OF COUNTRY: A self-governing territory of the United States, with the title of "commonwealth".
CAPITAL: San Juan.
GEOGRAPHICAL FEATURES: Central mountain ranges surrounded by coastal plains; many swift-running streams.
CHIEF PRODUCTS: Sugar, tobacco, bananas, rice, maize, beans; metal goods, chemicals, cement.
IMPORTANT TOWNS: San Juan, Ponce, Mayaguez.
EDUCATION: Children must attend school between the ages of 6 and 12.

storms of wind and rain, sometimes do great damage. The land was once thickly wooded but, except on the Luquillo Range about 30 kilometres southeast of San Juan, nearly all the forest growth has been cleared for cultivation. Few wild animals live on the island except fairly small ones such as turtles, lizards and toads.

Most of the people are descended from the Spaniards who conquered and settled on the island. Thus about three-quarters of Puerto Ricans are whites, the rest being of mixed white and Negro blood. Most of them are Roman Catholics and speak Spanish. Puerto Rico is very densely populated and many of its people have sought work in the United States. New York, for example, has about 600,000 Puerto Ricans. Children in Puerto Rico must attend school between the ages of 6 and 12.

The capital and chief port is San Juan, whose almost landlocked bay forms an excellent harbour on the north coast. Much of the city stands on a small island joined to the main island by bridges. The old palace of the governors, the cathedral and the Spanish fortified castles make a pleasing contrast with the marble capitol (government building) and tall modern hotels.

Agriculture is the chief occupation and about

four-fifths of the island is cultivated. The people grow rice, maize, beans and bananas for their own food and keep cattle for supplying milk and meat. The main crop, however, is cane sugar, which together with tobacco, fruit (grapefruit, oranges and pineapples) and coffee is sold abroad. Within the last 20 years great efforts have been made to set up factories in Puerto Rico, and the products include refined (purified) sugar, cloth and clothing, fertilizers, building

Paul Popper

A crowd outside a modern church in San Juan, Puerto Rico's capital. Most Puerto Ricans are Roman Catholics.

materials, plastics, petroleum products and cement. Copper has also been discovered.

A railway following the coastal plain runs most of the way round the island and there are good roads. The main airport is at Isla Verde near San Juan and is linked by several air lines with North and South America and Europe.

Puerto Rico was discovered on November 19, 1493, by Christopher Columbus. In 1508 Juan Ponce de Leon explored the island and discovered the bay where San Juan harbour is. He named it Porto Rico (later Puerto Rico) or "rich port", and this name was later applied to the whole island. The Spanish settlers ill-treated the Arawak Indians on the island so that by 1582 none was left. The fortifications built by the Spaniards made San Juan too strong to capture, as Sir Francis Drake found in 1595. After the defeat of Spain by the United States in 1898, Puerto Rico became United States territory. Its people were made United States citizens in 1917 and in 1946 they were given a Puerto Rican as their governor. The island became completely self-governing in 1952, but the people are still United States citizens. It is ruled by a governor who, with the legislature (parliament), is elected for four years by the votes of men and women over 21.

PUFFIN. The enormous striped beak of the puffin, brilliantly coloured in red, yellow and blue, has made it one of the best known British sea birds. It has this beak only in the breeding season, however. When the breeding season is over the bright colours fade and some parts of the beak are shed, leaving it much smaller and mainly yellow in colour. The beak is very powerful, and if a live puffin is handled it may give a very deep bite.

The puffin is sometimes called the sea parrot. It is about 30 centimetres long with a white breast and black back and wings. The sides of the face are greyish and the feet are bright orange. It has a peculiar rolling walk.

Puffins are silent birds, though they can make a deep sound like a growl. They spend the winter at sea, only coming on land to breed. Although they have become less plentiful in recent years, puffins can be seen in flocks on rocky coasts of

north and west Britain and on islands, together with guillemots and razorbills. All three birds belong to the auk family, the puffin being the smallest of the three. (See AUK.)

The hen puffin lays one white egg in a burrow. This is sometimes dug in turf by the puffins themselves, but they may take over a rabbit burrow. Only a few feathers or pieces of grass are

Puffins carry their fish neatly arranged in their beaks.

used to line the nest. When collecting fish for its young, the puffin sometimes carries as many as ten at a time, holding them crosswise in its beak, heads on one side, tails on the other.

These puffins are found all over the north Atlantic. The tufted puffin, a larger bird with long yellow tufts on the sides of its head during the breeding season, lives in the Pacific.

PULSE. The way the heart is beating can be known by feeling the pulse. It beats in all the arteries (largest blood vessels) of the body, but it is easiest to feel in the arteries just under the skin, especially those which lie over a bone. The wrist, about an inch below the thumb, is the best place to feel the pulse, but it can also be felt in the neck, at the temples, in the groin and armpits, behind the knee and at the ankles.

What happens is that the heart pumps blood into the arteries, which have walls that are like elastic, so that they swell up with each pumping and go down a fraction between beats. (The same effect can be seen just once when firemen turn a powerful jet of water into a long flat hose-pipe.) The pulse of human beings beats about 70 times a minute, but the pulse rate of children is quicker than that of old people.

Doctors and nurses feel a patient's pulse because it gives them a record of the rate of the heart's beat and also of the efficiency of the heart as a pump. (See HEART.)

PUMA.

The puma, which is also called the mountain lion or cougar, is one of the two big cats of America, the other being the jaguar. It is found from North America through to South America, although it is rare in the United States except in the Rocky Mountain region. Its fur is dull yellowish-brown or tawny, paler on the chest and under parts. A full grown male puma may be 2·5 metres long, of which about a third is tail.

The puma is carnivorous (flesh-eating) and eats a wide range of foods. In North America it preys on deer and may also kill livestock. In many regions the puma has been eliminated by man and it now lives only in remote areas.

Up to five kittens are born at a time. Young pumas have large blackish spots and are playful. They are easily tamed, but become less reliable as they grow older. However, adult pumas rarely attack people.

The puma is a big cat, yellowish or tawny in colour.

PUMP.

Machines for moving liquids are called pumps. Another type of pump, sometimes called a compressor, is used for compressing air and other gases. (Compressing means squeezing into a smaller space.)

One of the earliest needs of man in agriculture was a way of raising water from streams or rivers so that it could be used for the irrigation (artificial watering) of the land. Lowering a bucket on a rope was one way, but the ancient Chinese and Egyptians found a better method. They had waterwheels turned by the flow of the stream and with scoops fixed round the rim of the wheel. When the wheel turned, each scoop filled as it dipped into the water and poured it out into a trough as it reached the top. Sometimes the wheel was turned by donkeys or camels, or even by man-power, and sometimes it was connected to a windmill.

Most pumps, whether used for pumping air or water, are divided into two main classes—those in which the movement is reciprocating (to-and-fro) and those with a rotary (turning) movement.

Reciprocating Pumps

One of the oldest types of reciprocating pumps is the *lift pump*. The old-fashioned "village pump" is usually of this type. To understand the lift pump (sometimes called a suction pump) it is necessary to understand what happens when a person sucks a drink through a straw. Ordinarily, the Earth's atmosphere causes a pressure on our bodies of about 0·9 bar. We do not notice this because the outside pressure of air is balanced by the inside pressure of the air within us. (See ATMOSPHERE.) By sucking at the straw the air is removed from it and therefore the pressure on the surface of the drink in the tumbler forces the liquid up the straw.

The lift pump consists of a piston moved up and down in a cylinder by working the pump handle. The hole in the middle of the piston and the hole at the bottom of the cylinder are covered by *valves* (in this case flaps) which allow the water to pass in one direction only. The pipe beneath the cylinder leads down to the water in the well and can be compared with the drinking-straw. When the piston is lifted, the valve in it

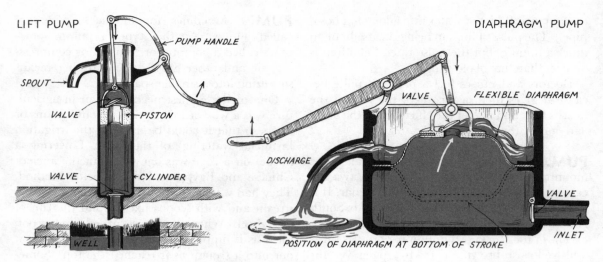

LIFT PUMP

PUMP HANDLE

SPOUT

VALVE

PISTON

VALVE

CYLINDER

WELL

DIAPHRAGM PUMP

VALVE

FLEXIBLE DIAPHRAGM

DISCHARGE

VALVE

INLET

POSITION OF DIAPHRAGM AT BOTTOM OF STROKE

closes and the atmospheric pressure forces water through the pipe into the cylinder. When the piston moves down, the valve at the foot of the cylinder closes and that in the piston opens, allowing the water to occupy the space above the piston. When the piston is lifted again, its valve closes and the water above it is discharged through the spout. A lift pump cannot raise water to more than a certain height—in theory about 10 metres, but in practice much less.

For raising water through greater heights the *force pump* is used. This can be placed near the bottom of the well with a long rod connecting the piston to the handle at the top. In this case the piston rod passes through a close-fitting hole in the top of the cylinder and there is an extra valve covering the passage through which water is discharged from the cylinder. The action is similar to that of the lift pump. When, however, the piston reaches the top of the cylinder and starts to move down again, the discharge valve is closed by the weight of the water in the discharge pipe and prevents the water from running back into the cylinder.

Pumps of these kinds were used by the ancient Romans and in the 16th century were much used for pumping the water out of deep mines in central Europe. Sometimes the cylinder was made by hollowing out a tree trunk. The 18th century steam engines invented by Thomas Newcomen and James Watt were used for driving reciprocating pumps.

The *diaphragm pump* is a reciprocating pump in which the piston is replaced by a flexible diaphragm made of leather, rubber, or thin metal. Pumps of this type are sometimes seen on building sites where they are used for getting rid of water. If a piston-type pump were used, the grit and dirt in the water would cause rapid wear of the piston and cylinder. In the diaphragm pump there can be no leakage past the diaphragm and therefore this type is often used to pump petrol from the tank of a motor car to the carburettor. The old-fashioned *bellows* used for blowing air into a fire to make it burn up are really a diaphragm pump.

The *bicycle pump* is a simple device whose piston acts as a valve. Air enters the cylinder at the handle end as the piston is drawn back, passing between the soft leather cup of the piston and the wall of the cylinder. On the forward stroke, the air is compressed and forces the cup outwards so that it fits tightly against the cylinder. The air is pushed out through the flexible connector into the bicycle tyre, whose valve prevents the air from escaping.

CYLINDER

HANDLE

LEATHER CUP

CONNECTOR

BICYCLE PUMP

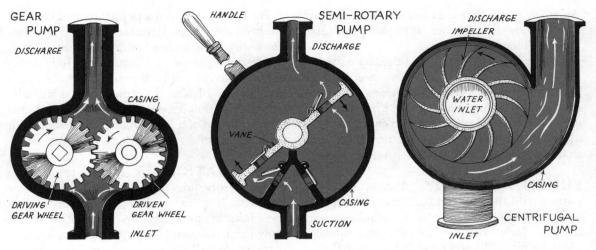

GEAR PUMP

DISCHARGE

CASING

DRIVING GEAR WHEEL

DRIVEN GEAR WHEEL

INLET

HANDLE

SEMI-ROTARY PUMP

DISCHARGE

VANE

CASING

SUCTION

DISCHARGE

IMPELLER

WATER INLET

CASING

CENTRIFUGAL PUMP

INLET

Rotary Pumps

A simple type of rotary pump is the *gear pump,* often used for supplying oil under pressure to the working parts of engines. Two gear-wheels are contained in a close-fitting casing, one of them being turned by the engine. The teeth of the two gearwheels are meshed together so that they turn in opposite directions. Oil is carried round between the teeth of the wheels and the inside of the casing. No valves are needed as the oil is prevented from flowing back between the two gearwheels by their interlocking teeth. Pumps of this kind are also used for working hydraulic machinery in aircraft, such as that used for lifting and lowering the wheels.

The *semi-rotary pump,* which is often fitted for pumping water out of launches and small craft, works on the same principle as a reciprocating force pump. Instead of a piston, its drum-shaped casing contains a vane which is turned first in one direction and then in the other by a to-and-fro movement of the handle.

Centrifugal pumps have a central turning part called the impeller. Water, or the fluid to be pumped, is supplied to the centre of the impeller and flung outwards against the casing of the pump by the curved vanes of the impeller (see CENTRIFUGAL FORCE). The casing of the pump forms a spiral chamber through which the water is discharged.

Turbocompressors. The large quantities of air required for the complete burning of the fuel in a gas turbine or aircraft jet engine are usually pumped in by a turbocompressor which in its simplest form consists of a fan spinning rapidly inside a casing. Usually the fan blades are arranged in several rows. (See INTERNAL COMBUSTION ENGINE.)

PUMPKIN. The pumpkins usually grown in England are enormous, round, orange fruits weighing many pounds, but some pumpkins are as small as oranges, some are grey or greenish and some are pear-shaped. The plant on which

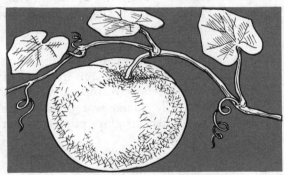

A pumpkin with leaves and climbing tendrils.

pumpkins grow is known by the Latin name of *Cucurbita pepo* and is cultivated in Europe and North America. The flowers are large and yellow. Some kinds of pumpkins are grown for cattle to eat. Cucumbers, marrows, melons and gourds are all closely related to the pumpkin.

Pumpkins can be boiled or baked in pies, but they are not eaten much in Europe. In North

America, where they are more popular, they are usually known as squashes. Pumpkin pie is eaten there on Thanksgiving Day.

Provided they have the right treatment, pumpkins are quite easy to grow. Seeds should be sown in early spring under glass with some heat and the young plants put out in the garden in May after the last frost, for even a little frost may kill them. They need a sunny place with rich soil and plenty of water at all times.

PUNCH AND JUDY.

Punch, the little puppet with the humped back and hooked nose who throws his baby out of the window, beats his wife Judy with his big stick and squeaks, "What a pity! What a pity! What a pity!" was once a real live actor. In Italian plays of the 16th century there was a rogue named Pulcinella, and this rogue was in plays in Paris throughout the 17th century, with his name changed to Polichinelle. This mischievous character was so great a favourite with crowds in fairs or at street corners that puppet showmen adopted him as their hero, and as a puppet. He became a favourite of Charles II and all other lovers of merriment in England.

At the beginning of the 18th century fashionable people crowded the theatre in Covent Garden where Punch, a wooden figure worked by wires, appeared as a commentator among puppets who represented characters in a serious play. When the subject was the Flood, Punch would thrust his long red nose into the scene of the Ark and squeak "Hazy weather, Mr. Noah". At that time his wife's name was Joan and he was still not at all like the glove puppet Punch of today.

Nobody knows now how our "Punch-and-Judy Show" began, with its real dog Toby in frilled collar, the showman with his musical pipes and his boxful of oddities like the beadle who wants to arrest Punch, the hangman who gets hanged himself when showing Punch how to put his head in the noose, the undertaker who brings a coffin to bury Punch and gets himself laid out instead, and Joey, the clown, who is the only one to get the better of the big bully. It was certainly part of English life throughout the reign of Queen Victoria.

For French children a puppet named Guignol has been a favourite since the time of Napoleon. For many years he has had a little theatre, four or five times the size of a Punch-and-Judy show, in their playground by the street in Paris called the Champs Elysées. Far from being a bully, he is a mild old simpleton who would come to harm but for the aid of a lively youth who rescues him from his enemies, who include a horned devil.

PUNCTUATION.

In writing or printing the system of dividing up sentences with signs or marks to help in reading and understanding them is called punctuation. Punctuation marks show the pauses and changes of expression that there would be if the sentences were being spoken instead of written. They include commas, full stops, semicolons, colons, question marks, exclamation marks, apostrophes, quotation marks, hyphens, brackets and dashes.

The Comma. (,) Commas are used to mark pauses in a sentence. They separate phrases and clauses from other parts of a sentence (phrases and clauses are explained in the article SENTENCE), and are also put between single words that form a list or series and are not connected by *and* or *or*.

Examples: The last runner, who had fallen into a pond on his way, arrived at the finishing post.

The basket contained apples, oranges, pears and nuts.

There are two important rules about when *not* to use commas. A comma is never used to end a sentence; and it should never be put between the subject of a verb and the verb, nor between a verb and its object or completing word. (That is, never use a comma like this: "The man, fell flat on the ice", or "The soldier rested, his tired feet.")

The Full Stop. (.) A full stop marks the end of a complete sentence that is a statement.

Example: The boy jumped over the wall.

If a sentence is a question or an exclamation it has a question mark or exclamation mark at the end, not a full stop.

A full stop is also used after an abbreviation or shortened form of a word. Examples are *Jan.* for January; *in.* for inch; *Co.* for Company.

The Semicolon. (;) A semicolon marks a less heavy and positive stop than a full stop, but more positive than a comma. It is normally used to separate statements which are complete but which are also very closely connected with each other.

Example : The wind blew from the north; the clouds darkened over the mountain tops; then the storm broke in fury.

The Colon. (:) This punctuation mark is not used very much nowadays, although it was in the past, as we can see from the Authorized Version of the Bible, for instance. It can be used in the same way as the semicolon, but its chief use in modern writing is to tell the reader that a list or series of some kind, or an example or quotation, is to follow.

Example : There are two alternatives : we can either go in the rain or we can wait till it clears.

The Question Mark. (?) As its name shows, a question mark is used at the end of a direct question.

Examples : Are you going tonight ?
Will you do this for me ?

Try to avoid putting a question mark in brackets like this (?) in letters to show that you feel doubtful or scornful about something. The words you write ought to make this clear so that you do not have to depend on punctuation to do it for you.

The Exclamation Mark. (!) This stop is used after words or sentences which show emotion, excitement or strong feeling of some kind.

Examples : Oh ! Ow ! Ah ! Good Heavens !
Great Scott !
What I endured !
How I hated what he had to say !

It is also used after wishes, like

God save the Queen !
Heaven help us !

Another use for the exclamation mark is in short, exclaiming "addresses" to people :

You stupid idiot !
You darling !

When you write yourself, particularly in letters, do not use exclamation marks too often, for if every sentence is an exclamation none of them will stand out as being specially important.

The Apostrophe. (') The apostrophe is used in two different ways. In the first use the apostrophe is a mark put with a noun to show ownership or possession. *The boy's book* means the book that belongs to the boy. When the noun is singular, or is plural but does not end in *s*, an apostrophe followed by the letter *s* is used ; when the noun is plural and ends in *s* an apostrophe alone is used.

Examples : The girl's satchel was lost.
Fashions in women's clothes change often.
Several boys' football boots needed cleaning.

When a singular word or name of one syllable ends in *s*, it is usually followed by an apostrophe and an *s*, as in *Keats's poems, St. James's Park*. When a word of more than one syllable ends in *s*, however, the apostrophe is often used alone, as in *for goodness' sake*.

The other use of the apostrophe is to show that a letter or letters have been left out for shortness or ease in speech.

Examples : Here's the very thing.
It's a shame you can't come.

Care is needed with *its* and *it's*. *It's* is the shortened form of *it is*; but in *its wheels were red*, *its* is the possessive form of the pronoun *it*. (This is explained in the article PRONOUN.) This possessive must never have an apostrophe, nor must *hers, yours, theirs* and *whose*, which are the possessive forms of other pronouns.

Quotation Marks (or *inverted commas*). (" " or ' ') These marks are used at the beginning and end of sentences or phrases that are quoting words that someone else has said or written. All conversation, in compositions or stories, must have quotation marks at either end.

Examples : He said "Good morning" in a growling voice.
"It was only yesterday", remarked Elizabeth, "that I found out his name."

Titles of books, papers, poems, plays, pictures or pieces of music may be shown by quotation marks, as "David Copperfield".

Both single and double quotation marks are used and there is no definite rule about which are best. When you wish to use quotation marks inside another set of quotation marks, you should use double ones if the outer ones are single, or single ones if the outer ones are double.

Examples : The man said : "I shall write to the 'Radio Times' about it."

The man said : 'I shall write to the "Radio Times" about it.'

The Hyphen. (-) A hyphen is used to join two or more words together to make one word, usually either a noun or an adjective.

Examples : stick-in-the-mud, bomb-proof, red-hot, will-o'-the-wisp.

Brackets and Dashes. (() and —) Both these punctuation marks are sometimes called *parentheses* (this is the plural of the word *parenthesis*). A phrase in brackets can be described as "in parenthesis". It means "put in as an aside."

Examples : He came (as we might have guessed) an hour late.

The black puppy—at least, it was black in patches—wagged its tail.

Dashes should not be used instead of either commas or full stops.

PUNIC WARS.

The word "Punic" means Carthaginian, and the three Punic Wars were fought between Carthage in North Africa, near where the town of Tunis now stands (see CARTHAGE), and Rome in Italy. Rome and Carthage were rivals because both wanted to control the trade routes of the Mediterranean.

The first Punic War, which broke out in about 264 B.C., was over possession of the island of Sicily. During the war, which lasted for 23 years, the Romans found a method of dealing with the skilled Carthaginian sailors. They fitted an instrument called a grappling-bridge to their ships and whenever a Carthaginian galley came alongside a Roman one the Romans dropped a bridge and clamped the two vessels together. They then leaped on board the enemy ship and fought hand-to-hand with sword and shield, as if the battle were on land.

Gradually the war turned in favour of the Romans, and in 241 B.C. they captured and sank most of the Carthaginian fleet. The Carthaginians then gave up their claim to Sicily and also paid a large sum of money to Rome.

The second Punic War brought a great soldier on the scene. He was Hannibal, the son of a Carthaginian general who had made him swear always to hate the Romans. (See HANNIBAL.) Hannibal stormed Saguntum, a town in Spain, so that the Romans declared that he had broken the peace treaty between Rome and Carthage, and war broke out again in 218 B.C.

Hannibal led a mighty army of men, horses and elephants across the Alps into the plains of northern Italy. Here he made his position secure by defeating the Romans on the banks of the River Trebia. Next he trapped a Roman army on the shore of Lake Trasimene and killed thousands of men.

Meanwhile the Romans had elected a dictator, Quintus Fabius Maximus, known as "the Delayer" because he believed in using his army to follow Hannibal and delay him by such means as cutting off his food supplies. The Roman people, however, preferred open battles, and they elected two men, Terentius Varro and Aemilius Paulus, to lead the army against Hannibal in 216. The two leaders took turns in commanding the army, but Varro knew nothing about war. The Romans met Hannibal by the fortress of Cannae. Hannibal formed his army in a crescent shape and caused it to close round the Romans. They were so closely packed that they could not use their weapons, and the fight became a butchery, with immense Roman losses.

The Battle of Cannae was Hannibal's greatest victory, but instead of marching on Rome he established himself at Capua, the second greatest town of Italy, whose people had joined his side. Gradually, however, the rest of the Romans plucked up courage and Fabius took up his delaying tactics again. Slowly Hannibal lost the ground he had gained, including Capua, which was starved into surrender. He pinned all his hopes on his brother Hasdrubal, who in 207 appeared in Italy with a fresh army. The Romans sent men under Claudius Nero against Hasdrubal and forced him to fight on the banks of the River Metaurus. Most of the army was destroyed and Hasdrubal himself was slain.

This was the end of Hannibal's attempt to conquer Italy. In 203 he returned to North Africa, but the Romans decided to defeat him there, and in 202, at Zama near Carthage, the Roman leader Scipio conquered Hannibal, thus ending the second and greatest Punic War.

The third Punic War broke out because of the Romans' fear of Carthage which, even after Zama, was not completely overcome. A Roman statesman, Cato the Censor, who was a hard and cruel old man, continually urged *"Delenda est Carthago"* ("Carthage must be destroyed"). The Romans therefore quarrelled with Carthage and insisted on impossible terms for a settlement. They then invaded Africa and in 146 B.C. destroyed Carthage utterly. Nevertheless, although this brought the Punic Wars to an end, Carthage was built again more than 100 years later by the Roman emperor Augustus.

PUNISHMENT. If a child misbehaves, he may be smacked, sent to bed early or not allowed to watch television. These are ways of punishing him for his misbehaviour. In just the same way, people who break the law are punished. Today, the punishments allowed by law in Great Britain are the paying of fines (for offences that are not very serious) and the loss of freedom resulting from imprisonment (for crimes such as robbery and murder). Some offenders may be sent to do social work as part of their sentence. Corporal punishment, for example flogging (severe whipping), is no longer allowed in Britain. Death by hanging as a punishment for murder was abolished in 1969. (See CAPITAL PUNISHMENT; PRISONS.)

Punishment usually has three main purposes: retribution, deterrence and reform. *Retribution* means causing pain to the wrongdoer, as a means of revenge for what he had done to his victim. *Deterrence* means making the punishment a warning to other people so that they will be deterred, or discouraged, from committing the same crime. *Reform* means the training of the wrongdoer to be a better person.

Today in many countries a great deal of effort is made to reform criminals, by "rehabilitation" so that they can lead decent lives after they are released from prison. The idea of reform is quite a new one in the history of punishment. For many centuries punishments were retributive and deterrent and were extremely cruel.

Execution

In England there were for a long time several methods of execution (putting to death). Until 1870 the legal punishment for treason was hanging, drawing and quartering. The criminal was first hanged, then his insides were taken out (drawn) and the rest of his body cut into four pieces (quartered), which were preserved in pitch and set up in prominent places as warnings to would-be traitors. This punishment was carried out for the last time in 1820.

Persons of high rank were usually beheaded— among them were Anne Boleyn, Lady Jane Grey, Mary Queen of Scots and Charles I. The last beheading in England was that of Simon Fraser, Lord Lovat, who was beheaded at the Tower of London in 1747 for taking part in the Jacobite rebellion against the king.

The recognized punishment for heresy (holding views not taught by the Church) was burning alive. Till 1789 burning was the legal punishment for women convicted of treason (which in the 18th century included the making of false coins) or murdering husbands or masters.

Torture and Harsh Punishments

In England torture was never allowed by the law as a means of punishment, but it was often used to make people confess to crimes. Among the commonest instruments of torture was the rack, which was a frame with a roller at each end. The victim was tied to the frame and the rollers were turned in order to stretch his joints. (We refer to the rack today when using such a phrase as "a racking pain".) The thumbscrews, which crushed the thumbs, and the "Scavenger's Daughter", which pressed the victim's head to his feet, were also used.

In the middle ages mutilation, which was the loss of a hand or an eye, was a common punishment. In the 11th century the punishments for killing game were very severe; in the reign of William the Conqueror anyone who shot deer was blinded.

From the middle ages until the beginning of the 19th century there were punishments which, as well as hurting wrongdoers, were also intended to put them to shame. Among these were

Reece Winstone

This ducking-stool, last used in 1809, is kept in the parish church at Leominster, Herefordshire.

the stocks and the pillory, where the victim was sometimes pelted with mud or stones (see STOCKS AND PILLORY) and the ducking-stool. This was a pole with a chair at the end of it into which the offender was put and then ducked under water. It was often used for nagging women.

Punishment in the 19th Century

From about the middle of the 19th century a great many wrongdoers were put in prison where they were kept in solitary confinement (shut up by themselves), or made to do hard and useless labour. Many were set to picking oakum, which meant untwisting old rope. The bits of thread they unpicked were used for stuffing between ships' planks in order to make them watertight. Prisoners also had to work machines called the treadmill and the crank, turning them endlessly round and round.

Such methods of punishment were useless, for long spells of bad treatment make people worse instead of better. People came to realize this, and since the beginning of the 20th century attempts have been made to reform criminals.

PUPA. Moths and butterflies, beetles, flies, ants, bees and wasps all start life as grubs or caterpillars which, when they have finished growing, have a pupal, or resting, stage before they turn into perfect adult insects. During this stage they do not feed at all and move little. A

pupa, in fact, is rather like a doll, which is what the word means in Latin.

Not all insects have a pupal stage. Grasshoppers and locusts just go on getting a little bigger and having larger wings each time they moult, or shed their skins, until they are fully grown. However, the changes from caterpillar to pupa and then to moth or butterfly are also only moults. The difference is that in insects such as grasshoppers these changes take place outside the insect and are easily seen and in moths and butterflies they take place internally, or inside the insect.

These internal changes start to take place slowly in the caterpillar long before it turns into a pupa, but it is only when the caterpillar sheds its last skin that they can be seen. Then the legs, wings, antennae (feelers) and eyes of the full grown insect which will eventually appear can all be seen in the pupa. In the pupae of butterflies and moths these parts are all pressed closely against the sides of the insect and covered by a cuticle, or hard shell. In the pupae of beetles these parts often stand out from the body and so these are called free pupae.

The pupa of a butterfly, which usually hangs from a leaf or twig, is generally known as a chrysalis, a name which refers to the silvery or golden marks it often has. The pupae of most moths are hidden away among rubbish, in the ground or in woven cocoons.

PUPPET. A puppet play is a play in miniature, acted not by live actors but by small figures of wood or some other substance, shaped and painted to look like human beings or animals and moved about by a "puppet-master" hidden behind the stage. Some puppet plays are silent, but when there are words they are spoken also by someone who is hidden away from the audience. The stage is a small version of a proper stage, there are bright lights on it to shine on the players and light them up for the audience, and there are often words and music. In fact, everything is like a real play except for the actors.

There are all kinds of puppets, and they can be as simple as the "rabbit" made with a handkerchief or as complicated as the greatest skill and cleverness can achieve. The most popular kind that people make for themselves when they want to give puppet plays of their own is the glove puppet, which is slipped over the hand like a glove and worked by moving the fingers about inside it. This is the kind to be seen in nearly all Punch-and-Judy shows. Another type is the stringed puppet or marionette. Strings are attached to its head, hands, feet and other parts, and the operator pulls on the tops of the strings to make the puppet move. Marionettes are more complicated to make and to work than glove puppets but they can act much more compli- cated plays too, and look more real and natural.

Rod puppets are very popular in the countries of the Far East, where there have been beautiful and elaborate puppet plays for centuries. Whereas a marionette is worked by strings from above, a rod puppet is moved from below by means of thin rods joined to various parts of its body. There are also shadow puppets. These are figures which are cut out of cardboard but are in separate pieces that are then joined with paper fasteners so that they can be moved up

and down from below by wires or rods. The cardboard shapes themselves are never seen by the audience, only their shadows cast on to a white screen, just as with the shadow of your hands on a wall you can make a dog's head or a rabbit or a goose.

Making a Glove Puppet

The most important part of a glove puppet is its head. The puppet will have to be seen from some distance away, and therefore all its features have to be exaggerated so that they will show up clearly. The nose, eyebrows, lips and ears, for instance, must be bigger and stick out more than if you were just making an ordinary model head.

A good way of making a human puppet head is to model plasticine on an old electric light bulb. Start by sticking on a good-sized knob of plasticine for the nose and two balls for the eyes. Then add more plasticine in strips, gradually building up the face and the expression you want on it—a grin, or a turned down mouth, for in- stance. Press the plasticine firmly into position with a small modelling tool; if you do it with your fingers you may squash the shapes and make them rather blurred. Make sure you "build out" the lips and do not leave them just as a flat mark on the plasticine. Ears should be large, and hair—or moustache or beard— should be modelled in with the rest of the head. When you have finished the modelling, the head must look right from the back and sides as well as from the front. It should look very exaggerated and "larger-than-life" at this stage, because the outlines become much softer and more rounded during the next process.

This consists first of covering the whole head and bulb with a layer of wet tissue paper, press- ing it well into all the hollows, and patching with another piece of tissue if it should split. Next, tear (do not cut) a coloured comic and an ordinary newspaper into pieces about the size of a postage stamp. Spread a coating of paste (made with flour and water) on the head and then stick pieces of coloured paper all over it—rub the edges well into the paste so that they are held firmly and the surface is even. A second coat of paste comes next, then a layer of the pieces of newspaper put on in the same way, so

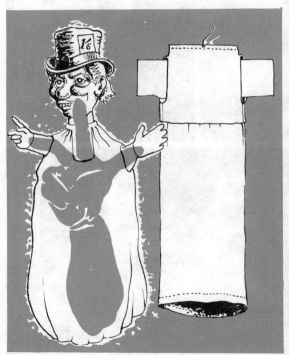

On the left is a glove puppet, representing a comic figure with a large nose and prominent teeth. On the right is the bag through which the puppet-master slips his hand. The top is pulled round the puppet's neck.

(1) Arts Council. (2) B.B.C. Television. (3) Rees Marionettes.
(4) Keystone.

Puppets and marionettes. (1) String puppets "acting" *The Merchant of Venice*. (2) Alison Uttley's *Little Grey Rabbit* stories being "acted" on television by glove puppets. Left to right: Little Grey Rabbit, Squirrel, Hedgehog and Hare. (3) Dutch boy and girl marionettes (notice the strings). (4) Two ballerina puppets.

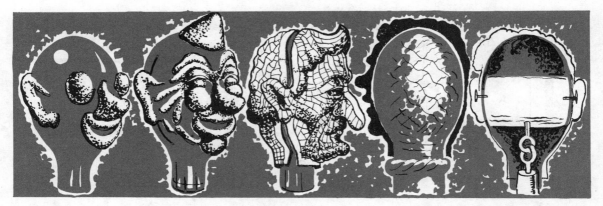

Modelling a puppet's head on a light bulb. Plasticine is stuck on for the features, then it is all covered with layers of paste and paper. This covering is then cut away and glued together on a dummy head. For a glove puppet, this is a knob of paste and paper on top of a tube. For a marionette a block of wood is used.

that no coloured pieces are left showing. (If you use some strips of bandage as well as newspaper they will give extra strength.)

Altogether five layers of coloured paper and five layers of newspaper have to be applied in turn like this, each layer being well "massaged" so as to mould it as closely as possible to the shape of the plasticine underneath. Lastly comes a final coat of tissue paper, its surface well worked in, and then the head is left until it is thoroughly dry.

When you are sure it is dry and firm, cut the outside in half with a razor blade or sharp knife, beginning cutting behind the ear at one side and going up over the head and down behind the other ear. The hardened paper "shell" can then be eased away from the plasticine model (which can be used again if you wish). Hold the halves of the head to the light and if you can see any thin spots strengthen them by putting extra layers of paste and paper *inside* the head.

You now need a strong cardboard tube cut the length of your forefinger. Make a rough head at the upper part of the tube by winding paper coated with paste round it until it will fill the hollow in the proper head. Then paste the two halves of this together again, fit in the tube with its knob and paste, and paper the join well until there is no danger of its coming apart. Glue a ring of coarse string round the tube just below the head : this forms a ridge to which the puppet's clothes can later be attached. At this stage some puppets are given a final coating of glue

and muslin to make a tougher head, and this is particularly necessary if a puppet is to be used in the knockabout of a Punch-and-Judy show.

This completes the main part of making the puppet. Now comes the painting of the face, colouring of hair, moustache and so on, and the making of the clothes. A glove puppet's clothes are a sort of bag, which should be long enough to reach from the neck of the puppet down to your elbow when you are working it. The bag must have sleeves, one for your thumb to go in and one for your second finger, to represent the puppet's arms.

For glove puppets the theatre can be a curtain or a three-sided screen with an opening in it in which the audience sees the puppets. There is no floor to the stage, of course, because of the puppeteer's hands and arms. Often people doing glove puppet shows have to hold the puppets high up above their own heads, but this is very tiring when you are not used to it. Instead, a muslin screen can be fixed up behind the stage and you can slip your hands with the puppets on them underneath it, and work the puppets in front of it at a comfortable chest level while the rest of you remains hidden.

Marionettes

The head of a marionette can be made in the same way as the glove puppet's head, but it may also be made of wood, plaster or stuffed cloth. The body may be in one piece, or in several pieces to make the marionette bend and move

☐ For a PUPPET PLAY, see the blue pages of this volume

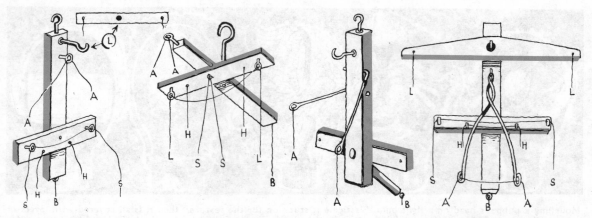

Controllers for marionettes. They are held by the person working the marionettes and used to move the strings. The L string is for legs; A for arms; S for shoulders; H for the head. B is attached to the lower part of the back.

naturally. Arms and legs can be of wood, or wire with padding round, or firmly stuffed cloth and there are many ways of making the hands and feet.

The joints in a marionette are very important, for they enable it to make movements much more natural and detailed than those of a glove puppet. There are joints at the neck, shoulders and elbows, the hips and the knees, and at the ankles, wrists and even sometimes at the fingers. They may be loops of wire, or "eyes" like the ones screwed into picture frames, leather straps or joints carved of wood.

The puppet hangs down by its strings from a wooden "controller" which the operator holds in his hand. By tipping the bars of the controller one way or another the person working the puppet raises or lowers certain strings, and the puppet moves accordingly. Besides the main positions for the strings, special ones are necessary sometimes. A puppet acrobat, for example, may need extra strings to enable it to turn upside down and walk on its hands.

The theatre for a marionette show has a rail at the back so that the "puppeteers" can lean against it and rest their elbows comfortably as they work the puppets. The stage below the rail must be deep enough to give the puppets plenty of room in which to move.

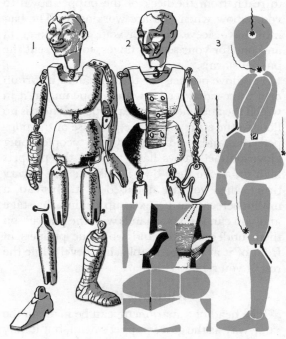

(1) and (2): two ways of putting a marionette together and making its limbs; under (2) are the rough shapes of hands and feet. (3) The points at which strings are attached.

PURCELL, Henry (1659–1695), was one of the greatest English composers. As a young boy he sang in the children's choir of the Chapel Royal (the sovereign's private chapel) and began composing at about the age of 12. It is thought that when his voice broke he studied the organ with John Blow, the organist at Westminster Abbey. We know that in 1679, when Purcell was 20, he took over Blow's place as organist, the fee paid to him being £10 a year. He married when he was about 22 and in 1682 was appointed organist at the Chapel Royal. He was present at the coronation of James II and at the funeral of Queen Mary, for which he composed the anthem "Thou knowest, Lord, the secrets of our hearts". He had six children, three of whom died before him. Purcell died on November 21, 1695. He was buried beneath the organ in Westminster Abbey.

In his short life Purcell wrote an enormous amount of music, much of it amongst the finest of his time. His church music includes many joyful anthems. As he was himself a singer he sang in performances of his own music. He wrote several odes and welcome songs—pieces offered as a present to mark a happy event such as the birthday of Queen Mary or the marriage of Princess Anne. He wrote four odes in celebration of St. Cecilia (the patron saint of music), the finest being "Hail bright Cecilia". Some of his most beautiful music is found in the fantasias and sonatas for strings and harpsichord.

National Portrait Gallery
Henry Purcell.

He wrote music for plays, among them Dryden's *King Arthur* (which contains the well-known song "Fairest Isle"), Shakespeare's *The Tempest,* and *The Fairy Queen,* which was a version of Shakespeare's *A Midsummer Night's Dream.* These plays with music were an early kind of opera. The greatest of Purcell's works of this kind is *Dido and Aeneas,* which was written for performance at a girls' school in Chelsea (London) and in which there is Dido's famous song of farewell, "When I am laid in earth". Purcell's music is poetic and song-like, but in many of his Welcome Songs it is jovial and gay.

PURITANS. When the Church of England broke away from the pope, most of its members were content that it should keep the greater part of the teaching of the whole Catholic Church (although the church services should be in English instead of in Latin). Others, however, felt that the church had not been reformed enough and that its worship should be as pure and simple as possible. They did not want to leave the church, but to get it to think as they did. These people were known as Puritans.

Some of the Puritans also disagreed with the system of having bishops appointed by the king. They preferred the new idea of government by presbyters, who were chosen by the people. This led to the founding of the Presbyterian Church. (See PRESBYTERIANS.)

Yet another group of Puritans thought that every gathering of Christians was a church in itself, and that it and its chosen minister should not be interfered with by anyone else. These were the Independents, now called Congregationalists. (See CONGREGATIONALISTS.)

In the reign of Elizabeth I laws were passed against the Puritans who broke away from the Church of England. James I, who had allowed Presbyterianism to be brought into Scotland, nevertheless refused to support the English Puritans when he became King of England in 1603.

The turn of the Puritans came during the reign of James's son Charles I. The article CHARLES I describes why the king became so unpopular with parliament that he was eventually

A Puritan reading the Bible to his children.

executed. Then the Puritans, under the leadership of Oliver Cromwell, who was an Independent, at last had their way in the church. Bishops were abolished, the use of the Prayer Book was made illegal and Independence became the state religion.

When Charles II was restored to the throne in 1660, the arguments between the Puritans and the Church of England began again. It was made law that all clergymen must use the Prayer Book again and teach the beliefs of the Church of England. From then on the Puritans outside the Church of England became known as Nonconformists; that is, people who would not conform to (agree with) the state church.

During the time that Puritans were persecuted for their beliefs many of them left England and made their homes in America. The most famous of these were the Pilgrim Fathers. (See PILGRIM FATHERS.)

Although the word Puritan originally meant those who wished to purify the church, it soon took on another meaning. Most of the early Puritans lived strict, simple lives. They wore plain clothes, often cut their hair short (which was why they were often known as Roundheads) and disapproved of fun and gaiety. So a person who is very strict, severe and rather narrow-minded is often referred to as a Puritan.

PUTTY made of powdered chalk and linseed oil is often used to hold window-panes in place. When freshly made it is soft and plastic and can be spread and moulded. It quickly hardens, owing to the action of the oxygen in the air on the linseed oil. It has been found that putty on metal hardens more slowly than that on wood, and so putty for use on metal is mixed with substances such as red lead in order to speed up the hardening.

The word putty is sometimes used to describe other soft materials. Among these is a fine lime cement used by workers in stone.

PYGMALION. The Greeks told how, long ago, Pygmalion, king of Cyprus, fell in love with a statue of Aphrodite, the goddess of love. In the version of Ovid, the Roman poet, Pygmalion was a young sculptor who found fault with every

Pygmalion carved an ivory statue of his ideal of womanhood, and fell in love with it.

woman he saw and determined never to marry. One day he set to work to carve an ivory statue of a perfect woman and when it was finished it was so beautiful that he fell in love with it. At the temple on the feast of Aphrodite he prayed to the goddess for a wife exactly like his statue, and then returned home to dote on it. As he gazed, the figure gradually turned into a living woman whom he married and called Galatea.

PYGMIES. Pygmies are small, dark people, the best known group of whom live in the hot equatorial forests of the Congo basin in Africa. Pygmy men are seldom more than 1·5 metres (about five feet) tall, and pygmy women are even smaller. Pygmies are not Negroes. Their skin is usually chocolate-coloured or yellow-grey. Their hair is crinkly and their noses are flat and broad.

The pygmies who live in the Ituri forest region of Zaire in West Africa are probably the earliest inhabitants of this part of the continent. There are only about 35,000 of them and their groups include the Twides, Aka and Efe. They are nomadic hunters and food gatherers, living in small bands, each of a few dozen people at most. A pygmy band has no chief and no council of elders. All the members meet to discuss and settle problems. Family ties are close and the people love to sing and dance, particularly on special occasions.

The tropical rain forest provides for all their

basic needs. The pygmies build simple huts from a beehive-shaped framework of sticks covered with leaves. They make temporary camps for a month or so before moving on. They wear only small loin cloths, and hunt game with bows and arrows, nets or spears. Poisoned arrows are often used to kill large game, such as elephants. The pygmies also dig pit traps, which they cover with branches and leaves.

Pygmies also trade with their Bantu neighbours. In what is known as a "silent trade" the pygmies take their goods—usually ivory or honey—and leave them in a prearranged spot. The pygmies watch from a distance as the traders arrive and put down the goods they are prepared to offer in exchange. If the pygmies are satisfied with the goods offered (salt is a favourite) they take them away. The traders then return to collect the goods·left by the pygmies. If the pygmies are not satisfied, they will wait to see if more is offered, before going away altogether. Although a group of pygmies speaks the same language as the non-pygmy people living close by, they remain quite separate.

These African people are not the only

pygmies, for small peoples live in equatorial forests in other parts of the world as well. The Bushmen of the Kalahari are also similar in many respects to the pygmies. (See BUSHMEN AND HOTTENTOTS.) The fact that pygmies are found in many different parts of the world may mean that long ago they lived in far greater numbers than at present, but have been driven out by other and more powerful peoples into the areas where they now live. Here the pygmies are at least left in peace to lead their own lives in the ways they have learned over many centuries. In Malaya are the Semang and in the Philippine Islands live the Aeta. Both these peoples are very dark-skinned and broad-headed with woolly hair and flat noses. Other pygmies are the Andaman Islanders in the Bay of Bengal. There are very few of them and they are much like other pygmies.

These pygmies are small as compared with other people but not so small as the pygmies mentioned in Greek legends. These were tiny people who fought battles with large birds called cranes and were protected by a giant called Antaeus. Hercules, while performing one of his 12 labours, came to Libya, which was known as the land of the pygmies, and slew Antaeus.

PYRAMID. The name pyramid comes from a Greek word *pyramis* and is used for the large triangular buildings which were placed over the graves of Egyptian kings of the Old and Middle Kingdoms (see EGYPT : ANCIENT). They are constructed of almost solid stone or brick, with the burial chamber usually cut in the rock beneath.

The Egyptian pyramids are the only true ones, although some similar monuments were built in Central and South America by the Mayas, Aztecs and Incas.

Until the end of the Archaic period in ancient Egypt (3200 B.C.) both the kings and the nobles were buried in tombs made of brick called mastabas. In the Third Dynasty, however (about 2700 B.C.), the kings began to use stone for building and the earliest pyramid was built for King Zoser at Sakkara, south of Cairo, by his famous architect Imhotep. This is called the Step Pyramid because it was built in a series of steps (six in all), developing out of the old flat-topped

Paul Popper

The white woman appears to tower over the pygmy mother, but actually she is only five feet tall.

113

mastaba. The pyramid was surrounded by a vast wall, inside which was a temple where funeral offerings could be made to the dead king, as he was regarded as divine. The Step Pyramid, which is 60 metres high and is built of Tura limestone, remains one of the finest of the ancient Egyptian monuments. Under the building were 11 shafts running into the ground and in these were found pink granite and alabaster sarcophagi (coffins) in which the kings and various members of the royal family had been buried. Unfortunately the tombs had been robbed so that the bodies themselves were not found. It is possible that many more pyramids were built, because in 1953 the remains of an unfinished Step Pyramid of the Third Dynasty were found at Saqqarah.

The best known of the pyramids are a group of three built at Giza south of Cairo by the kings of the Fourth Dynasty (2680–2565 B.C.). The largest of these was built by Cheops (his Greek name), or Khufu as he was known to the Egyptians. The sides of the base of the pyramid were 230 metres and the height 146 metres, although the loss of the outer casing now makes it about 9 metres lower. The core of the pyramid is of rock and the outside of limestone and granite. The latter consists of 2,300,000 blocks of stone, each averaging 2·5 tonnes in weight.

The stone was quarried (dug) on the other side of the Nile River. The limestone came from the Tura Hills near Cairo, but the granite had to be brought from Aswan. It was roughly shaped and dragged on rollers to the river where it was placed on barges and floated down to the nearest point to the pyramid. Here a wharf was built and a granite causeway constructed to the pyramid. The stone was dragged up the causeway on wooden rollers. The men who quarried and moved the stone carved their names and those of

A. F. Kersting

The oldest of the pyramids of Egypt is the Step Pyramid. Like many others, it has been plundered by tomb robbers.

their gang on the stones in red ochre, where they can still be read.

All the stone was cut with copper tools by means of wedges and chisels. The work was very accurately done and there is only half an inch difference between the cutting of one side and the other.

Other pyramids were erected by Chephren and Mycerinus, Cheops' successors, but they were not so large. The kings of the Fifth and Sixth Dynasties (2565–2258 B.C.) also built pyramids at Giza and Abu Sir. The kings of the Eleventh and Twelfth Dynasties (2134–1786 B.C.) built pyramids at Hawarah, Dahshur and Illahun, but after this period the use of pyramids as royal burial places was given up (probably to avoid robbery) and the kings were buried in rock-cut chambers in the Valley of the Kings near Thebes (Luxor), the capital of Egypt in the Eighteenth Dynasty (1570–1372 B.C.).

There were at one time many pyramids along the west bank of the river, and their building in the Old and Middle Kingdoms is thought to be connected with the worship of the sun god Ra and the introduction of mummification (see MUMMY). The ancient Egyptians believed in an after life which could be obtained if the body was preserved and supplied with food and drink. They therefore buried their kings with all that they might need in the after world, and with paintings and inscriptions on the walls of the tomb telling them how to avoid any dangers that they might meet.

PYRAMUS AND THISBE.

In Babylon in ancient times lived a pair of lovers called Pyramus and Thisbe. Their parents would not let them marry, but they used to talk secretly to each other through a hole in the wall between their houses. They agreed to meet one evening outside the city. Thisbe reached the meeting-place first, but was frightened by a lioness which had come from killing cattle to drink at a spring near by. In running away from it, she dropped her cloak, which the lioness chewed, thus staining it with blood. Pyramus came later, and finding the cloak and the tracks of the lioness, thought Thisbe had been killed. He took the cloak under a mulberry tree which grew near

Thisbe weeping over the dead body of Pyramus.

by, drew his sword and stabbed himself. Just before he died, Thisbe found him, saw what had happened and killed herself with his sword. Ever since, it is said, ripe mulberries have been black, though formerly they were white.

This is the story on which the clowns' play in William Shakespeare's *A Midsummer Night's Dream* is founded. The legend is told by only one ancient writer, the Roman poet Ovid.

PYRENEES MOUNTAINS.

The high mountain barrier of the Pyrenees divides France from Spain. The boundary between the two countries runs along the crest of the central and highest ridge. The range is about 430 kilometres long and its tallest peak is Pic de Aneto (3,404 metres). The higher peaks are always snowclad and there are tiny glaciers, or ice rivers, in the higher valleys. The main railways and roads between France and Spain pass close to the sea at each end of the Pyrenees, but there are two passes carrying roads and railways through the mountains. The first of these is the Col de Somport between Pau and Jaca. The second, farther east, is the Col de la Perche between Mont Louis and Ribas de Fresser. There are several other passes carrying roads between France and Spain.

Few people except shepherds live in the Pyrenees. The little republic of Andorra in the

Courtesy, French Government Tourist Office

The high peaks of the Pyrenees form a natural barrier between France and Spain.

heart of the mountains is one of the smallest states in the world. (See ANDORRA.) Water power obtained from the rapid rivers is used to make electricity. There are large vineyards on the southern slopes of the Pyrenees where they approach the Mediterranean Sea. Winter sports can be enjoyed in the high central Pyrenees and at the western end are several seaside resorts between Biarritz and San Sebastian. At this end live the Basques, a people who speak a language unlike any other in Europe.

PYROMETER.

An ordinary thermometer cannot be used at high temperatures because the glass would melt and the liquid boil. Therefore special types of thermometer must be used. These special instruments are called pyrometers.

Hot bodies give out electro-magnetic radiation (see HEAT; RADIATION). The hotter the body is, the more energy it gives out as radiation; the wavelengths of this radiation depend on the temperature of the body. As the body gets hotter it glows, and its colour changes from red through orange, yellow and white to blue.

Pyrometers use these properties to measure the temperature of a body by means of the radiation it gives out.

In the *total radiation pyrometer* the radiation is focused on one junction of a thermo-couple (see THERMOMETER; ELECTRICITY). The thermo-couple then gives a reading which depends on the total amount of radiation received. From this the temperature of the body may be found.

In an *optical pyrometer*, the colour of the hot glowing body is matched against the colour of a wire filament heated by an electric current. The temperature of the filament, or of the hot body, may then be found from the current used to heat the filament.

PYTHAGORAS

was a Greek who lived in the 6th century B.C. He is remembered for his work in mathematics and music and his ideas about the soul. He settled in Crotona in southern Italy with a group of some 300 people, the Pythagoreans, who devoted themselves to the rules laid down by Pythagoras and to his ideas about religion and philosophy.

As far as is known, the people of Crotona rose up against the Pythagoreans and set fire to the building in which they were gathered. After this Pythagoras retired to Metapontum where he remained until he died at the end of the 6th century B.C. The Pythagorean school continued until the 4th century B.C.

The name of Pythagoras is often mentioned in geometry (see GEOMETRY), but although many of the ideas and teachings of Pythagoras are still known, he himself wrote nothing down. He taught that the souls of dead people might appear on earth again, not only in new human beings but also in animals. This idea is called *metempsychosis,* or the transmigration (moving across) of souls. He also taught that one vegetable, the bean, had a soul, and forbade his disciples to eat it. His enemies said that beans gave him indigestion and that he invented this rule to protect his stomach.

Pythagoras said that the earth was a sphere revolving round a central fire and that as it revolved it made music. He was one of the first people to believe that the earth was a sphere—most people thought it was flat. Pythagoras also claimed to see into the future, and some of his teachings were later used in magic during the middle ages.

PYTHON. Pythons are found in tropical Asia, Africa and Australia, and, except for the anaconda, are the largest of all snakes. The reticulated python from Malaya (so-called because the markings on its body are in the form of a network, or *reticulum*) grows to about 9 metres in length, and both the African and Indian pythons have been known to grow more than 6 metres long.

Pythons are not poisonous snakes. They are closely related to boa constrictors and, like them, kill the warm-blooded animals on which they feed by coiling tightly round them until they are suffocated.

Young pythons hatch from eggs about the size of tennis balls, covered with a tough, parchment-like skin. The mother python lays up to 60 eggs and then coils herself round them until they hatch. Each baby python has a small, sharp, chisel-shaped tooth which sticks out from the front of its mouth, and with this it cuts slits in the shell and crawls out. It loses this egg-tooth in a few days.

In Australia the carpet python, which is about 3·5 metres long, is sometimes kept in warehouses to catch rats and other pests. The python used in stage performances is usually the Indian python, which becomes tame when frequently handled.

Photo Coverage

An Indian python, one of the largest of all snakes. It kills other animals by suffocating them in its coils.

QATAR is an independent Arab state on the west coast of the Persian Gulf. The country occupies a peninsula which is bordered in the south by Saudi Arabia and the United Arab Emirates. To the west lie the islands of Bahrain. Qatar is a monarchy, or *emirate*, ruled by an *emir*. Its capital is Doha.

Until the 1940s the people of Qatar lived mainly by pearl diving, fishing and camel breeding. Then came the discovery of oilfields which have since made the country one of the richest in the world.

Qatar has an area of 11,400 square kilometres. Its population, most of whom are Moslem, is about 200,000. (See also PERSIAN GULF.)

QUADRILLE is the name for a game of cards and also for a dance. The card game, which was played by four people with a pack of 40 cards, was popular in the 18th century but ceased to be played when whist became fashionable instead. The dance called the quadrille, however, is still danced as an "old time" dance.

QUAIL. Among the rarer birds that visit the British Isles in the summer and fly away to other countries later is the quail. It is only about 18 centimetres long and looks like a small partridge, mainly buff in colour with black markings. The cock has two black stripes on its neck. Its call has been described as "wet-mi-lips", and quails are far more frequently heard than seen, as they prefer to remain under cover. They haunt cornfields and pastures, feeding on grass, weed seeds and insects. The eggs vary from 7 to 12 in number and are yellowish with dark blotches and spots. They are laid in a shallow scrape made by the hen in a cornfield or on grassland and lined with a few pieces of dried grass. A few quails may remain for the winter in southern England and Ireland if the weather is mild.

Quails are found in Europe and in autumn large numbers migrate, or

The quail is a summer visitor to the British Isles.

journey, to Africa and India. They are very good to eat, and so many were caught in Egypt that they became very scarce. In 1936, however, a law was passed in Egypt forbidding the catching of quails in spring, and Great Britain also stopped buying live quails for fattening and selling in the London markets. After this quails became more common.

Relatives of the common quail include the rain quail of India and the Australian stubble quail. Other Australian quails are the brown or swamp quail and the beautiful king quail, which also lives in Indonesia and Malaysia. In North America the birds called quails are not true quails. They include the bob-white, whose whistling call resembles these words often repeated. It has been introduced into the British Isles but it soon died out.

QUAKERS are members of a religious group called the Society of Friends. It was founded in the middle of the 17th century by George Fox (see FOX, GEORGE), and almost from the first its members were known as Quakers. At first this name was intended to show bitter scorn. It originated in the law court at Derby where Fox was being tried. During the proceedings he warned the judge to "tremble at the word of the Lord", and the judge called him and his followers "Quakers" (tremblers). There was an additional reason for the name, because they were supposed to shake with awe when

they felt God's presence. They calmly accepted the nickname and it has long since ceased to sound like a jibe.

Quakers, or Friends, as they are also called, worship God in a very simple and straightforward manner. Let us suppose we are in London on a Sunday morning and that we are going to attend the meeting for worship (this is the Quakers' word for service) at Friends House, opposite Euston Station. This is the headquarters of Quakers in Britain. We shall see no minister or priest and there will be no set form of service. Instead of the hymns and set prayers that make up the services in many other churches there is a silence—a very still sort of silence—but members of the congregation may occasionally speak or pray aloud. This does not seem to break the silence but to express in words the reason for it.

If we ask a Quaker, "What was all that silence for?" he would reply, "So that we could know the presence of God." Quakers believe that as they wait quietly God makes His presence known, and that they can reach Him directly and quite simply if they listen and wait. This is possible at all times, whether at their meetings or when they are alone.

When George Fox, the founder of the Quakers, died in 1691 Quakerism was flourishing in the British Isles and North America, in spite of the fact that Quakers were often persecuted for their independent and unusual beliefs. Friends made many journeys in Britain, Europe and North America preaching their simple faith with great enthusiasm. William Penn, one of the early Quakers, founded the colony of Pennsylvania so that the Quakers could put their beliefs into practice. (See PENN, WILLIAM.)

Quakers believe that God loves all His people and that He has put something of His divine nature into every person's heart. They feel that they must act simply and directly in all things; for instance, they must state their opinions honestly and their "Yes" and "No" must really mean "Yes" and "No". For this reason they never swear on oath to tell the truth, for they consider it unnecessary. They do not believe in titles and they show as much respect to a humble person as to an important one. Above all, and

since the early days of the movement, they have refused to have anything to do with fighting—because, they say, it is utterly against God. However, although they refuse to join the armed forces they have done great work for the victims of war—for the wounded, the prisoners and the

Courtesy, Society of Friends

Jordans Meeting House in Buckinghamshire. William Penn of Pennsylvania is buried at Jordans.

refugees. In places where there is famine or some other emergency they are always to be found, doing what they can to relieve suffering. They played a big part in the freeing of the Negro slaves in North America.

Elizabeth Fry, a great Quaker who lived from 1780 to 1845, is particularly famous for her work in prisons and she did perhaps more than any other single person to improve the lot of prisoners. (See FRY, ELIZABETH.)

Friends still call for an end to war and would like to see all nations working together to help the poorer ones, and they are also working for an end to bitterness between people of different colours.

QUANTUM THEORY. In 1901 the German scientist Max Planck (1858–1947) put forward the Quantum Theory as a result of his observations of the way in which heat is radiated, or given out. Heat, light, X-rays, gamma rays and radio signals are all forms of energy radiated in waves. The difference between them lies in their *wavelengths*, or distance between the crests.

According to the quantum theory, the energy is not radiated in a steady stream but in little packets called quanta. This can be compared with the difference between the smooth flow from a running water-tap and the drops from a leaky tap. *Quantum* is the Latin for "a definite amount".

The amount of energy in the quantum of any kind of radiation depends on its frequency, which is the number of waves given out each second. The size of the quantum is obtained by multiplying the frequency of the kind of radiation concerned by a very small number called Planck's Constant. Thus the quantum of gamma radiation, which has a very high frequency, is much larger than that of radio waves with their comparatively low frequency.

QUARANTINE. A person suffering from an infectious disease is "isolated" for a period varying from one to four weeks during which he is advised not to mix with other people. This is called the "isolation period". A person who has been in contact with someone suffering from an infectious disease is often kept away from other people during a period when he may be developing the disease. This is called the "quarantine period".

Quarantine is a very old way of keeping infectious diseases from spreading. For a time people were kept in quarantine for 40 days, and this was how it got its name (from the Italian word *quaranta*, meaning forty). Now, however, quarantine is only about the same length of time as the incubation period. The incubation period is the time between the arrival of the germs in the body and the beginning of the actual signs of illness. In many infectious illnesses a rash appears soon after the first symptoms, and only then can it be known for certain what the disease is.

The quarantine period is just long enough for people who have been near a patient with an infectious disease to show the first symptoms. If they have not developed symptoms by the end of the quarantine period they are probably all right. During the quarantine period, however, they may be "incubating" the disease germs and may infect other people if they go out among them. So it is not only the person known to have

the illness who may spread infection to others.

The incubation and quarantine periods for some infectious diseases are as follows:

	Incubation (days)	Quarantine
Chicken pox	11–21	6 days from first appearance of rash
Diphtheria	2–5	Until free from infection
German measles	14–21	4 days from appearance of rash
Measles	10–15	7 days from appearance of rash
Mumps	12–26	While swelling is present
Scarlet fever	2–5	1 week

Because worldwide air travel is now so common, careful checks are made to make sure that people and animals travelling from country to country do not carry infectious diseases with them. Dogs, for example, must remain isolated in quarantine kennels for six months on arriving in Britain by air or sea. This is mainly to prevent the introduction of rabies, or hydrophobia, a terrible disease spread among dogs and other animals. People who are bitten by an infected animal also catch rabies and may die. It is a serious offence to try and avoid the quarantine regulations; for instance, by bringing pets across the English Channel from Europe where rabies is carried by wild animals.

The method of guarding against the spread of infectious disease from overseas is explained further in the article PUBLIC HEALTH.

QUARRYING. Quarrying is closely allied to mining. Indeed, it is not always easy to establish the difference between these two forms of mineral extraction. Usually quarrying describes the work of extracting from the Earth's crust the various kinds of hard stone or rock required for building, for road-making and for general industry.

The art of quarrying is one of the oldest skills of mankind. It became well established in the Stone Age when early man dug shallow quarries for the flints and the stones he needed for his tools. The quarrymen became especially skilful about 5,000 years ago when they were able to quarry the large, regular-shaped blocks of stone that were used for building the pyramids in Egypt. In fact, the name "quarry" comes from the Latin verb "quadrare" meaning to make something square. Similar skills in cutting and squaring huge blocks of stone were shown by quarrymen in Pembrokeshire when they quarried the massive pillars now at Stonehenge.

Nowadays the term quarrying has a somewhat different meaning from that used by the Egyptians and the Romans. The industry is divided into two main branches. One type of quarrying still produces large blocks of building or ornamental stone. The most important materials quarried in this way are granite, limestone, marble and sandstone for buildings and slate for roofing and cladding (facing).

Quarrying Blocks of Stone

Most rock masses have natural joints and cleavages and they break more easily along these than in other directions. The quarryman's knowledge of the position and extent of these cracks often enables him to break hard rock like slate or even granite without using explosives. Many of the blocks of stone are often roughly cut to shape while they are still partly attached to the rock in the quarry.

To cut blocks of softer rock such as Bath and Portland stones it is possible to use specially designed machines. The machines are mounted on rails and, as they are moved to and fro across the rock, power driven chisels or band-saws mounted on the machines cut deep grooves. In this way it is possible to cut out large blocks of shaped stone. Stones that can be freely cut in any direction are known as "freestones".

In very hard rock such as granite, that may not show any useful cracks or cleavages to help the quarryman, it may be necessary first to drill a row of holes in the rock. Into these holes the quarryman forces steel wedges until the block of rock cracks under the strain. It is sometimes even possible to split the rock along a line of drill holes by setting off small explosive charges in these holes.

Blocks of stone up to 30 metres long, 5 metres wide and 2 metres thick can be produced by these methods. If necessary, they can then be "dressed" into smaller sizes by suitable cutting machines that can saw, or plane, or polish.

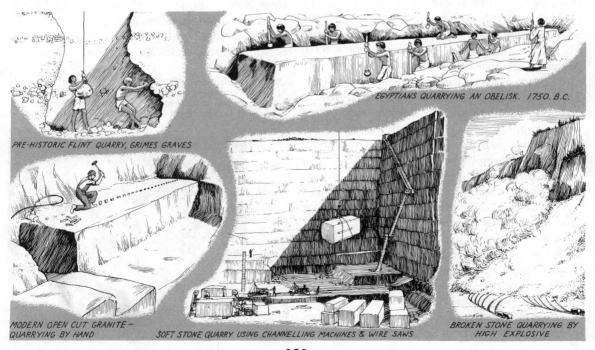

EGYPTIANS QUARRYING AN OBELISK. 1750. B.C.

PRE-HISTORIC FLINT QUARRY, GRIMES GRAVES

MODERN OPEN CUT GRANITE – QUARRYING BY HAND

SOFT STONE QUARRY USING CHANNELLING MACHINES & WIRE SAWS

BROKEN STONE QUARRYING BY HIGH EXPLOSIVE

Courtesy, Kingston Minerals Ltd.

The large quarrying complex at Penmaenmawr in North Wales where granite is worked for use as rail ballast and road materials.

Quarrying Broken Stone

The other main branch of the quarrying industry provides broken stone or aggregate. In "aggregate" quarries a series of small holes is drilled downwards from the surface ahead of the rock face. The holes are filled with explosives and these charges are fired in quick succession. In this way several thousand tonnes of rock can be broken from the quarry face by a single blast and irregular lumps of rock ranging in size from about 1 metre to fine powder are produced. Mechanical shovels load the broken stone into large trucks which carry it to a treatment plant. Here the bigger lumps are broken down in crushing machines and the stone is then sorted by screening through a set of large sieves.

The rocks most commonly worked for aggregate are "granite" (the word is here used as a trade name and includes a variety of hard igneous rocks), sandstone and limestone. Large quantities of granite and sandstone are used for road making, as "ballast" to support railway lines and in concrete. Limestone can also be used for these purposes and, in addition, it is frequently converted into lime for chemical and for agricultural use : it is also extensively used as a flux in the steel industry.

The rocks of most quarries are usually covered with a layer of weathered rock and soil that is of no value. This "overburden" must, of course, be removed before the rock can be quarried.

QUARTER DAYS. In England, Wales and Northern Ireland four days in the year are known as quarter days. They all have special names and are Lady Day (March 25, see LADY DAY), Midsummer Day (June 24), Michaelmas Day (September 29) and Christmas Day (December 25). Rents that are not paid weekly or monthly are usually paid quarterly, being due on each of the quarter days.

Quarter days in Scotland are quite different and are Candlemas (February 2), Whit Sunday (fixed for these purposes on May 15), Lammas (August 1, see LAMMAS DAY) and Martinmas (November 11).

QUARTZ is one of the most useful minerals and one of the most widely distributed.

Quartz is a particular crystalline form of silica —a compound of silicon and oxygen (crystalline means "having crystals"). It is harder than steel and clearer than glass. When pure, it is colourless or white, but when mixed with other substances it may be various shades of red, yellow, brown, green, blue, lavender or black. (Amethyst is an example of coloured quartz.) Quartz is sometimes found in large, clear, six-sided crystals with pyramidlike ends, called rock crystal. Many rocks are composed largely of

Quartz crystals are almost all alike, whether formed by nature or produced by man. The atomic pattern of four oxygen atoms joined to one silicon atom is repeated throughout the crystal and this determines its shape.

B. M. Shaub

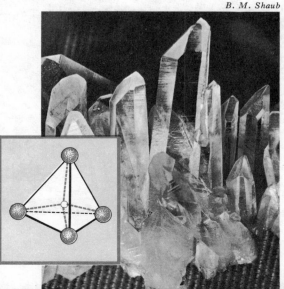

quartz. Sandstone consists of grains of quartz held together by a "cementing" substance. The "cement" may be made of more silica, of clay, or of other minerals. Quartzite is composed of grains of quartz formed into a solid block by the deposit of crystalline quartz between the original grains. Quartz also forms a large part of granite. White sand is almost pure quartz and all sand consists largely of quartz.

Quartz is used in the manufacture of optical instruments and of glass. Thin slices cut from pure quartz crystals are used to keep radio stations on their proper wavelengths. The very best quartz is needed for this purpose and only a few kilograms out of each tonne that is mined are of a high enough standard. Almost the entire supply comes from Brazil.

Fused quartz, made by melting pure rock crystal at a very high temperature, has a melting point of 1,710 degrees C. It expands and contracts less than most known materials and is more transparent than glass. These qualities make it very suitable for laboratory utensils. A dish made of fused quartz may be heated red hot and plunged into ice-cold water without cracking. Light and radiant heat waves travel through it very easily. As the health-giving ultra-violet rays (which are absorbed by glass) will go through fused quartz, a sanatorium is sometimes roofed with panes of fused quartz and special quartz lamps are used to give artificial sun treatments.

QUEBEC is Canada's largest province. It is about ten times the size of England and Wales. The great North American trade route of the St. Lawrence River splits the province into two parts, of which the northern is by far the larger. (See St. Lawrence River.)

North of the valley of the St. Lawrence, most of Quebec forms part of the region of forested rocky uplands called the Canadian Shield. (See Laurentian Mountains.) The vast region between Labrador and Hudson Bay is dotted with lakes and has many rapid streams. Few settlers live there. Most of the people live in the St. Lawrence lowlands, and in the eastern townships bordering on the U.S. state of Vermont.

The province has long severe winters and the Laurentides Provincial Park north of the capital has probably the heaviest snowfall in the continent. The St. Lawrence is open to shipping all year long as far as Montreal but, during the four winter months, navigation can go no further than this because of ice. The summers in the St. Lawrence valley are hot but grow cooler towards the Atlantic and in the north.

Much of Quebec is covered with forest. In the extreme north is the barren tundra region (see Tundra Plains). Farther south the trees are more numerous and bigger, and include spruce and pine. Nearer to the St. Lawrence valley there are both evergreen and leafy trees such as poplar, yellow birch and maple, but many have been cut down to clear the land for agriculture.

The multi-arch Daniel Johnson Dam. In the foreground is the power house which supplies electricity to Montreal and Quebec City.

Courtesy, Agent General for Quebec

People and Cities

Most of the people in Quebec are of French origin and are Roman Catholics. Although most of the city folk speak English, the common language of the countryside is French, spoken with an accent rather like that of Normandy and with a number of English words added. The motto of Quebec is *Je me souviens* (meaning "I remember") and expresses the Québécois love of tradition. (The people of the province are known as

National Film Board Photo

A memorial to the explorer Jacques Cartier on the Gaspé Peninsula, a mountainous piece of land in east Quebec.

Québécois.) Religious holidays are of great importance to the people, especially the feast of St. John the Baptist, who is the patron saint of French Canadians. On the evening of June 23 crowds gather round great bonfires which are blessed before being lit. Then there are speeches, folk-songs and dancing until late at night, followed on June 24 by parades and colourful processions. Children in Quebec must attend either a Catholic or a Protestant school, according to their religion, between the ages of 6 and 15.

The largest city in the province is Montreal (see MONTREAL) but the capital and centre of culture is Quebec on the north bank of the St. Lawrence. The city consists of an upper and lower town connected by steep winding streets. The lower town with its narrow streets, cobbled squares and old buildings is rather like the older parts of French towns such as Rouen or St. Malo. There is also a harbour able to take the largest ships. The upper town contains the chief public buildings and many churches, parks and gardens. The highest point, Cape Diamond, is crowned by the citadel overlooking the Plains of Abraham, where General James Wolfe fell when capturing the city in 1759 (see WOLFE, JAMES). Rail and road traffic is carried across the St. Lawrence River by the Quebec Bridge, completed in 1917, and the Pierre Laporte Bridge, opened in 1970. The population of Greater Quebec is about 550,000.

Other important towns in the province are Sherbrooke, which is a manufacturing city not far from the United States border; Trois-Rivières on the St. Lawrence between Montreal and Quebec, with important pulp and paper factories; and the thriving industrial city of Hull opposite Ottawa. On the south bank of the St. Lawrence is Sorel, with steelmaking and titanium industries and a fleet of dredgers which keep the river deep enough for large ships.

Farming and Industries

Most of the farms are in the St. Lawrence lowlands, although there are also agricultural districts around Lake St. John at the head of the Saguenay River and west of Senneterre on both sides of the railway. The most important products are meat, dairy products, eggs and poultry. The chief crops are hay, clover, oats, buckwheat (a cereal plant) and potatoes. Sheep are grazed on the foothills of the Appalachians.

The broad forest areas of Quebec supply timber, firewood and wood-pulp. Wood-pulp is used for making cardboard and paper and about a third of the Canadian supply comes from Quebec.

Quebec has little coal but its many rivers can provide almost unlimited water power for making electricity. There are large power stations near Arvida on the Saguenay River, at Shawinigan on the St. Maurice River and where some of the waters of the St. Lawrence are led into the Beauharnois Power Canal. Another is on the Bersimis River which enters the St. Lawrence near Baie Comeau. The most important

Courtesy, Aluminum Company of Canada

The Place Ville Marie building in Montreal is one of the largest aluminium-clad buildings in the world.

125

Courtesy, Canadian High Commissioner

A row of cannon on the Citadel of Quebec, once a French fort. In the background towers the Château Frontenac hotel.

power stations are on the Manicougan River and, in the northern part of the province, installations are being developed on James Bay.

The province is rich in minerals. Iron is obtained at Schefferville near the Labrador border and on the west coast of Ungava Bay. Gold, silver and copper are mined near Rouyn and Noranda in the west of the province. Titanium is mined near Lake Allard which lies inland from Havre St. Pierre on the north coast of the Gulf of St. Lawrence (see TITANIUM). Quebec is the world's largest supplier of asbestos (see ASBESTOS), which is mined at Black Lake, Thetford Mines and near the town of Asbestos itself.

The abundant supplies of cheap electricity are used in industry, transport and lighting. They are also used for obtaining aluminium from bauxite brought in ships from abroad. (The smelting of aluminium requires a large amount of electric current; see ALUMINIUM.) There are large aluminium smelting works at Arvida and at Baie Comeau on the north shore of the St. Lawrence estuary. Apart from pulp, paper and metals, there are industries making ships, chemicals, textiles, clothes, electrical goods, machinery and many other products.

Quebec, with its varied scenery, is popular with holidaymakers. Some hunt bear and moose in the forests, others go camping, canoeing or fishing and many come for the winter sports, skiing championships and curling matches in the Laurentians and at other resorts. The province is crossed by the Trans Canada Highway and its main rail and air centres are Montreal and Quebec. The chief trade route is the St. Lawrence River and the main ports besides Montreal and Quebec are Sorel, Trois-Rivières and Port Alfred, which is reached by the Saguenay River.

History

Quebec was first settled by the French. The explorer Jacques Cartier was sent out by the King of France and sailed up the St. Lawrence in 1535. The first settlement was made in 1608 at Quebec, when Samuel de Champlain built a fort at the foot of Cape Diamond. For some years most of the French living in Canada were traders, missionaries, explorers and soldiers. Slowly but surely settlers came in the 17th century. Forts grew into villages, missions became parishes and forests gave way to fields and pastures. By 1750 there were about 65,000 settlers in the St.

Lawrence lowlands. They called themselves "Canadiens", not Frenchmen, and attached great importance to their customs, laws and religion. Canada itself was called New France and one of its most able governors was Count Louis de Frontenac et Palluau (1620–1698). (There are separate articles on Cartier and Champlain.)

The long struggle between France and Great Britain for overseas possessions was ended in 1763 by the Treaty of Paris, which gave Canada to the British. An important act passed by the British parliament in 1774 was the Quebec Act, which besides setting up the province of Quebec promised the people that their language, laws, customs and religion would not be interfered with. The French Canadians fought loyally against the Americans who invaded Canada in 1775 and again in 1812. In 1791 Quebec became known as the Province of Lower Canada. Self-government was granted in 1841. The province again became known as Quebec in 1867, at the time of confederation.

Quebec has an elected parliament, and also sends representatives to the Canadian federal parliament in Ottawa. The "separatist" Parti Québécois wants "sovereignty-association" for the province—political independence but continued economic links with the rest of Canada. The population of Quebec is about 6,306,000.

QUEEN. A queen may have her title because she is the wife (or widow) of a king or because, like Queen Elizabeth II, she herself has inherited the throne and rules in her own right in the same way as a king. A queen who rules in her own right is called a queen regnant, or a ruling queen (from the Latin word *regnare,* "to rule").

In early history ruling queens were rare because sovereigns often led their troops in battle and thus a man was thought to be more suitable as a ruler. However, there are examples of ruling queens in early days. Queen Cleopatra, who ruled Egypt in the 1st century B.C., is perhaps the most famous of them. In the 1st century A.D. Queen Boadicea of the Iceni, a British tribe, led her own people and many others in a great revolt against the Roman masters of Britain. Actually, however, Boadicea ought not to be called a ruling queen because she was

merely the widow of a king who had just died. However, she took on the leadership of her people and acted as a ruling queen. (See BOADICEA ; CLEOPATRA.)

In the 16th century England was ruled by Queen Elizabeth I, who was one of the most brilliant of all British sovereigns. Queen Victoria, who reigned from 1837 to 1901, was a very different kind of woman, but she too had a great effect on her period. (See ELIZABETH I ; VICTORIA, QUEEN.)

There have been queens who ruled jointly with their husbands. King William III and Queen Mary II ruled Britain together from 1689 until 1694 when Mary died (see ENGLISH HISTORY), and in the 15th century Isabella of Castile and Ferdinand of Aragon were joint rulers of Spain (see FERDINAND AND ISABELLA).

A queen who is merely the wife of a king is called a queen consort. Although a queen consort is not given any official power, this has not prevented some of them from being very powerful indeed. During the Wars of the Roses in England it was often Queen Margaret, wife of King Henry VI, who led the Lancastrian forces, for the King was weak and suffered from madness. (See ROSES, WARS OF THE.) Queen Catherine de Medici, the Italian wife of King Henry II of France, exercised great power after he died and while their son Charles IX was still too young to rule. She ruled for him and was called the Queen Regent.

In Britain and some other countries the widow of a king is known as the Queen Mother if she is the mother of the new sovereign.

(See also the separate articles ELIZABETH II ; KING ; MONARCH.)

QUEEN ANNE'S BOUNTY was a fund that was established by Queen Anne in 1704 to help the poorer clergymen of the Church of England.

Queen Anne established this fund by giving up her right to receive annual payments from the Church of England, and she ordered instead that the money should be paid into the Bounty fund. It consisted of first-fruits and tenths. First-fruits were the payment that newly appointed clergymen had to make, usually the whole of their first year's salary. Tenths were a payment they made every year, and it consisted of one-tenth of their income for the year.

The church had made payments to the British crown ever since King Henry quarrelled with the Pope in the 16th century (see HENRY VIII). Before that they had been made to the Pope.

For more than 200 years Queen Anne's Bounty was the source from which help was given to needy parishes. It was used, for example, to help pay for the clergyman's house and salary and for new churches. Its wealth was increased by the gifts of rich men and occasionally, at the beginning of the 19th century, by grants from parliament. In 1878 it was amalgamated, or combined, with the Ecclesiastical Commission, the new name Church Commission taking its place. Today the Church Commission is the body responsible for managing all the property and income of the Church of England.

QUEENSLAND is the second largest state of Australia. It occupies the northeast quarter of the continent and is more than five times the size of the British Isles. On the northwest its low-lying coast looks over the lonely Gulf of Carpentaria. Between most of its northeast coast and the Pacific Ocean, this part of which is called the Coral Sea, a string of coral islands and reefs stretches for more than 1,700 kilometres (see GREAT BARRIER REEF).

The Eastern Highlands, much of which are made up of smaller mountain ranges, separate the fertile region along the eastern coastline from the vast grassy plains of western Queensland. (See EASTERN HIGHLANDS.) Their highest peak is Mount Bartle Frere (1,611 metres) on the Atherton Tableland. Here the country is green with tropical forest and grassland and starred with brilliant flowers. The mountains are rugged, with crater lakes and magnificent gorges and waterfalls, including the Tully Falls (293 metres). Farther south, on the ranges behind Mackay, there are palm groves, ferns and brilliantly coloured vines and creepers. South of Brisbane are Tambourine Mountain, its slopes covered with jungle forest; Lamington National Park, with its rugged heights and deep wooded

Australian News and Information Bureau
Queensland farmers with their horses and dogs on a sheep station at Goondiwindi, near the New South Wales border.

valleys; and the Stanthorpe region, with its granite rocks and magnificent trees. The rivers flowing eastwards from the Eastern Highlands are short and swift.

Except for the northwest uplands, which join up with the Barkly Tableland of the Northern Territory, most of Queensland west of the Eastern Highlands is a great stretch of lowland plain on which grow bluegrass and bushes such as mulga scrub. Except after the summer rains, several of the long rivers in this part, such as the Georgina, Diamantina, Thomson and Barcoo, are mere chains of water-holes. Also, they flow away from the sea, their water finally becoming lost in the huge low-lying Lake Eyre (see SOUTH AUSTRALIA).

The spiny anteaters or echidnas are common in Queensland, and the duck-billed platypus (see PLATYPUS) is also found there. Marsupials, or pouched mammals, range from the great grey kangaroo to the pigmy mice. Other land animals include the koala, the bandicoot,

Brisbane has become an industrial centre of growing importance. Shipbuilding takes place in the city along the banks of the Brisbane River.

the tree kangaroo and wild dogs or dingoes. Among the birds are the emu, the cassowary, the bird of paradise and the bower bird.

The capital is Brisbane in the southeast of the state (see BRISBANE). Other important towns are Townsville, the chief port and industrial centre of northern Queensland; Toowoomba, the centre of the Darling Downs agricultural and pastoral district; Ipswich, a coal-mining and industrial centre near Brisbane; Mount Isa in the northwest, a centre for new farming and mineral development; and the ports of Rockhampton and Gladstone. Much sugar is exported through Cairns, Lucinda and Mackay.

Animal farming is more important than crops in Queensland. Most of the water on the western plains is obtained from deep boreholes (see ARTESIAN WELL) and is too salty for crops, although animals can drink it. Beef cattle and sheep are bred, with dairy cattle and pigs on the downlands nearer the east coast.

Most of Australia's sugar is grown on the hot, damp plains of the Queensland coast. Other crops are wheat, maize and peanuts. Pineapples, bananas, pawpaws, mangoes and other tropical fruits are grown in the coastal districts and apples, peaches, plums and grapes around Stanthorpe near the New South Wales border.

Most of the wood used for building in Queensland comes from gum trees of the eucalyptus type, but the forests also contain trees yielding beautiful furniture woods such as Queensland maple and walnut. Thursday Island, off Cape York at the northerly tip of the state, is one of the chief Australian pearl fisheries.

Queensland is rich in minerals, including copper, coal, lead, silver and zinc, bauxite, petroleum and natural gas, tin, gold, rutile (see TITANIUM), uranium, phosphate rock and nickel. Coal is the state's most important mineral. The major coal fields are in the Bowen Basin and include Moura, Callide, Blackwater, Goonyella and Collinsville. The port at Hay Point, developed to serve the coal mines, is now the world's largest coal export outlet. Much of the coal goes to Japan. Mount Isa contains valuable minerals including gold, silver, copper, lead and zinc. Bauxite is mined at Weipa on the Cape York peninsula and is processed at Gladstone (see

BAUXITE). Oil (petroleum) from Moonie in the south travels by pipeline to Brisbane, and natural gas from Roma is also piped to Brisbane.

Many of Queensland's factories are concerned with food production, examples being sugar mills, meat-packing and fruit-canning works and butter factories. Other products include cement, machinery for mining and sugar mills, woollen and cotton mills, fertilizer, motor cars, farm machinery and furniture. Holiday-makers come to enjoy boating, fishing, swimming, surfing and sailing, to admire the wonders of the Great Barrier Reef and the beauty of the outback.

A railway runs up the east coast of Queensland as far as Cairns, with lines branching off inland from Brisbane, Rockhampton, Townsville and Cairns. The coastal road runs as far north as Cooktown and there is also an inland highway linking Brisbane with Townsville. The Northwest Highway through Cloncurry leads to the Northern Territory. A network of cattle roads covers western Queensland. Several of the airports are "flying doctor" bases, which the sheep and cattle stations can contact by radio.

History

The rather barren coast of the Gulf of Carpentaria in Queensland was discovered in 1606 by the Dutch explorer William Jansz and further explored by Abel Tasman in 1644. The more important east coast was discovered in 1770 by James Cook. (See COOK; TASMAN.) The Brisbane River was discovered by the explorer John Oxley in 1823, and a settlement was made there

Courtesy, Agent General for Queensland
A view of Brisbane, the capital of Queensland.

in the following year. By the 1840s about 2,000 settlers had come from New South Wales, mostly to the Brisbane and Darling Downs regions.

Queensland was created as a separate colony in 1859. Sheep and cattle rearing gradually spread westwards and the population was greatly increased by "diggers" seeking gold in the gold rushes of the 1860s (see GOLD RUSH). During the same period, sugar plantations were started along the east coast. Between 1894 and 1902, when there was a period of insufficient rainfall ending in a disastrous drought, tremendous losses of cattle and sheep were caused by cattle ticks (see TICK) and by lack of water. Many thousands of Pacific Islanders were brought into Queensland to work on the sugar plantations and for a long time there was argument as to whether this should be allowed. Finally the Australian government forbade it in 1904, and most of the islanders were sent home.

Queensland controls its affairs through a legislative assembly, or parliament, whose members are elected for a period of three years, and sends representatives to the Australian federal parliament at Canberra. It has a population of over 2,000,000.

QUICKSAND. Stretches of sand that will not bear the weight of a person or heavy object are called quicksands. The word comes from the old-fashioned use of "quick" to mean alive or moving, and quicksands are very easily moved. They are sometimes found near the mouths of large rivers where the beach is underlaid with stiff clay. As the water cannot escape through the clay, it forms a kind of bog with the sand. The grains of sand in these beds are smooth and rounded and when wet slide past one another easily, so there is nothing to support a heavy weight. This can be quickly swallowed up, leaving no trace.

The danger of quicksands may have been rather exaggerated by novels such as Sir Walter Scott's *The Bride of Lammermoor* or Wilkie Collins' *The Moonstone*, but some quicksands are dangerous to cross. A person who steps on a quicksand sinks far more quickly if he struggles and the best thing to do is to keep still and shout for help.

The Goodwin Sands off Deal on the Kent coast are continually shifting their position and form quicksands at some states of the tide.

QUINCE. The quince is a firm yellow fruit shaped like a very large pear or apple. Although it has been grown for more than 2,000 years in Asia Minor (Turkey), few varieties have been bred. Quinces grow on small, many-branched

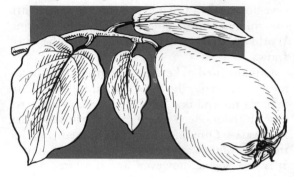

A quince.

trees or shrubs which belong to the rose family. The red or white flowers are large and look like those of the pear.

Quinces are sour, and are therefore seldom eaten raw, except in warm countries where they become sweeter by being exposed to the hot sun. They are usually made into jelly, and are sometimes cooked with other fruits to give them flavour and a sharp taste. Quince seeds were once used in medicine. The ripe fruit has such a strong scent that if stored with apples and pears it will affect their flavour. Some quince fruits, however, have a very pleasant smell and are placed among clothes to scent them.

In northern countries it is generally too cold for quinces to ripen. The Japanese quince is grown for the beauty of its flowers, which may be white, brilliant rose or deep red and bloom in early spring and summer. The fruits are not fit to eat. This plant is also called japonica.

QUININE is a strong, bitter-tasting medicine made from the bark of a tree called cinchona, which originally grew only in South America. There are many different kinds of cinchona, but only a few produce quinine.

Quinine has long been used to cure fever and

pain, and so much of the bark of cinchona trees was stripped off that for a time it looked as if all the trees might be destroyed. In the 19th century, therefore, the Dutch planted seeds of the cinchona in Java, an island of what is now Indonesia but was then part of the Dutch East Indies. Through skilful cultivation they grew trees which produced far more quinine in their bark than the wild South American variety had ever done. Java became the chief supply centre for quinine, although this ran short during World War II when Japan seized the East Indies.

Quinine used to be the main drug in the treatment of malaria, the fever caused by the bite of malaria mosquitoes, but it has been entirely replaced by modern chemical substitutes. (See MALARIA.) Quinine is also used in medicines for treating influenza and colds, and also in tonics. It is very strong, however, and if a large dose is taken it often makes people feel deaf and dizzy or even ill.

QUIZ. A quiz is a game in which people are asked how much they know. Generally, the questions can be on any subject. Of course examinations, too, are held to find out how much people know; but they are different from quizzes because the quiz is held only for fun.

People have always enjoyed being asked questions of all kinds so that they could have a chance to display their knowledge. The ancient Greeks and other peoples enjoyed riddles and "brain-teasers". However, it was not until reading was widely taught that general knowledge quizzes became popular among ordinary people. In the 19th century games for testing knowledge and spelling bees (see PARTY GAMES) became popular, and in the present century newspapers and magazines began printing quizzes for their readers and (sometimes) giving prizes. Then radio and television made quizzes more popular than ever.

There are many kinds of quizzes and all sorts of questions can be asked. Quiz questions should not be asked with the intention of "catching out" someone. For example, the question: "How fast can a laughing jackass run?" is unfair as the laughing jackass is a bird and not a land animal. Questions should not be too far-fetched, like this one: "Who chased whom how many times round what?" (The answer is that Achilles chased Hector three times round Troy.) Questions which have large numbers in the answers, such as: "How many metres high is Mount Popocatepetl?" are somewhat too difficult even for experts. Another example of an awkward and bad question would be "How do you spell Llanfairpwllgwyngyllgogerychwyrndrobwllllantysiliogogogoch?" (a village in Anglesey). A good question, although rather tricky, is: "What is the capital of New York state?" (It is not New York, but Albany.)

Another good question would be "Tell me the name of Henry VIII's third wife." (Jane Seymour is the answer.) When making up quizzes, ask only questions whose answers you know or think you ought to know.

Some schools run quizzes every now and then. A school in the Isle of Man gives the boys a long general-knowledge paper to take home for the Christmas holidays. They are allowed to look up the answers from books in libraries, but when the next term starts they have to answer the questions without books.

People good at answering quizzes are not always especially intelligent or clever; they may have no more than an excellent memory.

QUOITS is a game played by throwing heavy iron rings so that they encircle an upright *hob*, or post, or stick in the ground near it. It requires considerable skill. The quoit is about 20 centimetres across and is thrown from a distance of about 16 metres. The players are divided into two teams and throw their quoits in turn, each player having two quoits. If a quoit rings the hob it is a *ringer* and scores two. Each quoit nearer to the hob than any of those of the other side scores one.

In some English country districts the game is played with horseshoes instead of rings and "horseshoe pitching", as it is called, is popular in the United States. Quoits is played as a deck-game on board ships, using rings made of rope or rubber which are thrown at a wooden peg or into a bucket. Rope or rubber quoits are also used in playing the game known as deck tennis.

RABAT is the capital of Morocco in northwest Africa. It lies on the Atlantic coast at the mouth of the Bou Regreg River, which divides it from the town of Salé. Separated by a hill from the coast is the old part of Rabat, which is surrounded by ramparts, or defensive banks, and contains the Moslem and Jewish quarters. Above it towers an ancient fortress, the Kasbah des Oudaya, which is entered by a beautiful 12th-century gateway. At the southern end of the old town, overlooking the valley, is the magnificent Hassan tower, a minaret also of the 12th century, at the foot of which are the ruins of a large mosque. ("Minaret" and "mosque" are explained in the article MOSQUE.) The modern part of the city is partly enclosed by a great fortified wall which also surrounds the Dar Al Makhzen, which is the king's palace. Most of the government buildings are on the slopes of a hill overlooking villas and houses in flowered gardens outside the city walls.

A bridge across the river connects Rabat with Salé and prevents ships from entering the harbour, which has been abandoned. The population of Rabat and Salé is about 642,000.

RABBIT. Although the wild rabbit is an attractive animal to look at, it is known as a pest because of the damage it does to growing crops. It is a mammal (see MAMMAL) and it is found in most parts of Europe. It seems to have been brought to Great Britain in the 12th century and gradually spread all over the country. In the 19th century rabbits were taken to Australia and New Zealand and in those countries they became a terrible pest. Australia suffers millions of pounds' worth of damage from them every year.

The rabbit can be distinguished from the hare by its smaller size and the fact that it has no black tips on its ears. Its general colour is brown with white beneath. The scut, or short tail, has a splash of white on it which serves as a warning signal when a rabbit, outside its burrow with other rabbits, senses danger and bolts down its burrow. Many burrows are made close together and known as warrens.

Rabbits live mostly on grass, but they will eat almost any growing plants. They do great damage in woodlands by eating seedlings and nibbling bark from trees.

The reason why rabbits spread so quickly is the rate at which they breed. A rabbit may mate when it is six months old and the litter, or family, is born a month later. One pair of rabbits can produce between four and eight litters in a year, and each litter has between three and nine young. The baby rabbits are naked and blind when they are first born, but within a fortnight their eyes are open and they can run about. A male rabbit is called a buck and a female is a doe.

Rabbits have many enemies, for in England they are hunted and eaten by foxes, badgers, weasels and stoats. Their chief enemy, however, is man, who shoots and traps great numbers of them every year. Not only is their flesh good to eat, but their skins are used to make clothing. The whole skin is made into fur coats, after it has been dyed to imitate a more valuable fur. (See the article FURS.)

Far more rabbits in Britain, however, were killed in the 1950s by the virus disease known as myxomatosis than by any other means. Myxomatosis was deliberately spread among rabbits until a law was passed in 1954 forbidding people to do so. By that time, however, the disease was widespread. It was a painful death for the rabbits, but it saved the farmers much money by killing so many. In the late 1950s rabbits began to increase again, through the breeding of some that escaped the disease or were immune to it.

Many rabbits are kept in captivity to be killed for their meat and fur, and many others are kept as pets. There are a great many breeds of tame rabbits, all descended from the wild ones. (For

Left: Camera Press, photo by Georg Quedens. Centre and right: W. Suschitzky
Left: A wild rabbit. Centre: An Angora, one of the rabbits kept for its wool.
Right: A Chinchilla rabbit, whose fur is very valuable.

instructions on how to look after tame rabbits, see the article PETS, CARE OF.)

The lop-eared rabbit has very long ears which hang down. The Angora (named after Ankara, the capital of Turkey) is kept for its wool, which is clipped every three or four months and is sold for a very high price. Some of the most popular fancy breeds are the English, Dutch, Rex, Netherlands Dwarf and Satin. The most valuable of the rabbits kept for their fur, however, is the Chinchilla rabbit, whose fur is rather like that of the beautiful little South American rodent called the chinchilla.

The rabbits that have been bred for their meat are often very heavy. The largest of all are the Flemish giants, which sometimes weigh as much as 10 kilograms.

RACCOON. The tail of the raccoon is large and bushy and strikingly ringed with black and white. It is the most noticeable feature of the animal, which is related to the bear family and is found only in America. There are two species, or kinds, of raccoons—the common raccoon of North and Central America and the crab-eating raccoon of South America.

The common raccoon is about the size of a large cat and has thick, long, greyish-brown fur. Its face is fox-like and it has a band of black across the eyes. The crab-eating raccoon is larger in body, with longer legs, and has shorter fur, but its habits are much the same as those of the common raccoon.

Raccoons, or coons as they are sometimes called, live high up in the hollow branches of large trees. They remain in the trees all day and climb down at night to look for food. Raccoons are good swimmers and catch fish and frogs. They also raid fields of green maize for food, rob birds' nests and catch birds and small animals. They have a habit of washing their food in water before eating it.

Baby raccoons are born blind and stay with their mothers for about a year. Raccoons sleep through the coldest part of the winter.

An interesting relative of the raccoon is the kinkajou. It lives in the forests of Central and South America and is about the size of a cat, with

The common raccoon lives in trees during the day but climbs down at night in search of food.

yellowish-brown fur. Its tail is prehensile, which means that it can be used to grip things. Kinkajous live on fruit, honey, eggs, small birds and mammals. Like raccoons, they are sometimes tamed as pets.

The coati or coatimundi, another relative of the raccoon, lives in woods in the southwestern United States and South America. Coatis are about the same size as raccoons, with reddish-grey fur and long tails which they carry erect as they walk. They climb trees, and often wander about in groups, looking for fruit, eggs, and small animals to eat.

RACES AND PEOPLES. The human beings of the world are divided into peoples and races. A *people* consists of men and women who speak the same language and have the same customs and way of life. A *race*, on the other hand, consists of those people who share the same physical features—dark or light skins, tall or short bodies, and so on. Those different features evolved in the ancestors of modern man to allow them to live successfully in the different climates found on the Earth. Thus the Negroes of Africa and the United States, whose ancestors came from Africa as slaves, are a race, while the English, French and Zulus are separate peoples. Some peoples, such as the Gipsies, are scattered among others, but usually a people lives together in a single country.

In this article are described some of the races and peoples found in the world today, although there are so many that all cannot be mentioned. Each group is only one out of many thousands of different peoples. Some of these groups are very large, like the Chinese, who number many millions. Others are very small, like the Bushmen who live in the Kalahari desert of South Africa and may have only 60 people in a group, or the peoples of the many little islands of the Pacific Ocean, where there may be only 200 men and women on an island hundreds of kilometres away from the nearest land.

The peoples of the world differ in the colour of their skins, their height, the type of their hair, the shape of their skulls and in other physical features. They differ also in their culture, which means their language, religious beliefs, ways of thinking about the world, ways of getting a living, of building their houses, of marrying and of burying their dead. The culture of some peoples that have now died out is known through writings or buildings that they have left, but their societies are dead. (Society in this sense means a community of people with the same culture living in the same area.) An example of such a people is the ancient Greeks.

The first true man, *Homo habilis*, appeared on Earth about 2,000,000 years ago, although the ape-man *Australopithecus* first appeared much earlier, about 3,500,000 years ago. *Homo habilis* developed into the more advanced *Homo erectus* about 1,500,000 years ago and later, about 200,000 years ago, *Homo erectus* evolved into our own species, *Homo sapiens*. (See MAN.) True men seem to have appeared separately and at different times in different parts of the world. However, this is still not certain and they may all have come from one place.

Since then, their descendants have wandered about the surface of the earth, often moving when the climate changed or when the animals and plants on which they lived could no longer be found. People have occupied every part of the world except the Antarctic, the area nearest the North Pole and the centres of the thickest forests and the driest deserts. They have mixed together and intermarried for many thousands of years, so that in many countries the people are a mixture of different races. Because of this mixture, it is impossible to say how many races there are. Different physical features grade into each other, making it impossible to draw a clear dividing line between one race and another. Migration, or the movement of people from country to country, has affected the distribution of the Earth's population since ancient times. (See EMIGRATION.)

The peoples of the world can be divided roughly into three main groups, or stocks. These are the *Caucasoids*, or white-skinned people, the *Negroids*, or black-skinned people, and the *Mongoloids*, or yellow-skinned people. There are also other races who do not fit into any of these three classes. Each stock consists of many races, each slightly different from the others.

The Caucasoids have light-coloured skins,

(1) Courtesy, National Film Board of Canada. (2) Crown Copyright Reserved. (3) Courtesy, Pan American Airways
Although they live in very different lands, these peoples all have Mongoloid features. (1) An Eskimo mother and her baby. (2) Japanese wearing kimonos. (3) A Quechua Indian of Peru—a descendant of the Incas.

straight, wavy or curly hair, narrow noses, thinnish lips, smallish teeth, high foreheads and well-developed chins. They live mostly in Europe, but also in India, North Africa and the islands of the Pacific known as Polynesia. The Mongoloids have dark, straight hair, high cheekbones, large teeth and a little fold of skin on the upper eyelid which gives the eye a slit-like appearance. They have very delicate skeletons and are found in Asia and the Americas. The Negroids all have dark skins, either almost black or various shades of brown, from dark yellow to chocolate. They have woolly hair, broad noses and thick lips. Some are very tall, while others are extremely short. Most live in Africa, but there are others in Melanesia (north of Australia) and various parts of the East.

Besides these main stocks there are various small groups who are probably the last remnants of once widely spread peoples. These are the Australian Aborigines, the Veddahs in Ceylon, the Ainu of Japan and the many aboriginal tribes of southern India who are not Hindus but who lived there before the Hindus entered India from the north. These groups are together called *Australoids* or *Archaic Caucasoids*, because they may be the ancestors of the main Caucasoid stock. However, this is mostly guesswork only.

Differences of Culture

Each of the many races within a single stock contains several different peoples. It is not always easy to describe a people by physical features, since they often look very alike, so they are described by the differences in their culture. All men and women who speak the same language, do the same sort of work for their living and have the same religion and beliefs are members of the same society. They also realize that they are members of a single society and live together in a distinct territory, or area. The word tribe is often used for a society.

From the very beginning man has lived in societies. He is a social animal and no person can live as a real human being outside a society. The few cases we know of children who have been brought up outside a society, by wolves in most cases, have really hardly been human beings at all, since they could not talk or even walk properly.

The first people of whose culture we know anything lived by collecting nuts and roots and by hunting wild animals for food. They made tools by chipping flints. These were the societies of the Old Stone Age. No people living today are so primitive. It was only about 7,000 or 8,000 years ago that people began to till the soil and to tame animals, and this occurred somewhere in what is called the "fertile crescent", which crosses from Egypt through Arabia and Persia into India. Similar developments probably took place in China. This is usually called the Neolithic Revolution or the New Stone Age, and it was then that people began to make pottery, to weave and to use ground and polished stones for tools. Later in the history of the world people discovered how to smelt metals, at first bronze and then iron. (See BRONZE AGE and

(1) Odhams Press Ltd. (2, 3) Crown Copyright

Peoples of Asia. (1) A man of Pakistan, from the old province of the Punjab (now divided between India and Pakistan). (2) A Sinhalese woman of Sri Lanka. (3) An Indian woman, heavily ornamented, from the Punjab hills.

IRON AGE.) There are a few peoples in the world today who still live as people did elsewhere in the New Stone Age; they include some Australian Aborigines and the Tasaday of the Philippines.

Peoples of Asia

The first civilizations of which we know were in southwest Asia at the eastern end of the Mediterranean. Armies from there invaded the surrounding countries, such as China, India and beyond, and eastern Europe. The Caucasoids, or white races of Europe, seem to have begun in southwest Asia, and Asia is also the homeland of the Mongoloid races. The barbarians of central Asia were pastoral nomads (they wandered from place to place and herded cattle, horses and reindeer) and were both Mongoloid (Mongols) and white (Huns, Aryans, Avars, Turks and others). At times they invaded the quieter cultivators of the soil around them and formed enormous empires. The greatest of them all, the Mongol Empire of Jenghiz Khan, which flourished in the 13th century, included all central Asia, China, Turkey, Russia, Poland and Hungary.

The barbarians had a more backward culture than most of the people they conquered but they were fiercer, richer and better organized. Because they had horses, they were able to move over great distances in a short time. In most cases the empires soon collapsed and the conquerors adopted the language and religion of the people whom they had conquered. Now the Mongols are a small people living almost surrounded by Chinese, while the Huns, Turks and

others have become lost in the general population of Europe, and the Aryans in that of India.

Today more than half the people in the world live in Asia, including the two largest groups, the Chinese and Indians. The main cultural groupings of Asia include the Chinese, the peoples of India, Bangladesh, Sri Lanka (Ceylon) and Pakistan, Japanese, Koreans, Malays, Indonesians, Sinhalese, Persians and Turks. Most of these groups are not single peoples but clusters of peoples, distinct from each other, who regard themselves as different even though they may have the same religion or language. All, except the peoples of the Indian sub-continent, the Persians and Turks, are Mongoloids. With the Mongoloids must also be counted the Indians of the Americas and the people of Madagascar, off the African coast, who are Malays who sailed across the Indian Ocean.

Primitive Peoples. Besides these great civilized peoples of Asia there are many smaller peoples in the continent. Some are representatives of earlier peoples who do not believe in any of the greater Asian religions (such as Buddhism, Islam, Hinduism and Confucianism) and who, although living surrounded by the larger peoples, have kept their own cultures to the present day.

In Japan there are the Ainu, who are white-skinned and hairy. They once occupied all Japan but have been driven into the far and barren north and today there are very few Ainu left. Little is known about them except that their religion is centred round the bear, and shamans (priests or prophets) perform religious

(1) Crown Copyright. (2) Paul Popper. (3) Courtesy, Swedish Tourist Association
(1) A Malay woman and her baby in Singapore. Although Singapore is close to the Malay Peninsula, there are many more Chinese than Malays there. (2) Land Army girl from the Jewish state of Israel. (3) A Swedish child.

dances dressed as bears. In Malaysia are the forest dwellers, Semang and Sakai, who live in the dense forests, hunting game with arrows from blowpipes.

In the Andaman Islands in the Bay of Bengal there exists a cluster of very small tribes of pygmy-like people who live mainly on forest roots, nuts and berries and on turtles and a sea animal called the dugong. They have no kings or chiefs and the largest groups are hunting bands of a few dozen people who live in the jungles on their small islands. In Sri Lanka there are the Veddas, a small, flat-nosed people who eat much honey, and throughout India there are found small tribes in the more difficult country. Because of their primitive way of life, these tribes are looked down upon by most other Indians.

Lastly, there are the original tribes of Siberia, the descendants of the Mongols. The Yakut, Tungu and Chukchee wander from place to place and keep reindeer, and the Mongols also wander but keep horses. They have no kings, and the only people with special authority are the shamans, who are thought to be able to speak directly with God. They fall into trances and claim to foresee the future.

Europeans

Today the peoples of Europe are much mixed together (intermixed), although their cultures are still a good deal different from each other. Most of the Caucasoid peoples live in Europe, and five Caucasoid races are found there. The oldest is probably the Mediterranean, and includes the Italians, Spaniards and Portuguese on the northern shores of the Mediterranean and the Berbers on the southern shores. (See ARABS.) It also includes the Semitic peoples of the Middle East (Arabs and Jews) and the people of Persia, Afghanistan and parts of central Asia. Then there is the Nordic race, with fair hair and blue or grey eyes, of Scandinavia, Poland, west Russia and eastern Germany. The other Caucasoid races are the Alpine race of central Europe, who are shorter and have darker hair; the East Baltic race of northeast Germany, Poland and the Baltic states, with very blue eyes and almost white hair; and the Armenoid race of European Turkey, with round high heads, dark hair and large noses.

Languages. The invaders (Huns, Goths and others) who came to Europe from the nearer parts of Asia, mostly across the Russian plains and Turkey, spoke languages known as Indo-European which are related to Sanskrit, the sacred language of the Aryans of India. In Europe today most languages spoken are Indo-European, and there are four main divisions. First the Teutonic or Germanic (including English, German, Dutch, Flemish, Norse, Swedish, Danish, Icelandic); then the Romance (including Italian, Spanish, Portuguese, French, Romanian); then the Slav (including Russian, Ukrainian, Polish, Czech, Slovak, Serbo-Croat, Bulgarian, Montenegrin); and lastly the Celtic (Erse, Gaelic, Welsh, Manx, Breton and the old dialect of Cornwall). (See CELTS.)

(1) Courtesy, High Commissioner for New Zealand. (2, 3) Crown Copyright Reserved
Three types of Pacific people. (1) A much-tattooed Maori. (2) The peoples of New Guinea are Negroid. This man keeps his pipe in his ear-lobe! (3) An Australian Aborigine girl carrying home a pail of mussels.

There are also other European peoples of different origin who do not speak Indo-European languages at all. They are the Finns and Estonians, who are related to the Samoyedes and other Siberian peoples; the Lapps, a Mongoloid race; the Magyars of Hungary, also of close Asiatic origin; and the Basques of northern Spain, whose language seems to be unrelated to any other known. The Gipsies are descended from a Caucasoid people of India, and have wandered westwards into Europe, bringing their own language with them. (See GIPSIES.)

Peoples of the Pacific

This vast area contains members of several different races, and peoples of many different types and cultures.

In the cluster of great islands which includes Java and Sumatra in Indonesia, Borneo, the Philippine Islands and the lesser islands to their southeast, the people are mainly Malayan, of the Mongoloid race. They live chiefly on rice, which they grow in carefully irrigated, or watered, terraces. Some, such as the people of the island of Bali, are renowned for their elaborate religious dances, performed by dancers dressed in heavy embroidered costumes. Some are Buddhist, others Moslem, and there are small pagan groups, such as the Aeta pygmies of the Philippines and the Punan of Borneo, who live hard lives, travelling in search of the sago palm.

Melanesia includes New Guinea and Papua, the Solomon Islands and Fiji, and its peoples are Negroid. They have no metal and use stone tools. Perhaps the best known are the Trobriand islanders, who live on the coral islands of the Trobriands, fishing and growing yams. They have an elaborate religious system and a clan, or family, system, based on descent through women. They are great travellers and a large part of their working year is concerned with collecting valuables (shell armbands and necklaces) which they exchange with much ceremony with their trading partners from neighbouring islands.

East of Melanesia live the Polynesians, who made great voyages in outrigger canoes and settled the many islands of the Pacific by sailing eastwards over vast distances. Some people, like Thor Heyerdahl who sailed the raft Kon-tiki, say that they came from South America, but this is not generally accepted by scientists. The Polynesians settled in New Zealand, where they are called Maoris, and almost all the islands eastwards, such as Samoa, Hawaii, Tahiti and Tonga, right across to Easter Island with its giant statues. (See MAORIS and POLYNESIANS.)

Micronesia consists of the scattered and small islands, including the Mariana, Marshall and Caroline Islands, between Melanesia and Japan. The Micronesians are also great sailors, but they are now much reduced in numbers, owing to foreign conquest. They are probably a mixture of Polynesian and Malayan.

In the continent of Australia live the Australian Aborigines. (See AUSTRALIAN ABORIGINES.) Of all the peoples in the world today, their culture most closely resembles that of early man. Until the end of the 19th century there were also Tasmanian Aborigines, whose culture was even simpler than that of the Australians. The last true Tasmanian, a woman called Truganini, died in 1877.

Peoples of the Americas

All the original peoples of the Americas are Mongoloid in race, and came in the first place from Siberia. They crossed the Bering Straits into Alaska and slowly spread southwards until some even reached Patagonia and Tierra del Fuego at the very southernmost tip of South America. In the far north (Canada, Alaska and Greenland) live the Eskimoes, who are very interesting as an example of how people can manage to live in a difficult country and climate. (See ESKIMOES.)

South of the Eskimoes live the North American Indians. In Canada most of them used to live by hunting caribou (wild reindeer) and led an extremely hard and simple existence. In the United States there used to be many Indian tribes. But their numbers were reduced in wars against the white settlers. Some lived half-wandering lives in very small groups, rarely numbering more than a few thousand people. Others lived in much larger societies and were farmers, while some moved out onto the plains to hunt bison. The spread of white settlers drove many of the Indians from their tribal lands; whites killed most of the bison and the hunting tribes were forced off the great plains of the mid-west. (See INDIANS, AMERICAN.)

In Central America there were many small tribes living by themselves, both on the mainland and in the islands of the Caribbean (so called from their original inhabitants, the Caribs, who are now almost extinct). In Mexico and other Central American countries live the Mayas. Today they are peasants living in countries where Spanish-speaking settlers predominate, but once they had a great civilization which lasted from about the 1st century A.D. until the early 16th century, when it was destroyed by the invading Spaniards. The early Maya people lived in cities of stone, each built around a centre of several pyramids, on which were ornamental temples and palaces. The Mayas had a kind of picture alphabet, a system of numbers, a calendar and a good knowledge of astronomy. They had no

wheels, but made beautiful pottery. The rich civilization of the Aztecs of Mexico and the empire of the Incas of Peru were also destroyed by the Spaniards. (See AZTECS and INCAS.)

In the vast area of the Amazon basin of South America are small tribes living mainly on manioc, or cassava, a root from which tapioca is made. They live in hot and unhealthy forests. Some tribes dry and shrink the heads of their enemies. The culture of the Amazon Indians is being destroyed as roads, settlements and industries spread farther into the forests. To the south, in Argentina and Chile, live small tribes who hunt the guanaco, a kind of wild llama. On the west coast, in Peru, Ecuador and Bolivia, are peoples who cultivate the soil.

African Peoples

Africa is divided by the Sahara desert. To the north of the Sahara live non-Negro peoples who speak Hamitic and Semitic languages such as Berber and Arabic. They are mostly Moslem and are Caucasoid by race, although many have some Negro blood. Long ago the Sahara was a fertile area, but it has since dried up and today the only places where large numbers of people live are Egypt and the Nile Delta and the Mediterranean coast.

To the south of the Sahara is Africa proper, Black Africa, occupied by the Negro peoples. (See NEGROES.) Most of these peoples were pagans or spirit-worshippers, and only one or two invented their own form of writing. In the past there were large states, many of which have now vanished and are known only by their remains dug out of the earth and from the tradi-

John J. Hayward, Camera Press
A pair of Bushmen drinking through hollow reeds.

(1) Anthony Howarth, Camera Press. (2, 3) Crown Copyright Reserved
(1) An Ibo woman of Nigeria. (2) A sheikh of El Fasher in the western Sudan. (3) A pygmy mother and child from the forests of Zaire.

tions of past glories still held by people today. One such state was centred on Zimbabwe in southern Africa (see ZIMBABWE). Others still exist in an altered form : examples are the Hausa emirates of northern Nigeria.

The Negroes seem to have originated somewhere in what is now the area between Lake Chad and Lake Victoria, and to have spread southwards and westwards until they covered Africa. They found other, non-Negro, peoples there and drove them before them, killed them or left them in thick forest or dry desert which they did not want themselves. These peoples are today represented only by a few remnants; the Pygmies of the West African forests and the Bushmen and Hottentots of southern Africa. (See BUSHMEN AND HOTTENTOTS; PYGMIES.)

In Africa there are many societies very different from one another. They differ in language (African Negro languages contain some as different from each other as are English, Russian and Urdu), in physical appearance (from ebony black to almost yellow) and in their family arrangements. By tradition, the most usual family is a large, so-called joint family, consisting of a number of brothers, their wives and children and perhaps grandchildren also. Descent is traced sometimes through the father, as with Europeans, but often through the mother, so that a boy inherits not from his father but from his mother's brother. Some peoples have kings and courts but others have councils of old men to rule them, and they also differ in religion, which may be ancestor worship or belief in a single

god. Witches and sorcerers are still common in some areas. (See WITCHCRAFT.)

The African peoples can be divided into groups according to the languages they speak. In West Africa they speak what are called Sudanic languages, and there are many different kinds of people in this area. In Nigeria alone there are many different peoples, of which the best known are the Yoruba people, the Ibo and the Hausa. The Hausa are divided into a number of Moslem emirates, or kingdoms. They live in northern Nigeria, a drier area than the south, grow grain and keep many cattle. Yoruba, Ibo and other southerners live in forest regions, growing yams and other root crops, and selling cocoa and palm oil. Benin in southern Nigeria is known for its beautiful carvings and bronze castings.

In present-day Ghana (which took its name from that of an empire which arose in the savannah region to the north during the middle ages) are the Ashanti people. They formed a group of small states, each ruled by a king, and with a single head of all the states set above the others. His symbol of office is a golden throne, called the Golden Stool. (See ASHANTI.)

Another group is that of the Nilotic Negroes of the Upper Nile Valley, most of whom live in the southern Sudan. Among them are the Dinka and Nuer, cattle keepers in the papyrus swamps of the Nile, and the Shilluk, who have a sacred king. He is said to be strangled in old age, as it is thought that if he grows feeble the country will become weak and poor.

In East Africa are also the Nilo-Hamites,

141

(1, 2) Camera Press. (3) C.O.I., Crown Copyright

(1) A boy from Dar es Salaam, in Tanzania, helping with the sisal crop. (2) Young Masai warriors smeared with red ochre. (3) A Basuto from Lesotho. The Basuto are among the Bantu group of Negroes.

among them the Masai of Kenya and Tanzania, who live in the Rift Valley and herd cattle. They are warriors and very proud; the Masai have preserved their ancient way of life, in spite of changes in the countries where they live.

The last Negro grouping is that of the Bantu, who speak Bantu languages. They live in East, Central and South Africa and include peoples very different from one another in almost every respect. The Baganda of Uganda and the Ruanda of Rwanda and Burundi are Bantu. Both tribes formerly had kings and there is a strong aristocracy of Nilo-Hamites who herd cattle and look down upon the Bantu cultivators of the soil whom they rule. They have a feudal system not unlike that of mediaeval Europe. (See FEUDALISM.) In Kenya are the Kikuyu, who have no king but are ruled by councils composed of the elders (senior men) of clans.

Then there are the Bantu tribes of Tanzania, including the Chaga, who live on the southern slopes of Mount Kilimanjaro and grow much coffee, and the Nyamwezi of the central Tanganyika plains. In Zambia are the Lozi of Barotseland and farther south in Zimbabwe the Ndebele or Matabele. Both tribes were known for their fighting abilities in the past and ruled over large areas. In southern Africa are the Zulus (see ZULUS), Swazi, Basuto, Tswana or Bechuana, and Xhosa, who fought bravely against the Europeans during the 19th century. In Namibia (South West Africa) live the Herero, who rebelled against the Germans in 1904.

The people in the Republic of South Africa called Cape Coloureds are not Africans but the descendants of many people who have lived in Cape Town and the surrounding countryside since the Dutch first settled there in 1652. They have Dutch, English, Hottentot, Bantu, Negro and East Indian peoples among their ancestors. They speak Afrikaans, a form of the Dutch language which is spoken by many white South Africans.

Other articles to read on this subject include FAMILY; FOLKLORE; MAN; and PRIMITIVE ART.

RACES AND PEOPLES: ANCIENT.
The previous article explains the difference between a race and a people. This article describes the history and customs of some of the races and peoples who lived in the past and no longer exist as separate nations.

Since the days, thousands of years ago, when men first began to till the fields and to build cities, many nations have grown rich and powerful, have conquered other nations and have even formed empires of varying sizes. Some of these empires lasted for centuries but eventually, because of rebellion by some of the conquered countries or conquest by younger, stronger nations, they vanished completely, their people became scattered and their languages were lost.

So much happened later in the parts of the world once covered by those ancient empires that it is often difficult to find out anything definite about their inhabitants. There are many legends about them and a few histories have been written, notably that of the Greek Herodotus, who lived in the 5th century B.C. Much more reliable information, however, is that provided by archaeologists, whose business it is to excavate, or dig out, the actual objects that such long dead people built or used. Such objects include statues, tombs, temples and written records, but they are few and hard to find.

(There are separate articles AZTECS; CHINA; EGYPT: ANCIENT; GREECE: ANCIENT; INCAS; ROMANS; and ROME: ANCIENT, so the ancient Aztecs, Chinese, Egyptians, Greeks, Incas and Romans will not be described in this article.)

The ancient peoples all tended to live in the rich land which bordered great rivers. There they were able to settle down and build cities without continually having to struggle for existence against drought (lack of water) or barren soil. The ancient Egyptians lived in the valley of the Nile and several other peoples flourished in the green strip enclosed by the two great rivers Tigris and Euphrates. These flowed through Mesopotamia, which is now part of Iraq in the Middle East, and it was here, it is said, that the Garden of Eden was planted.

The Sumerians

The earliest civilization which grew up in the Mesopotamian region was that of the Sumerians, who had their beginnings in about 5000 B.C. They lived in southern Mesopotamia, not far from the Persian Gulf. The Sumerians seem to

The courtyard of a Sumerian temple.

have been the first people to have invented a method of writing, although they did not use letters. Instead they drew signs to stand for various words on soft tablets of clay, which were afterwards baked and hardened. The earliest of these tablets so far discovered date from about 3000 B.C.

The art of working in metals and the use of arches in buildings and of the potter's wheel spread to other countries from the Sumerians. Boats carrying goods such as rugs and linen passed up and down the Euphrates, and Sumerian tradesmen exported much to Syria. Both the Babylonians and the Jews used the Sumerian legends and laws.

The most famous cities of the Sumerians were Ur of the Chaldees, Lagash and Eridu. Ur is mentioned in the Old Testament as the city where Abraham lived (although that was much later). A leading archaeologist, Sir Leonard Woolley, carried out excavations at Ur which added greatly to modern knowledge of the Sumerians. In 1928 he opened the grave of Mes Kalam Dug, a Sumerian king who reigned in about 3300 B.C. This tomb contained vessels of clay, copper, gold and silver, as well as a solid gold bowl and helmet.

In both graves were the remains of a large number of other people, evidently attendants on the royal pair. From this it is known that the Sumerians believed in a life after death in which the dead needed the same things that they had needed in life. Therefore the attendants of the king had to be sacrificed and buried with them so that their souls could continue to wait on them in the life after death.

One of the most interesting results of the work of Woolley has been to find proof of the Biblical story of the Flood. The writers of Sumerian records do not give precise details of it, but they mention that certain cities existed both before and after the Flood, so it seems that some were able to survive even that terrible event. One of these cities was Ur itself.

The Babylonians

The Sumerians were gradually replaced by a race of another kind—Semites, like the Jews of today. These people, the Babylonians, also settled in the southern part of Mesopotamia, which therefore became known as Babylonia. They probably arrived about 4,000 years ago. After a period of settlement and fighting a king called Sargon, who probably lived in about 2550 B.C., overran the old Sumerian cities and lands to the west of Mesopotamia. Sargon, like Moses, is said to have been cast adrift as a child in an ark of bulrushes.

Between 100 and 400 years later the Sumerians became powerful again and the land was ruled by kings at Ur. They were, however, conquered by the armies of Elam, from across the Tigris to the east.

Three city states—that is, independent states consisting of a city and the land round it—then grew up in Mesopotamia. Isin and Larsa were the first two of these, then came Babylon. Some time after 2100 B.C. its wisest and strongest king, Hammurabi, came to the throne. It was Hammurabi who broke the power of the Elamites in Babylonia and thus set the stage for Babylon's first period of splendour.

Hammurabi drew up a series of laws, now known as the Code of Hammurabi, which were carved on a pillar of black basalt (a kind of rock). Many of these laws seem sound and just, even to modern people, although many of the punishments for crime were savage, including drowning and the putting out of eyes.

Meanwhile, although Babylonia was still strong and prosperous, another Semitic people, the Assyrians, were rising to power in the north of Mesopotamia, and in time the Assyrians conquered Babylon, some time after 1300 B.C., and the first period of Babylonia's glory was over.

For hundreds of years the Assyrians remained the leading peoples of the East, but in their turn they fell. In 612 Nineveh, the Assyrian capital, was taken and destroyed by the Babylonians, Medes and Scythians, and Babylonia again took over Mesopotamia.

From 604 to 562 Babylon was ruled by Nebuchadnezzar, who is often mentioned in the Old Testament. It was Nebuchadnezzar who raised the mighty temples, walls and gates that made Babylon one of the most splendid cities of the ancient world. (The Bible describes it as "that great city that was clothed in fine linen, and purple, and scarlet, and decked with gold, and precious stones, and pearls.") It was Nebuchadnezzar also who carried the Jews captive into Babylon. (See BABYLON and NEBUCHADNEZZAR.)

The empire of Nebuchadnezzar extended from the Euphrates to Egypt and from Armenia to the wastes of Arabia. Nevertheless it was short-lived. In 538 B.C. Cyrus, King of Persia, conquered Babylon, and that was the end of the Babylonian Empire, although the city continued to exist for several centuries more.

The Babylonians followed to a great extent the achievements and learning of the Sumerians who went before them. Like the Sumerians they wrote on tablets of clay, but their writing was in the form of wedge-shaped letters and is known as cuneiform writing (from *cuneus*, the Latin for wedge). An interesting piece of information discovered from a tablet is that one of the governors of Babylon brought honeybees into the city from the mountains.

The Babylonians' buildings, such as temples and palaces, were also made of bricks baked from mud and were often crowned by high towers. Some were made in the form of seven mighty steps, and these were known as *ziggurats*. One of them may have been the Biblical Tower of Babel.

Like almost all ancient nations the Babylonians worshipped many gods, making idols, or images, and carrying out religious ceremonies which shocked the Jews. Of these gods, Marduk, who fought and overcame the dragon Tiamat, was the most important. The legend of how he created heaven, earth and man was written down in clay tablets and scholars found that it resembled the Biblical story of the creation in several places.

The chief goddess of the Babylonians was Ishtar, who was rather like Aphrodite, or Venus, the Greek goddess of love. Another very important character in Babylonian mythology was the hero Gilgamesh. The story of Gilgamesh contains an account of the Flood, and this, too, resembles the Biblical story of Noah.

The Chaldeans. When Babylon rose to power again after the fall of Assyria, the ruling class were the Chaldeans. These people had probably come to Mesopotamia at a very early date, settling round Ur. Nebuchadnezzar was Chaldean, and by that time the Chaldeans had become part of the Babylonian nation.

The Chaldeans laid the foundations of astronomy, although they themselves to a large extent studied the heavens because they believed that the future could be foretold from the stars and planets. Because of this, the word Chaldean later came to mean magician or prophet. The Chaldeans were also the first people to divide the equator into 360 degrees and to map the stars. They also made a system of weights and measures which was afterwards used by the Greeks and Romans.

The Assyrians

Like the Babylonians, the Assyrians were a Semitic race. They probably came to the north of Mesopotamia about the time of Sargon, and at first they lived only in the city of Assur on the Tigris. For a while they were ruled by the Babylonians and the Sumerian kings of Ur, but in time their land grew in strength and Babylon was conquered.

The names and histories of many Assyrian kings, greatly feared in their lives, have come down to us, either through archaeology or in the pages of the Bible. The first king of whom much is known is Shalmaneser I, who reigned about 1280 B.C. The records of his time show that even then Assyria had a large empire. Two

An Assyrian chariot outside an enemy city.

hundred years later Tilgath-Pileser I became king and conquered more lands to the north, besides raising great temples and palaces and laying out gardens and parks.

For a time Assyria was weakened by the Aramaeans, a Semitic race who settled in north Syria and the upper Euphrates and controlled the trade routes of the area. Under Assur-nasir-pal, who reigned from 885 to 860, the Assyrians reconquered the lands they had lost, and from then until the fall of Nineveh in 612 the Assyrian Empire was more powerful than ever before.

In 722 a general of the army, Sargon II, seized the throne of Assyria. His successors included Sennacherib, who fought against the Jews and sacked Jerusalem, and Assur-bani-pal, a king who was interested in the arts of peace as well as those of war. Carvings showing scenes of Assyrian life in Assur-bani-pal's reign have been found, so has his library of 22,000 clay tablets covered with cuneiform writing.

The capital city of Assyria was Nineveh on the right bank of the Tigris, which was greatly enlarged and strengthened by Sennacherib. Nineveh was a great city, but when it was captured by the Babylonians it fell so completely that all traces of it were lost for more than 2,000 years. Only legends and references to it in the Bible were left. For instance, the prophet Jonah was sent by God to Nineveh to call the people to repent of their sins.

The Assyrian Empire fell with Nineveh, for the countries that made it up were in rebellion. The greatness of Assyria melted away, and eventually it became part of the Persian Empire.

The Assyrians, although like the Babylonians in many ways, were a more cold-blooded and savage people. Their empire was a military one, and they often cruelly tortured the captives they took in war. They had fast chariots, driven by the sons of their leading men, who looked on chariot-driving as a new and exciting adventure. Yet they were also a highly efficient people. Their cities, such as Nimrud and Nineveh, were ruled and built as well as the army was organized. Leading up to them and to the palaces were avenues flanked by huge figures in the dark grey stone that the Assyrians used— figures half man and half bull. Great aqueducts were also made to bring water to the cities. The Assyrians wrote hymns and poems, as well as scientific, historical and legal documents, which scholars today find to be of very high quality.

The Hittites

Until the 20th century very little was known about the Hittites or, as they were also called, the Hatti. There are a few references to them in the Old Testament—King David caused the death of a man called Uriah the Hittite—but these uses of the name have been found to be rather vague and uncertain. The patient work of archaeologists has now proved that the Hittites were a mighty people before the greatest days of Babylon and Assyria.

The most remarkable thing about the Hittites is perhaps the fact that they seem to have been the first people to use iron instead of bronze for making their weapons. They were thus the beginners of the period known as the Iron Age. (See IRON AGE.)

The Hittites began in Asia Minor, which is now Turkey, not in the valleys of the Tigris and Euphrates. Between 4,000 and 5,000 years ago they lived in various places all over Asia Minor and were already fairly civilized, being skilled builders and craftsmen. Gradually they spread to Syria and towards Palestine, coming into conflict with Egypt. They also spread across the upper valleys of Mesopotamia and took control of some important trade routes.

The Hittite Empire was at its height between about 1350 and 1200 B.C., during which time a peace treaty was made with Egypt. Like the later empires of the Assyrians and Babylonians, that of the Hittites collapsed suddenly, when hordes of people who were pouring into the countries around the Aegean Sea invaded them.

It is interesting to realize that if the Greeks who attacked the city of Troy in the 12th century B.C. had arrived a little earlier they would have been opposed by the power of the Hittite Empire. As it was, the empire was by then in decay, if not actually in ruins.

The capital of the Hittite Empire was at Hattusas, now Bogazkoy, in Turkey; other important cities were Halpa, now Aleppo in Syria, and Carchemish in Asia Minor. Most of the important documents about the Hittites have been found at Bogazkoy. It was here that tablets covered with cuneiform writing were first discovered in 1906. This marked a great advance in the study of the Hittites, for the only documents discovered before were in a kind of picture language that was very difficult to read. The cuneiform writing was found to be rather like Latin, and when translated it provided a good deal of new information about the Hittites, particularly about their laws, although many gaps remain to be filled.

Sculptures of the Hittites have also been found, and they much resemble those of the Assyrians. Some of these show the gods and goddesses whom the Hittites worshipped. The most important was the sun-goddess, whose husband was god of the storm.

The Hittite kings were high priests who led the worship of the gods. The king was the earthly representative of the storm god and himself became a god when he died. Noblemen served as judges and officials, and formed a warrior class whose armed chariots were the backbone of the army. The ordinary people lived mostly in villages as peasants, artisans or slaves.

The Phoenicians

Phoenicia was an ancient country that covered part of what are now Syria and the Lebanon in the Middle East. The Phoenicians were the only Semitic tribe to become a seafaring people. They sailed across the Mediterranean beyond the Pillars of Hercules (now called the Straits of Gibraltar) to England in the north and, so it is said, they were the first people to sail round Africa. By their voyages the Phoenicians linked the old civilizations of Egypt and Mesopotamia with the younger powers of the Mediterranean, for they were great traders and people of all nations bought from them.

They were not only sailors, however, for they built Tyre and Sidon, which still exist on the coast of Lebanon, although now shrunk almost beyond recognition from the cities they once were. Tyre, the younger of the two, was once on an island but has been joined to the mainland by causeways (raised roads). Carthage, on the north coast of Africa, was founded by

descendants of the Phoenicians. (See CAR-
THAGE; TYRE AND SIDON.)

The Phoenicians left few records of themselves, although they were among the first
people to use an alphabet instead of having a
whole sign to stand for each word. For a long
time all that is known about them was learned
from the writings of other people, such as the
Old Testament, two Greeks—the historian
Herodotus and the poet Homer—and, where
Carthage is concerned, Roman historians.
Archaeologists, however, besides discovering
Egyptian documents which give information
about Phoenicia, have excavated Phoenician
houses and tombs at Ungarit (now Ras Shamra)
and at Byblos (now Jubeil) in Lebanon.

The first definite information about the
Phoenicians dates from about 1600 B.C. when
they were conquered by the Egyptians. For
several centuries the power of Egypt over
Phoenicia strengthened and weakened, until,
from about the middle of the 14th century B.C.
to the rise of the Assyrian Empire in the 9th
century, Phoenicia was independent. Tyre was
the ruling town and one of its kings, Hiram, who
reigned from 970 to 936, gave Solomon "cedar
trees and fir trees according to all his desire" for
the building of the Temple at Jerusalem.

The Assyrian Empire brought Phoenicia's
independence to an end for a time and its cities
were forced to pay tribute to Assyria. Only
Tyre withstood conquest until Nebuchadnezzar
took it in 573. Later both Tyre and Sidon
passed peacefully into the power of Persia.

Under the Persians Phoenicia remained quiet
for a time and fought with them against the
Greeks at the Battle of Salamis. Gradually, however, it turned towards Greece, and when
Alexander the Great conquered the Persian
Empire in 333 all the cities of Phoenicia except
Tyre surrendered to him. Tyre prepared for
another great siege, but Alexander took only
seven months to capture it. He and his successors ruled Phoenicia until, in 64, the Roman
general Pompey made Syria, including Phoenicia, a province of Rome. It was absorbed into
the Roman Empire and the Phoenicians ceased
to exist as a separate people.

The prophet Ezekiel in the Bible says that at

Phoenician merchants unloading wine from their ship.

the height of their power the Phoenicians of
Tyre traded gold, silver, iron, tin, ivory, ebony,
emeralds, coral, agate, wine, spices, honey, linen,
horses, mules, lambs, goats and slaves. For a
long time it was thought that the Phoenicians
sailed out into the Atlantic as far as the mainland
of Cornwall and mined tin there, for they
reached islands which they named the Cassi-
terides. It now seems that these were the little
group known as the Scillies off the coast of Cornwall and that they never reached the mainland.

The Phoenicians visited Greece and searched
its shores for the murex, a mollusc (shellfish)
from which a purple dye, known as Tyrian
purple, was made and greatly prized. The
Greeks, however, thoroughly disliked the
Phoenicians and thought them greedy.

From Tyre the Phoenicians went to settle in
Sicily, Sardinia, Corsica and Cyprus, as well as
North Africa. In Spain they founded Tarshish,
from which they gained much wealth, including
silver. For a time Tyre was supported to a considerable extent by its colonies, but later
Carthage became the leading town.

The Jews traded with Phoenicia and provided
the country with oil and wheat, but the religion
of the Phoenicians horrified them. One of their
chief gods was Moloch, to whom children were
sacrificed. The chief goddess was Astarte or
Ashtoreth, who resembled Ishtar of the Babylonians. Tyre was under the patronage of
Melkarth, who was part god and part hero.

The Medes and the Persians

Media, the land of the Medes, is the ancient name of the northwestern part of the modern country of Persia. The tribe of the Medes is first heard of in 836 B.C., when they paid tribute to Shalmaneser II, King of Assyria. It was not until about 200 years later that the Medes broke away from Assyria and set up their own kings. They were among the people who overthrew Nineveh in 612, and their king gained much of the northern part of the Assyrian Empire.

The first Persians were a tribe who lived in the southwestern part of modern Persia. One of their kings, Cyrus, rose against the Median king, defeated the Medes and took Ecbatana, the capital, in 550 B.C. From Media Cyrus went on to conquer the rich province of Lydia in Asia Minor, the Greek colonies of Asia Minor and Babylon and Syria. He released the Jews whom Nebuchadnezzar had taken to Babylon, allowing them to return to their own land.

Cyrus was a great commander, who achieved his successes within about 20 years. The men he led were tough mountain-dwellers and skilled bowmen who proved too much for the softer, luxury-loving peoples of the rich river valleys. Nevertheless Cyrus treated the people he conquered well and allowed them to keep their own customs of life. He probably died in 529, and it is said that on his tomb were the words, "I am Cyrus, the founder of the Persian Empire. Envy me not the little earth that covers my body."

Cambyses, the son of Cyrus, conquered Egypt in 525 and also took Cyprus and the Greek islands near the coast of Asia Minor. He was, however, a tyrant who eventually went mad and killed himself. After his death pretenders to the Persian throne caused trouble until Darius, a member of the royal family, gained the crown.

He found himself ruler over an empire greater than had ever been known before, apart from that of China. It covered Asia Minor, Armenia, much of what is now the Middle East and even touched part of India. Darius divided the empire into 20 provinces, known as *satrapies,* and fixed the amount of tribute money each was to pay. The Persians began to use coins, instead of merely bars of gold and silver. It was in the days of Darius, also, that the Persians first wrote in ink on parchment, using a different writing from the cuneiform, which was still sometimes used for stone and clay.

Darius explored the shores of Sicily and Italy and one of his captains sailed across the Indian Ocean. In 512 he led a great expedition across the Danube to conquer the wild Scythian people and reached Russia, but was obliged to turn back because his supplies failed. In Egypt he cut a canal from the Nile to Suez (not, of course, the same as the present-day Suez Canal) and his ships sailed from there through the Red Sea.

The decay and fall of the Persian Empire was due to a great extent to the rise of the cities of Greece—not then a single country. Darius sent commanders against the Greeks, but they failed to conquer them, and these attempts were finally checked by the Battle of Marathon in 490.

Darius was succeeded by his son Xerxes (pronounced "Zerkseez"), who led a mighty army into Greece. It was defeated by the Athenian fleet at the Battle of Salamis in 480. After this the Persian Empire gradually lost more and more of its possessions, the kings grew weak and the satraps (provincial governors) became rebellious. For a time the empire returned to its former strength, but in 333 it was conquered by Alexander the Great.

The laws and religion of the Persians were both much in advance of those of most other ancient peoples. The phrase "the laws of the Medes and the Persians" comes from the Book of Daniel in the Bible and means a rule that never changes. The religion of the Persians had been taught to them by the prophet Zoroaster, who lived in solitude in the desert, probably in the time of Cyrus. Zoroaster taught that good and evil were always striving against each other and that the god he worshipped was the god of the whole world as well as of the Persians.

The Etruscans

Few ancient races are so little known to present-day scholars as the Etruscans. They lived in Italy long before the days of the Roman Empire and were a highly civilized people. It has not been found possible, however, to translate their language, which is not like the Latin spoken by the Romans, and the Romans wrote very little about them. Herodotus says that they came from Lydia in Asia Minor. Carvings and statues of the Etruscans have been found, and as they resemble those of the Assyrians and Egyptians it is almost certain that they were an eastern people. The towns the Etruscans built along the coasts of Italy were the oldest, so it seems clear that they came by sea. Some time after 1000 B.C. they settled in the region between the rivers Arno and Tiber, which became known as Etruria.

The Etruscans were mainly a warrior race, although they were also great sailors who gained wealth and power from their trade with Greece. Much of their art is very striking, particularly their sculpture, in which they used bronze, terracotta and clay. They were, however, a rather cruel, proud and luxury-loving people.

Strange to say, the Etruscans never formed a single, united nation. The inhabitants of the different towns did not fight each other and in the 6th century they formed a league of 12 cities, but they hardly ever joined together against their enemies the Romans. This was why they were swallowed by Rome even before the days of the Roman Empire.

Tarquinii, one of the earliest of all, was the city from which the Tarquin kings came. These ruled in Rome until 510 B.C., when the last, Tarquin the Proud, was driven out by the Romans. The Tarquins made an alliance with Lars Porsena, King of Clusium, an Etruscan city farther north. In about 500 Lars Porsena led an army on Rome to restore the Tarquins to the throne, but was held back by Horatius (see HORATIUS) until the bridge leading across the Tiber to Rome had been cut down. Lord Macaulay's famous poem "Horatius" begins:

> Lars Porsena of Clusium
> By the Nine Gods he swore
> That the great house of Tarquin
> Should suffer wrong no more.

Tarquinii, as well as Populonia, not far from the island of Elba, was inhabited by an even earlier people, the Villanovans, before the Etruscans came.

Veii, about ten miles from Rome, warred with Rome until 396 B.C., when Veii was finally overcome. At the town of Caere, near the coast northwest of Rome, was discovered an Etruscan tomb in the form of a room with ornaments and furniture. In it had been buried a warrior and a woman decked in jewellery.

The later history of the Etruscans is a long, losing struggle against the rising power of Rome. They made an alliance with Carthage in North Africa and took part in various sea battles. They were finally defeated by Rome in 283 B.C. and gradually became absorbed into it.

Rome in its early days learned much from the Etruscans, particularly the ways by which they administered their cities. Their gods, too, were not unlike those of the Romans.

Macedonian Empire

Between three and four centuries before the birth of Christ there was a state called Macedonia which covered the northern part of modern Greece and the southern parts of what are now Albania, Yugoslavia and Bulgaria. It was made a powerful state by its king, Philip II, who saw in the quarrels and wars between the other states of Greece an opportunity to become the master of the country. In spite of opposition by the great orator (speaker) Demosthenes, Philip had almost succeeded in this when, in 336 B.C., he was murdered at a festival by one of his own men, possibly urged on by Philip's wife.

Philip's reign was only the beginning of the

Macedonian soldiers riding through a village.

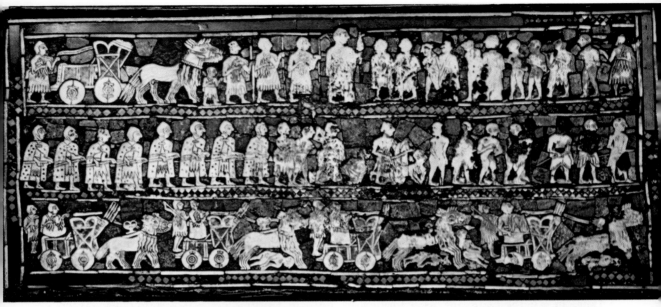

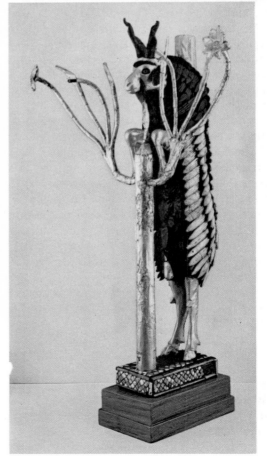

Top: This inlaid standard from Ur, the great city of the Sumerians, is a mosaic made of lapis lazuli, shell, coloured stones and mother-of-pearl. It shows a battle and victory scene. Above: A copper lion's head from the temple of a Sumerian goddess, about 2400 B.C. Right: This figure of a goat, made of gold and silver, lapis lazuli, red sandstone and shell is one of a pair found in a royal tomb at Ur. It is 45 centimetres high.

greatness of Macedonia. His son Alexander, who succeeded him, was one of the most extraordinary men who have ever lived. In his short life—he died at 32—he overcame the Persian Empire, founded the city of Alexandria in Egypt and even penetrated into northern India. (His story is told in the article ALEXANDER THE GREAT.)

Alexander died of a fever in Babylon in 323, when he was at the height of his glory. Not long afterwards the new Macedonian Empire that he had founded began to crumble, for no one like Alexander or his father was left to rule it. A line of kings known as the Seleucids (after Seleucus, one of Philip's and Alexander's generals), was set up, but the more distant parts came again under the rule of their original kings. The Romans finally overcame Macedonia, and in 146 B.C. it became a Roman province.

There were Macedonian kings in Egypt, however, until more than 100 years later. Another of Alexander's generals, Ptolemy, took over Egypt after Alexander's death, and his descendants ruled it until 30 B.C. The kings usually married their sisters, whose names were generally Arsinoe, Berenice or Cleopatra. The last of the Ptolemy line was the beautiful and fascinating Cleopatra who was beloved by both Julius Caesar and Mark Antony.

Although the Macedonian Empire at its greatest lasted for such a short time, it had the very important effect of spreading Greek learning much farther east than before. New cities were built or old ones remodelled according to Greek plans, Greek was generally spoken and Greek interests, such as athletics and drama, were taken up by the people.

The Goths

All the peoples that have been described so far flourished before the birth of Christ. We now come to those who entered history in the years A.D., when the teachings of Christ were spreading and being understood in different ways by different people.

When the Roman Empire began to weaken and decline under foolish or wicked rulers, peoples who are often described under the general heading of "barbarians" overran some of its lands. They were savage and fierce, with none of the efficiency of the Romans or the learning and love of beauty of the Greeks. Therefore the centuries when the barbarians swarmed over western Europe after the Roman Empire had finally fallen are sometimes known as the Dark Ages—the times when the light of learning died out.

One of these peoples was the Goths, another was the Vandals and a third was the Huns. There were also the Vikings, who crossed the sea from Scandinavia and plundered the coasts of several countries, including those of the British Isles. They are described in a separate article VIKINGS.

Probably the Goths came originally from Sweden, but they gradually journeyed southeast until they reached the northern shores of the Black Sea. The language they spoke does not closely resemble any other language, although here and there it is a little like Norwegian. Nearly all the knowledge of Gothic today comes from studying a translation of the Bible made by the Gothic bishop Ulfilas, who probably lived between 310 and 383.

It was the work of Ulfilas that was largely responsible for the conversion of the Goths to Christianity. They followed the Arian religion, which taught that Christ was not equal with God the Father and God the Holy Spirit.

The Goths had many clashes with the Romans, and during one of them, in A.D. 251, the Roman Emperor Decius was killed. After settling by the Black Sea they became divided into two separate peoples, according to where they lived. Those in the west, from the River Danube to the River Dniester (now in the U.S.S.R.), were called the Visigoths. Those in the east, around the River Dnieper (also in the U.S.S.R.) were called the Ostrogoths.

For a time the Ostrogoths were very prosperous, but in 370, during the reign of their most celebrated king, Hermanaric, they were overrun by the ferocious Huns. Hermanaric killed himself in despair and the Ostrogoths surrendered to the Huns.

The movement of the Huns westward caused the Visigoths to take fright and cross the Danube in 376 into the Roman Empire. They did not, however, become absorbed into the empire in the way the Etruscans had done centuries earlier, but remained a separate race of warriors.

It was not long before the Visigoths turned against their Roman masters. Under Alaric, who became their king in 395, they raided first Greece and then northern Italy. Alaric attacked Rome three times, and in 410 it fell and was sacked by the Goths. Alaric carried away great riches from Rome, and when he died later in the same year he was buried with much treasure beneath a river, so that no man should know his grave. (See ALARIC.)

The Visigoths, not content with taking Rome, also conquered much of France and Spain. They adopted Roman customs to a large extent, but their Arian religion was never acceptable to the conquered people of the Roman Empire. A German tribe called the Franks, who had the backing of the Roman church, succeeded in conquering the Visigoths in France in 507.

The Spanish kingdom of the Visigoths remained until 711. For a long time the Romans of Spain resented the Goths because of their religion, but one of their kings, Reccared, who ruled from 586 to 608, became a Catholic Christian and many of the Visigoths did the same. The Gothic language began to go out of use as the two separate nations, Gothic and Roman, found it easier to mix.

It was an entirely different people who brought about the fall of the Spanish Visigoths. In 711 Moslems from North Africa crossed into Spain and conquered the land. These people, the Moors, remained rulers of southern Spain until 1492, and were in many ways a most enlightened and cultured people. (See MOORS.)

The Ostrogoths, meanwhile, remained under the power of the Huns until the death of Attila, their leader, in 453. They then turned to the south, and began to give trouble to the Byzantine Empire. (This was the eastern part of the Roman Empire, with its capital at Byzantium, now Istanbul. How this division came about will be explained later.) The Ostrogoths invaded first the Balkans and then, in 493, they became the masters of Italy and Sicily.

The king of the Ostrogoths at that time was a remarkable man called Theodoric, who was far less of a barbarian than most of the other Gothic kings. He lived in peace with the Romans of Italy and also married one of his daughters to the Visigothic king Alaric II. With the death of Theodoric in 526, however, the Gothic Empire that he had held together began to fall apart. The Byzantine emperor Justinian made war against the Goths of Italy, and after a long struggle he had driven them out by 555.

The Visigoths and Ostrogoths gradually mixed with the Franks and other Germanic races, as well as with the Celts and remnants of the Romans, until they ceased to exist as separate peoples.

Today tall cathedrals with pointed arches are described as being in the Gothic style of architecture. This did not begin to be used, however, until about 1200, long after the days of the Goths. (See ARCHITECTURE.)

The Huns

The most ferocious people of the Dark Ages were the Huns, who were a good deal more destructive and savage than the Goths. They seem to have come from Mongolia and were small, flat-nosed, yellow-skinned people. The Huns were nomads, or wandering people, who spent much of their lives on horseback.

Some Huns penetrated into India and others attacked Persia, but the best known are those who swept across Europe and did so much to bring about the downfall of the Roman Empire.

A Hun herdsman on horseback before his tent.

They reached the height of their power under Attila, "the Scourge of God", who became king in 433. (See ATTILA.) He ruled over all the lands between the River Rhine in Germany and the Caspian Sea in Russia. Under him some of the Huns gave up their wandering lives and settled down in wooden houses. They traded with the Byzantine Empire, which also had to pay the Huns large sums of money in order to keep the peace with them.

In 451 Attila attempted to extend his empire to the west, and led a mighty army across the Rhine. The Huns and the Ostrogoths, whom they had conquered, fought the Romans and the Visigoths at the Battle of Châlons in France but were defeated. Next year Attila invaded Italy.

Attila, like Alexander the Great, stood out so much from his followers that after his death in 453, following his own wedding-feast, his empire quickly fell apart. The conquered peoples turned against the Huns and drove them back to the East. Today several races of Europe, particularly the Bulgarians, show traces of Hunnish descent.

The Vandals

The Vandals were a Germanic people who settled on the north coast of Germany in the 1st century A.D. After various battles with Goths and Romans they swarmed into France in 406, where the Franks defeated them, and crossed into Spain. They took possession of the country and divided into two groups, the Asdingian Vandals, who settled in Galicia in the northwest, and the Silingian Vandals of Andalusia in the south. The Silingians, however, were wiped out by the Visigoths when they conquered Spain.

In about 429 Gaiseric, King of the Asdingian Vandals, led an army into North Africa (which was then a province of Rome) and swiftly overran it, although the city of Carthage was not taken for ten years. Thus Rome was cut off from the province which supplied most of its corn and Carthage became a pirates' stronghold. The Vandals regularly issued from it to attack what Gaiseric described as "the dwellings of the men with whom God is angry". He also built up a powerful fleet, which made him the master of the Mediterranean.

In 455 Gaiseric set sail with his fleet to Italy and marched on Rome. There, it is said, he was met by the pope, who persuaded him not to set fire to the city or murder the people. However, Gaiseric allowed his men to strip Rome of all the treasures which Alaric's Goths had left 45 years before and to carry them back to Africa. This treasure included the sacred vessels from the Temple at Jerusalem, which had been brought to Rome in the 1st century A.D., and gold from the roof of the great temple of Jupiter. The Vandals also took captive the widowed Roman Empress Eudoxia and her daughters.

Gaiseric tried to make sure that the Vandal kingdom would remain together after his death by making it the law that a king should be succeeded only by his eldest son. (The rule before had been that kingdoms were divided up among each king's sons.) Nevertheless, after Gaiseric died at a great age in 477, the power of the Vandals began to decline.

Gaiseric and many of the Vandals were Arian Christians, and they fiercely persecuted the Catholics among them. A later king, Hilderic, was a Catholic, but as he was old and feeble his fiercer cousin Gelimer overthrew him. This gave the Catholic Byzantine Emperor Justinian an opportunity of conquering the Vandals. He sent his greatest general, Belisarius, to deal with them, and after two battles in 533 Belisarius and his army defeated them. Some months later Gelimer was captured, together with many of his men, who became soldiers in the Roman army. Although some of them rebelled in 536, this was the last of the Vandals as a nation.

"Vandalism" is a word often used nowadays to describe the destruction of beautiful things or works of art by people ignorant of their value. The Vandals were to a large extent robbers and pirates, but towards the end of their career they copied the Roman way of life. Rich Vandals built themselves palaces and feasted at banquets and many of them learned to speak Latin.

The Byzantine Empire

In the year 330 A.D. the Roman Emperor Constantine, the first Christian ruler of Rome, made the old Greek city of Byzantium the capital of the eastern half of the Roman Empire. It was renamed Constantinople after the emperor and quickly grew to rival Rome in size and splendour. Constantine's action was a wise one, for, as has been described, Rome was several times plundered by barbarians. Constantinople, standing on the harbour known as the Golden Horn, where Europe and Asia meet, became the storehouse of Greek learning and Roman order and the centre of the eastern or Byzantine Empire.

Many times Constantinople was threatened by barbarians, but the Byzantine Empire did not finally fall until 1453. Its fall was a most fortunate thing for western Europe, as will be seen later. After the overthrow of the Byzantine Empire, Constantinople became the centre of the Ottoman (Turkish) Empire, but today it is no longer a capital city and its name has been changed to Istanbul. (See CONSTANTINOPLE; ISTANBUL; OTTOMAN EMPIRE.)

Under Attila, the Huns threatened Constantinople in 450, but the city had walls and gates strong enough to keep them out. By 527, when the Emperor Justinian came to the throne, things had settled down to a certain extent, and Justinian considered it possible to reconquer the parts of the Roman Empire that had fallen to the barbarians.

Justinian was a peasant by birth and became emperor on the death of his uncle Justin, who was ignorant of almost everything and could not even write. Justinian himself, although he accomplished much, was not a brilliant man. He was extremely vain and apt to be jealous of anyone under him who was at all outstanding. He was, however, very religious (in fact hymns by Justinian can be found printed in hymn books even today) and, being a devout Catholic who took his religion seriously, he was anxious to do as much as possible to bring to an end the many divisions that existed in the Christian Church.

Justinian was helped very greatly in his plans for the Christian Church and the eastern Empire by his wife, Theodora, whom he had married before becoming emperor. Theodora was the daughter of a bear-keeper at the Hippodrome, which was the entertainment centre of Constantinople. She was beautiful, clever and brave, but she could also be cruel and deceitful.

Courtiers bowing as a Byzantine empress passes by.

Theodora gave Justinian guidance and help in almost everything, and after her death in 548 his character and rule rapidly grew worse.

One of the most lasting of Justinian's achievements was the collecting together and rearranging of the laws of the Roman Empire, which had fallen into great confusion. This rearrangement, known as the Code of Justinian, is the basis of the law in many modern countries. Justinian also spent great sums of money on magnificent buildings, especially churches. The most remarkable of those that can still be seen today is St. Sophia, which is now a museum.

Justinian's plans for reconquest of the empire were carried out by his two finest generals, Belisarius and Narses. Belisarius first took North Africa from the Vandals and then recaptured Italy and part of Spain from the Goths. He also beat back the Persians from the east. Narses finally defeated the Goths in Italy. Therefore when Justinian died in 565 the Byzantine Empire had been much enlarged, but it was very liable to be attacked, and the treasury was almost empty.

Three years after Justinian's death most of Italy fell to the heathen Lombards, whose name is still recalled by the Lombardy plain of northern Italy. The Persians were also pressing strongly on the eastern frontiers, and the empire seemed to be crumbling rapidly when a man who was strong enough to deal with the situation

Some examples of the art of the ancient peoples of Europe and the Middle East. Above: Etruscan bronze incense burner in the form of a two-headed bird with four legs, mounted on wheels. 10th–8th century B.C. Top right: Greek gold earring. 4th–3rd century B.C. Left: Bronze bull from Sabaea, South Arabia. 6th century B.C. Right: Greek scent bottle with mouth in the form of a lion's head. About 650 B.C. Below left: Greek wine jar, with black-figure decoration. About 530 B.C. Below right: Jewelled brooch from a Jutish grave in Kent. 6th–7th century A.D.

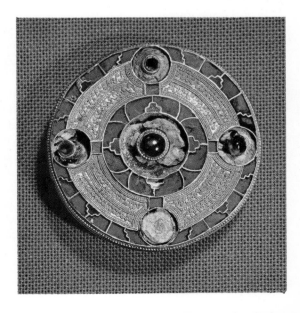

appeared on the scene. This was Heraclius, the son of the governor of Africa, who seized the Byzantine throne in 610. He reorganized the army and in 627, a year after a mighty siege of Constantinople by the Persians and some other savage tribes, he marched his army into the plain of the River Tigris and finally defeated the Persian army.

Once more the Byzantine power was saved, but a new danger threatened. This was the rise of the Arabs, who had recently been converted to a new religion, Islam (see ISLAM), founded by the prophet Mohammed (570–632). The Arabs conquered not only Persia but also the Byzantine possessions of Syria, Egypt and North Africa. They aimed at Constantinople itself, but were beaten back in 678 after a long siege.

Gradually the Byzantine Empire, although shrunk in size, became more secure, and in the 10th century it was at the height of its splendour. Its frontiers were strongly guarded, its navy was powerful and Constantinople was a centre of riches and wisdom. Its people did not merely copy the Greek and Roman way of painting and architecture, however. Their paintings and sculptures are very distinctive, and they developed a special style of architecture which included large round domes on the top of square buildings.

A very important result of the separation of Constantinople and Rome was the formation of the Greek Orthodox Church. After the death of Justinian Greek became the official language of the Byzantine Empire and church services were held in Greek instead of in Latin, as in Rome. The patriarchs (bishops) of Constantinople and the popes of Rome had disagreements and the final break came in 1054, leaving two distinct churches, one in the East and one in the West.

In the middle of the 11th century the Byzantine Empire began to be menaced by the Turks. The Catholic peoples of the West, including the English and French, sent armies known as the crusades against the Turks, but in 1204 a terrible thing happened. The western and eastern Christians had long been unfriendly to each other, and the soldiers of the fourth crusade went so far as to seize Constantinople and to set up a western ruler there. It was not recaptured

for the Byzantines until 1261, when Michael Palaeologus reconquered it and was crowned emperor as Michael VIII.

The danger from the Turks was not over, however. Under Mohammed II, the sultan (ruler) of the Ottoman Turks, Constantinople was besieged in 1453. The Byzantine people fought bravely but the Turks were too strong for them. On May 29, 1453, Constantinople fell to the Ottomans.

This was the end of Constantinople's isolation from Christian Europe. Its scholars, forbidden by the Turks to use the Greek language, wandered into Western countries and spread the learning that the Byzantine Empire had jealously guarded for so long. This was one of the causes of the Renaissance, or rebirth, of learning, when people began again to follow the ideas of the Greeks and seek for the truth about things, instead of relying on superstitions. (See RENAISSANCE.)

RACKETS is a game in which the ball probably travels faster than in any other game in the world. It should not be confused with squash rackets, on which there is a separate article. Rackets is played in a rectangular court 60 feet long and 30 feet wide. There are four hard, smooth, flat walls and a floor, with a heavy door in the back wall through which the players enter and leave the court. Across the front wall is a board whose top is 26 inches from the floor. The ball must strike above this board during the game to remain in play. Higher across the front wall, $9\frac{1}{2}$ feet from the floor, is a red line called the service line.

The hard white ball is about $1\frac{1}{2}$ inches in diameter and is made by winding thread tightly round a plastic centre and covering with white tape. The racket is longer than a lawn-tennis racket and has a thinner shaft and a smaller and rounder head.

The game is played either by two players (singles) or by four players (doubles). A match consists of games, each of which is played by points. A game is won by the first player or pair to reach 15 points. To start, one of the players becomes "hand-in" and stands inside one of the two small squares marked on the floor and called the service box. He strikes the ball with the racket so that it hits the front wall above the service line and rebounds to land within a given area. The player receiving the service is "hand-out" and must return the ball above the board before it has bounced twice on the floor. The rally continues until one of the players fails to return the ball above the board. Points can be scored only by hand-in. If hand-out wins a rally, he does not score a point, but becomes hand-in and serves at the start of the next rally.

The game of rackets calls for rapid thinking and quick footwork, as the ball sometimes travels at 100 miles an hour. The game became popular in Great Britain, and especially in London, during the 19th century, but is no longer widely played. This is because the large courts are expensive to build and the rackets are liable to be broken or damaged. Also, the quickness of re-action needed makes it a game for men only. However, the speed and skill in rackets keeps the game alive. There are about 25 courts in England and the game is also played in the United States and Canada. The British amateur championships, army championships and the public schools competitions are played at the Queen's Club in Kensington, London.

RADAR is an electronic system for locating distant objects. It works by squirting out radio energy from an antenna (aerial) in a thin beam of very short pulses and listening for echoes to return to the antenna. (For an explanation of radio energy, see under RADIO.) By measuring the time a single pulse of energy takes to return to the antenna (the speed of radio waves is 300,000 kilometres a second) it is possible to work out the *distance* the pulse travelled. If the *direction* of the pulse is known, then the combination of distance ("range") and direction ("bearing") gives the position of the object (known as a "target" in radar jargon) which caused the reflection of the pulse.

Clearly, a process like this which works just as well at night or in fog is very useful for detecting aircraft and ships. If the radar is fitted to an aircraft, it can be used to detect high ground. If it is on a ship, it can locate land and other ships. These are the most common uses

for radar, but an enormous number of other uses have been found.

Pioneers of Radar

From the early days of radio, scientists knew that very short radio waves could be reflected from solid objects. Heinrich Hertz, who discovered how to generate radio waves, was aware of this. Guglielmo Marconi, the pioneer of radio, outlined a system like modern radar in 1922 but did no practical work on it. In 1925, the Americans Gregory Breit and Merle Tuve began a series of experiments to find the height of the reflective part of the atmosphere, called the ionosphere, and used a technique later used widely in radar. However, it was the threat of war in the 1930s that gave a big boost to the development of radar.

In 1935 the British government asked the scientist R. A. (later Sir Robert) Watson-Watt to look into the possibility of a "death ray" using radio waves. He told them such a ray was impossible but instead suggested that radio waves might be used to detect aircraft long before they could be seen or heard. A practical demonstration followed. On February 26, 1935, Watson-Watt succeeded in detecting a bomber aircraft using radio waves.

The ability to give early warning of enemy air raids was so important that Watson-Watt's ideas were quickly adopted. By the time World War II started in 1939, some 40 secret radar stations had been built around the south and east coasts of England.

They were called "RDF" (standing for "radio direction-finding") stations. While the British were in the lead, both the United States and Germany were also developing radar systems. In 1940, the public were told something of the secret, and newspapers called the new system "radiolocation". However, in 1942, Britain officially adopted the American word "radar" which stands for "*RA*dio *D*etection *A*nd *R*anging".

By this time the radar principle had been extended to a number of other purposes besides aircraft and ship detection. Guns were being armed by radar and radar was also fitted to night fighters to help them find and attack enemy bombers. Radar-aimed bombing devices were also developed.

So radar was first developed for wartime use. Since the 1940s, however, radar has come to play an important part in navigation, both at sea and in the air. How do these different radars work?

How a Simple Radar Works

A simple radar system, as found on many merchant ships, has three main parts. These are the antenna unit (which used to be called the scanner), the transmitter/receiver or "transceiver" and the visual display unit.

The antenna is about 2 or 3 metres wide and focuses pulses of very high frequency radio energy into a narrow vertical beam. The frequency of the radio waves is usually about 10,000 MHz (that is 10,000 million cycles per second)—equal to a wavelength of three centimetres. The antenna is rotated (turned round) at a speed of from 10 to 25 revolutions per minute so that the radar beam sweeps through 360 degrees all round the ship out to a range of about 90 kilometres.

In all radars it is vital that the transmitting and receiving in the transceiver are in close harmony. Everything depends on accurate measurement of the time which passes between the transmission (sending out) of the pulse and the return of the echo. About 1,000 pulses per

Courtesy, Marconi Company

A long-range air defence radar, intended to give warning of approaching aircraft.

second are transmitted (though this is varied to suit requirements). Short pulses are best for short-range work, longer pulses are better for long-range.

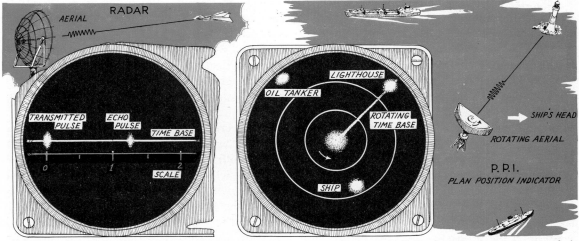

Left: Ground radar detecting aircraft. The calibrated scale on the display unit shows how far away the aircraft is. Right: A ship's radar (labelled "Rotating Aerial"). The "range ring" and the position of a lighthouse and two other ships can be seen.

An important part of the transceiver is the modulator circuit. This "keys" the transmitter so that it oscillates, or pulses, for exactly the right length of time. The transmission power is generated in a device called a magnetron, which can handle these very short pulses and very high frequency oscillations.

Between each pulse the transmitter is switched off and isolated. The very weak echoes from the target are picked up by the antenna and fed into the receiver, amplified (made stronger) and then passed to the display unit.

The display unit usually carries all the controls necessary for the operation of the whole radar. It has a cathode ray tube, very like the tube which provides the black-and-white picture in a television set, but specially adapted for radar work. (See TELEVISION.) In the neck of the tube is an "electron gun" which shoots a beam of electrons at a chemically coated screen at the far end. The chemicals on the screen

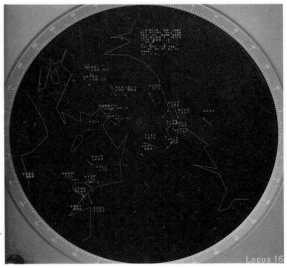

Courtesy, Marconi Company

Above: With the help of a computer, this radar screen shows the position of aircraft over Britain. Below: Air traffic controllers use this information to keep aircraft at safe distances from one another.

Courtesy, Marconi Company
A radar plan position indicator or P.P.I. The white dots are aircraft echoes, shown on a video map.

glow when they are hit by the electrons and, although the screen is on the *inside* wall of the tube, the resulting spot of light can be seen through the glass face exactly as you view a television picture. Unlike a television tube, however, a radar tube has a circular screen marked off ("calibated") in degrees around its edge. The electron beam travels out from the centre to the edge. This radial motion of the electron beam, known as the "trace", is matched with the rotation of the antenna. So when the trace is at O degrees on the tube

calibration, the antenna is pointing dead ahead.

The beginning of each trace corresponds exactly with the moment at which a pulse of radar energy is transmitted. When an echo is received it brightens up the trace for a moment. This is a "blip", and its distance from the centre of the tube corresponds exactly with the time taken for the radar pulse to travel to the target and return. So the "blip" on the screen gives the range and bearing of the target. As the trace rotates, a complete picture is built up from the "afterglow" of the chemical coating of the tube. This type of display is called a P.P.I. (Plan Position Indicator) and is the most common form of presenting radar information.

Computers and Radar

From this simple description, you can see that *timing* is important to the way radar works. By using computers, various "tricks" can make the display easier to read and also get rid of unwanted echoes.

For example, in an air traffic control radar (controlling the movement of civil and military aircraft) it is important to be able to see *only* the aircraft. Other echoes, such as rain or high ground, only confuse the display. A computer can be programmed to display only those targets which are moving fast enough to be aircraft. Also, the computer can "draw" the radar

Royal Air Force
(Germany) photo
The R.A.F.'s Rapier anti-aircraft missiles are directed by the Blindfire radar (shown nearest the camera). The radar spots approaching aircraft and, if necessary, will aim the missile at its target.

picture and show targets as crosses, squares or triangles, more easily read than the old-fashioned blip.

Whether the air traffic controller sees blips or computer-generated symbols, he must be able to identify the targets He also needs to know the height of aircraft, so that those on the same course but flying at different levels can be kept apart. (For more about this, see AIR-CRAFT and AIRPORT.)

To give the controller this information, a second radar, called a "secondary surveillance radar", is used. This works differently and needs the "help" of the aircraft. It sends out a sequence of pulses to an electronic "black box", called a "transponder", fitted on the aircraft. The transponder is linked to the aircraft alti-meter (the device that measures the plane's altitude or height) to transmit back to the radar a coded message identifying the aircraft and its altitude. Military aircraft use a similar radar system with secret codes to identify "friend" from "foe". A "hostile" aircraft does not know what code to transmit.

To work out the height of unidentified air-craft, special height-finding radars are used. There are two methods of height-finding: one called "nodding" radar and the other "three-dimensional" radar. A nodding height-finder is like an ordinary radar standing on its side. When the controller wants to find the height of a target displayed on the screen, he rotates the height-finder to the bearing of the aircraft, whereupon the radar nods up and down. By measuring the angle of the antenna at the point when the beam strikes the target, the height of the aircraft can then be worked out. There are also what are called "3-D" radars. Instead of using two radars, the two functions are com-bined in a single antenna system. Here the "nod" is an electronic signal instead of a mechanical movement.

There are many other uses for these radars. Most missiles are guided by radar. (See GUIDED WEAPONS.) Quite often the radar is mounted in the nose of the weapon. Radars are also fitted on board some aircraft to warn the pilot of air turbulence and thunderstorms. Radars now play an important part in weather forecasting and

are also found on board spacecraft, mapping the surface of the Earth below.

Radars using continuous wave transmission (rather than pulses) are fitted in devices such as the proximity fuse, which causes a missile or shell to explode when close to its target. Lastly, as some car drivers discover to their cost, radar can be an effective way to catch the motorist who exceeds the speed limit.

RADIATION is a word which comes from the Latin *radius*, meaning a beam or ray. In science, it is used for anything which travels in rays: for example, light, radio waves, X-rays, the rays given out by radioactive substances like radium, and cosmic rays are all forms of radiation.

Some forms of radiation are tiny particles of matter, while others are waves. Among the par-ticle radiations are the alpha and beta rays given off by radium and also cosmic rays, which are atomic particles travelling through outer space. These particles collide with atoms in the upper layers of the Earth's atmosphere to produce "cosmic ray showers" of other atomic particles which can be detected at sea level.

Among the several kinds of wave radiations are electro-magnetic waves. Gamma rays, X-rays, ultra-violet light, ordinary visible light, infra-red "light", microwaves used in radar, and radio waves are all forms of electro-magnetic radiation. Of these, only two kinds can be de-tected without instruments: visible light, which enables us to see, and infra-red rays of long wave length which we feel as heat. Radio waves can be detected by radio receivers and there are various ways of detecting the other radiations. They are all waves, however, and may be com-pared with the waves of the sea, or with the ripples caused in a pond when a stone is thrown in.

The electro-magnetic waves differ from water waves, however, in two important ways: they can travel through empty space, and they travel at an enormous speed (about 300,000,000 kilo-metres a second).

The only difference between the different kinds of electro-magnetic radiation is that they have different wave-lengths. The wave-length is the distance along the wave between one crest

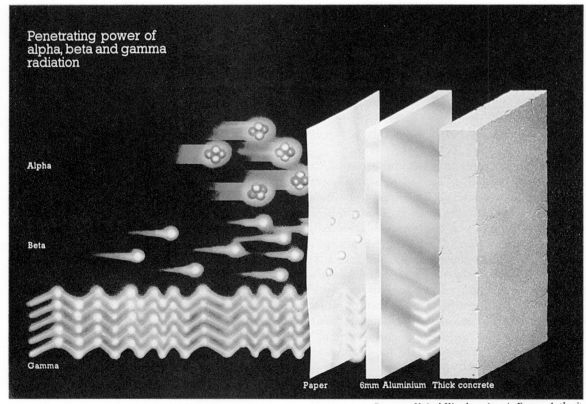

Penetrating power of
alpha, beta and gamma
radiation

Alpha

Beta

Gamma

Paper   6mm Aluminium   Thick concrete

Courtesy, United Kingdom Atomic Energy Authority

Top: This diagram illustrates how different kinds of radiation penetrate; alpha rays are blocked by paper, while gamma rays can pass through aluminium sheeting. Below: Radiation therapy is used in the treatment of cancer and other illnesses. This machine gives computer-controlled doses of cobalt-60 radiation.

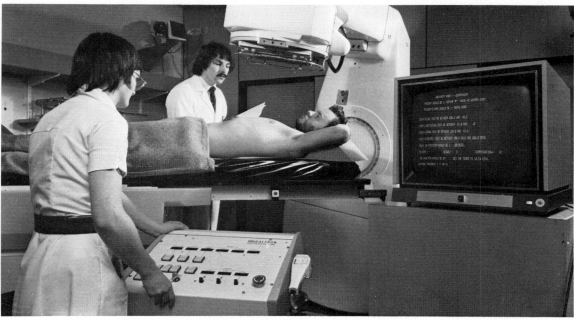

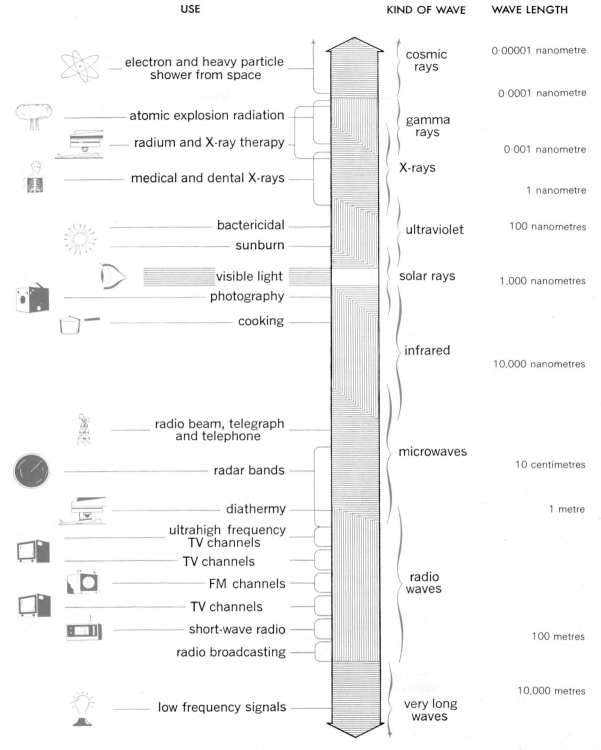

USE	KIND OF WAVE	WAVE LENGTH

electron and heavy particle shower from space — cosmic rays — 0·00001 nanometre

0·0001 nanometre

atomic explosion radiation — gamma rays

radium and X-ray therapy

0·001 nanometre

medical and dental X-rays — X-rays

1 nanometre

bactericidal — ultraviolet — 100 nanometres

sunburn

visible light — solar rays — 1,000 nanometres

photography

cooking

infrared

10,000 nanometres

radio beam, telegraph and telephone

radar bands — microwaves — 10 centimetres

diathermy — 1 metre

ultrahigh frequency TV channels

TV channels

FM channels — radio waves

TV channels

short-wave radio — 100 metres

radio broadcasting

10,000 metres

low frequency signals — very long waves

This diagram shows the different kinds of radiation arranged according to their wave-lengths. At the top are cosmic rays, which are particles of matter. From gamma rays downwards, the rest are electro-magnetic waves, which have no solidity and all of which travel at the speed of light.

and the next, but the wave-lengths of the shorter electro-magnetic radiations are so tiny that they are usually measured in nanometres : a nanometre is $\frac{1}{1,000,000,000}$ of a metre. An older unit called the angstrom unit is also used and is equal to 0·1 of a nanometre.

The shortest radiation wave-lengths are those of gamma rays, which can be as little as 0·05 of a nanometre. Gamma rays are given out by naturally radioactive substances such as uranium and radium, and also when atomic nuclei are split in a nuclear reactor or atomic bomb explosion (see NUCLEAR POWER). Gamma rays, although harmful to life, are useful in medicine for killing unwanted growths and for sterilizing hospital equipment.

X-rays have wave-lengths of between half a nanometre and 100 nanometres, about 500 times as long as gamma rays. They can be used, for example, to examine a bone which may be broken. The arm is placed between the X-ray source and a photographic plate. The rays pass more easily through flesh than through bone, and so a dark shadow of the bone is seen when the photographic plate is developed.

Ultra-violet rays have wave-lengths ranging from those of the longest X-rays up to nearly 400 nanometres· Sunlight contains ultra-violet rays, which are important because they enable our bodies to produce vitamin D.

Visible light ranges from violet, with a wave-length of just under 400 nanometres, to red, with a wave-length of about 720 nanometres. The colours of the spectrum which are seen in a rainbow are simple light waves arranged in order of decreasing wavelength—red, orange, yellow, green, blue and violet. (See LIGHT.)

Infra-red rays have wave-lengths from about 720 to 100,000 nanometres. The shorter infra-red rays travel through mist and cloud which stops visible light, and can be used to take photographs in bad weather and at night. Longer infra-red rays are felt as heat, and the heat of the sun's rays is due to these.

Longer electro-magnetic waves of up to a kilometre or more in wave-length are all different kinds of radio waves. Microwaves have wave-lengths of between a few millimetres and a few metres. Rays with wavelengths of about 3 cm are used in radar (see RADAR)· Rays with a wave-length usually of 12 cm are used in microwave ovens. The rays are converted to heat when they are absorbed by the food in the oven. Waves of up to a few metres in length are used in television and longer ones for ordinary radio broadcasting.

See also HEAT; LIGHT; RADAR; RADIO; RADIO-ACTIVITY; and X-RAYS.

RADIO.

In nature there exists a vast range or spectrum of electro-magnetic radiation. At the top end of the scale (in terms of the number of oscillations or vibrations per second) are cosmic rays, followed by gamma rays, X-rays, ultra-violet rays, visible light, infra-red rays and, lowest of all, radio waves. (There is more about this spectrum in RADIATION.)

Radio communication makes use of the fact that electro-magnetic waves can carry electrical copies of sounds, when the sounds have been transformed into electrical oscillations of the same frequencies. An electrical oscillation is an electric current which, instead of flowing steadily in one direction, reverses its direction of flow at regular intervals. One complete sequence is called a "cycle", and the number of times the cycle repeats itself every second is called the "frequency".

Radio waves cover a range of frequencies from about 30,000,000 kHz to 10 kHz (kHz= a kiloHertz, an oscillation of 1,000 cycles a second). These waves travel through space at a uniform speed of 300,000,000 metres a second. This article outlines the history of radio communications to the present day. The article BROADCASTING, RADIO explains how radio programmes are planned and produced. RADAR explains the use of radio echoes for finding the position of distant objects, and TELEVISION describes how radio waves are used to bring pictures into the home.

Early Days of Radio Communication

Until the 19th century no-one knew anything about radio waves. Then in 1864 James Clerk Maxwell, a brilliant mathematician, showed that in theory electro-magnetic waves, lower in frequency than infra-red waves, must form part of the spectrum. However, 22 years passed before a German scientist, Heinrich Hertz, became the first to generate these mysterious invisible waves and to recognise them for what they were. Hertz showed that the waves obeyed the optical laws governing reflection, refraction and interference (see LIGHT), but neither he nor any other scientist of the day could find a practical use for them.

Hertzian waves, as they were called, remained merely a puzzling subject for laboratory research until 1894–5. There is some doubt as to who first used a Morse key (see MORSE) and an antenna system in conjunction with a Hertzian transmitter. It was either a Russian, A. S. Popov, or Guglielmo Marconi, then an unknown young Italian. Popov worked for the Imperial Russian Navy and his work was secret, and Marconi too worked in secrecy, so no firm date can be given. However, there is no doubt that Marconi went on to become the greatest influence on the development of radio. (See MARCONI.)

In 1896 Marconi arrived in England and demonstrated his "wireless apparatus". The transmitter was similar to that used by Hertz. It consisted of an induction coil which, when connected to a battery, developed a high voltage across two metal spheres placed close to one another. The air gap between the spheres broke down under the electrical strain and a stream of sparks jumped across the gap whenever the Morse key (which Marconi had added to Hertz's apparatus) was pressed down.

To one side of the spark gap Marconi connected an elevated wire or antenna and the other side he connected to earth. The stream of sparks produced a series of oscillations which radiated into space from the antenna. By pressing the Morse key for a longer or shorter period, the radiations surged from the antenna in long or short bursts to form letters in Morse code.

The receiver used a device called a *coherer*. This was a small glass tube containing loosely-packed metal filings and was connected between an antenna and earth. In the absence of any signals on the receiving antenna, the electrical resistance of the filings remained high. But as soon as a signal arrived, the metal filings "cohered" or came together and the resistance dropped considerably. Whenever the resistance dropped in this way it caused electro-mechanical relays to come into operation and work a Morse printer. One disadvantage of the coherer was that every time a signal caused the filings to cohere, they had to be tapped to restore them to high-resistance condition. This was done automatically using the hammer of an electric bell mechanism.

When an operator at the transmitter tapped out a message in Morse code, it was picked up by the receiver and printed in Morse characters on a paper tape. The range of the new wireless apparatus was only a few kilometres and sending messages was slow work. There was no way of tuning, so two transmitters within range of each other could not work at the same time. If they did, the receivers would pick up both messages simultaneously, with chaotic results.

But between 1896 and 1901 Marconi made great progress. Transmitters grew from a simple, battery-operated, table-top version to a high-power station on the cliffs at Poldhu in Cornwall. The tuned circuit was developed, so that stations could operate without interfering with one another, and receivers were improved. In December 1901 Marconi announced that signals from Poldhu had crossed the Atlantic Ocean and been received at St. John's in Newfoundland.

The Ionosphere

Yet, in the light of the knowledge of the time, this was theoretically impossible. Hertz had shown that radio waves travelled in optical paths. To cross the Atlantic, surely antenna over 150 kilometres high would be needed on each side to allow the waves to travel in a straight line between Europe and America? Marconi had no independent witnesses, so his claim was not accepted until 1902, when he repeated his transmission in the presence of observers.

What was causing the waves to follow the curvature of the Earth, when in theory they should have left the Earth's surface just beyond the horizon to vanish into space? No-one knew. But in 1902 an American, Arthur E. Kennelly, and an Englishman, Oliver Heaviside, suggested that high above the Earth was a layer of *ionization* (electrified particles) which acted as a mirror and reflected the radio waves down to Earth again.

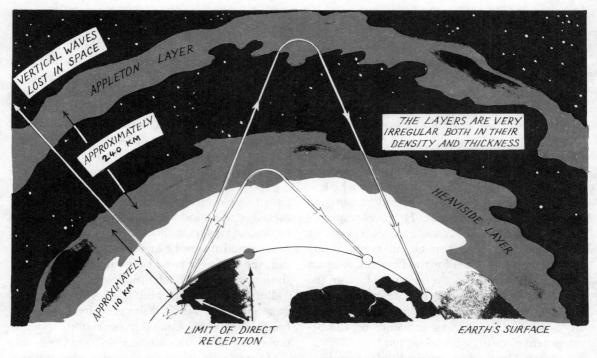

Radio waves are reflected from the ionized Appleton and Kennelly-Heaviside layers of the Earth's atmosphere. These "reflectors" make long-distance radio transmissions possible.

Very few people accepted this at first. However, in the 1920s the British scientist E. V. (later Sir Edward) Appleton proved that the Kennelly-Heaviside theory was correct.

In fact several layers of ionization surround the Earth, at different levels and in two main groups. They are caused by the Sun's action on gases in the upper atmosphere, where ultra-violet radiation frees some of the electrons from the gas atoms (see ATMOSPHERE; ELECTRON). These free electrons reflect part of the radio wave back to Earth while the remainder is absorbed into the ionosphere. The amount reflected depends on various factors, including the density of the layer, its height, the frequency of the radio wave and the angle at which it encounters the layer.

One of the two main layers (from 80 to 140 kilometres above the Earth) is called the Kennelly-Heaviside layer. The other, known as the Appleton layer, is about 240 kilometres up. Without these layers, long-distance radio transmissions would have been impossible until the first satellite launches.

The Radio Wave Spectrum

The spectrum of radio waves is divided into seven main bands. The divisions are artificial ones, made on the basis of different transmission characteristics. In each case, there is a gradual shift from one band to the next, rather than a sudden break.

In ascending order of frequency, the first division is the *very low frequency* (v.l.f.) band. Only a few stations operate in this band and these are for special purposes. Their transmissions are almost wholly reflected from the ionosphere and are thus guided round the Earth in a "channel" formed by the ground and the atmosphere. This gives them reliable worldwide coverage, but they are large and costly to operate.

In the *low frequency* (l.f.) band, the ranges are not so large because of absorption by the ionosphere. Nevertheless, l.f. stations can cover considerable areas by day and night. Many radio sets have a "long wave" or l.f. band. But few stations broadcast on this, although their signals are fairly good.

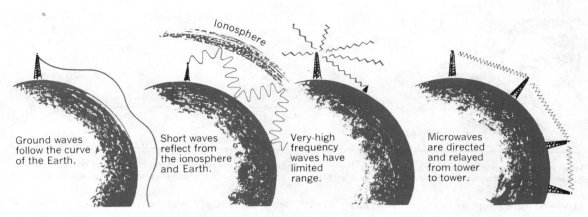

How radio waves travel around the Earth.

Medium wave or *medium frequency* (m.f.) stations behave quite differently. After dark, m.f. stations which cannot be heard by day are received at great strength, often causing serious interference with other transmissions. Also, their signals tend to fade. These effects are caused by the ionosphere.

All radio transmissions have two components or parts, the ground wave and the sky wave. In daylight, the sky wave of a m.f. station is almost completely absorbed by the ionosphere and the station's receiving area receives only the ground wave, which gives a steady signal over reasonable distances. But because the ionized layers are produced by the Sun's action, they are affected in density and height, both by seasonal changes and by the change from day to night. When darkness falls, the reflection of the sky wave becomes much stronger and at a greater angle. The reflected waves which return to Earth within the ground wave area add to or substract from the strength of the signal, causing fading. They are also reflected again from the Earth's surface back to the ionosphere, only to be reflected once more. This "bouncing" process may be repeated several times, and in this way signals can reach areas after dark which they cannot reach during the day.

The *high frequency* (h.f.) band is most important in long-distance communications, although for many years it was regarded as useless for anything other than short-range broadcasts. This was because the ground wave extends only a short distance and no-one knew anything about

the sky wave until the 1920s. Then it was discovered that the sky wave penetrates the lower layers of the ionosphere, but is reflected by the Appleton layer higher up. The first reflection returns to Earth at a point far beyond the limit of the ground wave and, by making several "bounces", can reach immense distances—even around the world. Between the limit of the ground wave and the first bounce is a zone where no signals can be heard. This is known as the "skip distance" effect.

The sky waves of *very high frequency* (v.h.f.), *ultra high frequency* (u.h.f) and *super high frequency* (s.h.f.) radio stations penetrate all the

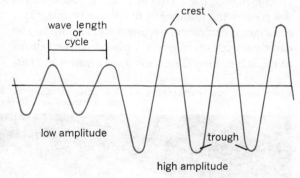

Radio Waves

The paths of radio waves can be shown by curving lines. The high point of a wave is called the *crest*. The low point is the *trough*. One complete wave (from crest to crest or from trough to trough) is a *cycle*. *Amplitude* is the strength of a wave. The strength, or loudness, of a radio signal increases as the amplitude becomes greater. *Frequency* is the number of waves per second. By increasing or decreasing the amplitude of the radio wave, it can be mixed with the slower audio or "voice" wave; it is then said to be *modulated*.

167

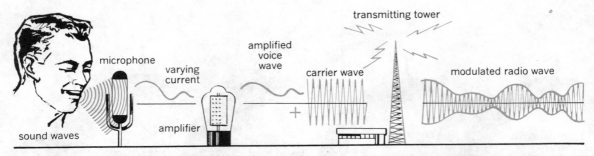

How radio broadcasting works. Sound waves (voice) are changed into varying electrical currents by the microphone. These modulate the radio "carrier" waves sent out by the transmitter. The receiver picks up the waves, amplifies

layers of ionization and escape into space. Their ground waves become shorter and shorter in range with increasing frequency, until at the upper end of the s.h.f. band the range does not extend much beyond the horizon. Engineers try to increase this distance as much as possible by siting the stations on hills or mountains.

In spite of their short ranges, these bands are very useful. For technical reasons, the complicated signals which give us our television pictures cannot be transmitted on the l.f., m.f. and h.f. bands. So they are sent by v.h.f. and u.h.f. stations, whose ranges may be only about 60 kilometres and 35 kilometres respectively. This means that many television stations are needed to cover even an area as small as the British Isles.

The higher the frequency of the radio wave, the greater the number of telephone or telegraph messages it can carry. For instance, an s.h.f. wave can deal with up to 900 telephone conversations at the same time. The short range limitation can

be overcome by placing a chain of stations at intervals between two cities and repeating the messages along the line from one station to the next. This can be done automatically, and distances of up to 1,500 kilometres can be crossed, linking cities separated by deserts or forests.

If a v.h.f. wave is directed skyward at a low angle, most of the energy escapes into space. But a small fraction of it is scattered by the ionosphere and some of this returns to Earth at a distant point, where it can be picked up by a highly sensitive receiver. This approach, called "ionospheric scatter", provides reliable reception over distances of about 1,500 kilometres .

The scatter principle is also used for medium-range communication using the ultra high frequencies. Here the scattering is caused by pockets of turbulence in the troposphere about 8 kilometres above the Earth. The ranges are around 300 to 500 kilometres, suitable for communication between mainland stations and islands or oil rigs.

Radio waves can reach thousands of kilometres round the Earth by means of multiple reflections or "bounces". The "skip distances" are different for day and for night.

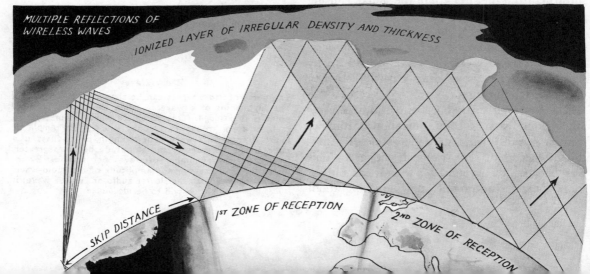

MULTIPLE REFLECTIONS OF WIRELESS WAVES

IONIZED LAYER OF IRREGULAR DENSITY AND THICKNESS

SKIP DISTANCE

1ST ZONE OF RECEPTION

2ND ZONE OF RECEPTION

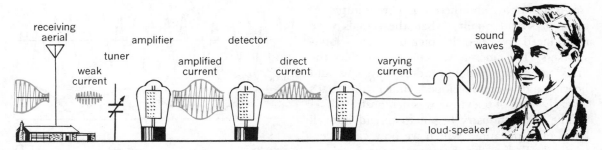

receiving aerial | amplifier | detector | sound waves
weak current | tuner | amplified current | direct current | varying current
loud-speaker

them, changes them to direct current (by means of a diode detector or rectifier) and sifts out the carrier waves. They can then make the diaphragm of the loudspeaker vibrate and send sound waves to the ears.

The Thermionic Valve

Until the 1920s nearly all the world's radio stations sent messages in Morse code. This is known as *wireless telegraphy*. The transmitters used no valves; the main methods of generating the radio waves being by spark, Poulsen arc, or by the Alexanderson high-frequency alternator. None of these methods were suitable for *radio telephony*, the electrical copying of sounds, including speech.

In 1904 Sir Ambrose Fleming had invented the thermionic diode valve, to which Lee de Forest added an extra element, called the grid, in 1906. The triode, as this device came to be known, could amplify (strengthen) weak signals. But not until 1913 was it discovered that the triode could also generate oscillations of a very pure character, which were ideal for radio telephony. (Both the diode and triode are explained in ELECTRONICS.)

During World War I there was a big step forward in the efficiency and power-handling of the triode valve. By 1918 the armed forces were using large numbers of low-power radio telephony sets. When the war ended, radio manufacturers looked around for new markets.

Radio Broadcasting Begins

Entertainment broadcasting started by accident. When testing a new station, an engineer would read out a list of names (such as railway stations) so that his colleagues listening on distant receivers could report on the strength and quality of the transmission. This was a boring business, so to give their voices a rest, they would play a gramophone record instead. People

wrote in, asking for more music. Many were amateur radio enthusiasts who had been radio operators during the war and had taken up radio as a hobby.

So the manufacturers began broadcasting music concerts and making cheap, simple receivers for sale to the public. In the United States, where almost anyone could set up and operate a radio transmitter if he wished, a number of stations soon began broadcasting. In Britain, however, the Post Office alone could grant transmitting and receiving licences. At first, it refused to grant more licences.

At last, under pressure from various "wireless societies", the Post Office issued one experimental licence, authorizing the Marconi Company to build a transmitter and broadcast a concert for half an hour each week. On February 14, 1922 the first regular broadcasts in Britain began from station 2MT in the village of Writtle in Essex. It was so successful that the Post Office issued a second licence and in May 1922 the first London station (using the call-sign 2LO) began broadcasts from London. Later that year the British Broadcasting Company, now the British Broadcasting Corporation or B.B.C., was formed and licences were issued to build stations in various parts of Britain. (See BRITISH BROADCASTING CORPORATION.)

"Listening-in" quickly became very popular. Many people built their own receivers, often known as "crystal sets", from simple kits.

The development of the triode valve led to rapid growth in this new branch of electrical engineering. The gramophone industry revived, when the use of microphones and valve amplifiers made it possible to make records electrically (see RECORDING), and there was a great improvement in sound quality when the signals were reproduced by electric pick-ups, and loudspeakers. The cinema was able to introduce the "talking picture"; public address systems and hearing aids were developed; and in the 1920s an early form of television was demonstrated.

The radio industry began to spread into all kinds of applications which we now call "electronics". Today, the thermionic valve has been largely replaced by the transistor, although it is still used where large output powers are required.

The valve also revolutionized radio communications. In 1921 a 100-kilowatt transmitter, using 54 valves, came into service at Caernarvon and sent signals to Australia. This was the end of the spark, arc and high frequency alternator systems, which could send only telegraphic messages. The new valved transmitters could now send telephony (sounds).

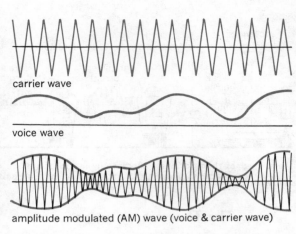

carrier wave

voice wave

amplitude modulated (AM) wave (voice & carrier wave)

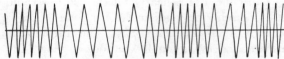

frequency modulated (FM) wave (voice & carrier wave)

How Radio Works

Sound waves, vibrating at different frequencies (see SOUND) are picked up in the studio by microphones (see MICROPHONE) and changed into electrical oscillations of the same frequencies. These signals are then passed through amplifiers to magnify them. The "audio frequencies" are then "impressed" upon higher-frequency radio waves generated in the transmitter. These radio frequencies carry the audio frequencies. The signals are "modulated" to combine them into the same wave pattern; they are then fed into the antenna from which they radiate in the form of electro-magnetic waves.

Inside the radio receiver is an arrangement of conductors (coils) and capacitors (see CAPACITOR). These provide the "tuning", so that the circuit accepts the correct signal and rejects others. Transistors (or, less often, valves) amplify the signals, which are weak when they arrive. The audio frequencies are separated and operate a loudspeaker, which changes the electrical oscillations back into sound vibrations.

Transmitting Telegraphy

Along with the development of radio transmitters, there have been many improvements in the methods of sending and receiving messages since the first days of radio. An operator tapping messages with a Morse key can transmit at only about 25 words a minute. In the modern teleprinter system, an operator types the message which is then translated into a binary number code. This is transmitted and, at its destination, the message is decoded and used to operate a teleprinter which types it out in letters again.

The telegraphic system is in the form of a pre-arranged sequence of two kinds of impulse. One is called a "mark", the other a "space". Each letter and figure has a particular combination of five marks and spaces. Fading of the signal can cause gaps or errors on the transmitted message. So the 5-unit teleprinter code is converted into a more complex one, usually a 7-unit A.R.Q. code (A.R.Q. stands for Automatic Request repetition, the Q standing for "Query".) It needs a transmitter and a receiver, as well as error-detecting equipment at each end of the radio path. As soon as an error is detected, a transmitter at the receiving station sends a signal to the "home" transmitter, which causes it to return to that point in the message where the mistake occurred and repeat it correctly. Another version of the teleprinter system uses punched paper tape to carry the coded message. (See SIGNALLING and TELEGRAPHS.)

Satellite Transmissions

By far the most important advance in recent years has been the widespread use of satellites in Earth orbit (see COMMUNICATION; SATELLITE.) In "along-the-ground" broadcasting, the ranges that v.h.f. and other high frequency bands can achieve is roughly limited to just beyond the horizon. Bouncing the signals off a satellite in space extends the "horizon" very considerably.

Suppose that a u.h.f. station in Britain wishes to contact a similar station in the United States. Normally, this can not be done because of the curvature of the Earth. If, however, a satellite is placed in orbit above the Atlantic there is a clear line of sight between it and both ground stations. Signals are transmitted from the first station to the satellite, where a receiver picks them up and amplifies them. They are then passed to a small transmitter in the satellite, which beams them towards the receiving station, where they are again amplified. One such amplifier is the maser (a word obtained from the initials of Microwave Amplification by Stimulated Emission of Radiation).

A communications satellite of this type contains all the necessary transmitting and receiving equipment, usually in duplicate. It is placed in orbit by a rocket with great precision, so that it will remain at a height of about 36,000 kilometres over a chosen spot on the Earth's surface. This is known as a "synchronous orbit". In this way the satellite is always in position to receive from the Earth stations it serves. Satellites are powered by batteries or by solar cells (which change the Sun's rays into electricity). In the future, perhaps, nuclear power will be used to give the satellites almost endless working lives. For interplanetary travel it is possible that lasers might be used. The laser's very intense beam of light can be modulated by signals to serve as a carrier wave for speech. (See LASER.)

RADIOACTIVITY. Radioactive substances are those which shoot out tiny particles or rays. Some of these substances occur in nature but others are made artificially.

Radioactivity was discovered accidentally in 1896 by the French scientist Henri Becquerel, who had stored some new photographic plates near a substance containing uranium. (A photographic plate is like a camera film except that the light-sensitive chemicals are on a glass plate instead of on a flexible film.) When the plates were developed they were found to be black all over, just as if they had been exposed to light.

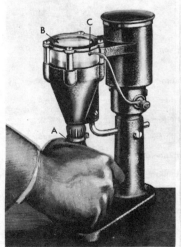
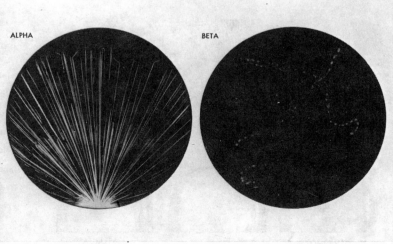

Above: A cloud chamber for studying radioactivity. It is partly filled with liquid. Squeezing the bulb (A) compresses the air inside; releasing it suddenly reduces the pressure. This creates a fog which condenses on any ions present. (See the article ION.) Tracks of ions are made by alpha and beta rays from a radioactive substance at C. Under a bright light the tracks can be seen at B. Photographs of tracks show that heavy alpha particles are rarely deflected by collisions with ions until near the end of their flight. The light beta particles are deflected and leave thin, wavy trails.

RADIOACTIVITY

Becquerel realized that some kind of radiation from the uranium must have gone through the wrapping around the plates with the same effect as light. His studies were continued by Pierre and Marie Curie (on whom there is a separate article). They discovered other radioactive elements, among them the very active one called radium. (See ELEMENT.)

The atoms of most naturally radioactive elements are heavy ones. Nearly all the weight of any atom is the weight of its nucleus, or central core (see ATOM). The nuclei of these radioactive atoms are "unstable" because they are so heavy. This means that they cannot remain permanently as they are; so they give off particles or rays and in doing so change into other atoms, ending finally as lead.

How Atoms Can Change

The atoms do not change all together. Each one changes unexpectedly at a moment that cannot be predicted. However, the time it takes for half (or any other fraction) of the atoms in a piece of radioactive material to change is always the same. The time depends on the fraction we choose. This time is called the *half life* of the substance. For example, radium has a half life of 1,622 years. If 4 grams of radium were left alone for 1,622 years, 2 grams would change into a gas called radon. After another 1,622 years, half of the remaining radium would in turn have changed into radon, leaving only 1 gram. The amount of radium remaining would be reduced by half every 1,622 years.

The nucleus of an atom is made up of two kinds of particles called protons and neutrons. The protons have electrical charges but the neutrons do not. The number of protons in a nucleus is always the same as the number of electrons moving round the nucleus and making up the rest of the atom. The way that an atom behaves chemically depends on the number of its electrons and therefore on the number of its protons, but hardly at all on the number of neutrons. Atoms with the same number of protons are called atoms of the same element.

For example, uranium, which is element number 92, has 92 protons in its nucleus and 92 electrons going round. There are several different kinds of uranium with different numbers of neutrons in the nucleus. Uranium-238, which is the most usual kind has 146 neutrons which together with the 92 protons make up its "atomic weight" of 238. On the other hand, uranium-235 has only 143 neutrons with its 92 protons.

HALF LIFE OF RADIOACTIVE MATERIALS

24-HOUR HALF LIFE

MONDAY   TUESDAY   WEDNESDAY

THURSDAY   FRIDAY   SATURDAY

ISOTOPE	HALF LIFE
Uranium—238	4,510,000,000 years
Radium—226	1,622 years
Actinium—227	21.6 years
Berkelium—249	314 days
Polonium—210	138 days
Einsteinium—253	20 days
Radon—222	3.8 days
Fermium—251	7 hours

The length of time it takes radioactive material to reduce its volume by half is the material's half life. The material above has a half life of 24 hours, so each day the pile contains only one-half as much material as it did the day before. The table on the right shows the half life of some radioactive isotopes.

Containers holding isotopes are handled with special tools which are designed so that the scientist's hands do not come too close to the isotopes. The scientist is shielded by a wall of lead bricks and a lead-glass window.

Atoms with the same number of protons but with different numbers of neutrons are called *isotopes.* Most elements have stable isotopes and radioactive ones but, for most of the lighter elements, only the stable isotopes are found naturally. Their radioactive isotopes can be made artificially by placing substances inside a nuclear reactor (see NUCLEAR POWER). Some of the neutrons moving about inside the reactor are absorbed by the nuclei of the substance which has been put in, making the nuclei unstable. Other isotopes are prepared in a particle accelerator or cyclotron, which is a machine that bombards nuclei with fast-moving particles. (This process is described in PARTICLE ACCELERATOR.)

Radioactive substances give off one or more kinds of rays, of which the best known are alpha, beta and gamma rays. *Alpha rays* are the same as the nuclei of helium atoms and so each particle consists of two neutrons and two protons. (The complete helium atom has two electrons moving around the nucleus.) They are usually shot off at tremendous speeds (up to 20,000,000 metres a second), but soon slow down and travel only a few centimetres in air. They cannot get through the human skin. *Beta rays* consist of electrons, which are tiny particles of electric charge (see ELECTRON). *Gamma rays* are electro-magnetic waves of very short wave-length (see RADIATION). They are like X-rays, but usually have higher energies; this increases their penetration (their ability to go through matter).

The rays given out by radioactive substances are *ionizing* rays, which means that they are able to break up the molecules of gases into pieces each bearing an electric charge. This property is made use of in the Geiger counter, an instrument for measuring the strength of the rays (see GEIGER COUNTER). This is the most widely used detector for radiation although other instruments which work in different ways have since been invented.

Uses of Radioactivity

Besides their use in making atomic bombs, radioactive substances have many more valuable uses in science, medicine and industry. For example, gamma rays are able to penetrate deep into human flesh and destroy particular kinds of living cells, and so can be used to destroy unwanted cell growths in the body, for example, in the treatment of some kinds of cancer. Unfortunately the rays also destroy healthy cells, so treatment must be given very carefully.

Radioactive atoms can be used to "label" substances by replacing normal atoms in them and tracing the path of the substance by detecting their radiation. In medicine, they are used to show which substances go to which part of the body—when testing a new drug, for instance. Radioactive labelling is used in chemistry and biochemistry to trace parts of molecules through a series of chemical reactions.

Gamma radiation from radioactive isotopes such as cobalt-60 are used instead of X-rays in industry for taking photographs through metal parts in order to detect flaws, cracks and faults, especially faulty welds (see WELDING). High-powered gamma rays can be used to sterilize (make germ-free) medical supplies for hospitals.

Radiocarbon Dating

One of the most interesting uses of radioactivity is in archaeology, or the study of the distant past. It is a method of finding the age of things by radiocarbon dating. Most of the carbon contained in all living things is the stable isotope carbon-12, but there is always a very tiny but constant fraction of radioactive carbon-14. This carbon-14 breaks down into other elements and has a half-life about 5,570 years.

As long as a plant or animal lives, it takes in fresh carbon (including carbon-14) from the atmosphere and in its food, and the proportion, or relative amount, of carbon-14 in its body remains unaltered. When it dies, however, the amount of carbon-14 begins to decrease. Knowing the half-life of carbon-14, scientists can find the age of any object that was once living matter, such as wood, bone, horn, grain, wool or the ashes from a wood fire, by measuring the proportion of radioactive carbon to ordinary carbon. (This does not work with coal, which although made of dead trees and plants, is so ancient that all its carbon-14 has long since decayed.) Charcoal (burned wood) taken from a pit near Stonehenge gave a date of about 1850 B.C. when tested by this method. The more recent the object's age, the more accurate radiocarbon dating is. (See also ARCHAEOLOGY.)

The age of the Earth can also be found by radioactive dating, but by using uranium (which changes into lead) and helium instead of carbon.

RADIO ASTRONOMY.

Until the middle of the 20th century, astronomers could explore the universe only by using optical telescopes to study the light from planets, stars, glowing clouds of gas, and galaxies. However, many other objects in the universe are brightest at wavelengths of radiation that are invisible. In order to "see" the stars and galaxies that emit radio waves, infrared radiation or X-rays, special telescopes and detectors are needed. The longest-established kind of "invisible" astronomy is radio astronomy. Radio astronomers have found many objects whose existence had never been suspected in optical telescopes because they do not send out much light.

The Radio Universe

The view of the universe through a radio telescope is very different from the picture obtained by optical astronomers. Radio waves can be detected from our Sun, the strength of which varies with the sunspot cycle (see SUN). One planet, Jupiter, is also a powerful radio source. This planet is surrounded by an extensive and strong magnetic field. Electrically charged particles (electrons) passing through this field emit radio waves. Beyond the solar system, radio telescopes pick up a glow of emission from the Milky Way (see GALAXIES and MILKY WAY) as well as from several of the large clouds of gas, called nebulae. Within our Galaxy there are rapidly-flashing radio sources called pulsars; these are thought to be the remains of extinct stars. Beyond the Milky Way lie remote but extremely powerful radio galaxies and quasars. From the far depths of space there is a background of radio emission left over from the fiery birth of the universe itself.

The telescopes used by radio astronomers are actually large and complicated radio antennas (aerials), generally operated by computers. In 1932 an American electrical engineer, Karl Jansky, constructed the first telescope capable of picking up waves from the Milky Way, which caused a faint hiss in an ordinary radio set. In the 1940s an English scientist, J. S. Hey, realised that strange interference on radar equipment was in fact caused by radio waves from the Sun. About this time, an American amateur astronomer, Grote Reber, built the first true radio telescope with which he detected a strong source of radio waves at the centre of the Milky Way. From these small beginnings the giant radio telescopes of the present day have evolved.

Radio Telescopes

A radio telescope has three essential components : something to reflect the cosmic radio waves, a detector to pick them up and a receiver for amplifying and recording the extremely feeble signals. The reflecting "mirror" can be either an array of many aerials connected in a special way, or a metal sheet or wire netting. It is not necessary for the reflector to be solid, and even wire netting reflects radio waves very well. Nor does the mirror need to be particularly smooth unless it is going to be used at wavelengths smaller than 10 cm. (The article RE-FLECTION explains why this is so.)

Radio telescopes are usually far bigger than optical ones. This is mainly because radio waves are about a million times longer in wavelength than light, and for that reason alone large reflectors and arrays are needed in order to make detailed maps of cosmic radio emission. A second reason for the size is that the radio signals are extremely weak, and therefore undetectable unless a large collecting area is used.

The detector is generally a simple dipole aerial or rod. This is positioned at the focus of the dish-shaped telescope; its protective housing includes an amplifier as the incoming signal is too weak to be sent to the receiver. The radio receiver is complex and normally part of a computer system. The information collected by the telescope can be processed by computer to make maps of the radio sky or to produce a "photograph" of the radio image. The receiving system may include a radio spectrometer which is capable of recording the strength of the radio signal over a narrow range of wavelengths. This particular technique can be used to identify, by means of characteristic radio signals, the atoms and molecules in gas clouds in the Milky Way.

The biggest dish telescope in Britain is the 76-metre instrument at Jodrell Bank, completed in 1957 and modernized in 1971. Other telescopes in this class are at Parkes, New South

Wales, at Goldstone, California, and Effelsberg, West Germany, where the 100-metre instrument is the world's biggest, fully-steerable reflector. In Puerto Rico engineers have constructed a 300-metre telescope by lining a natural crater with wire netting. It cannot be pointed anywhere in the sky; some flexibility results from moving the detecting dipole instead. In addition, the Earth spinning on its axis makes it possible to observe different parts of the sky at different times. The huge size of these single-dish telescopes makes them expensive and they take years to build. For these reasons a different type of telescope, in which several smaller dishes are linked, was developed.

By joining two or more dishes together electronically, some of the qualities of a very large telescope can be obtained, in particular the ability to see fine detail in a radio source. Each dish in the array is pointed at the same radio source. The Earth spinning on its axis causes the array to rotate beneath the sky. Computer analysis of the signals obtained over many days of observing the same object can then mimic the effect of a huge telescope.

A telescope of this type, 4.6 kilometres long, at Cambridge in England stands on the site of a former railway line (see the picture on the page after this one). There are others in the Netherlands and Australia.

Radiations from the powerful galaxy Cygnus A are 500 million light-years away from the Earth.

Photograph from the Hale Observatories

Courtesy, The Marconi Company

This radio telescope at Cambridge in England has eight dish aerials, four of which can be moved along a disused railway track.

At Socorro in New Mexico is the largest telescope of this type, the Very Large Array (V.L.A.), completed in 1979. It has 27 antennas, each of which is movable along the three arms of a Y-shaped array; each arm is 20 kilometres long. The V.L.A. can map small radio sources with the same precision as the best optical telescopes.

Radio telescopes on different continents can be linked electronically. This arrangement allows fine structure to be mapped in very distant radio sources in greater detail than any optical telescope has achieved.

Pulsars and Supernovas

The first pulsars were detected in Cambridge in 1968. Their radio emission consists of a series of extremely regular pulses separated by a second or less. For a time scientists thought the pulses might be interference, but they soon realized that they came from far beyond the solar system.

Hundreds of these pulsars are now known. Some send very rapid signals: 30 times a second for the one located in the Crab Nebula, and 642 times a second for one found in 1982 in the constellation Vulpecula. Pulsars are very small stars called neutron stars. They are only a few kilometres in diameter but may have nearly as much mass as the Sun. They are millions and millions of times denser than ordinary matter, consisting almost entirely of neutrons. When a supernova explosion occurs, the central core of the dying star gets compressed into a neutron star. This spins very rapidly, with a pulse being sent out every time it rotates. The neutron star in Vulpecula is spinning over 600 times every second.

The gas thrown into space by a supernova explosion may itself be a detectable radio source. One of the strongest of these is the Crab Nebula in the constellation Taurus. This glowing cloud is the remnant of a star seen to explode in 1054 A.D. Some supernova remnants are almost invisible optically but show up strongly in radio maps of the sky.

Radio Galaxies

1951 was a crucial year for the new science of radio astronomy. One of the strongest sources was found to be a galaxy 500 million light years away, then considered a fantastic distance. Astronomers realized that this object, called Cygnus A, had to be making the radio waves in some extremely powerful way in order for them to be detectable at such a distance. In fact the radiation from Cygnus A is about a million times more powerful than the waves from our own Galaxy. Hundreds of similar galaxies are now known to be radio galaxies.

The radio waves are produced by electrons travelling at the speed of light through magnetic fields that surround the galaxies. Some sources are double, some have jets and yet others have long tails as if leaving a wake caused by motion through the universe. The investigation of these energetic and remote galaxies led to an even more intriguing discovery—quasars.

Quasars

In 1963, while trying to pin-point some of the radio sources to galaxies that had been photographed, astronomers noticed one radio source that seemed to match the position of a star. The light from this "star" was found to be very much redshifted, like the light from the farthest galaxies. (Redshift is explained in the article UNIVERSE.) Astronomers deduced that radio source 3C 273 was connected with a starlike object that was shining 100 times more brightly than a whole big galaxy. (This conclusion was based on the idea that a redshift could be converted into a distance, something that some astronomers still dispute.)

Hundreds of these quasars are known. Their optical images are smaller than those of galaxies; their redshifts seem to indicate that they are farther away than most galaxies; and at that

Courtesy, Max-Planck Institute

The Effelsberg radio telescope in West Germany, with its 100-metre dish, can study quasars up to 5,000 million light-years away.

distance their radio and light emission must be hundreds of times stronger than for a "normal" galaxy in order for us to be able to detect it.

Theoretical astronomers have suggested that radio galaxies and quasars are powered by immense black holes. A black hole is a region of space where the matter has collapsed in on itself. As a consequence, the gravitational field is extremely high—so strong that even light cannot escape. If black holes have formed in the central regions of some galaxies they could grow quickly by capturing, and swallowing, other stars. A black hole of a few million solar masses would explain the power requirements of many active galaxies. A strong radio galaxy would need a black hole containing 100 million times the Sun's mass to explain the radio emission. The details of the processes are still mysterious; even the presence of such black holes has not been proven beyond doubt.

The Nature of the Universe

Radio astronomy has made two major contributions to our understanding of the universe.

Photograph from the Hale Observatories

Radio astronomers are interested in distant galaxies, such as this one in Centaurus, which give off radio waves.

The first is connected with radio galaxies and quasars. The work of radio astronomers suggests that there were once a lot more radio galaxies than there are now, because there seem to be many more of them at great distances (and therefore earlier times) than there are nearer to us. This suggests that the "steady state" theory of the universe is wrong, for according to it, the universe never changes its basic appearance.

The second discovery was that of the "microwave background radiation" in 1965. Many theorists consider this the most important finding in astronomy in the last half century. Radio astronomers in the U.S.A. found that surprisingly strong radiation was reaching the Earth, which did not seem to have any particular source. It was equally strong in all parts of the sky. Most astronomers accept that it is left over from a much earlier phase of the universe. It may even be the remains of the fireball that started the expansion of the universe. Scientists find this discovery of great interest because it suggests that the universe evolved from a very hot and dense beginning.

RADIUM is a very rare metal. It is white and shiny but darkens when exposed to the air, as it combines with the oxygen in air. It dissolves in water, giving off hydrogen gas. For most purposes a radium salt is used, made by combining radium with another substance. Examples of these salts are radium chloride, radium bromide and radium sulphate.

Radium was discovered in 1898 by Pierre and Marie Curie, on whom there is a separate article. The metal itself was not obtained in a pure state until 1910. The Curies obtained radium from a substance called pitchblende mined at a place now called Jachymov in Czechosolvakia. Supplies of pitchblende were later found at Shaba in central Africa and on the shores of the Great Bear Lake in Canada. Radium is also obtained from the ore (rock) called carnotite, which is mined in the United States and other countries.

Radium is one of the radioactive substances. These substances continually give off particles and rays, and in the process they change into other substances at a fixed rate (this is explained in the article RADIOACTIVITY). Thus the mineral uranium changes slowly into radium, which in turn changes into other substances and finally into lead. That is why some radium is always found in uranium mines. However, even the richest ores contain less than 0·3 of a gram of radium in a tonne of rock.

Radium is used because of the radiation of rays and particles which it gives off. These radiations cannot be controlled or altered, although they can be prevented from escaping by sealing the radium in a thick lead box. The radiations destroy cells in the human body, and radium in the form of radium salts or the gas radon is used in needles or capsules (small containers) for destroying unhealthy growths such as those caused by the disease cancer. As the radiation also destroys healthy cells the treatment has to be given with great care. Before the effects of radiation were understood, Marie Curie's hands suffered badly from exposure to radium.

The radiation from radium is so powerful that its rays can pass through thick pieces of steel and most other materials. Although these rays cannot be seen they affect photographic film in the same way as light. This is the principle of radiography, for "X-ray" photographs are really shadow pictures of material which is transparent to radiation. A small capsule of radon or radium salt is placed on one side of the materials being X-rayed and a piece of photographic film (shielded against light) on the other. According to the density of the material, so more or less rays pass through and show up as darker or lighter patches on the film. For instance, cracks allow more rays to pass through and they appear as dark streaks on the film. Thus X-ray films show conditions in materials which may be invisible from the outside. This is important in industry for checking for minute cracks and internal flaws in iron and steel and other metals.

RADNORSHIRE was a small county in Wales which after local government reorganization in 1974 joined with the former counties of Montgomeryshire and Brecknockshire to form the new county of Powys (see POWYS), The Radnor district is on the border with England next to Hereford and Worcester and Shropshire. The area is more English in character than most

Welsh counties, except in the extreme west, and very few of the inhabitants can speak Welsh. But the customs of the people are more Welsh than English. The Welsh name of the old shire is Sir Faesyfed.

The River Wye forms the southwestern boundary of Radnorshire while the Teme, a tributary, or branch, of the Severn, forms a large part of the northern boundary. Other rivers are the Elan, Arrowe, Lugg and Ithon.

There are many hills in Radnorshire and much of the higher ground is moorland covered with heather or bracken. In the centre of the region is Radnor Forest, where, in spite of its name, there are hardly any trees, because so many of them were cut down for shipbuilding in the past.

In the Elan Valley, or Cwm Elan, in the north-western corner of Radnor, are reservoirs from which comes water for the city of Birmingham. The valley was first taken over by the Birmingham Corporation at the beginning of the 20th century. *The House under the Water*, a novel by Francis Brett Young, describes the drowning of the Elan Valley. The Claerwen Dam stands on a river close by.

Many different kinds of wild flowers, including some rare ones, grow in Radnorshire. Among

polecat

sheep sale
Knighton

Pen-y-gareg dam

birds, buzzards are common and their mewing cry is often heard. There are also curlews and ravens. Badgers and foxes are common, and the rare polecat is also found. The Wye is a well-known salmon river and trout are found in the smaller streams.

Comparatively few people live in Radnor, the largest town being Llandrindod Wells in the west, with a population of about 3,400. This town has springs containing minerals and people drink these waters to improve their health. Although the springs have been known for several centuries, Llandrindod Wells was no more than a village until the middle of the 19th century. The town is still an active tourist centre.

Although Llandrindod Wells was the administrative centre of Radnorshire, the former county town was Presteigne, which is on the border near Hereford and Worcester and on the River Lugg. Only two other places in Radnor can be described as towns. One is Knighton, on the border between Wales and England. The other, Rhayader, is near the Elan Valley. It is a small market town and sheep fairs are held there.

Radnor is a farming area, hay and oats being grown in the valleys. Sheep-raising is the most important industry, and buyers come to the autumn sheep sales—mainly at Knighton—from all over Wales.

Ancient remains in Radnor include stone circles and burial mounds from prehistoric times, and also Roman camps. There is also the great earthwork known as Offa's Dyke, which was made by King Offa in the 8th century as the boundary between Wales and his kingdom of Mercia. Its remains are still clearly visible.

There are also ruined castles, many of which were built by the Mortimers, a powerful family of nobles who ruled the Welsh border in the middle ages. The Mortimer colours of blue and gold appear on the county coat of arms and are the colours of the grammar school at Llandrindod Wells. At Pilleth (mentioned in Shakespeare's play *Henry IV*) the Welsh under their great leader Owen Glendower defeated the English under Edmund Mortimer in 1402.

The poet Percy Bysshe Shelley lived near Rhayader in 1811 and 1812 with Harriet Westbrook, his first wife. He wrote of the Elan Valley,

"Nature is here marked with the most impressive characters of loveliness and grandeur".

RAFFLES, Sir Thomas Stamford (1781–1826), was the founder of Singapore. He was born on a ship commanded by his father off Jamaica but was educated in London. In 1805, he went to Penang in Malaya, learnt to speak Malay and became secretary of the East India Company. This British company then managed the trade affairs of India and the Far East. (See EAST INDIA COMPANY.)

It was Raffles who persuaded the British authorities to take the rich island of Java from the French, who then owned it. Troops were sent to Java in 1811 and the French were defeated. Raffles was made governor of the island and ruled it well, aiming in particular at close friendship between the Javanese and the British.

In 1881 Raffles became governor of Sumatra, another East Indian island. He governed it as well as he had governed Java, and also explored the rain forests of the island. On one expedition he discovered an enormous flower, measuring 60 centimetres across and smelling like decaying flesh. This was named *Rafflesia arnoldi*.

The Dutch, who were the rivals of the British in the East Indies, were at that time trying to seize all the rich trade of the islands for themselves. In 1819, therefore, Raffles took possession of the island of Singapore, and it became the chief port of Malaya. (See SINGAPORE.) For a long time, however, Java and Sumatra belonged to the Dutch, but in 1949 they became part of the republic of Indonesia. (See INDONESIA.)

In 1824 Raffles set sail for England, but on the way his ship blew up and he lost many of his possessions. When he finally got to England he found himself in some trouble with the East India Company, which disapproved of the freedom he had given to the local people. For the last two years of his life (he was never in good health), Raffles helped to found the Zoological Society of London.

RAGGED SCHOOLS were so called because the children who attended them were very poor and were often dressed in rags. Many of the children were homeless; some slept in doorways and passages and one little boy at a London ragged school used to make a bed for himself each night inside a big roller in Regent's Park, climbing the railings to get to it. One of the first of these schools was opened in 1818 at Portsmouth, Hampshire, by a kind-hearted cobbler called John Pounds. He persuaded about 40 "down and outs" to come to school in his small workshop. When not mending shoes, he taught them the "three Rs" (reading, writing and arithmetic), fed them and cared for them.

Other people with kind hearts started similar schools. Another cobbler opened one in London and a chimney sweep ran one at Windsor. In time influential people heard of this good work.

Radio Times Hulton Picture Library
A ragged school in London. Several classes were held in one room, the children standing round the teachers.

One was the novelist Charles Dickens, who wrote about a ragged school. It was situated in a part of London known, because of its many criminals, as "Jack Ketch's Warren". (Jack Ketch was the name of a famous hangman of the 17th century.) Describing the school, Dickens said: "it was held in a low-roofed den, in a sickening atmosphere, in the midst of taint and dirt and pestilence." However, as a result of the good work done by the school, he found it two years later to be "quiet and orderly, full, lighted with gas, whitewashed, numerously attended and thoroughly established." Eventually in 1844 Lord Shaftesbury founded the Ragged Schools Union; it collected money for the existing schools and started new ones. To the end of his life Lord Shaftesbury was the great champion of the ragged schools; when he died in 1885 there were in the crowded areas of big towns ragged schools of many kinds—day, Sunday and night schools. But by then the national system of education, begun in 1870, was already making them less and less necessary. (There is a separate article SHAFTESBURY.)

RAGTIME was a forerunner of jazz music (see JAZZ). It became popular between 1890 and 1920 in the United States, particularly in the south. Ragtime was a mixture of minstrel songs, syncopated or off-beat dance rhythms, and banjo tunes. It was usually played on the piano, and the best known of all black ragtime musicians was the composer Scott Joplin. Other ragtime musicians, such as Jelly Roll Morton and Fats Waller, became celebrated jazz artists. A typical ragtime tune has a fast, bouncy melody over a regular, almost march-like beat.

RAGWORM. Ragworms are also known as nereids or bristle-worms. Most kinds live in salt water, on the seashore. They are "segmented" worms; in other words, their bodies are divided into many segments or rings. On each segment is a pair of bristles, which the worm uses for walking and swimming. When swimming, the worm beats its body from side to side, using its bristles as paddles.

Ragworms may be brown, red or green in colour. They live in U-shaped burrows and catch other worms and small creatures for food. They defend their burrows against rivals with bites from their sharp jaws, which can give a nasty nip. The largest ragworms reach 90 centimetres in length, but most are much smaller. (See also SEASHORE.)

RAILWAYS made it possible to carry goods and people overland for long distances at high speed. Railways were first built in Great Britain and in the 1800s, as the Industrial Revolution

Photo, Science Museum, London
A horse-drawn coal wagon running on wooden rails in 1765.

developed (see INDUSTRIAL REVOLUTION), the railways were the most important and fastest-growing form of transport.

There were railways long before there were railway engines or "locomotives". As early as the 16th century, wagon-ways made of wooden rails were used to convey wagons loaded with coal from the mines in Durham and Northumberland in northeast England. It was found that horses could pull heavier loads along a smooth track than on a rough road. Later, iron plates were used to protect the wood and around 1800 L-shaped rails came into use for guiding the wagon wheels. These "plateways" and "tramways" were also used in south Wales and it was there in 1804 that the Cornish mine-owner Richard Trevithick worked a steam locomotive able to haul a 20-tonne load. With the development of the steam engine, the way was open for the start of the railway age. (See STEAM ENGINE; TREVITHICK, RICHARD.)

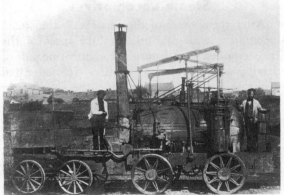

Photo, Science Museum, London
"Puffing Billy", built by William Hedley in 1813 and used to pull coal trucks in Durham.

The first public railway was the Stockton and Darlington, opened in 1825. It had been intended to use only horse-drawn carriages on this railway but George Stephenson persuaded the owners to use steam and drove "Locomotion No. 1", which was designed by himself, to pull the first train.

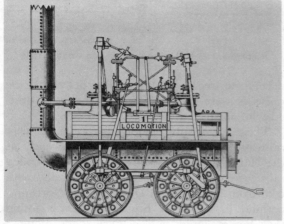

Photo, Science Museum, London

A drawing of Stephenson's "Locomotion".

In 1829 the owners of the Liverpool and Manchester Railway offered a £500 prize for the best engine. The competition was won by George Stephenson's "Rocket" which drew a train 56 kilometres in a little under two hours. This success made Stephenson and his son famous and the little "Rocket" set the design for locomotives for many years to come. (See STEPHENSON, GEORGE AND ROBERT.)

Steam Locomotives

After the success of the "Rocket", the steam locomotive was established. Like most of the early engines, the "Rocket" had only one pair of driving wheels and two cylinders. Its boiler had multiple fire-tubes rather than the single flues previously used, and the steam pressure in the boiler was almost 3.5 bars. The tender of the "Rocket" was a large water barrel fixed to a wooden frame carried by four cast-iron wheels. Together the locomotive and tender weighed about $7\frac{1}{2}$ tonnes.

For comparison, the "Britannia" class—the last standard mixed traffic steam locomotives built for British Rail—weighed 141 tonnes and carried 7 tonnes of coal. The boiler pressure of these locomotives was around 35 bars.

The weight of the steam locomotive made stronger tracks necessary, so the plates and L-shaped rails were replaced by the upright rails used today, the flange for guiding the wheel being transferred from the rail to the wheel itself. The early rails were only about 1 metre long and were supported at the joints.

The steam locomotive carries water to generate the steam and fuel (usually coal but sometimes oil or wood) to heat the boiler. The power of a steam locomotive depends largely on the boiler pressure. The boiler has tubes running through it from end to end. The flames and hot gases from the fire-box are drawn through the tubes to the smoke-box at the front, thus heating the water around the tubes and changing it into steam. The steam is usually collected under a steam-dome at the top of the boiler. It then passes through the regulator, a valve which controls the amount of steam admitted into the cylinders. In the cylinders the steam acts on the pistons which turn the driving-axle and wheels by means of the connecting rod and cranks. (See also BOILER; STEAM ENGINE.) After leaving the cylinders, the steam is led into the smoke-box through a tapered nozzle called the blast pipe underneath the chimney, or funnel. The very powerful blasts of steam from the blast pipe are the cause of the puffing noise made by the engine. They create a powerful draught which sucks the flames and hot gases from the firebox through the tubes.

Like the "Rocket", later steam locomotives still had two cylinders. But they were much larger. Many locomotives had three or four cylinders. Three- and four-cylinder engines caused less "hammer blow" (a pounding effect on the rails) and so gave a smoother run.

In a *compound* engine the steam, after being used in two high-pressure cylinders, is used again in one or two low-pressure cylinders. After being used once the steam is at a lower pressure and therefore the low-pressure cylinders, in order to give the same force as the others, have to be larger. Compounding was not widely adopted in Britain. It was considered more important to have simple engines which were easy to repair.

Three kinds of brakes were used on steam locomotives : the hand brake, the steam brake and the automatic brake. The hand brake is worked by screwing down a handle; hand and steam brakes act only on the wheels of the engine. The automatic brake, which may be either of the vacuum or the Westinghouse type, is connected between the locomotive and the coaches by flexible pipes and brakes the train as well as the engine. In Britain the vacuum brake was used on steam trains. The Westinghouse, sometimes called the air brake, is used on today's diesel and electric trains. The vacuum brake is smoother and the Westinghouse more powerful. Either will stop a 500-tonne express train running on a level line at 95 kilometres an hour within 330 metres.

A special practice in Britain was the picking-up of water from troughs between the rails. This was done at speeds of up to 120 kilometres an hour, using a scoop lowered from the tender. This made it unnecessary to stop the train in order to take on water, as was done in most other countries. It also allowed small tenders to be used and thus saved weight.

Although the great days of steam are over, steam locomotives still have a fascination for the railway enthusiast. Possibly this is because they seemed almost to be alive, and no two steam locomotives behaved in exactly the same way, even if they belonged to the same class. Even the way in which the wheels of a steam locomotive were arranged reflected the history of railway engineering, and the individuality of different locomotives.

Wheel Arrangements

With a single driving-axle the wheels tended to slip, especially on an up gradient (slope) when the rails were wet or greasy. To overcome this two axles were coupled together by a coupling-rod and thus the oO wheel arrangement of the "Rocket" became OO. This was known as a four-coupled engine. To give smoother riding round curves a leading-axle was added at the front. This also helped to distribute the weight better at the forward end and gave a oOO arrangement. The single leading-axle, called a pony-truck, was replaced by a four-wheeled bogie, giving the arrangement ooOO.

At the end of the 19th century a larger firebox became necessary for the bigger boilers. To prevent the driver's cab from overhanging at the rear end a carrying-axle was added beneath it, thus making the arrangement ooOOo. This wheel arrangement is known as the "Atlantic" because it was first used on engines serving Atlantic City, New Jersey (United States). In more mountainous districts three-coupled axles became necessary to prevent the wheels from slipping when pulling heavier trains, and thus developed the ooOOOo, or "Pacific" arrangement. An example of the Pacific wheel arrangement in Britain was the "Britannia" class of steam locomotives.

Photo, Science Museum, London

This locomotive, no. 990 of the Great Northern Railway, built in 1899, was the first British locomotive to have the 4-4-2 "Atlantic" wheel arrangement.

For freight (goods) trains and shunting work, where speeds were low, there was no need to have a leading-axle or bogie, so the six-coupled type with OOO arrangement became common in Great Britain. Then came the OOOO arrangement and, when the weight at the front became too heavy, leading axles were added to give the classes oOOO and oOOOO.

The wheel arrangements are divided into classes by a method called the Whyte notation. This is a group of three figures. The first figure represents the number of uncoupled or idle wheels at the front of the locomotive. The second figure represents the number of driving wheels and coupled wheels. The third figure gives the number of trailing wheels at the rear. Thus a Pacific locomotive, ooOOOo, becomes "4–6–2". Some of the named arrangements were:

Freight Engines

oOOO	2–6–0	Mogul
oOOOO	2–8–0	Consolidation
oOOOOo	2–8–2	Mikado
oOOOOO	2–10–0	Decapod
oOOOOOo	2–10–2	Santa Fé

Passenger Engines

ooOOo	4–4–2	Atlantic
ooOOOo	4–6–2	Pacific
ooOOOoo	4–6–4	Hudson
ooOOOOo	4–8–2	Mountain
ooOOOOoo	4–8–4	Northern

For shunting engines or those on short runs it was found convenient to replace the tender by a bunker behind the cab for coal and by tanks each side of the boiler for water. These tank engines did not have to be turned round at the end of each journey, as they allowed the engine crew quite a good view of the track and signals when going backwards. A tank engine is described by wheel arrangement or, in the Whyte notation, by adding a T, so that an "Atlantic" tank is ooOOoT, or 4–4–2T. In some European countries the types were classified by axles instead of by wheels. Hence in France an "Atlantic" is known as a 2–2–1 and a "Pacific" as a 2–3–1.

The classification for electric and diesel locomotives uses letters. B stands for a four-wheel bogie and C for a six-wheel bogie. If the axles of the bogie are separately driven without being coupled together a small "o" is added. Thus an electric locomotive carried on two six-wheel bogies, all axles separately driven, is Co-Co.

Special Locomotives

Steam locomotives used on European railways were generally larger than those used in Britain. Because they ran on longer routes they needed to carry more fuel and water. The largest United States steam locomotives had 14-wheel tenders carrying up to 28 tonnes of coal and 95,000 litres (25,000 gallons) of water.

To give greater tractive power for drawing heavy freight, special types of locomotive were developed. These included articulated locomotives such as the Garrett and Mallet designs. The word "articulated" means "jointed", and these locomotives had two separate engine units under a common boiler. The front engine was articulated, or hinge-connected to the rear engine, so that the very long locomotive could negotiate curves in the track. Some Garrett locomotives with the wheel arrangement 2–6–0 +0–6–2 were used in Britain on the Midland Region, but articulated locomotives were more often used abroad.

The largest articulated ever built was the Union Pacific Railroad's "Big Boy", built in 1941 in the United States. Considered to be the largest steam locomotive of all time, "Big Boy" weighed nearly 600 tonnes and was used for hauling freight in mountainous areas.

Other special locomotives are used on rack railways, which are found in mountainous districts. If the gradient is steeper than 1 in 14 (that is a rise of 1 metre for every 14 metres travelled) an ordinary locomotive wheel with its smooth rim may not grip the track. So a steel rack with teeth rather like the blade of a saw is fixed between the rails. The driving-axle of the locomotive carries a pinion, which is a wheel with teeth round the rim. The teeth of the pinion mesh with those of the rack, enabling the locomotive to climb the gradient without risk of its wheels slipping.

Electric Traction

In spite of all the improvements made to their design, steam locomotives are inefficient since heat loss dissipates most of the energy of the fuel burned. For this reason steam locomotives gradually became obsolete, despite their advantages of simplicity and reliability. By the 1970s there were virtually no steam locomotives left in North America and western Europe, including Britain, although they were still used (but in declining numbers) in Africa and Asia, particularly in India. Everywhere the more efficient and economical electric traction has taken over.

The first electric locomotive was demonstrated in Berlin in 1879. In 1890 the City and South London Railway opened an underground service of electric trains running beneath the River

British Rail operates some of the busiest commuter routes in the world. This electric commuter train has sliding doors.

Thames. (See UNDERGROUND RAILWAYS.) Italy had a main-line electric service in 1902 and electrification quickly spread to other parts of Europe and beyond.

Electric locomotives have several advantages. They are more economical and efficient than steam locomotives, are quieter and produce no smoke or fumes. They can develop greater power, particularly when starting or climbing a gradient. The higher power allows an electric train to reach top speed in a shorter time than a steam train. Against this must be set the cost of installing the power lines and other equipment needed—and the rising cost of generating electricity.

The principle of electric traction, or hauling power, is to make electricity at a power station and carry it to an electric locomotive or to a "motor car". A motor car is an ordinary passenger coach with a cab for the motorman, or driver, at one end. The electric motors are placed near the axles and drive them through gearing (see ELECTRIC MOTOR; GEARS), all the motors being controlled by handles in the cab.

The train obtains electric current either from a third rail fixed on insulators (see ELECTRICITY) between or to one side of the rails for the wheels or from an overhead wire. On suburban lines, which generally use fairly low voltages (about 660 volts), the third rail system is suitable. The current is collected by steel shoes on the motor cars which press against the third rail. This system is used on the Southern Region of British Rail, which is the largest suburban electric railway in the world. It uses direct current. A French electric locomotive, operating on 1,500 volts direct current, set a world speed record of 330 kilometres an hour in 1955.

Many main-line electric railways use alternating current, which can be sent long distances through wires with little loss if at high voltage, say 25,000 volts. Such high voltage is unsafe to use in the motors, so it is changed to a lower voltage by transformers in the locomotive (see TRANSFORMER). The locomotive collects the current from the overhead wires by means of a pantograph, which consists of a metal wiper mounted on rods and pressed against the wire by springs. This is the system used on fast Inter-City passenger services by British Rail.

Diesel Locomotives

Diesel locomotives were first used for shunting in 1925 and grew steadily more popular, espe-

Courtesy, British Rail

(1) The "Caledonian" running between Euston and Glasgow in the days of steam. (2) A diesel engine hauling the "Flying Scotsman" between King's Cross and Edinburgh. (3) The "Torbay Express" running beside the sea in Devon on its way from Paddington. (4) An electric locomotive using the overhead system hauling a passenger train beside the M1 motorway south of Rugby. (5) The "Bournemouth Belle" in the days of steam. This line now uses the third-rail system of electrification.

cially in the United States and Canada, where they rapidly replaced steam locomotives. British Rail has several hundred diesel main-line and shunting locomotives as well as a large number of diesel-car trains.

Diesel rail traction usually depends on the use of diesel engines to drive dynamos which make electric current (see DYNAMO). The current is led to electric motors called traction motors which drive the axles in much the same way as those of an electric train. The diesel engine itself is an internal combustion engine that works in the same way as those in buses and large lorries. It is explained in the article DIESEL ENGINE. A diesel-electric locomotive is really an electric locomotive which carries its own power station.

A German design of diesel locomotive uses hydraulic instead of electric transmission, and locomotives of this type have worked on the Western Region of British Rail. For shunting, where only low powers are required, direct mechanical drive may be used. In the United States and Canada a diesel may haul its train over distances of 4,500 kilometres. In these countries "slave" diesels are positioned in the middle of trains 1,000 metres long and controlled by radio from the head-on locomotive.

Gas-turbine-electric locomotives are the most powerful engines in the world. In this type of locomotive the dynamo, instead of being driven by a diesel engine, is driven by a gas turbine (which is explained in the article INTERNAL COMBUSTION ENGINE). The French Train à Grand Vitesse (TGV) reached a speed of 380 km/h in 1981, making it the world's fastest train.

British Rail's High Speed Train (HST) is diesel-powered, capable of 200 km/h on straight stretches. The even faster Advanced Passenger Train (APT), capable of 240 km/h, has a special tilting suspension to give a smooth ride round curves but has not proved as successful as had been hoped.

Railways in Britain

The earliest line in southern England was that between Canterbury and Whitstable, opened in 1830. It included the world's first railway tunnel, but since much of the line was uphill the trains were hauled up the slopes by a cable worked by a fixed winding-engine.

From these beginnings railways sprang up in all parts of Britain. Most of them were short lines separated from each other and it was not for many years that they were linked together. An early example was the Liverpool and Manchester Railway, built with double tracks for its whole length of 50 kilometres, a distance which was usually covered in about 90 minutes. It was opened in 1830 and later was linked with the first long-distance main line, which was opened in 1838 between London and Birmingham. These railways were united in 1846 to form the London and North Western Railway, which later spread to the Scottish border at Carlisle and to Holyhead, whence it ran steamers to Ireland. It spread westwards to Hereford and Swansea and eastwards to Huddersfield, Leeds, Peterborough and Cambridge. The Great Western

Two very different trains. Right: The last broad-gauge through train leaving Paddington station in 1892. After this, the G.W.R. changed to standard-gauge track. Below: The French Train à Grand Vitesse (TGV) capable of speeds up to 380 km/h.

Right: photo, Science Museum, London.
Below: courtesy, French Railways

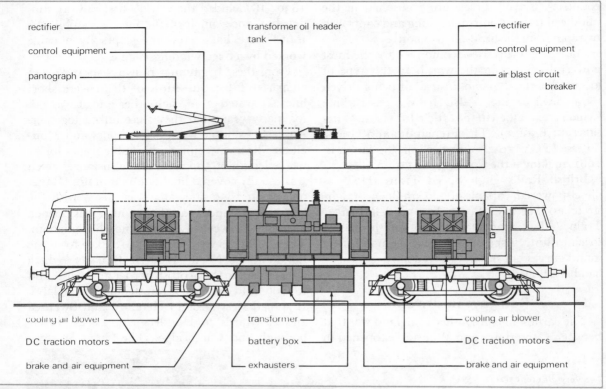

rectifier

control equipment

pantograph

transformer oil header tank

rectifier

control equipment

air blast circuit breaker

cooling air blower

DC traction motors

brake and air equipment

transformer

battery box

exhausters

cooling air blower

DC traction motors

brake and air equipment

Photograph: courtesy, British Rail

The diagram above shows an electric locomotive of British Rail. For electrified services many bridges over the track were rebuilt to make room for the overhead power wires. The electric current, which is supplied at 25,000 volts, is transferred from the wires to the locomotives by the flexible pick-up (called a pantograph) seen on the roof. The Class 86 locomotives have the Bo-Bo wheel arrangement, with two four-wheeled bogies each axle of which is separately driven, and a maximum power of more than 2,000 kilowatts. Notice the excellent view ahead provided by the driver's position. In front of him is the dial of the automatic warning system. His right hand is on the speed controller and the lever just below it is the forward-and-reverse handle.

Railway ran from London to Bristol, stretching to Exeter, Plymouth and Penzance and also through Birmingham and Worcester to Chester and Birkenhead.

The engineer of the Great Western was the famous Isambard Brunel (see separate article) who, to permit high speeds, adopted the broad gauge of 7 feet (2·1 metres) between the running rails instead of the 4 feet 8½ inches (1·4 metres) chosen earlier by George and Robert Stephenson. This narrower gauge was the distance between the rails in the old wagon-ways and, so it is said, the distance between the wheels on Roman chariots. The G.W.R. broad gauge was altered to 4 feet 8½ inches in 1892.

In southern England there was the London and South Western Railway running to Southampton, Exeter and Plymouth and also the London, Brighton and South Coast Railway. The Kent coast towns were served by two railway systems: the South Eastern and the London, Chatham and Dover, each of which had its own cross-Channel steamboat service to France. They were united as the South Eastern and Chatham Railway very early in the 20th century. The S.E.C.R. joined the L.S.W.R. and L.B.S.C.R. to form the Southern Railway in 1923.

In eastern England the Great Eastern Railway linked London with Essex, Suffolk, Norfolk and Cambridgeshire and the Great Northern Railway formed an east-coast route between London and Doncaster. From Doncaster northwards to Berwick-on-Tweed ran the trains of the North Eastern Railway. These three lines and the Great Central, which ran from London to Manchester and Sheffield, were united to form the London and North Eastern Railway in 1923. The other railway to join them was the North British, which was the biggest of the Scottish lines. It ran from Berwick through Edinburgh and Dundee to Aberdeen, and through Glasgow to Mallaig in the west Highlands.

The Midland Railway fanned out from Derby to York, London, Bournemouth, Swansea and Carlisle, where it linked with the Glasgow and South Western. From Carlisle the Caledonian Railway formed the northern part of the west-coast route to Glasgow, Edinburgh, Perth and Aberdeen. The Highland Railway ran northwards from Perth to Inverness and Wick. The Railway Act of 1921 united the L.N.W.R., the M.R., the C.R., the H.R. and the G. and S.W.R., together with the Lancashire and Yorkshire Railway joining Liverpool with York and Goole, to form the largest system in Great Britain. This was called the London, Midland and Scottish Railway.

There were many other smaller lines, but from 1923 onwards almost the whole railway system in Great Britain was divided between four large railways. These were the Southern, which was 3,470 kilometres long; the Great Western (6,550 kilometres); the London and North Eastern (10,193 kilometres) and the London, Midland and Scottish (10,911 kilometres).

On January 1, 1948, these four railways, which had been built and managed by private companies, were "nationalized", or taken over by the state. They were called British Railways and in 1965 renamed British Rail. They are divided into five regions—Southern, Western, Eastern, London Midland and one called the Scottish Region which includes all the lines in Scotland. The railways in Northern Ireland were operated by the Ulster Transport Authority.

The four great railway companies owned other property besides railways. They had fleets of steamers on cross-Channel and short sea routes and large numbers of hotels. For the most part they built locomotives, carriages and wagons in their own works at Crewe and Derby (L.M.S.R.), Doncaster and Darlington (L.N.E.R.), Swindon (G.W.R.) and Ashford and Eastleigh (S.R.). Also they owned fleets of lorries and carts for collecting and delivering goods and held part of the ownership of a number of the large provincial bus companies. They owned and operated ports such as Southampton, Cardiff and Hull. These properties were taken over by the state when the railways were nationalized. The Underground railways in the London area are not operated by British Railways but, together with the bus services in the capital, come under the London Transport Executive. (See UNDERGROUND RAILWAYS.)

Some figures will give an idea of the size of British Rail (B.R.) and what has happened since

Courtesy, British Rail

The old-style signal box with windows overlooking the track and rows of shining steel levers is disappearing with the semaphore-type signal and the steam locomotive. British Rail's signal box at Watford Junction on the London Midland Region has an illuminated diagram of the track, and switches on the control panel operate the colour-light signals and points along the permanent way.

it was nationalized in 1948. The length of track open is about 18,600 kilometres (31,600 in 1948). This figure is obtained by adding up the distances between all the places linked by rail. The actual length of track is much more, partly because some stretches have 2, 4 or even 8 parallel tracks and partly because of the many sidings. The total is about 49,400 kilometres (84,000 in 1948).

From 1955 there was a rapid and complete replacement of steam locomotives, of which there were 20,200 in 1948, by diesel and electric units, many of them "multiple-unit" trains, where the power unit is incorporated in the passenger-carrying vehicles. Multiple-unit trains may consist of 2 to 12 or more cars and can be driven from either end, thus saving time at terminal stations and avoiding locomotive movements. On some S.R. electric trains the locomotive remains at one end of the train in whichever direction the train is running. This arrangement is also possible with diesels.

British Rail finished with steam traction on its standard gauge lines in August 1968; Britain had started with steam in 1825. British Rail has about 3,700 diesel, and more than 300 electric locomotives. Locomotive-hauled passenger coaches number more than 7,000 and multiple-unit diesel cars 3,600, with 7,000 electric cars, compared with a total fleet of 40,350 in 1948. Parcel, mail and other vans total about 6,200. Freight train vehicles, including company-owned, oil-tank and bulk cement wagons, total about 240,000; in 1948 the railways owned no less than 1,160,000.

The use of containers for carrying road-rail freight has developed rapidly and "freight-liner" trains, carrying containers only, operate at high speeds between industrial centres such as Glasgow, Manchester, Cardiff and London. A container may be shipped from Liverpool to Budapest or Istanbul, or from Tilbury or Felixstowe to Montreal, New York, Freemantle or Sydney. Each container can carry about 20 tonnes and this system greatly speeds the carriage of freight.

The number of stations has been reduced to about 2,400 for passengers and 600 for freight in order to provide worth-while loads between important places and to get rid of stops and staff at wayside stations. British Rail carries about 800 million passengers each year; the average passenger journey is about 35 kilometres. Freight traffic amounts to nearly 189 million tonnes, of which more than half is coal and coke; the average journey is about 100 kilometres and the average load 223 tonnes, although some train loads are over 1,500 tonnes. Speeds vary according to weight of train, gradients and curves, but "freightliner" trains can run at 110 kilometres an hour.

British Rail's fastest passenger trains, the diesel-powered high-speed trains (HSTs) run at up to 200 kilometres an hour. The record speed for a steam train of 203 kilometres an hour was reached for a short distance downhill between Grantham and Peterborough with a train of eight coaches drawn by L.N.E.R. Pacific-type locomotive "Mallard" on July 3, 1938.

Railways outside Britain

The first steam railway in France was opened near Lyons in 1830 and the first in Germany, between Nuremberg and Fürth, was opened in 1835, the engine driver being an Englishman. Belgium opened its first line between Brussels and Malines in the same year. The first Italian railways began in the 1840s and the earliest Spanish line was opened in 1848.

The railways of continental Europe are owned and run by the governments of the different countries. This is the general practice nearly everywhere, the important exceptions being the railways in the United States, which have always been owned by large companies, and the Canadian Pacific Railway. One of the most exciting railway contests was held in the 1860s between two American companies to see which could build the longer line. The Union Pacific Railroad started westwards from the Missouri River and the Central Pacific Railroad started eastwards from the Pacific coast. The two met at Promontory, Utah, where a golden spike was driven in 1869 to celebrate the completion of the first line across America.

Although there are many different gauges, the United States and Canadian lines have the same standard 4 feet 8½ inches gauge as the British, and so have most of the railways of continental Europe except mountain lines. This is partly because many of the locomotives for the earliest railways were built by British engineers. Spanish and Portuguese lines have a gauge of 5 feet 6 inches (1·7 metres) and those of the U.S.S.R. and Finland one of 5 feet (1·5 metres). However, a locomotive built at Glasgow could, if it were not too heavy for the bridges or too big for the tunnels, travel all the way to Istanbul in Turkey and then, after being ferried across the Bosporus, go on to Baghdad or Cairo.

Steamers have been built to carry locomotives, carriages and wagons across the North Sea between Harwich and Zeebrugge and across the English Channel between Dover and Dunkirk. Thus a wagon loaded in Sicily can be hauled to Inverness for unloading. Similar train-ferries run across the Baltic Sea, between Italy and Sicily, and across Lake Michigan (United States).

Australian railways have been built to several gauges. New South Wales uses 4 feet 8½ inches, South Australia and Victoria use 5 feet 3 inches (1·6 metres) and Western Australia and Queensland 3 feet 6 inches (1·1 metres). The Trans-Australian Railway, which links Kalgoorlie in Western Australia with Port Augusta in South Australia across more than 1,500 kilometres of waterless desert, was completed in 1917 with a gauge of 4 feet 8½ inches. Railway engineering has presented great problems in New Zealand, where the mountains have made steep slopes and long tunnels necessary. A gauge of 3 feet 6 inches is used, as is also the case in South Africa, Rhodesia, Nigeria, Ghana, Sudan and some other parts of Africa. Other African lines, however, have a gauge of 1 metre. They include the East African Railways of Kenya, Uganda and Tanzania. Most South American lines are either 5 feet 6 inches or metre-gauge, as are those of India and Pakistan. Ireland has a gauge of 5 feet 3 inches.

The chief advantage of narrow gauges is that they allow the line to follow sharper curves, so that in mountainous country there is less need for cuttings, tunnels, embankments and bridges. The broader the gauge, however, the greater the loads that can be carried. Broad gauges help towards faster and more comfortable travel.

Canada is served by two great railways and several smaller ones. The Canadian National Railway, which claims to be the largest on the continent, is a government-owned line running right across Canada. The Canadian Pacific Railway belongs to a private company. It was intended from the beginning as a trans-continental line and ran its first train from Montreal to Port Moody near Vancouver in 1886. Nowadays the journey takes three-and-a-half days.

The United States has a network of lines belonging to a number of companies, of which the oldest is the Baltimore and Ohio, which started in 1830 using horse-drawn cars. Some of the most beautiful railway runs in the world are those crossing the Rocky Mountains through passes such as the Yellowhead Pass, the Kicking Horse Pass and the Raton Pass. Most of these lines go through long tunnels, such as the Cascade Tunnel, 12·5 kilometres long between Skykomish and Appleton (Washington). The Southern Pacific route crosses the Great Salt Lake in Utah by an embankment about 45 kilometres long.

Other continents have examples of great feats of railway engineering. There is a separate article on the Trans-Siberian Railway, which crosses nearly the whole of the U.S.S.R. The

Swiss railways are famous for their tunnels under the Alps, of which the greatest is the Simplon Tunnel to Italy. It is more than 19 kilometres long and consists of two tunnels, one for trains in each direction. The St. Gotthard Tunnel farther to the eastward is about 14 kilometres long. The oldest of the Alpine tunnels is the Mont Cenis between France and Italy, which was opened in 1871. Another long railway tunnel is that under the Apennine Mountains in Italy with a length of 18 kilometres. The longest railway tunnel in Great Britain runs under the estuary of the River Severn and is 6·9 kilometres long.

All along the southern coast of France and into Italy as far as Leghorn, the railway hugs the Mediterranean coast for more than 800 kilometres, passing through many tunnels. The whole of the Italian part of this route is electrified. An interesting railway in northern Europe is the line built to carry iron ore (earth and rock containing iron) from Kiruna in northern Sweden to the port of Narvik in Norway. This railway passes through many snowsheds, which are structures built over the track to prevent it from becoming blocked by drifting snow.

In South America the railways from the Pacific coast have to climb great heights to reach places near the Andes Mountains or to cross the ranges. At Punto Alto in northern Chile the metre-gauge line reaches a height of 4,800 metres above sea level. The Central Railway of Peru, which is of standard gauge, zigzags its way up to a height of 4,829 metres above sea level at La Cima. Instead of going round a sharp curve at the end of each stretch of the zigzag, the train stops and the points are changed so that it can reverse up the next stretch. It is very difficult to work a locomotive at these heights because of the thin air, which gives people headaches and makes physical effort exhausting. It also affects the efficiency of the locomotive.

For gradients steeper than about 1 in 14 it is usual to have rack railways, which are explained in the previous article. This type of railway is used for crossing the Andes between Argentina and Chile but is to be found mainly in Switzerland, where the metre-gauge Jungfrau Railway reaches a height of nearly 3,500 metres above sea level. The only example in Britain is on a sec-

Barnaby's Picture Library

The mountain railway in the Bernese Oberland, Switzerland, leading from Mülenen to the top of the 2,355 metre Niesen peak.

tion of the Snowdon Mountain Railway in Wales.

In crowded districts where land is expensive monorail (single-rail) railways are sometimes built. The single rail is mounted from tall towers and the carriages are hung from it. A railway of this kind is used for local passenger traffic at Wuppertal in Germany.

The Permanent Way

The finished track of a railway is called the permanent way. The word permanent means "lasting for ever", but in fact the rails wear out and the road-bed needs constant attention. The track is laid on firm soil on which is first put a layer of ashes to provide good drainage. Above the ashes is spread a bed of ballast about 22 centimetres thick, consisting of granite, limestone or slag broken into small pieces. On top of the ballast are laid at intervals of about 75 centimetres wooden sleepers which have been treated with creosote or other chemicals to make them last longer. A thinner layer of top ballast is laid to fill the gaps between the sleepers. Steel sleepers are sometimes used in tropical countries where there are insects which eat wood. Reinforced concrete sleepers (see CONCRETE) may also be used but they are heavy and liable to crack. The rails are usually made with flat bottoms in lengths of up to 30 metres or more and fixed to the sleepers by means of springy steel spikes driven into the wood on both sides of the rail. This flat-bottomed rail is sometimes called a "vignole", after the English engineer Charles Vignoles who is credited with its invention in the 1830s. Another kind of rail which was for long popular in Britain was the so-called "bullhead" type, which has a fairly narrow base. It is supported in a cast-iron "chair" which is perman-

ently screwed to the sleeper. A wooden or metal wedge called a key holds the rail in position.

One length of rail is joined to the next by fishplates, which are pairs of steel plates bolted to the ends of each rail. These joints are the cause of the "clicking" noise made by the train and also of most of the wear of rail-ends and wheels. On main lines the rails may be welded into lengths of 400 metres or more. This "ribbon rail" is laid on concrete sleepers by British Rail.

The weight which the permanent way has to carry is measured by the greatest weight borne by any particular axle or group of axles. With a heavy British locomotive this is about 25 tonnes, but on some railways abroad it may be as much as 35 tonnes. To strengthen the track the sleepers are laid closer together, the depth of ballast beneath them is increased and heavier rails are used. The rails used in Great Britain weigh about 55 kilograms a metre.

British Rail has laid some experimental paved track, which has neither sleepers nor ballast, the rails being fastened directly to a continuous slab of reinforced concrete. This kind of track can be laid by a paving machine, similar to those used to build motorways.

Signals

When railways began, the engine driver had to stop his train if he saw another train or an obstacle in front of him. The brakes in those days were weak and in an emergency the driver had to reverse his engine. The first recorded accident occurred near Manchester in September 1830, when the statesman William Huskisson was knocked down and killed by the engine "Northumbrian" on the day the Liverpool and Manchester Railway was opened.

To give increased safety, the railways introduced a system in which a ball was raised on a high post to let the driver know the time interval since the passing of the last train.

The coming of the electric telegraph made possible a much better system as it allowed one signalman to communicate without delay with another in the next block post. (The *block* is the distance between two signalmen's posts.) The important principle which is still followed is that two trains must not be allowed to be in the same

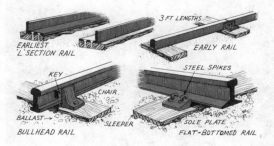

EARLIEST 'L' SECTION RAIL   3 FT LENGTHS   EARLY RAIL

KEY   STEEL SPIKES   CHAIR   BALLAST   SLEEPER   SOLE PLATE   BULLHEAD RAIL   FLAT-BOTTOMED RAIL

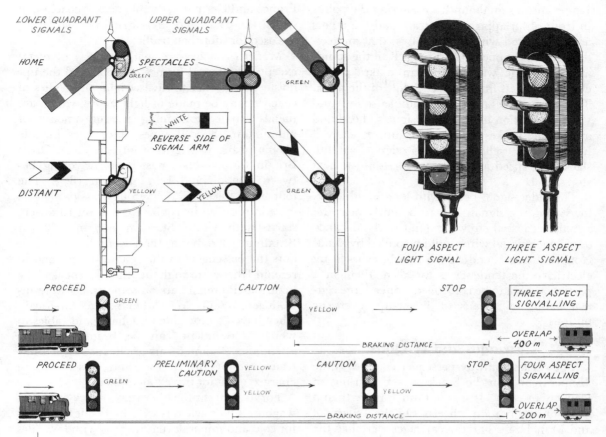

LOWER QUADRANT SIGNALS

UPPER QUADRANT SIGNALS

HOME

SPECTACLES

GREEN

REVERSE SIDE OF SIGNAL ARM

WHITE

GREEN

DISTANT

YELLOW

YELLOW

GREEN

FOUR ASPECT LIGHT SIGNAL

THREE ASPECT LIGHT SIGNAL

PROCEED

GREEN

CAUTION

YELLOW

STOP

THREE ASPECT SIGNALLING

BRAKING DISTANCE

OVERLAP 400 m

PROCEED

GREEN

PRELIMINARY CAUTION

YELLOW

YELLOW

CAUTION

YELLOW

STOP

FOUR ASPECT SIGNALLING

BRAKING DISTANCE

OVERLAP 200 m

block section on the same track at any one time.

The semaphore arm later took the place of the hoisted ball. It was easier to see and for use at night was fitted with "spectacles" of coloured glass arranged so that a lamp fitted to the signal was covered by the red glass when the arm was horizontal and by the green glass when the arm was sloping down.

Some countries use three-position semaphores whose third position—sloping upwards—is used as a warning signal. In Great Britain the warning signal shows a yellow light and warns the driver that his next signal is likely to be at danger, showing a red light. He must on no account pass a red-light or stop signal. The warning signal is known in Great Britain as a "distant". If of semaphore type, the blade has a fish-tail end and is painted yellow with a black band. Stop signals have square-ended blades painted red with a white band.

The modern signal is usually of colour-light type without a semaphore arm and shows green to mean "clear", yellow as "warning" and red for "stop". The advantage of the colour-light signal is that it appears the same to the engine driver by night as by day. It can be seen from long distances even in bright sunlight and is operated from a power supply. The signal system is so arranged that a driver should never meet a signal at red without being first warned of it by a signal at yellow. Two lights at yellow, one above the other, mean that the next signal is at yellow.

Signalling systems vary widely in different countries but the general principles are the same. To obtain the greatest safety, automatic train control can be used. One method uses an electric current sent through the running rails which can be made to apply the brakes if the train passes a signal at danger when the block section it enters is occupied by another train. Another safety system is called the "track circuit" as the track acts as a circuit, or path, for the electric current.

It prevents a signalman from altering the points in front of an approaching train and the points are interlocked with the signals so that an accident cannot happen. On British Rail the standard automatic warning system makes use of electro-magnets fitted in the middle of the track. This system gives the driver audible (sound) and visual indication in his cab of signals ahead and applies the brakes of the train automatically if he passes a yellow warning signal without slackening speed in readiness to halt at the next stop signal.

The older signal boxes with long hand levers for setting the signals had to be fairly near the signals because there was a limit to the distance over which signal wires could be pulled by hand. Now that points and signals can be worked by electricity the tendency is for all of them in a particular area to be controlled from a large central cabin by means of finger-tip levers or buttons.

Carriages and Wagons

The earliest railway passenger coach was the "Experiment" on the Stockton and Darlington Railway in 1825. It was not much more than a horse-drawn box on wheels. On the Liverpool and Manchester line the carriages were like the stage-coaches used on the roads except that they ran on railway wheels. Thus railway carriages are still called coaches and the man in charge of them, like the man in charge of the stage-coach, is called the guard.

For many years passenger coaches had two axles and four wheels but as they became longer a third central axle was added to make six-wheelers. The standard passenger coach has a steel underframe mounted on swivelling trucks called "bogies". The bogies ease the movement around curves and each bogie may have four or six wheels. The latest British Rail "Inter-City" coaches are more than 22 metres long and 3 metres wide, weighing 34 tonnes and supported on four-wheel bogies. They provide 72 second-class seats in open saloons and 48 seats in the first-class version. British Rail's Advanced Passenger Train has a suspension system which automatically tilts up to 9 degrees as it glides round curves. In some parts of the United States,

France and Germany, double-decker coaches, in which the passengers are carried on two levels, are used for suburban traffic.

Modern coaches are made entirely of metal except for internal fittings of wood and the upholstery. In order to save weight, the bodies of coaches may be made of light alloys, which are metals usually containing a large amount of aluminium. Special types of coaches include sleeping cars, which were introduced in Great Britain for first-class passengers travelling between London and Edinburgh in 1873. The four-berth "sleepers" for second-class passengers were introduced in 1928. Restaurant cars were started in the United States in 1867 and in Great Britain in 1879, but as there were then no corridors the passengers in the restaurant car had to remain there throughout the journey. The luxurious Pullman cars on some trains were introduced by G. M. Pullman, an American. They have comfortable armchairs and tables to which refreshment can be brought by the attendants. Pullman cars are available on a few trains run by British Rail and passengers are charged extra for travelling in them.

For freight traffic there are many kinds of wagons. Open wagons with high sides are used for coal and minerals, flat wagons with low sides or no sides at all or timber, steel and goods of that kind, and roofed or box vans for goods liable to be damaged by weather. Some wagons have end doors, some have side doors and many for coal and minerals have bottom doors in the form of a "hopper" through which their contents can be allowed to pour out. Many special kinds of vans and wagons are used for goods such as salt, acids, bananas, meat, oils, lime, tar and so forth. A modern method of reducing delay and avoiding damage to goods is by the use of containers. The goods are packed into the containers at the works or factory and the containers are then lifted bodily on to lorries which take them to the freight station. There the containers are lifted on to specially designed railway wagons. The process is reversed at the far end of the journey.

RAIN is caused by the water vapour in the atmosphere condensing. A good deal of the Earth's water takes part in a kind of repeated

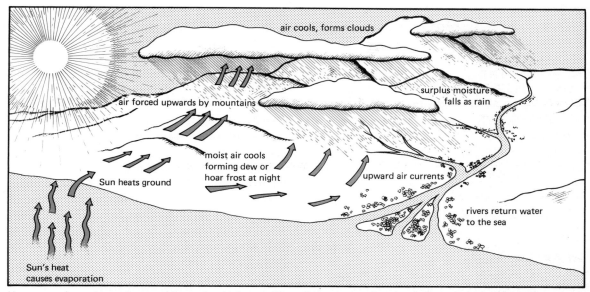

air cools, forms clouds

surplus moisture
falls as rain

air forced upwards by mountains

moist air cools
forming dew or
hoar frost at night

upward air currents

Sun heats ground

rivers return water
to the sea

Sun's heat
causes evaporation

How water from the sea is turned into rain. Moisture rising off the sea on a hot day passes over sun-warmed ground and
rises to condense in cooler air. Where there are mountains it has to rise still higher.

movement called a cycle. After the rain falls some of this water is evaporated, or turned into vapour, with the help of the sun and the wind. This happens both to the water on trees and fields and to that in seas and lakes. In some conditions, the water vapour in the air changes into clouds and later falls as rain, and so the cycle begins again.

The way in which heat changes water into water vapour, or steam, can be seen every time the sun draws the water out of wet clothes hung on the line. In just the same way, the sun draws moisture from all stretches of water, from the dew on the grass and from damp ground. The process is explained in the article EVAPORATION.

On the other hand, people can see their breath on a cold day because the water vapour in the warm air they breathe out is changed to mist, or tiny drops of water. This formation of water from its vapour is called *condensation*.

The air of the atmosphere always contains a certain amount of water vapour and some of this, if cooled sufficiently, condenses into droplets. The droplets may form on dust particles in the air, and to begin with they are tiny. If the air continues to cool the drops grow bigger and begin to fall. Droplets about one-fifth of a millimetre across may fall at the rate of about one

metre a second. Those in heavy tropical showers may be several millimetres across.

Condensation in the atmosphere, caused by cooling, arises in three main ways. The first way is when air passes over ground at a lower temperature. This condensation is often visible as dew or hoar frost (see DEW). Again, air may mix with other air at a lower temperature and result in fog or cloud (see FOG). Condensation may also be caused by rising air. This is the main cause of cloud and rain. As air rises the atmospheric pressure becomes less and the air expands, or becomes rarefied. This results in the air becoming cooler. The air can then hold less moisture and the surplus moisture forms clouds and finally falls out as rain or snow. Rising air may be caused by the sun in heating the ground, resulting in *convectional* or *instability* rains, as in thunderstorms and monsoons (see MONSOON and THUNDER). Rising air also occurs when a warm air mass rises over colder air and this gives what is known as *cyclonic* or *depressional* rain (see WEATHER). A third type of rising air occurs when air is forced over hills or mountain ranges, and this gives what is known as *orographical* rain. Most rain is due to a mixture of these three causes, although generally one has been playing a more important part than the other two.

The amount of rainfall is also influenced by other factors (see WEATHER). Areas over which little moist air passes are naturally dry. In general air masses which have travelled over a long stretch of ocean give a greater rainfall than those which have passed over land surfaces. Air masses travelling towards the poles—that is, advancing into higher latitudes—can give more rain than those travelling from colder into warmer areas, where the air can hold more moisture. The fall in the polar areas, mainly in the form of snow, is usually less than 250 millimetres a year. Air masses which have travelled over mountains become drier and also warmer. Thus some of the deserts are under the lee of mountain ranges. The wettest parts of Australia are all on the fringe of the continent and the interior has less than 250 millimetres a year.

The direction of the flow of air over any area may change during the year and give rise to rainy and dry seasons, or a seasonal rainfall. Most tropical areas, except the equatorial belt and the great hot deserts, have rain in summer. This rain is chiefly convectional. India and southeast Asia have in summer a great inflow of moist air called the monsoon. (See MONSOON.) In the cool season these tropical lands are dry. The equatorial belt, on the other hand, has heavy rain all the year round.

Places in middle latitudes, such as the British Isles and New Zealand, and on the western sides of the continents, such as western Europe and British Columbia, have no dry season. In similar positions but somewhat nearer the equator are a group of areas which are sometimes said to have a Mediterranean rainfall, when the rainy season is the winter half of the year. Besides the Mediterranean countries themselves these areas include California, central Chile and the southwest corners of Africa and Australia.

Rainfall is measured either in inches or millimetres. It is measured by a special instrument known as a rain-gauge. The meteorologist uses the word "rain" to cover all condensation, or precipitation, caught in a rain-gauge. This includes rain, hail, snow, dew and hoar-frost (rime). Any solid precipitation, such as hail or snow, is converted to water before it is measured. A measurement of 25 millimetres of rain for a day means that if the rain had been allowed to accumulate the depth would have been 25 mm.

Wet and Dry

The figures for average annual rainfall (in millimetres) in some large cities are : Berlin 580, Bombay 1,725, Cairo 25, London 580, Madrid 405, New York 1,090, Paris 700, Tokyo 1,625. (The expression "average rainfall" is explained in the article AVERAGES.)

The wettest place in the world is probably Cherrapunji in Assam (northeast India), with an average of 10,820 millimetres a year, most of which falls during the summer monsoon, from April to September. As for the driest, it seems that no measurable rain has fallen in the Atacama Desert of northern Chile for centuries.

Rain-making

Without rain, few plants or animals can thrive. A long period without rain (a drought) can cause enormous damage to crops and livestock. Where rains fall only at certain seasons, the failure of the rains to arrive can mean hunger and even death for many people.

So it is not surprising that since ancient times people have prayed to rain gods and spirits and also performed special ceremonies to "make rain". Scientists too would like to be able to make it rain, and there have been various experiments at rain-making.

One method tried is to "seed" clouds with solid crystals of carbon dioxide, either from an aircraft or small rocket. The crystals act (like the natural ice particles in the clouds) as "cores" around which tiny water droplets can grow large enough to fall as raindrops. Seeding has also been carried out by dispersing (spreading) silver iodide in the form of smoke from generators on the ground. Rain has been made to fall from clouds by these methods but artificial rain-making has not yet been done on a large scale. In any case, there must be suitable clouds to start with. Rain cannot be made to fall from a cloudless sky.

RAINBOW. The arch of many-coloured light in the sky called a rainbow is caused by the reflection and refraction (bending) of sunlight by raindrops. In the article COLOUR it is explained that sunlight, or ordinary white light, is a mixture of all colours. When light passes from one transparent substance to another it is refracted, or bent. The different colours are bent through different angles, red being bent least and violet most. Thus when a ray of sunlight strikes a raindrop it is split into beams of different colours. These beams are reflected from the inside curved surface at the back of the raindrop, which acts like a mirror. As the beams leave the water of the raindrop again they are refracted once more and each beam now follows a separate path. Since there are millions of raindrops at every level, anyone standing between the sun and the rain will see all the colours one above the other, with the red on the outside edge of the bow and the violet inside. A rainbow may be due to raindrops at any distance from the observer, from a few metres to several kilometres.

ZEFA

A rainbow's arc above the English countryside.

Sometimes a second and fainter rainbow is seen outside the first. This outer bow has the colours reversed, with the red inside and the violet outside, and is caused by the beams of light being reflected twice inside each raindrop.

The lower the sun is in the sky, the bigger the rainbow. When the sun is just rising or setting a rainbow forms half a circle. When the sun is more than 42 degrees above the horizon no rainbow can be seen. Therefore rainbows are more common in the early morning or late afternoon, although in Great Britain they can be seen at any time in winter because the sun then never rises higher than 42 degrees.

In Great Britain the wind is generally blowing from the west so the rain travels eastwards. Therefore a morning rainbow, with the rain in the west and the sun in the east, usually means approaching rain while an evening rainbow usually means clearing weather.

A halo, or ring, sometimes seen around the sun or moon, is caused in the same way as a rainbow except that the rays of light are refracted by tiny ice crystals instead of by raindrops. These ice crystals are the frozen specks of moisture forming the wispy sheets of high cloud called cirrostratus. A bright halo sometimes shows a red inner edge but generally the colours are so mixed up that the halo appears white.

In earlier days haloes were often regarded as foretelling approaching storms. Modern meteorologists regard haloes as too common to be reliable indications of definite weather.

RAIN FOREST. The lands within about ten degrees of the equator are generally covered with dense forests called rain forests. This is chiefly because there is no cold winter or dry season to stop the growth of vegetation. In the lowland regions, where the growth is thickest, one day is very much like another all the year round. The sun rises quickly and is high in the heavens during most of the 12 hours of daylight. Only at night and when clouds cover the sky is its power reduced. Even then the air remains hot and damp. Rain falls nearly every day and at all seasons, so that the total rainfall in the year is high, being seldom less than 2,000 millimetres and in many places more than 2,500 millimetres.

The change from one season to another is slight. In the early morning a brilliant sun rises and its rays are reflected from foliage drenched with dew. Towards noon clouds gather and soon there is a downpour of rain, often with vivid lightning and rolling thunder. After a period of steaming heat, the sun appears again in the afternoon and soon dries the open spaces. Sunset is about 6 p.m. and the still, warm darkness comes swiftly. In these conditions plants grow at an amazing rate, but metals rust and mildew (a form of fungus) quickly covers leather or cloth articles. Timber rots and food decays unless kept dry and covered. Many diseases spread rapidly because the climate encourages the growth of the microbes causing them and of the insects that carry them.

The tangled mass of vegetation that springs up in these conditions is called rain forest, or sometimes equatorial forest, to distinguish it from the forests covering large areas in colder lands. Rain forest is also sometimes called tropical forest and jungle, but neither is a suitable name, for although it is found between the tropics of Cancer and Capricorn it is very unlike jungle, which is a waste of grass and bushes with few large trees. (See JUNGLE.)

By far the largest rain forest is found in South America, where it covers much of the basin of the Amazon River. In Africa the rain forest is usually called the "big bush" and spreads inland from the Gulf of Guinea and over part of the basin of the Congo-Zaire River. In Asia it is found throughout Malaya, Indonesia and Indochina. (See also AMAZON; CONGO RIVER; INDOCHINA; INDONESIA; MALAYSIA; NIGERIA.)

Forest Growth

In the rain forests plant life runs riot. Every scrap of land except rock cliffs is covered with vegetation of some sort and hills and valleys alike are clothed with trees. The rivers are always full and with every storm wash down soil to the sea. The forest covers their deltas (that is, the channels near their mouths) and the muddy shores where grow the plants called mangroves (see MANGROVE).

Where the coasts are sandy, the mangroves are replaced by the tall graceful coconut palm (see COCONUT) and clumps of trees with drooping branches, like overgrown bushes of broom, hang out over the water.

Inland the forest is very different. The tall trees have slender trunks which break out in a cluster of branches near the top. The leaves form a sort of roof which shuts out the sun. Their trunks are draped with climbing plants and laced together by rope-like creepers. Beneath these tall trees are other smaller ones, often palms or similar trees with very large leaves. Sometimes there are giant ferns, clumps of bamboo, and plants like the banana.

The rotting trunks of fallen trees cover the ground, where grow lesser ferns and palms, trailing plants and fungi. Only in the few scattered clearings is there any grass. So little light reaches the ground that flowers are few. They are to be found on the trees and climbers that reach the sunny upper layers.

As there are no great seasonal changes there is no period of general flowering. Trees of the same kind may be found close together, one in

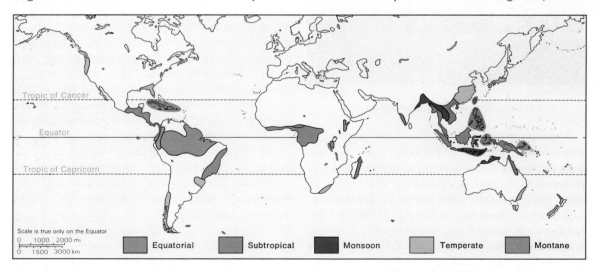

This map shows the Earth's main areas of jungle and rain forest. Five different types of forest are shown.

Scale is true only on the Equator

0   1000   2000 mi
0   1500   3000 km

Equatorial   Subtropical   Monsoon   Temperate   Montane

Tropic of Cancer

Equator

Tropic of Capricorn

Marion Morrison

In this picture of Amazon rain forest, you can see a huge liana, or climber, spiralling upwards from the forest floor into the treetops.

West Africa

The rain forests in different lands have much in common and a description of forest life on the coasts of the Gulf of Guinea, in West Africa, gives a good general idea of the conditions.

The coast is lined with swamp forest growing in a maze of muddy islands separated by countless shallow channels. Many of these banks of black mud are completely covered at high tide. Here are the mangroves, 15 to 20 metres high, their leggy roots exposed at low tide and forming a tangled mass of twisted stems. Crocodiles and other reptiles lie resting on the mud-banks or swim in the creeks.

Farther inland are other wet areas through which flow branches of the rivers but which are covered by water only when the rivers flood. Instead of mangroves there are raffia palms, which provide fibre for making brooms, ropes and baskets and whose sap is made into palm wine. The raffia leaf-stalks are used for hut building and its leaves for thatch. As the forest stretches inland, timber trees begin to appear amid the palms and reeds wherever the soil becomes a little drier.

full bloom, another with ripe fruit and a third with newly opened leaves. Some may bloom two or three times a fortnight and then not again for more than a year. Generally speaking, trees of one kind are not found covering large areas but many kinds are found intermingled. This means that when valuable trees are cut down for timber, many other trees may also be destroyed.

The swamp forest changes gradually into true rain forest. Here grow great trees with smooth shiny bark. Often their trunks are buttressed at the base; that is, they are supported by thin ridges growing out in such a way as to help keep them upright. Many rise 20 or 25 metres before putting out a single branch. Then they spread in

Rain forest can be quickly destroyed. First, loggers arrive to make a road.

The new road brings more people, planters who cut down trees to clear the ground for crops.

The planters "slash and burn" to clear the forest. For a few years the crops thrive, but then the soil is exhausted.

Without the protection of the trees, the soil is worn and washed away by wind and rain. The planters move on, leaving a wasteland behind.

a great crown of branches and leaves beneath which grow many climbers and other plants depending on the trees for support. The biggest trees often grow to 45 metres in height, with tree-ferns, bananas and plants of many kinds beneath, fighting with one another for sunlight.

The forest floor is often dark, silent and rather gloomy, for little wind or sunlight reaches it. Travel is difficult because of the woody climbers called lianas, the spiny, low palms and the rambling and creeping plants spread over the ground, but the usual tracks are marked by well-trodden paths.

Many forest animals and plants thrive in the treetops, in what is known as the forest canopy. They find food more plentiful on the "top floor" of the forest.

Although nearly all the plants shed their leaves, the different kinds do so at different times of the year so the forest is evergreen in most places. On its northern edge, however, there is a short rainless season when most of the trees shed their leaves. There are over 1,000 kinds of large trees and within a small area there may be 100 different sorts. Common trees are mahogany, rosewood, walnut, sapele, guarea, iroko, cottonwood and ebony, and many palms grow along the river banks. The most important is the oil-palm, whose fruits provide a valuable export.

Rain forests contain fewer large animals than is often supposed. Elephants are rare and hippopotamuses are found in only a few rivers. A few types of antelope live in the African rain forest, and the bush cow or dwarf buffalo and giant hog are also found in some areas. The aquatic mammal called the manatee dwells in some of the rivers and is believed to have given rise to the stories about mermaids. (See MANATEE.) Apes and monkeys include the chimpanzee and the black colobus monkey. The leopard is found over a wide area although it is not common. Bats and squirrels are common. The hornbill and the bright-coloured banana-eater are two of the many kinds of birds. Many European birds such as the swallow and nightingale spend the winter months in the African rain forest. There are vast numbers of insects and other small creatures.

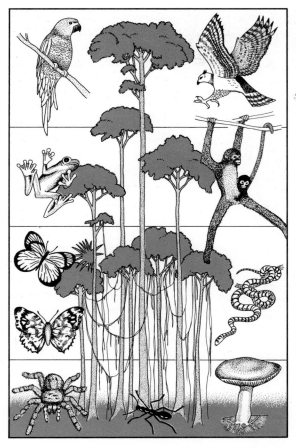

Each level of the rain forest, from forest floor to treetops, supports a variety of plants and animals.

Ants are perhaps the most interesting of West African insects. Some, like the driver ant, have no fixed home but wander about in swarms that may contain 1,000,000 insects. When on the hunt for food these ants sometimes kill and eat quite large animals. Other insects carry diseases.

For millions of years the rain forests flourished undisturbed. Human beings made little changes to them, until recently. Today, rain forests are being cut down at an alarming rate in many areas. Trees are felled for timber. Land is cleared for farming and development. How this will affect the life not only of the rain forests, but of other areas besides, is still not properly understood. But without special reserves to protect wildlife and proper management of forest resources, it is possible that the rain forests and their unique animals and plants could soon disappear from the face of the Earth.

For more about forest management, see FOREST and FORESTRY. For information about the world's largest rain forest, see under AMAZON RIVER.

RAISIN is the name given to certain kinds of dried grapes. Nowadays when people talk about raisins they mean the dark, deliciously flavoured dried grapes used mainly, in Britain, in puddings and cakes or eaten with nuts or cereal. At one time sultanas and currants, which are also dried grapes, but of a different variety, were called raisins (see below). In the middle ages raisins were often mixed with meat dishes. In Greece, Turkey and Arab countries they are added to rice dishes called pilaffs, and to stuffings for chicken and lamb.

There are several varieties of raisin. The very best come from Malaga in Spain. These start as black grapes with seeds, and they are dried and packed while still in bunches on the stalk. At one time they were part of the traditional Christmas dessert. These are called Muscatel raisins. From California in the United States come seedless raisins, which are particularly useful for cooking. All wine-growing countries produce raisins, but the chief exporters are the United States, Greece, Turkey, Iran, Spain, South Africa and Australia.

Sultanas are prepared from a small and seedless yellow grape, which came originally from Smyrna in Turkey. They were at one time known as Turkey or Smyrna raisins. The best sultanas are pale yellow.

Currants which are used in cakes and puddings are prepared from very small black grapes and get their name from Corinth in Greece. They were at one time known as Greek raisins to distinguish them from sultanas which were called Turkey raisins. They are in no way related to the red, white and black berried fruit which we grow in our gardens (see CURRANTS, BLACK, RED AND WHITE).

RALEIGH, Sir Walter (1554–1618). Among the most bold and dashing men of Elizabeth I's days was Sir Walter Raleigh (sometimes spelt Ralegh), who was a soldier, courtier, poet,

Left: "The true and lively portraiture of the honourable and learned knight, Sir Walter Raleigh", an engraving from the title page of the 1614 edition of Raleigh's "The History of the World". Right: A contemporary map of the coast of Virginia, showing wrecked ships and others anchored off Roanoke Island.

historian and explorer. He was born near Budleigh Salterton in Devon, probably in 1554 (but possibly two years earlier). Another famous adventurer, Sir Humphrey Gilbert, was his half-brother. (See GILBERT, SIR HUMPHREY.)

Raleigh became a student at Oxford University, but left to fight against the Spaniards with Sir Humphrey Gilbert when he was only 16. After this he went to Ireland to suppress a rebellion there, returning to England in 1581. He then came to court, where he attracted the Queen by his handsome appearance, gay manners and wit. The story may be true that he threw his velvet mantle over a puddle so that the Queen could cross it without wetting her feet.

In 1584 Raleigh sent an expedition to North America, and another a year later under his cousin, Sir Richard Grenville. The members of the second expedition tried to settle in what is now North Carolina, but without success. They brought back tobacco, and Sir Walter Raleigh was one of the first Englishmen to smoke a pipe. He also brought potatoes from the New World to Ireland, where he lived for a time during 1588 and 1589.

Raleigh organized the defence of Devon against the Spanish Armada in 1588. In 1592, however, he angered the Queen by marrying one of her maids of honour, Elizabeth Throckmorton, and was imprisoned in the Tower of London for a time.

Inspired by the stories of gold in South America, Raleigh sailed there in 1595 and brought back quartz (a kind of rock) with specks of gold in it. After his return a year later he helped to capture Cadiz in Spain.

With the death of Elizabeth in 1603 and the accession of James I to the throne of England, Raleigh's fortunes changed. The new king disliked him and lost no time in accusing him of treason. Raleigh was tried very unfairly and imprisoned in the Tower for 13 years. He was, however, well treated, and set to work to write a great history of the world, of which only one volume was published. He also carried out chemical experiments.

In 1616 he persuaded the king to send him on another search for gold in South America. If he failed he was to be beheaded on his return. A year later he set sail on his last and unluckiest voyage. Storms attacked his ships and he fell ill with fever. On reaching the mouth of the River Orinoco he sent ships up it to search for gold, and with the ships went his son Walter. They found not gold but Spaniards, and in the fight that followed young Walter was killed.

Raleigh returned without gold to face the executioner. The night before his death he wrote a poem referring to Time—

> Who in the dark and silent grave,
> When we have wandered all our ways,
> Shuts up the story of our days.
> And from which earth, and grave, and dust,
> The Lord shall raise me up, I trust.

He was beheaded on October 29, 1618, in Old Palace Yard, Westminster.

RANGOON is the capital of Burma. It lies 40 kilometres from the sea on the north bank of the Rangoon River, which is deep enough for large ships to use the wharves on the city's waterfront. The Rangoon River connects with the Irrawaddy River, which is the chief trade route in Burma. (See IRRAWADDY RIVER.)

The modern part of Rangoon is laid out in square blocks and contains the Burmese government offices and many fine public buildings. Towering over the city on a hilly ridge to the north is the Shwe Dagon pagoda, a sacred building which is the centre of Burmese religious life. It is a cone-shaped tower of brick above a chamber said to contain relics of Gautama the Buddha. (See BUDDHA AND BUDDHISM.) The pagoda is the largest in the world and around it is a broad terrace, usually thronged with pilgrims.

When this part of Burma was taken under British rule in 1852, Rangoon was a small fishing village but it soon became the trading centre of the whole country. It has grown considerably. On the south bank of the river and on the outskirts of the city are busy rice mills and saw mills where great teak trees are cut into logs.

The population of Rangoon is about 2,200,000.

ZEFA

Rangoon's most famous landmark is the Shwe Dagon pagoda (centre), almost 100 metres high and decorated with gold.

RANJIT SINGH

RANJIT SINGH (1780–1839). Ranjit Singh, maharaja (ruler) of the Punjab in India, was a soldier and Sikh leader. He led Punjabi armies against the Afghans and Pathans who for centuries had invaded India. His success as a military leader earned Ranjit Singh the proud title of "Lion of the Punjab".

Ranjit Singh's army, which he modernized with French and British help, contained soldiers of all religions—Sikhs, Moslems and Hindus. He was so shrewd a leader that the British sought his aid when invading Afghanistan in 1838. Ranjit Singh became ill during the victory celebrations, and he died at Lahore, the capital of the Punjab, which he had captured from the Afghans forty years earlier.

RANKS (MILITARY).

From the earliest times, when wars were waged between tribes, warriors have usually been divided into ranks, graded from the highest leader down to the humblest man-at-arms. As armies became larger and more complicated, this led naturally to the creation of more ranks. The word rank can be used for the lines or rows in which troops are arranged when drilling, but it is more generally used to describe the position occupied by someone in one of the three fighting services, the Navy, Army and Air Force.

The higher or commissioned ranks in the forces, both for men and women, are held by officers. Next come the warrant officers and certain other ranks in the army and air force, followed by the non-commissioned officers, who in the navy are called senior ratings. In the army, all ranks below warrant officers are called soldiers. In the navy, they are called ratings; and in the air force, airmen or airwomen.

Officers and Warrant Officers

The highest naval officers are sometimes called flag officers because their ships or headquarters fly special distinguishing flags. They include commodores, first class, and above. In the same way, army officers of the rank of major-general and above are called general officers and air commodores and above are called air officers.

There are also *acting ranks* in the navy, army and air force. An acting rank is a higher rank held temporarily (for a time) by an officer. However, in the British Royal Navy, there is a permanent rank called acting sub-lieutenant.

The word lieutenant comes from the French word *lieu* meaning "place" and *tenant* meaning "holding". Thus a lieutenant is junior to a captain because he is holding the captain's place. But a lieutenant-general is above a major-general because in this case the word lieutenant in front of general means that he takes the place of a general.

The Royal Air Force was formed in 1918 by uniting the Royal Naval Air Service with a branch of the army called the Royal Flying Corps. As would be expected, its ranks show traces both of the navy and the army. Thus "air *marshal*" and "flight *sergeant*" are of army origin while "air *commodore*" and "wing *commander*" follow naval use.

In days of old, officers often wore special clothing to distinguish them from the others, such as a more splendid hat or armour or a special coat. This enabled soldiers to recognize their officers but it also helped the enemy to pick out and shoot down the officers. Nowadays, there is less difference between the uniforms of the various ranks, although distinguishing badges of rank are still worn. In the army the badges showing an officer's rank are worn on the shoulder. In the navy and air force they may be on the sleeve or the shoulder.

In addition to badges of rank on the sleeve or shoulder, senior officer wear various kinds of gold lace or oak leaves on the peaks of their caps.

Other Ranks and Ratings

The most senior ratings in the navy are called fleet chief petty officers. They can be distinguished from other ratings by a more elaborate cap badge and a cuff badge incorporating the royal arms. Next come chief petty officers, distinguished by the badges on the lapels of their jackets and the type of cap badge. Next come the senior ratings of petty-officer rank, who can be distinguished by the crown and crossed anchors worn on the sleeve above the elbow. Below them are the leading rates with a single anchor on the sleeve. Then come the able rates and ordinary rates. Able rates are fully trained

Ranks of the British Armed Services

Royal Navy	Army	Royal Air Force
Officers		
Admiral of the Fleet	Field Marshal	Marshal of the Royal Air Force
Admiral	General	Air Chief Marshal
Vice-Admiral	Lieutenant-General	Air Marshal
Rear-Admiral and Commodore, 1st class	Major-General	Air Vice-Marshal
Commodore, 2nd class	Brigadier	Air Commodore
Captain (see Note ii)	Colonel	Group Captain
Commander	Lieutenant-Colonel	Wing Commander
Lieutenant-Commander	Major	Squadron Leader
Lieutenant	Captain	Flight Lieutenant
Sub-Lieutenant	Lieutenant	Flying Officer
Acting Sub-Lieutenant	Second Lieutenant	Pilot Officer
Midshipman	Cadet	Cadet
Warrant Officers, etc.		
(no equivalent)	Conductor, Royal Army Ordnance Corps; Master Gunner, 1st class; Staff Sergeant-major, 1st class	(no equivalent)
Fleet Chief Petty Officer	Warrant Officer, Class I (Regimental Sergeant-major)	Warrant Officer; Master Aircrew
(no equivalent)	Warrant Officer, Class II (Squadron or Company Sergeant-major)	(no equivalent)
Non-commissioned officers or senior ratings		
Chief Petty Officer	Squadron or Company Quartermaster - sergeant; Colour - sergeant; Staff-sergeant	Flight Sergeant; Flight Sergeant Aircrew; Chief Technician
Petty Officer	Sergeant	Sergeant; Sergeant Aircrew
Leading rate	Corporal; Bombardier	Corporal
(no equivalent)	Lance-corporal	(no equivalent)
Others		
Able rate	Private (or equivalent)	Junior Technician; Senior Aircraftsman/woman; Leading Aircraftman/woman
Ordinary rate		

NOTES: (i) The ranks in the Royal Marines are the same as those in the army except for colonels-commandant, Royal Marines, who rank with brigadiers. Army lance-sergeants rank with but before corporals, and lance-corporals with but before privates. (ii) Captains R.N. of six years' seniority or more rank with brigadiers.

while ordinary rates are those whose training is not complete. However, the titles "able" and "ordinary" do not apply to all branches; some use "first class" and "second class".

In the army the senior non-commissioned officers are the quartermaster-sergeants, colour-sergeants and staff sergeants. Then come the sergeants. (In the Household Cavalry these ranks are somewhat different and a sergeant is called a corporal-of-horse.) The junior non-commissioned officers are the corporals (called bombardiers in the artillery and lance-sergeants in the Foot Guards) and the lance-corporals.

Non-commissioned officers in the army and air force can be distinguished by their chevrons, which are V-shaped stripes worn on the sleeve above the elbows. Lance-corporals have one chevron, corporals have two chevrons and sergeants and above have three. Staff sergeants, or their equivalent, wear a crown above their chevrons.

The senior air force non-commissioned officers are of sergeant and flight-sergeant rank. Flight-sergeants can be distinguished by the metal crown worn above their chevrons.

The men below non-commissioned rank in the British army may be called troopers, gunners, sappers, signalmen, guardsmen, privates, fusiliers, riflemen, air troopers, drivers or craftsmen— according to which regiment or corps they are serving in. Those in the air force are divided into junior technicians, and senior and leading aircraftmen (or women).

In many armed forces (such as Israel's), men and women serve on equal terms and both are trained for fighting. In Britain, the three armed services have separate branches for women. The Women's Royal Naval Service's officer ranks are commandant, superintendent, chief officer and then first, second and third officer. Ranks in the Women's Royal Army Corps and the Women's Royal Air Force are the same as those for male officers. The names of the non-commissioned and other ranks are generally the same for women as for men (although in the W.R.N.S. ratings add the word "wren", as for example, "leading wren").

There is a separate article WOMEN'S SERVICES which explains how they came into being.

Ranks in Other Countries

The ranks in other countries are generally much the same as those in Great Britain. The Americans have the rank of fleet admiral instead of admiral of the fleet and besides lieutenants their navy has lieutenants, junior grade. Instead of sub-lieutenants they have ensigns. The highest rank in the United States Army is general of the army, which is equal to field marshal. Instead of brigadiers it has brigadier-generals and its lieutenants are called first lieutenants. Additional non-commissioned ranks are master sergeant, first sergeant and sergeant first class.

The Royal Air Force and other Commonwealth air forces are unusual in having rank titles for officers which are unlike those used in the army. Most air forces use army rank titles for their officers.

RANSOME, Arthur (1884–1967). Some of the best and most popular books for children are the ones written by Arthur Ransome about the two families of Walkers and Blacketts. The first, *Swallows and Amazons*, tells of their adventures in the Lake District of northern England. Each family has a small sailing boat and from the names of the boats—*Swallow* and *Amazon*—come the nicknames of their crews and the title of the book. Nearly all the stories are about sailing, sometimes on lakes, sometimes on the Norfolk Broads and sometimes at sea. Arthur Ransome gave his readers all the details accurately and with expert knowledge, for he himself was very keen on sailing all his life. In *Peter Duck* the Swallows and Amazons sail in a bigger boat, a schooner, with their uncle Captain Flint and the old sailor Peter Duck to the South Atlantic in search of treasure. In *Winter Holiday* two friends named Dick and Dorothea Callum join the Walkers and

Courtesy, Jonathan Cape, Ltd.
Arthur Ransome.

Blacketts for the Christmas holidays and carry out explorations in the snowbound countryside. One of the most exciting of the series is *We Didn't Mean to go to Sea*. The Walkers, in a boat belonging to a young man named Jim Brading, are swept out of Harwich harbour in a dense fog and, after a nerve-racking night voyage, end up in Holland. The last book, *Great Northern?* takes all the children—Walkers, Blacketts and Callums—to the Outer Hebrides, where they find the nest of a rare bird, the great northern diver. The villain of the story is an unscrupulous egg-collector.

Before he started to write children's books, Arthur Ransome was for many years on the staff of the newspaper called the *Manchester Guardian* (it is now called *The Guardian*). He had travelled all over the world—Russia, China, Egypt, the Sudan and Syria. While he was in Russia he made a collection of Russian folk tales, called *Old Peter's Russian Tales*, and he also wrote a book for adults called *Racundra's First Cruise*.

RAPE. You may see whole fields of yellow-flowered plants, making great patches of colour in the countryside. The plants are called rape, and belong to the mustard family. Farmers grow rape for its seeds, which give a useful oil.

Rape is an annual plant, and grows to 30 centimetres or so tall. It has a very long and thin taproot reaching down into the soil. The leaves are a bluish green colour, and the yellow flowers appear in clusters. Each round flower pod is full of seeds, containing an oil (sometimes called colza oil) used for cooking, for lubricating machinery, and also to make soap and synthetic rubber. Warning : rape is a poisonous plant and should not be eaten. Eating rape can cause blindness in cattle.

A native of Europe, oilseed rape is also grown in Canada, India and Pakistan.

RAPHAEL (RAFFAELLO SANTI or SANZIO) (1483–1520). Although Raphael was only 37 when he died, he is recognized as one of the world's greatest painters. As a man he was described as "gentle and modest, jealous of none, kindly to all", and these qualities seem to shine out in his paintings. He painted many pictures of the Madonna and Child—the Virgin Mary and the infant Jesus—and in them all the Madonna is gentle and sweet, often smiling, while the Christ-child is a delightful baby. Reproductions (printed copies) of his works are very well known, but they cannot show the dignity and glorious colour of the paintings themselves. When Raphael painted a crowd scene, all the details of people were very natural and realistic, yet at the same time every tree, every figure and every movement that he showed fitted in as part of the general pattern of the picture.

Raphael was born in Urbino, in Italy. His father was a talented painter who taught him to draw when he was still only little but who died when he was 11. Raphael was able to go on having lessons, however, and later worked in the studio of an artist named Perugino. Perugino's paintings were fresh and tranquil-looking, and some of the pictures Raphael painted at this time were rather like his master's.

Raphael's painting of Pope Julius II. It was Julius who called Raphael to Rome in 1508 and encouraged him to do his greatest work.

Raphael went to Florence after his time with Perugino and there painted some of his most famous pictures, including many of the Madonna. In 1508 he was invited to Rome and it was there that he developed his particular genius for large and magnificent paintings. He was asked to decorate the walls of several rooms in the Vatican, the Pope's palace, with paintings. On opposite walls of one room he painted two scenes, one showing the glory of the holy church on earth and in heaven, and the other in honour of human learning. The latter showed a gathering of the great philosophers, poets and men of science of ancient Greece.

Now Raphael's life became very full. He was one of the architects of the basilica (church) of St. Peter, and also studied the history and legends of ancient Rome. The Pope appointed him inspector of all the excavations—diggings for the remains of past ages—in Rome and within ten miles around. Raphael had many assistants and produced an immense amount of work. He was always willing to learn from other artists, and two whom he specially admired were Leonardo da Vinci and Michelangelo.

One of his later works was to design mosaics (see MOSAIC) for the domed roof of a chapel in Rome, which showed God enthroned in clouds in the centre, surrounded by the planets. Raphael also planned and supervised the construction of many splendid buildings. He died of fever before he could finish the picture he was working on, of the Transfiguration of Jesus.

Many of his pictures can be seen in the National Gallery, London. The designs he made for tapestries to be hung in the Vatican are in the Victoria and Albert Museum.

There is another colour picture of one of Raphael's paintings in the article PAINTERS AND PAINTINGS.

RASPBERRY. The raspberry is closely related to the blackberry, but, unlike blackberries, ripe raspberries will come away, without breaking, from the white core or plug in the centre. The fruit is really a collection of drupelets (small fleshy fruits with stones or pips). The raspberries grown for market are red, but there are also yellow and white kinds, and in North America there is a black raspberry known as the black-cap. It is smaller and less juicy than the red European raspberry.

The raspberry plant is a type of shrub with rather prickly stems called canes, which die after producing fruit in their second year. The small white flowers appear in clusters, usually in June.

Courtesy, Hortico
A cluster of raspberries.

The genus, or group, of raspberries is *Rubus* and the European raspberry is called *Rubus idaeus*, after Mount Ida in Greece, because the Roman historian Pliny said it came from there. The European raspberry is found wild in Europe (including Great Britain), North Africa and northwestern Asia, and from it were bred most of the cultivated raspberry plants. Raspberries were gathered in early times from plants growing wild, but they do not seem to have been cultivated until the 16th century.

Raspberry canes grow best in a cool, moist climate in rich, well-drained soil. Usually they are grown in rows, supported by wires stretched between posts. The old canes should be cut down after they have died. The largest raspberry-growing area in Britain is in the Tayside region of Scotland, where the fruit is chiefly grown for jam, canning and freezing.

RASPUTIN, Grigory Yefimovich (1872?–1916). A mysterious "holy man" and healer called Rasputin gained great power at the court of Tsar Nicholas II of Russia. A Siberian peasant, Rasputin won the confidence of the Russian royal family by treating their sickly only son, Alexis. The Tsar's wife, Alexandra, came under his spell and, despite the many tales of Rasputin's evil way of life, refused to part with him.

From 1905 until the outbreak of World War I in 1914, Rasputin's power in Russia, and the scandals surrounding him, were equally great.

At last, a group of plotters decided to murder him. They poisoned him, shot him and finally drowned him in the River Neva. Rasputin's behaviour did much to harm the reputation of the Tsar's court, and his bad influence on Nicholas and Alexandra helped to cut them off from the government and the people in the years leading up to the Russian Revolution. (See RUSSIAN REVOLUTION.)

RASTAFARIANS are members of a religious movement which began in Jamaica. They believe that the former Emperor of Ethiopia, Haile Selassie (1891–1975) was the Messiah, appointed to champion the cause of black people. Before his coronation, the Emperor was called Ras (Prince) Tafari.

According to Rastafarian belief, Africa is the spiritual homeland of all black people. Their teachings include African and Biblical religious ideas.

RAT. Few animals are more disliked by human beings than rats. They are rodents, or gnawing animals, and are found in nearly every part of the world. There are wild and generally harmless rats—some as small as a mouse, others as large as a hare—and there are also rats which probably do more harm than all other animals put together. These rats live wherever there are houses and towns.

In Great Britain there are two quite different kinds of rats. They are the house rat or black rat, and the brown rat. Their names are in-accurate and their colours are not a reliable way of telling them apart. The brown rat, however, is distinctly larger, weighing up to 450 grams, and its tail is always shorter than its body. The black rat, which only weighs about 200 grams, has a tail longer than its body.

Both kinds reached Britain from the East by ship. The black rat was the first to arrive and may have come in the ships bringing crusaders home from fighting in Palestine during the 11th, 12th and 13th centuries.

The brown or Norway rat came later and apparently reached Europe at the beginning of the 16th century. It is fond of water and (unlike the black rat, which is an excellent climber) keeps mostly to the ground, travelling through sewers and entering basements. The brown rat is much the more common of the two.

Rats do terrible damage by eating and spoiling stored foodstuffs. They may also cause fires by gnawing through gas pipes or flooding by making holes in water pipes. In history black rats are chiefly known as spreaders of bubonic plague, one of the world's worst diseases. This was the disease that killed so many people during the Black Death in the 14th century and the Plague of London in 1664–1665. The germs of bubonic plague are passed to human beings by fleas which leave a sick or dead rat to find another creature on which to live.

Rats are able to live in all kinds of climates. They are even known to live in the refrigerated holds of meat ships, where they grow long coats to keep themselves warm.

One of the main reasons why rats are so widespread is that they breed very quickly. A female rat may have eight litters in a year with anything up to 20 young in each litter. In about three months each of these young rats can start breeding.

Many animals and birds prey on rats, and in Britain these include owls, hawks and stoats. People wage continual war against rats, poisoning, gassing and trapping them. Modern poisons are more effective than the old ones and also painless. However, rats can develop an immunity to a poison in time so new methods of control are constantly sought.

Tame rats, mostly white, have been bred from

The two kinds of rats found in Britain—the brown rat (left) and the black rat (right). They do not interbreed.

brown rats and are often kept as pets. They are also much used in scientific research. Other kinds of rats are the bamboo rats of Malaysia, the crested rat of Kenya, the pack and kangaroo rats of America, the giant pouched rats of Africa and the fishing rats of South America.

RATES.

The upkeep of roads, schools and libraries, the collection of refuse and the provision of street lighting all cost a great deal of money. In Britain, such things are provided by county and district councils (see LOCAL GOVERNMENT). But where do they get the money? Apart from receiving grants from the government, the councils get their money by charging taxes called rates on property such as houses, shops and factories.

The sum that has to be paid is based upon the value of the property. So, generally speaking, people who live in a big house pay more rates than people who live in a little one. Officials of a government department called the Inland Revenue Department state what value a house or shop should have, and that is known as its *rateable value*.

When a local council has decided how much money it needs for the coming year it fixes the rates; that is to say, it tells the ratepayers how much money must be paid on each £ of rateable value.

RATIONING

is a means of ensuring that everybody has a fair share of food and other goods. The word "rations" was originally used for the amounts of food issued to soldiers.

During World War I Germany began to ration food much earlier than Great Britain, where rationing was not seriously introduced until the summer of 1918. In World War II rationing in Britain began in the early part of the war, was much stricter and applied not only to food but also to clothing, petrol and other things. People were given coupons which entitled them to buy, for example, small amounts of butter, cheese, sugar, clothing or petrol during a certain period.

Rationing continued in Britain and some other countries long after the end of World War II, for certain articles were still very scarce.

RATTLESNAKE.

There are about 30 species, or kinds, of rattlesnakes, all of which live in America. They get their name from the "rattle", which is a number of joints of dry horny skin fitting loosely into each other at the tip of the tail. When the tail is held in an upright position and vibrated at great speed, the rattle makes a shrill whirring sound which can be heard as much as 30 metres away. The purpose of the rattle is not known, but it is generally thought to be a means of warning off animals that might step on the snake.

Diamond-back rattlesnake. The rattle can be seen to the left of the snake's head.

Baby rattlesnakes have no rattle, but each time the skin is shed a joint is added. The joints are brittle and easily broken, so few full-grown rattlesnakes have a complete rattle.

Rattlesnakes are poisonous, having two large, hollow fangs in the front of the upper jaw with which the poison is injected into the wound when the snake bites. The fangs are folded back out of the way when not in use. Like most snakes of the viper family, however, rattlesnakes are sluggish and will bite only if trodden on or otherwise provoked. They are more likely to flee than to attack.

The family of snakes to which rattlesnakes belong is that of the pit-vipers, so named because they have a deep pit on each side of the head, between the eye and the nostril. It may be that these pits are special organs with which the snakes can trace the animals on which they feed. The smaller rattlesnakes feed on lizards and frogs; the larger snakes take anything they can overpower, such as lizards, frogs, mice, rats and even half-grown rabbits, as well as birds.

Like most members of the viper family, female rattlesnakes give birth to young snakes instead of laying eggs. The young rattlesnakes are fully equipped with poisoned fangs at birth.

The diamond-back rattlesnake, which is found in the southeastern parts of the United States, grows to well over 2 metres in length and is the largest poisonous snake in the United States. It is also the heaviest of all known poisonous snakes and its bite usually causes death. The skin is olive or brown with yellow-bordered diamond markings down the back.

The prairie rattler lives on all the great plains of North America from Canada to Texas. The horned rattlesnake, which lives in the desert area of the southwest United States, is small, with two prominent horn-like scales projecting over each eye. Its colour is a pale brown or yellow with a series of darker markings. This snake is also known as the side-winder because of its peculiar way of moving. The timber rattlesnake is a kind found in the eastern United States. Only one species of rattlesnake is found in South America.

RAVEL, Joseph Maurice (1875–1937).
Ravel was a French composer who introduced bright new harmonies into music (see HARMONY) and whose works, both for the piano and the orchestra, show the witty and elegant French style in modern music at its best.

Maurice Ravel, to give him the Christian name by which he is usually known, was born at Ciboure in the Basque country, not far from Spain. Ravel's mother was a Basque, and several of his works have a Spanish character. In 1889 he entered the Paris Conservatoire, but his early works were considered so revolutionary that he was not allowed to compete for the famous first prize awarded at that school. However, when he left he was soon recognized as one of the most important composers of his time. He wrote the *Spanish Rhapsody* for orchestra, and the ballets *Daphnis and Chloe* and *La Valse*. In these the orchestration is brilliant. *Boléro* became immensely popular. His piano works, too, are glittering, such as his *Jeux d'eau* (Fountains),

though sometimes there is something sad in them, such as his *Pavane pour une Infante défunte* (Pavan for a Dead Princess). Ravel never married and in many ways he was a lonely man. But he loved children, and he also had a passion for collecting and playing with mechanical toys. This can be seen in his music—in his *Mother Goose* suite, for instance, and in his opera *L'Enfant et les Sortilèges* (The Child and Magic), which is based on a story about a mischievous child by the French writer Colette. In 1932 Ravel had a mental breakdown, and he wrote nothing in his last five years.

RAVEN. The raven belongs to the crow family. It is a large, entirely black bird, very like the carrion crow in appearance but bigger. It croaks, but can utter other sounds as well, and is able to mimic other birds.

Ravens live mostly in mountain areas in Great Britain and by the sea. Their nests are built in cliffs and quarries or sometimes in trees, and are made of sticks and stems mixed with earth and lined with moss, hair and wool. Four to six blue or greenish egggs, blotched with brown, are laid, often as early as February.

It is said that ravens attack and kill sickly or wounded sheep and lambs, but this is very unusual. The food of ravens is mainly carrion (dead flesh) and small mammals such as rabbits.

Ravens do very well in captivity and have lived to 26 years, although the average age is 15. They often learn to repeat many sounds and words. Since early times one of the sights of the Tower of London has been the tame ravens that are kept in its courtyards.

The common raven also lives in many other

A. T. Moffett—Aquila Photographics

A raven feeding on a dead rabbit. Ravens are found in mountainous areas and by the sea.

countries of Europe and in northern Africa, northern Asia and North America. In South Africa lives the Cape raven, which is a common bird near the mountains, where it nests on the ledges of rocks. It is not so big as the European bird and has a large white patch on the back of the neck. It is considered a great pest by farmers as it destroys poultry and attacks lambs.

RAY and SKATE.

These fishes are closely related to sharks, and therefore are not "bony" fishes. Their skeletons are made of cartilage, or gristle, and the gill openings through which they breathe do not have a cover over them as those of bony fishes do.

Rays and skates have flattened bodies covered with prickly scales. They live on the sea bottom, and the shape of their bodies has become flattened to adapt them to this life. (They are not flatfish, as plaice, halibut and dabs are.) The pectoral fins below the head are enlarged and form the main part of the sides of the body. It is by means of these fins that the fishes swim. A wave-like motion passes along the fins and the fish moves forward. The tails of rays and skates are narrow and often spiny and the spines may be poisonous, as in the case of the sting ray. The fish uses them to protect itself.

Rays and skates have a special way of breathing. When resting on the sea bed they avoid breathing in sand by taking water in through two holes on the upper surface of the head, just behind the eyes. These openings, called spiracles,

Rays and skates are related to the sharks. The common skate is plentiful in the seas around Britain. The thornback ray has hooked spines on its back and tail.

can be closed by means of flaps of tissue.

Unlike most fish, male rays and skates fertilize the eggs inside the females. Before the eggs are laid they are each encased in a horny cover. At each corner this cover is extended to form a hollow tube with slits in it and through these slits water enters and surrounds the growing fish. When the fish is able to look after itself, the case splits and releases it into the sea. Often the empty cases are cast up on the beach and are called "mermaids' purses".

As the developing young are very well protected, they have a good chance of escaping their enemies, and so the female does not need to produce many eggs. Some rays and skates give birth to young which are already well developed.

There are various species, or kinds, of skates in the waters around Great Britain, the most usual being the common skate. The rays include the thornback ray, the spotted ray and the bottle-nosed ray. There is also the electric ray, which can give electric shocks.

Rays can be very large. The manta ray or devil fish may grow to 7 metres across and weigh 450 kilograms. The eagle ray may reach a width of over 4 metres and weigh 350 kilograms.

RAZOR.

Nobody knows exactly when men first shaved the hair from their faces, but we do know that the Egyptians were shaving in 3400 B.C. and that the ancient Greeks considered shaving to be a mark of good manners.

Instruments used for shaving in Britain between about 1000 and 500 B.C. have been found at Syon Reach on the River Thames. They are rough knives made of bronze. In other parts of the world shaving was carried on—and in some parts still is—with sharpened shells and flint.

After about the mid-1600s the "cut-throat" razor was in general use in England. Some men still use this type of razor and barbers shave their customers with them. The earliest type had wedge-shaped blades with straight sides that tapered to a sharp edge. They were strongly made and often lasted the lifetime of their owners. Early in the 19th century the sides of the blade began to be ground, or hollowed out. This made it easier to sharpen the blade and improved the fineness of the cutting edge.

1

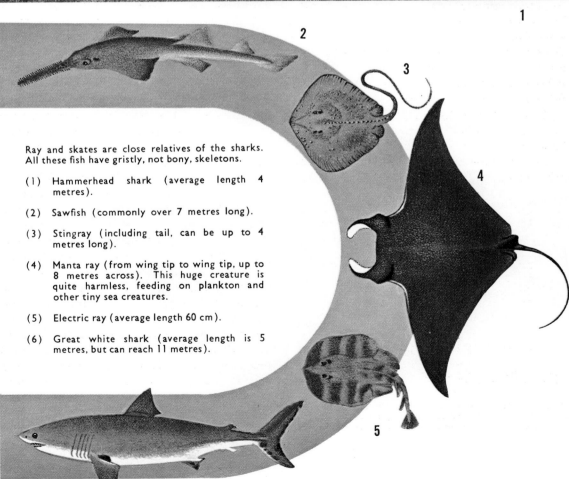

Ray and skates are close relatives of the sharks. All these fish have gristly, not bony, skeletons.

(1) Hammerhead shark (average length 4 metres).

(2) Sawfish (commonly over 7 metres long).

(3) Stingray (including tail, can be up to 4 metres long).

(4) Manta ray (from wing tip to wing tip, up to 8 metres across). This huge creature is quite harmless, feeding on plankton and other tiny sea creatures.

(5) Electric ray (average length 60 cm).

(6) Great white shark (average length is 5 metres, but can reach 11 metres).

Great skill is needed to make cut-throat razors and the best ones are thinner in the centre than nearer the cutting edge.

Such a razor is a dangerous instrument, however, and many attempts were made to make it safer. Guards to prevent the blade from cutting the face were brought out and the handles were improved. In 1771 a Frenchman, Jean Jacques Perret, invented a new razor that was very like the modern safety razor. The blade was fixed between a cap above and a guard below, so that only the very edge was left bare. Strangely enough, little notice was taken of Perret's invention and it was not until 1895, when King C. Gillette brought out his safety razor, that this type of razor became at all common. Gillette's, also, had the blade fixed between a cap and a guard. The guard comes between the skin and the cutting edge of the blade, which can there-

fore pass over the uneven surface of the skin without cutting it.

Nowadays, many people prefer to use an electric razor. This has tiny shears or spinning blades, and can be mains or battery powered. With an electric razor, the shaver has no fear of cutting himself.

RAZORBILL. This sea bird has a large beak which looks rather like the open blade of an old-fashioned "cut-throat" razor. The razorbill is often seen with its relative the guillemot (see GUILLEMOT), but it is slightly smaller than the guillemot and darker in colour on the upper parts. It is also stouter-looking and has a white line across its beak.

When swimming, the razorbill lifts its tail into the air. It is a fairly quiet bird. In May the hen birds lay their single eggs in a crack of rock or

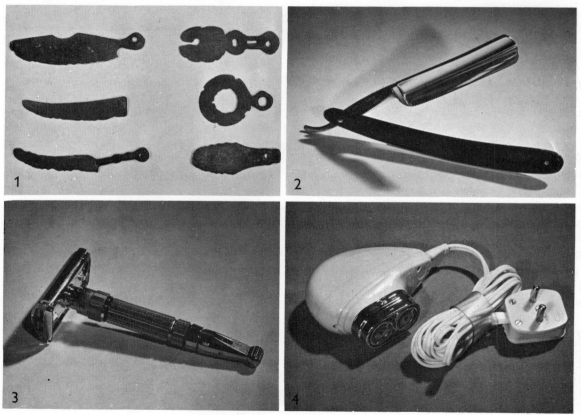

Courtesy, Gillette Industries Ltd.

Razors from prehistoric times to the present day. (1) The earliest shaving implements found in Britain, made by Bronze Age man. (2) A cut-throat razor, which shaves well but is rather dangerous. It fits into a long curved case. (3) A safety razor, its blade so placed that it passes over the skin without cutting it. (4) An electric razor.

G. W. Ward—Aquila Photographics

Razorbills breed in colonies on cliffs. They are diving birds that spend most of their time over or in the sea.

under a boulder. Razorbills often breed in company with guillemots.

Razorbills are found in the North Atlantic and in parts of the Arctic Ocean. They go south in winter.

READING. We live in a world of words and other signs (such as figures). Whether it is a library book, an advertisement in a newspaper or the instructions for a video game, reading plays a major part in our lives. Through reading, we learn and increase our knowledge. Because reading is so important, schools spend a great deal of time showing people not only how to *learn* to read but also how to *use* reading—to gain information and for enjoyment.

You probably learned to read while still quite young. But not everyone does. Adults are often "reading beginners" too. In the developing countries, most young people may be able to read, but many older people may not. So reading classes are held for grown-ups as well as for children.

Although reading is something almost all of us do, it is very difficult to describe. There are a number of ways in which we use the term

"reading" : we talk of "reading a person's mind" or "reading the sky for changes in the weather". This article is about the ways in which we read *print*, which can be books, newspapers, words on paper or TV screen, numbers on a page, and so on.

Because we can define "reading" in several way, teachers have different ways of teaching us to read, depending on what definition they choose. This choice is very important. It can govern the kind of reading programme used in a school, the selection of books read, the reading activities completed, and even the kinds of questions asked in the classroom.

Teaching Reading

Here are two definitions of reading. Each will affect what takes place in the classroom. Let's say one teacher believes that :

"Reading is saying all of the words correctly";
while another teacher says that :

"Reading is understanding".

These two definitions of reading are quite different. And there are reading materials based on each idea.

Our first teacher believes in the importance

of students being able to *say*, or pronounce, each word in a book correctly. So in the classroom reading would be organized around activities concerned primarily with the *sounds* of words and letters. Students would learn the sound of each letter and then how to combine them into complete words. They would be shown how to divide words into smaller parts for better pronunciation. Oral reading (reading out loud) would be encouraged, particularly in the early stages of reading. Questions from the teacher would emphasise the learning of specific *facts* and *ideas* presented in the material being read.

In contrast, our second teacher would be much more concerned with what the reader was able to *understand* through reading. Less emphasis would be given to the sounds of language and to oral reading. Instead, students would practise silent reading, and would frequently discuss what they had read, drawing on their own everyday experience. Questions from the teacher would be less concerned with specific facts and details, but would encourage readers to give their own ideas and opinions.

Most teachers today probably agree with at least part of each of these views. Teachers do, however, often disagree on the place in reading instruction that should be given to *comprehension* or understanding.

Reading Comprehension

"Reading comprehension" is the ability to know and understand what has been read. It is a part of all reading instruction. "Reading comprehension" is what you, the reader, learn or comprehend from what you see on the printed page. For example, when you read a passage about trains, you learn certain facts about this form of transport. Once you have finished reading, your teacher may ask you questions to find out how well you understood the passage. Very simply, the meaning of a passage lies within the material being read and you, the reader, understand or comprehend when you read it.

Recently, another idea about "reading comprehension" has become common. Instead of simply saying that meaning is obtained by the reader from the printed page, a teacher may stress the importance of what the words on the page stimulate the reader *to remember*. These memories or feelings are influenced by people's own experience of what they are reading about. So when you read about trains, you may remember your own experiences when travelling on or looking at trains. Words such as "engine", "station", or "passenger" have their own special meaning for you. For one person, an article about trains might bring memories of the time when a train he was in was three hours late because of a snow storm. Another person might remember a train journey to the seaside on holiday. A third person might recall a story she read about an exciting railway trip in a foreign land. Each reader "comprehends" in a different manner.

These differing ideas about reading comprehension affect the way we learn to read. Teachers who prefer the first definition of reading will frequently emphasise the importance of knowing specific facts following the reading of a passage. So they may ask questions, such as "what are the names of the characters in a story?", or "when did the story take place?", or "what colour was the car they drove?". On the other hand, teachers who prefer the second approach to reading comprehension might encourage students to relate their own personal experiences as they describe what they had read. Questions about the passage might include "why do you think the characters felt the way they did?", or "do you think this story was true or false?", or "how would you change the ending of the story if you could rewrite it?". Here the teacher is trying through questioning to encourage students to comprehend the reading material based on their different background and experience.

Reading Readiness

"Reading readiness" is a term which describes those abilities which a child must have before he or she can become a successful reader. Factors influencing reading development include physical growth, intelligence level and the kinds of experiences young children have before starting school. Reading readiness schemes can help not only teachers but also parents to prepare children for reading. In some schools tests may be used before reading instruction begins to try to

United Nations

Learning to read is a big step forward for children everywhere—but especially so for those in developing countries, like these children at school in Burma.

determine how well the child is going to read. But such tests are less often used nowadays.

However, there is no set list of abilities or tests to tell whether a young child is ready to read or not. It is not always the case that a child who is "ready to read" actually starts learning to read. Some children successfully complete various stages of a "reading readiness" scheme and yet still find reading itself difficult.

Most decisions about when a child is ready to read are made by the class teacher, who relies to a great extent on what he or she knows about each child from working with them in the classroom.

Starting to Read

There are as many different types of reading lessons as there are different books. Teachers select from a wide variety of activities according to the needs and interests of the children. Although reading lessons can vary a great deal, most follow the same general outline.

In the first part of a typical reading lesson, and to prepare the children, the teacher finds out how much the children already know about the story to be read. The teacher first reads the book with the child and discusses new words.

They talk about the pictures and how these also tell the story. The child then reads the book, or part of it, out loud. The teacher sometimes asks the children to read stories silently. Afterwards they may discuss the characters and the plot together. The children might also be asked how they would feel or behave if they were part of the story. Children might be asked to read out loud a favourite part of the story and then say why they liked it.

The fourth and last part of a typical reading lesson can be some kind of related activity, such as craft projects based on the reading material. It can be finding out how to use the library and its reference books, such as encyclopaedias and dictionaries. Children may be asked to write a piece of work based on what they have read. In this way, the teacher can extend the reading beyond one book to other books.

Reading Materials

There are many different types of reading material (books, cards, charts) which schools use in the teaching of reading. This was not always so, as you can see if you turn to BOOKS FOR CHILDREN and SCHOOL BOOKS in this encyclopaedia. Today, there are books at all levels which are both interesting and enjoyable as well as helping children to become better readers. Many contain pictures and diagrams designed to help and encourage the young reader. Often a whole series of books offers a step-by-step development of reading skills. Each is designed to build on what has been taught in previous books and prepare the reader for what follows in later books.

In the past, most text books used for the teaching of reading had a "controlled vocabulary". Each story in the book used only a very small number of words. Because there were so few words, (in some cases as few as 20) the stories were not very original or interesting.

Pictures can help young children to read. Young readers find it difficult to tell the difference between words such as *on* and *in*; or *under* and *over*. Simple pictures (cut from a magazine, even) can help explain the differences.

Today's reading books are more interesting, and the vocabulary used in them is often large and varied. Long before they begin to read, young children often have had a great deal of experience with language. They come to school already equipped with a large speaking vocabulary and, in many instances, knowledge of written words as well. They have learned this vocabulary from television and from seeing other forms of writing, such as street signs and advertisements.

Older material for early reading was rather out of touch with the modern world. The stories were not typical of the kind of lives led by most

of the children reading them. So modern reading schemes have tried to include materials which more accurately depict the world in which many young people live today. A reading programme produced by an educational publisher is not designed as the children's *only* reading material, but is intended to be just part of wide-ranging reading activities which should also include magazines, library books, newspapers and other reading material.

Reading Problems

Some people (of all ages) have problems learning to read well. These reading difficulties may be caused by poor health, such as problems with eyesight. Sometimes, children do not learn properly at school. This can happen when children move house a great deal and go to several different schools during their early years. There are children who just do not like to read (for various reasons) and would rather do something else with their time.

Special teachers are trained to help children who have trouble learning to read. They use tests designed to find out why a child does not read as well as he or she should. Once the problems have been determined, special teaching solves the reading difficulties of many children. One form of reading difficulty is known as dyslexia, although it is not very common. Some people think that it is brought about by a condition known medically as "perceptual aphasia". A dyslexic may, for example, read "p" for "q", or "on" for "no". He or she may find it very difficult to put words in the correct order. This results in a reading difficulty, although the person concerned is of perfectly normal intellectual ability. Dyslexia is now usually spotted early on, and special reading instruction does help, though experts do not agree on its causes.

The first aim of parents and teachers should be to encourage young people to become lifelong readers. Children should not only learn to read well but also come to see reading as an essential and rewarding part of their lives. Given this encouragement, reading will be seen not as a chore but as the avenue leading to the wide world of books and learning.

See also BOOKS FOR CHILDREN.

REAGAN, Ronald Wilson (born 1911). The 40th President of the United States was Ronald Reagan, who took office in 1981. He was born in Tampico, Illinois and worked as a radio sports broadcaster before becoming a film actor in 1937. He went on to make more than 50 films (including several Westerns) and also became leader of the film actors' trade union.

Camera Press
Ronald Reagan.

Ronald Reagan did not seriously enter politics until the 1960s. In 1966 he was elected governor of California. A conservative Republican, he twice unsuccessfully sought his party's nomination for President before being chosen in 1980 to challenge President Jimmy Carter (Democratic Party).

Reagan won the 1980 election easily. It was the first time since 1932 that a President had been beaten by a challenger and, at 69 years of age, Reagan was the oldest person ever elected President.

His policies as President included cutting government spending and having tougher talks with the U.S.S.R. on international matters such as disarmament. In 1981 President Reagan survived an assassination attempt, and in 1984 he was re-elected for a second term.

REAPING AND THRESHING. In prehistoric times corn was reaped, or cut, with a tool made from a sharp piece of flint fitted into a handle of wood or bone. Then as people learnt to make iron tools the flint tool was replaced by the sickle, which was used in Britain in Roman times. It has a curved iron blade fitted into a wooden handle and is held in one hand. The scythe was also used for reaping in Roman times. In shape it is not unlike the sickle, but the blade and the handle are much longer, so it is held in both hands. It cuts far more at one swing than the sickle.

When the crop had been reaped and gathered in (see HARVEST) it had to be threshed to separate the grain from the straw and chaff. The people of the Bible did this by spreading corn on the floor and driving oxen over it. Another early way was to take handfuls of corn and beat the heads against a stone. In Britain, at least since Roman times, people used the flail. This was a stick which had a heavy beater loosely fixed to the end of it. The corn was laid on the floor and beaten with flails until they loosened the grain and chaff. This was then collected together and thrown into the air on a windy day in order to winnow it; that is, to separate the grain from the chaff. The light chaff was blown away while the grain fell to the ground.

Threshing and winnowing by hand took most of the winter. However, at the end of the 18th century threshing machines were invented. Andrew Meikle, a Scot, built the first in 1786. They did the threshing much more quickly, but at first the winnowing still had to be done by hand. During the 19th century, however, they were much improved and were made to winnow the grain also. At first they were driven by horses or water mills but by 1850 they could be driven by steam engines.

The first successful mechanical reaper was invented in 1831 by an American called Cyrus H. McCormick. But reapers were not common until some years later. They had a long blade with many small knives, and were first pulled by horses and later by tractors. The early reapers could not bind the corn into sheaves, but towards the end of the 19th century they were fitted wih a binding mechanism. The reaper and especially the reaper-binder saved labour, but after the corn had been cut and bound it still had to be put into stooks—groups of six or eight sheaves stood against each other—to dry. Then it had to be made into stacks, which needed thatching, or stored in the barn to await threshing.

Both the reaper-binder and the thresher in turn became old-fashioned. A large machine called the combine harvester now combines their work, cutting the corn *and* threshing it as it goes along. They are either pulled by a tractor or driven by their own engine. The threshed corn

(1, 3) *Radio Times Hulton Picture Library.* (2, 4) *Courtesy Massey-Ferguson (U.K.) Ltd.*

Ways of harvesting corn. (1) Using the old-fashioned sickle. (2) A 19th-century reaper-binder. (3) Scything corn which has been beaten flat by rain. (4) Combine harvesters at work.

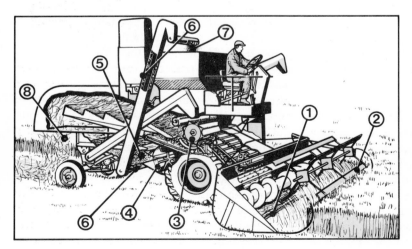

How a Combine Works

Key to diagram

1 Cutter bar's teeth cut grain
2 Paddles lift grain onto feeder
3 Toothed threshing cylinder separates grain from straw and chaff
4 Fan blows away chaff
5 Clean grain falls through sieve
6 Clean grain is drawn up into elevator
7 Clean grain falls into bin
8 Straw falls onto field

drops into sacks on the combine harvester or straight into a trailer. The straw is thrown to the ground. Another machine called a baler picks it up, presses it into squarish bales, ties them up and drops them. They are then collected and piled into "stacks". Sometimes, however, the straw is burnt. After grain has been threshed by a combine harvester it often has to be dried by hot air before it can be stored or milled.

The Americans began experimenting with combine harvesters as early as the 1850s, but these machines did not really catch on until the 1880s. They were ideal for use on the huge grain fields of the North American prairies. Because British farms are much smaller, combines did not become common in Britain until much later, during the 1940s. Today, combines are seen at work wherever corn is grown on a large scale.

RECIPES. If you have read the article COOKING, you may like to try some recipes for yourself. You will probably be able to make some of the things that are described in this article on your own. But for others you may need to ask someone older to help you, especially if the instructions say that the oven is to be used. Ask a grown-up to light or switch on the oven for you and set it so that it gives the correct heat by the time you want to put the food in it.

Begin by collecting all the ingredients you are going to use in the recipe and then all the bits of equipment you will need. Otherwise you may find yourself in difficulties after you have started because it turns out that you have not got enough of one of the ingredients you want or the suitable tin or basin that is needed !

The recipes in this article are traditional ones, and the old measures (ounces, tablespoons and so on) are used. But you can quite simply convert them to metric measures if you like. There are some helpful tips on this in COOKING under the heading "Measuring the Ingredients".

Lastly, a word of warning. Kitchens can be dangerous places, especially when boiling water or hot fat are around. Always take great care when at the cooker, and when handling knives and other kitchen equipment.

How to boil eggs. Choose a small saucepan and put into it the amount of water which will just cover the eggs when they go in. Heat it until the water is boiling and then gently lower the eggs into it, putting them in one at a time with a large spoon. Leave them boiling for 3 or 4 minutes, according to how soft you like to eat them, and then as quickly as possible lift them

out with the spoon. Use a timer if you have one in the kitchen.

If you want hard-boiled eggs to eat cold, put the eggs into a pan of cold water and then heat it until it boils. Leave the eggs boiling for about 10 mintues after this, then take them out with a spoon and put them into the sink where the cold water can run over them to cool them down. Once they are cold it is easy to peel the shells off.

How to scramble eggs. For scrambled egg for one person, you need two eggs. Get a small basin, break the eggs into it and then beat them with a fork so that the whites and yolks are quite mixed together. Shake a little salt and pepper into the basin too and stir them in. Now put two table-spoonfuls of milk and half an ounce of butter into a saucepan and put the pan on to a low heat, so that the liquid becomes warm but does not boil. While it is warming, make some toast under the grill (or in an electric toaster), spread it with butter and put it on a plate to keep warm.

When you have done this, pour the beaten eggs from the basin into the saucepan, still keeping it on a low heat. Stir with a fork until the

mixture begins to thicken; then take the pan off the heat but continue stirring until the eggs look creamy. Then spoon them out in a pile on to the buttered toast.

How to fry bacon and eggs. Before you begin, put some plates to warm. Any hot food is spoilt if it is put on to cold plates, but this is specially important with anything greasy.

Prepare the bacon by cutting off the rind with a pair of kitchen scissors. If there are any little white bones cut these out too. Lay the rashers (slices) of bacon in a frying pan. There is no need to add fat or oil in unless the bacon is very lean. Put the frying pan on a low heat so that the bacon cooks gently and does not frizzle up. Turn each rasher over once or twice during cooking (you can use a spatula or "fish slice" for this) to make sure both sides are done. When the bacon is done, lift it out on to the plates to keep hot while you fry the eggs.

The bacon will have made some fat in the pan and this should be enough to cook two or three eggs in. Fry them one at a time if you want to be sure of keeping them the proper shape. Break the egg into a cup first, then slide it gently out of the cup into the hot fat in the frying pan. Let it cook gently, and pour a little of the fat over the top with a large spoon. When the yolk is just set, lift the egg out of the pan with the slice and put it on one of the hot plates. Cook the other eggs in the same way.

How to cook sausages. Sausages can be cooked in several ways—two easy ones are frying and baking. The first step in each method is to separate the sausages. Some people like to prick each one in several places with a fork, to stop the skins from bursting. If you are going to fry them, put a little oil into the frying pan first and melt it over a low heat. Then put in the sausages and let them cook gently. The skins will almost certainly burst if you cook them too fast. Turn them several times so that they become brown all over. They will take 12–15 minutes to cook. After that, turn off the heat and lift them out of the pan on to a hot dish or hot plates.

To bake sausages, lay them either in a shallow oven-proof glass dish or in a baking tin which you have greased by rubbing the inside with a piece of paper off some butter or lard. Then put them into a moderately hot oven. They will take about 20–30 minutes to cook and should then look well browned.

How to cook vegetables. There are many ways of cooking vegetables, but the quickest and simplest is by boiling them. Prepare the vegetables, scrubbing or peeling potatoes, washing cabbage and shelling peas, for instance. Put on a pan containing about 3 cm (just over an inch) of water when you are cooking green vegetables and rather more for root vegetables. When the water boils put in about a teaspoonful of salt and the vegetables. Only old potatoes are put on in cold water.

Vegetables are best cooked quickly with the lid on. Over-cooking makes them less nutritious as well as less tasty. Be careful that the water does not all boil away before they are cooked. Look at them occasionally while they are cooking and if it seems that the pan might boil dry add a little cold water. This will stop the vegetables boiling for a minute but they will very soon come back to the boil again.

You can test whether vegetables are cooked

by lifting off the saucepan lid and poking them with a fork to see if they are tender enough. Here is a list of vegetables and cooking times:

Broad beans	20–30 mins.	Cauliflower	20–30 mins.
Runner beans	15–20 mins.	Onions	30–45 mins.
Brussels		Peas	10–20 mins.
sprouts	10–15 mins.	Potatoes	20–30 mins.
Cabbage	15–20 mins.	Swedes	30–45 mins.
Carrots	20–45 mins.		

How to make salad. The easiest salad to prepare is the kind made of lettuce, with tomato, cucumber and beetroot if you like it. Spring onions—the little white onions with long green stalks—are good in salad too, and so are watercress and mustard-and-cress. To begin with, the green things, especially the lettuce, need to be very carefully washed. Wash each lettuce leaf separately under the cold water tap, then shake it to get rid of as much of the wet as you can. When you have washed all the green stuff you are going to use, you can dry it either by putting it on to a clean tea towel, gathering the edges together and then shaking very well, or else by shaking in a special lettuce-shaker.

Watercress and mustard-and-cress will have to be washed two or three times (in fresh water each time) to make sure they are quite clean.

Tomatoes are usually cut in quarters for salad. Wash the tomatoes first under the tap and wipe them dry on a clean tea towel. (Some people like to remove the skin from tomatoes, which can be done by putting them into a basin and pouring boiling water on them. If this is done they need not be washed first.)

Cucumber is cut across into thin round slices. If you do not like the outside skin, slice it off before you begin cutting the slices. If you like to leave the skin on, wash and dry the cucumber.

Beetroot is usually bought from shops already cooked, and if it has been grown in the garden it will have been cooked before you come to use it for salad. Peel off the rough dark skin, and then cut the beetroot into slices or into little squares. If you have to cook the beetroot, do not peel it until afterwards, when the skin will come off quite easily.

If you are using spring onions, cut off the little bits of root at the white end, but leave most of the green stalk. Just cut the tops to make all the onions about the same length.

When all your ingredients are ready, you can put them into a bowl and mix them up with the kind of salad dressing your family likes best. Another way is to arrange all the ingredients on a large dish so that they make a nice pattern. It is a good idea to start with the lettuce, then arrange the tomatoes, cucumber and beetroot on top, and put the spring onions round the edge with their green stalks sticking out from the dish. Or the salad can be arranged in the same way on separate plates, one for each person.

Two Meat Recipes

Lancashire Hotpot. These are the ingredients you will need for four portions :

12 ounces of lean beef or stewing steak	1½ pounds of potatoes
1 tablespoonful of plain flour	4 medium-sized onions
	¾ of a pint of water
Some pepper and salt	A little dripping

This is the equipment you will need :

A stewpot with a lid, or a glass or earthenware casserole with a lid
A knife for cutting the meat and onions and peeling the potatoes
A large kitchen plate for the flour, pepper and salt
A chopping board for cutting meat and onions

Lancashire hotpot takes two hours to cook, so be sure you put it in the oven early enough to be cooked by meal time.

The meat has to be cut up into small pieces, removing any unwanted fat or gristle. Cutting up raw meat at home requires a really sharp knife and sometimes takes quite a long time, so it is a good idea to ask the butcher if he will cut it up for you when you buy it.

To get the meat ready when it has been cut up, spoon a tablespoonful of flour on to a plate, sprinkle on pepper and salt, and mix them in with the flour. Then put the chunks of meat on to the plate and roll them in the flour mixture until they are covered all over.

Now prepare the potatoes and onions. Peel the potatoes and cut them into quarters, or, if they are very big ones, into eighths. Peel the thin brown skin off the onions and then cut them into

slices—try not to lean over the onions as you peel and slice them, or they will make you cry !

Now is the time to ask for the oven to be lit or switched on and set to "moderate"—about 180°C for an electric oven and number 3 or 4 for a gas one. You are then ready to put the ingredients into the stewpot or casserole. The sliced onions go in first, at the bottom of the pot. Then on top of the onions comes the meat, and last, at the top of the pot, the potatoes. Pour the water into the pot and finally place a few little lumps of dripping on the very top. Put on the lid of the pot or casserole, and the Lancashire hotpot is ready to go into the oven. When you have put it in, put the plates to warm on top of the oven, and then there will be no chance of your forgetting them.

The only other thing you have to do comes 20 minutes before the two hours' cooking time is up. Open the oven door ; then very carefully, using an oven cloth, lift the stewpot on to the table, take off the lid and put the pot back into the oven. This allows the potatoes to become brown and crisp at the top during the last 20 minutes of the cooking.

Roast pork with gravy and apple sauce. These are the ingredients you will need :

A large piece, or joint, of pork	Some sugar
A little dripping	Some plain flour
1 pound of cooking apples	Some pepper and salt
1 ounce of butter	Some gravy browning

This is the equipment you will need :

A meat tin for roasting the joint
A saucepan for cooking the apples
A knife for peeling the apples
Two wooden spoons, one for beating the apples and one for making the gravy
A big fork and spoon for lifting the meat
A basin for the hot fat

The time a joint takes to cook depends on how much it weighs, so first of all find out the weight of the piece of pork. If you fetch the meat from the shop yourself, ask the butcher to tell you how much it weighs. It's a good idea to check the weight on the kitchen scales. This recipe is for the *slow* way of roasting, and the time for pork is :

25 minutes for each pound of meat
+ an extra 25 minutes
+ one-third as long again.

(Ask someone to help you work the sum out if you are doubtful !) This is how it works out for a joint that weighs about three pounds :

25 minutes × 3 = 1 hour and 15 minutes
+ 25 minutes
= 1 hour and 40 minutes
1 hour and 40 minutes ÷ 3 = roughly, 35 minutes
Total time for cooking = 2 hours and 15 minutes.

This means that if you are going to have lunch at, say, 12.30 p.m., you should put the meat into the oven at about 10.5 a.m., and take it out at 12.20 p.m. This will leave you with 10 minutes for making the gravy.

Now for what you have to do. Wipe the meat with a clean cloth or a piece of kitchen paper, and then lay it in the meat tin with the rind uppermost—this turns into the crisp brown crackling. Spread a little dripping (a lump about as big as a small egg will be plenty) over the top and sides of the meat. Put the lid on to the tin or cover with foil. Now ask for the oven to be lit or turned on and set at 180°C if it is an electric one or number 3 or 4 if it is gas. Put the meat tin straight into the oven on the shelf one rung from the top, and close the door. Now you can forget all about the meat for about 1 hour and 45 minutes.

To make the apple sauce, first peel the apples and cut out the cores. Slice the peeled pieces into the saucepan. You do not need any water with them. Put on the lid of the saucepan and then place the saucepan on the cooker over a *very* low heat. The apples will cook gradually until they become a soft pulp and there are no separate slices showing.

When they are done, take the saucepan off the stove and beat the apple pulp with a wooden spoon until it is nice and smooth. Put the butter in and stir it until it melts, then add some sugar. Drop the sugar in, one spoonful at a time, stir it in and then taste the sauce to see how sweet it is. When it is sweet enough, put the saucepan lid back on, and then all you need to do is to heat the sauce up again just before you are ready to serve it, when the meat is cooked and the gravy made.

Not everyone likes apple sauce with roast pork. It is a traditional "extra", similar to eating horse-radish with beef, red-currant jelly with mutton or lamb or Cumberland sauce (a mixture of red-curant jelly, oranges and raisins) with gammon. So serve the sauce in a sauce boat of its own.

From now on, you need an older person around to help you handle the hot dishes. About half an hour before the meat finishes cooking, lift the tin out of the oven (using an oven cloth). Very carefully, put it safely on the table where no one will touch it by accident and get burnt. Close the oven door again so that the heat does not escape. Then with a spoon pour some of the hot dripping in the tin two or three times over the top of the joint (this is called "basting"). Put the tin, without its cover, back into the oven.

Now fetch the dish that the joint is to be

served on and two sauce boats, one for the apple sauce and one for the gravy, and put them on top of the oven to warm. Put the other plates to warm as well.

When the meat has cooked for the correct time, turn off the oven and take out the meat tin. Put the hot dish on the table beside the tin and with a big fork and spoon gently lift the joint out on to the dish. Then put the dish back on top of the oven, or else in the oven now that it is turned off, to keep hot. The next thing to do is to pour most of the fat from the meat tin into a basin. Ask a grown-up to do this for you, because if you spill hot fat on yourself, it can cause severe burns.

You should now have a little fat left in the meat tin. Put in about a dessertspoonful of flour and stir it into the fat until there are no lumps. Then, bit by bit, add about half-a-pint of water (water that the vegetables have been cooked in is the best), stirring to mix well together. Put the tin over the heat and go on stirring all the time until the gravy boils and becomes thick and creamy. Sprinkle in some salt and pepper, and pour in a little gravy browning; then cook for two or three minutes more. While the gravy finishes cooking, heat up the apple sauce again, and your roast pork, apple sauce and gravy will all be ready to eat.

Two Dishes with Cheese

Welsh Rarebit. These are the ingredients you will need :

¼ of a pint of milk and water mixed	1 teaspoonful of some sharp-tasting sauce
1 ounce of soft breadcrumbs	Some pepper and salt
2 or 3 ounces of cheese	Some slices of bread to be toasted
Some butter	

This is the equipment you will need :

A grater for cheese and breadcrumbs
Two kitchen plates
A small saucepan
A wooden spoon
A knife for buttering the toast

Begin by making the breadcrumbs, unless there are some already prepared in the larder. If possible use a thick chunk of bread from the end of a loaf. Rub the soft side up and down the grater (with the grater standing on a plate) until there are enough crumbs. (You will not want to grate the crust, but it will save your fingers from being grated as well as the bread !) Next, grate the cheese on to a separate plate. It does not need to be very finely grated.

Now put the milk and water into a saucepan and stand it over a medium heat. When the liquid is warm, put in the breadcrumbs and stir

with the wooden spoon until the mixture becomes thick. Sprinkle in some pepper and salt and add *half* the grated cheese and the teaspoonful of sharp sauce or a little mustard. Stir well, then turn off the gas or hot plate but leave the pan standing on the stove so that it keeps hot while you make the toast.

Toast slices of bread, under the grill or in an electric toaster, and butter them. Then spread the mixture from the pan on the slices of toast, being careful that you cover them right to the edges. Sprinkle the rest of the cheese on top, put the slices on the rack in the grill pan and slide them under the hot grill. Grill them until the cheese on the top is bubbly, crisp and brown. Then slide each toast slice on to a hot plate.

Macaroni Cheese. These are the ingredients you will need for four portions :

2 ounces of macaroni	1 teaspoonful of sharp-tasting sauce
1 ounce of butter	Some mustard (already mixed)
1 ounce of flour	Some salt
¾ of a pint of milk	
4 ounces of grated cheese	

This is the equipment you will need :

2 saucepans
A grater for the cheese
A kitchen plate
A wooden spoon
A colander or sieve for draining the macaroni
A pie-dish, or a casserole without a lid

227

This dish takes about half-an-hour to make, or perhaps three-quarters of an hour when you are doing it for the first time.

First, fill a medium-sized saucepan with water to about three-quarters of the way up. Sprinkle in a little salt, cover the saucepan with its lid, and put it on the cooker with the burner or hotplate full on. If you have the kind of macaroni that is supplied in long lengths, break them up into small pieces. They will take about 20 minutes to cook. If your macaroni is the special quick-cooking sort, however, it will already be broken up. It takes much less time to do; the instructions on the packet will tell you how long.

While you wait for the water in the pan to come to the boil, grate the cheese on to a plate; as for Welsh Rarebit, it does not need to be grated very finely. When the water boils, put the macaroni in. Turn the heat down a little so that it does not boil over, but still have it high enough to keep the water boiling fast.

Now you can make the sauce in your other saucepan. Put the butter in and let it melt over a gentle heat. When it has melted, stir in the flour carefully with a wooden spoon so that there are no lumps and then gradually, stirring all the time, add the milk. Turn the heat up a little and go on stirring thoroughly all the time until the mixture boils and becomes thick. (What you have made so far is white sauce.) After it has thickened, sprinkle in a little salt, add the mustard and the sharp-tasting sauce if you like it, and stir well in. Then turn the heat down again and let the sauce bubble very gently for about 10 minutes. Still stir it occasionally so that it does not stick or go lumpy.

By now the macaroni will probably be cooked —pick a piece out with a spoon to see if it is soft enough. When it is, put the colander or sieve into the sink, take the pan off the cooker and pour the water and macaroni into the colander or sieve. The boiling water will run away down the sink, and you can then shake the macaroni a little to get rid of any water that is left.

Then is the time to stir nearly all the grated cheese into the sauce, which is still simmering over a low heat. (Keep a little of the cheese to be sprinkled on later.) Add the macaroni, mix well

and then pour the whole mixture into the pie dish or casserole. Sprinkle the top with the grated cheese you have left over. To finish, put the dish under a hot grill (or else into a hot oven) to brown the top.

Two Puddings

Apple Cornflake Crunch. These are the ingredients you will need for four portions:

1 pound of cooking apples   2 ounces of butter or
2 cupfuls of cornflakes   margarine
2 ounces of brown sugar

This is the equipment you will need:

A knife for peeling and cutting the apples
A pie-dish or casserole without a lid
A kitchen plate

Apple Cornflake Crunch takes about 45 minutes to cook in the oven.

First of all peel the apples, take the cores out and cut the apples into slices on a plate. When you have done this, ask for the oven to be turned on and set to "moderately hot"—200°C if you are using an electric cooker or number 6 on a gas cooker.

Now for putting the ingredients into the pie-dish. Start with a layer of apple slices at the bottom of the dish. On top of this put a layer of cornflakes, then a good sprinkling of brown sugar, and then a few little lumps of butter dotted about. Fill up the dish with other layers —apple first each time, then cornflakes, sugar

and lumps of butter—until all the ingredients are used up. Make sure that you finish with the sugar and butter on top.

Put the pie-dish into the oven and let it bake until the apples are cooked and the mixture is crisp. You can see whether it is done by taking the dish out of the oven for a moment and sticking in a fork or a skewer to test the softness of the apples.

Banana Trifle. These are the ingredients you will need for four portions :

1 pint of milk	Some apricot jam
1 pint packet of custard powder	5 bananas
	Some castor sugar
3 or 4 small oblong sponge cakes	

Some cream (about ¼ of a pint if possible)
Some cherries, angelica and chopped nuts

This is the equipment you will need :

A saucepan for heating the milk for the custard
A basin for the custard
A wooden spoon
A knife for cutting and slicing
A glass or china bowl or dish
A whisk for whipping the cream
A basin for the cream

First, make the custard by following carefully the instructions on the packet. When the custard is made, leave it standing in the basin while you prepare the rest of the trifle. Split the sponge cakes in two and spread a thick layer of apricot jam on each piece. Peel the bananas and slice them. Then arrange the sponge cakes and the bananas in layers in the bowl or dish. Pour the hot custard over the top, and leave it to cool.

The time to do the decoration on the top is just before the meal, when the trifle is thoroughly cold. Put the cream into a basin, and whip it with the whisk until it is just beginning to get thick. (Sometimes this seems to take a long time, but if you go on it will come thick in the end!) Then sprinkle in a little sugar—about a level dessertspoonful—and go on whipping until the cream thickens a little more, so that it is solid enough to stay where it is put on the trifle.

Pile the cream in little heaps on top of the trifle and arrange some cherries, little pieces of angelica (strips of sticky sugary green stuff) and chopped nuts on the trifle as well to make a pretty decoration. Of course, you can leave out the cream, which is rather expensive, and also the other decorations, but it will be a more special and delicious trifle if you use them.

Tarts, Buns and Biscuits

Jam or Lemon Curd Tarts. These are the ingredients you will need :

6 ounces of plain flour
A pinch of salt
3 ounces of fat (lard, or vegetable fat, or half lard and half margarine)
A little water
Some jam, of any flavour you like, or lemon curd
A little extra flour

This is the equipment you will need :

A large mixing bowl for the pastry
A knife
A flour dredger
A pastry board
A rolling pin
A round pastry cutter
A baking tin with hollows for 12 tarts
A piece of the greasy wrapping paper off some butter or lard
A teaspoon
A broad knife or spatula
A cake rack

Jam or lemon curd tarts take about 15 minutes to cook in a hot oven.

To make the pastry, put the flour and the pinch of salt into the mixing bowl, and add the fat. When it is in the bowl cut it up into fairly small lumps and then begin what is called rubbing the fat into the flour. Put both your hands into the basin and rub the fat and flour between your fingertips and thumbs, as lightly and gently as you can. This breaks up the lumps of fat and mixes them thoroughly into the flour, so that when you have finished the mixture looks rather like breadcrumbs. (If you have never done this before or seen it done, ask someone to show you how and to start you off.)

When you have rubbed all the fat into the flour and there are no lumps left, make a "hole" in the middle of the mixture and pour in a very little water. Mix this in with your hand, then add another little drop and mix in again. When the mixture begins to stick together, you have got enough water. Squeeze the mixture gently together with one hand until it forms one lump and leaves the side of the basin clean. (Be careful not to add too much water or the pastry will

229

be sticky and hard to handle—the less water the better. If you find you have put too much water, sprinkle in a little extra flour.)

This is the time to ask for the oven to be turned on and set to hot—425 degrees or number 7. Also, before you go on with the pastry, grease each of the hollows in the baking tin by rubbing it over well with the greasy side of the butter or lard paper.

Now put the extra flour into the flour dredger if you have one, and sprinkle it over the pastry board and the rolling pin. (If you have no dredger, sprinkle the flour on with your fingers.) This is to stop the pastry sticking. Put the pastry on to the board, shape it lightly into a neat piece with your hands, and then roll it out with the rolling pin until it is quite thin—about an eighth of an inch thick. Try to roll as quickly and lightly as possible, and turn the pastry round a little on the board after each roll to keep it an even thickness.

Next, with the pastry cutter, stamp out as many rounds as possible from the pastry. You probably will not get 12 out of the first rolling of pastry, so after you have lifted out the rounds, gather the left-over pieces of pastry together, squeeze them gently in a new lump, and roll out again. This time you should be able to cut out the rest of your 12 rounds.

Now put each round into one of the hollows in the baking tin, pressing it in gently at the middle first and then round the sides. Spoon a teaspoonful of jam or lemon curd into the middle of each pastry round, and the tarts are then ready to be put into the oven. After about a quarter of an hour the pastry should have swollen a little and be crisp and just brown.

Ease the tarts out of the tin with a broad knife or spatula and put them on a cake rack to cool.

Rock Buns. These are the ingredients you will need :

12 ounces of plain flour	6 ounces of butter or
A pinch of salt	margarine
2 teaspoonfuls of baking	6 ounces of sugar
powder	3 ounces of currants
¼ of a teaspoonful of	1½ ounces of finely
grated nutmeg	chopped peel
¼ of a teaspoonful of	1 egg
mixed spice	A little milk

This is the equipment you will need :

A baking sheet
A sieve
A mixing bowl
A small basin
Two forks
A large spoon
A teaspoon
A flour dredger
A piece of paper from butter or lard
A broad knife or spatula
A cake rack

Rock buns take about 15 or 20 minutes to cook in a hot oven.

The ingredients to be mixed together first are the flour, salt, baking powder, grated nutmeg and mixed spice. Instead of tipping them straight into the basin, hold or stand the sieve over the basin and then put the ingredients into the sieve and shake them through into the basin. This makes sure there are no tiny lumps. Now rub the fat into the flour mixture in exactly the same way as for pastry (described in the instructions for jam tarts). When the mixture looks like

breadcrumbs, stir in the sugar, currants and chopped peel and mix all the ingredients well with the large spoon.

Next, ask for the oven to be turned on and set to "hot"—425 degrees or number 7. At the same time prepare the baking sheet by rubbing it all over with the greasy butter or lard paper and then sprinkling a little flour on to it from the dredger or with your fingers. Tip the baking sheet this way and that so that the flour gets all over it, then shake off any that has not stuck on.

To finish mixing the buns, break the egg into a small basin and beat it up with a fork until the white and yolk are thoroughly mixed together. Make a hole in the middle of the mixture in the large basin and pour the beaten egg in. Stir it well in. Then add milk gradually, a few drops at a time, and stir this well in, until the mixture sticks together but is still stiff. (If you put in too much milk and the mixture becomes too soft, it will not keep its shape when you put it on the baking sheet.)

When the mixture is right, use a teaspoon and a fork to put it out in little heaps on the baking sheet. Do not try to make the heaps round and smooth or they will not be *rock* buns when cooked, but do your best to make them all the same size. Put them into the oven, and after about a quarter of an hour they should be ready.

Lift the cooked buns off the baking sheet with a broad knife or spatula and put them on a cake rack to cool.

You may find that you cannot get all the mixture on to one baking sheet, and if so you will have to put another batch into the oven after you have taken the first one out.

Flapjacks. These are the ingredients you will need:

2 ounces of sugar
2 ounces of butter or margarine
2 teaspoonfuls of water
5 ounces of rolled oats (porridge oats)

This is the equipment you will need:

A saucepan
A wooden spoon
Two sandwich tins (shallow cake tins) measuring 6 inches across
A piece of paper from butter or lard
A knife
A cake rack

Flapjacks take about 30 to 45 minutes to cook in a moderate oven.

First of all, grease the two cake tins by rubbing the greasy butter or lard paper over them, and also ask for the oven to be turned on and set to moderate—350 degrees or number 3 or 4—as it will not take you long to make the flapjacks.

Put the sugar, butter and water into the saucepan and warm it over a very low heat, stirring all the time with a wooden spoon until the ingredients are dissolved and well mixed together. Then stir the porridge oats in. Spoon the mixture into the cake tins, and spread it evenly and press it well in all over with the back of the spoon. Put the tins in the oven and bake for

about 30 to 45 minutes; when the flapjacks are done they are a golden-brown colour.

Take the tins out of the oven and put them on the kitchen table. Then cut the mixture into triangles while it is still in the tins. Leave the pieces in the tins for a few more minutes before you take them out to cool on the cake rack, otherwise they may crumble.

Chocolate Corn Roughs. These are the ingredients you will need:

1 ounce of corn flakes
¼-pound bar of chocolate
Hot water

This is the equipment you will need:

A baking sheet
A basin
A saucepan big enough for the basin to fit over but not go right in
Two forks
A piece of waxed paper (the inner bag from a corn-flakes packet, spread out, does nicely)
A pastry board

First of all ask for the oven to be turned on and set at "slow"—300 degrees or number 1. Spread the cornflakes out on the baking sheet and put them into the oven for five minutes to crisp them up. Then take the baking sheet out and let the cornflakes cool.

Put some hot water into the saucepan, and stand the basin over the pan. (It is a good idea to keep the water hot by having the pan over a very low heat.) Break up the bar of chocolate into the basin and let it melt. Watch it carefully, because if it becomes too hot it will spoil. When the chocolate is *just* melted and soft, stir in the cornflakes with a fork, very gently so that you do not break them. Then take the basin out of the pan.

Spread the waxed paper out on the pastry board. Then, using two forks, put the chocolate mixture in little heaps of the same size on the paper. Leave them till they are quite set, and they are then ready to eat.

RECORDER. Certain cities and boroughs in England and Wales used to hold law courts of their own which were higher than the magistrates' courts, or petty sessions. These higher courts were called quarter sessions and each was presided over by a recorder. Usually he held his court once in every quarter, but he could hold it more often if necessary. Recorders were paid a salary and could continue to practise as barristers. Quarter sessions in the *counties* were held by a bench of magistrates presided over by a legally qualified chairman or deputy chairman.

Quarter sessions both in towns and counties were abolished by the Courts Act 1971. A criminal court called the Crown Court was set up to try all the graver cases. The judges who sit in it include full-time judges and also a number of part-time judges called recorders of the Crown Court. Solicitors as well as barristers can now be appointed as recorders.

Towns that had recorders under the old system now have honorary recorders, to preserve the links between the law and local government.

RECORDER FAMILY. Formerly known as
"English flutes", recorders are wood-wind instruments in which the player's breath causes a lip in the mouthpiece to vibrate, thus producing sound by the same method as an organ flue-pipe or a whistle. The name comes from the verb "to record", which in early times meant "to sing like a bird".

The recorder is a straight pipe having seven finger-holes and a thumb-hole. The four chief members of the recorder family are the descant recorder, whose lowest note is one octave above middle C; the treble recorder, whose lowest note is the F above middle C; the tenor recorder, with middle C as its lowest note; and the bass recorder, whose lowest note is the F below middle C. In addition, there is the sixth flute (above the descant), the alto recorder an octave above the tenor and the soprano recorder an octave above the treble. Each has a range of rather more than two octaves, except the bass, which has a smaller range.

The recorder was known in England in the middle ages, at a period before orchestras existed. The fashion grew for having a "consort", or group, of recorders playing together, and this gave rise to the family of instruments able to cover a wide range of notes. King Henry VIII played the recorder and it was popular in

Shakespeare's time, being mentioned in his plays *Hamlet* and *A Midsummer Night's Dream.* In his diary in 1668 Samuel Pepys mentioned having bought one. (See PEPYS, SAMUEL.)

With the rise of orchestral music in the 18th century the recorder began to fall into disuse, giving place to the cross-blown flute with its much fuller tone. (See FLUTE FAMILY.) Although some compositions by Bach and Handel have parts for recorders, the instrument almost died out in the 19th century. In about 1925, however, the researches of Arnold Dolmetsch into early instrumental music brought a revival of popularity, and under the influence of his son Carl, who became a brilliant performer, the recorder was soon a favourite instrument with amateurs. Edgar Hunt introduced the recorder to schools in Great Britain, where it is now widely played, and in 1937 the Society of Recorder Players was founded. Several modern composers have written works for the recorder, among them Paul Hindemith and Lennox Berkeley.

The six-holed flageolet and "tin whistle" (or "penny whistle") are instruments of recorder type but are not usually included as members of the recorder family.

Three young recorder-players. Below are five kinds of recorders, once known as English flutes. From top to bottom they are: soprano recorder, descant recorder, treble recorder, tenor recorder and bass recorder.

RECORDING is the science of storing sounds so that they can be listened to again. Playing them back again is called reproducing. Sounds come to us in the form of vibrations in the air.

Forming a stamper, the final stage of making a record.

The higher the note is the more rapid its vibrations are; a very low note vibrates so slowly that its separate throbs can be distinguished. The vibrations can be compared with ripples whose crests are close together for high notes and far apart for low notes.

To record sounds it is necessary to make their vibrations cause physical changes in some substance which can be stored. There are three main ways of doing this, and they depend on three kinds of physical change. The earliest method, and the most common, is that used for gramophone records, where the sound vibrations are represented by changes made in a groove cut spirally in the surface of the record. The vibrations either vary the *depth* of the groove (called *hill-and-dale* recording) or cause it to waver slightly from side to side (*lateral* recording). On a two-channel stereo record both the depth and the width are continually varying. Another method is that used for the "talkies", or sound films. In this method the sound vibrations are represented by photographic changes in a narrow band called the *sound track* along one edge of the film. There are two types of sound track. One has a fixed width and is made to vary in darkness (called *variable-density* recording) and the other has an all-black track which is made to vary in width (*variable-area* recording).

The third main system is called *magnetic recording*, in which the sound variations are made to cause magnetic changes in the surface coating of a tape. The tape is covered with a form of iron oxide which, like iron, can easily be magnetized. Magnetic recording is employed in tape recorders and dictating machines, and is also an important feature of computers, in which it provides the memory storage. (See COMPUTER.) It is also used for recording sound on cinema films and can be used to record television pictures on video-tape. The magnetic system has the great advantage that a recording can be magnetically erased (wiped out) when it is no longer wanted, and the tape used again.

Recording Discs

There have been several changes in the methods of making gramophone records. Until 1926 they were made by bringing together the sound vibrations by means of a horn so that they fell on a *diaphragm*, or thin plate, to which a cutting *stylus* like a needle was attached. A revolving disc of wax was moved at a constant speed under the stylus, which was made to track towards the centre and therefore cut a spiral groove in the wax. So long as the horn caught no sounds the diaphragm remained still and the groove was perfectly smooth. If, however, a sound came through the horn, the diaphragm vibrated in sympathy with the sound and caused the stylus to make tiny indentations in the walls of the groove.

In 1926 the system was altered. A microphone like that in the mouthpiece of a telephone (see TELEPHONE) was used to change the sound vibrations into a varying electric current, which was then amplified, or magnified, by a valve amplifier (see RADIO). The amplified current was led to the record-cutter, which was an electro-magnetic device which vibrated in sympathy with the current and operated the stylus. In this way the force operating the stylus was no longer limited by the strength of the sound vibrations and the recording was more faithful.

After 1947 the system was again altered. First

a magnetic tape recording was made in the manner described later in this article. This was then played back and its electrical vibrations were amplified and led to the record-cutter. At about the same date a metal disc coated with a special kind of lacquer was used instead of a wax disc.

When the disc has been recorded, its surface is sprayed with a fine silver solution which, as it is a conductor of electricity, allows the disc to be electroplated (see ELECTROPLATING). In this process a thin skin of nickel is deposited on the surface of the disc. The skin when peeled off has ridges on it corresponding to the grooves in the disc. The skin is given metal backing to strengthen it and is called the *master*. It could be used to stamp out records from some soft substance, and these records would be similar to the original disc, but this would soon wear out the master. Therefore further electroplating processes are carried out to obtain any desired number of what are called *matrix shells*. These are mounted in heavy plates and become the *stampers* used for stamping out the final records. The records are made of a plastic substance which is heated to soften it and placed in a powerful press which squeezes it between two stampers, one above and the other below.

Long-playing Records

Until 1949, records were played at a speed of 78 or 80 r.p.m. ("revolutions per minute") and had about 100 grooves for each inch of radius. A 12-inch record had grooves over about 4 inches of its radius and therefore its 400 grooves gave a playing time of about $\frac{400}{78}$, which is roughly 5 minutes. This was not enough for long pieces such as whole acts of an opera.

Then a new substance for making records was discovered. This was *vinylite*, a much smoother plastic than the older shellac mixture, which was slightly gritty. The use of vinylite made it possible to reduce the size of the grooves so that 250 grooves could be packed into each inch of radius and also to reduce the playing speed to $33\frac{1}{3}$ r.p.m. These *microgroove* records last more than 20 minutes for each 12-inch side and enable a far wider range of notes to be recorded. They are used with sapphire or diamond needles and with light-weight *pickups*. These are devices which

change the mechanical vibrations of the needle into electrical vibrations.

The 20-minute record was too long for pieces such as songs so the 7-inch record was introduced, using vinylite and microgrooves but with a playing speed of 45 r.p.m.

The first of all long-playing records were the "Talking Books" produced in 1933 for the use of blind people. These were recorded on discs rotating at a speed of 24 r.p.m. About eight discs were needed for recording one book. Nowadays the Talking Books are recorded on magnetic tape, which is contained in a holder known as a cassette that can be slotted into place on a special tape recorder for playing back. Using this method, a book can be recorded on a single tape cassette.

Magnetic Tape Recording

To produce a magnetic tape record the electrical vibrations from the microphone are led to an amplifier which magnifies them so that they can be made to work an electro-magnet called the *recording head*. This has a stronger field as the current increases and a weaker field as the current decreases (see ELECTRO-MAGNET). A plastic tape coated with a magnetic iron oxide is drawn across the face of a tiny gap between the two pole-pieces of this magnet, where the magnetic force is greatest. The strength of the electro-magnet varies according to the sounds picked up by the microphone and therefore it creates a pattern of magnetism in the coating of the tape, as it is drawn past the pole-pieces at a steady speed.

To play back, the recorded tape is drawn at the same speed past the pole-pieces of another electro-magnet called the *playback head*. The variable magnetism of the tape induces, or creates, variable currents in the coils of wire wound round the electro-magnet in the playback head. These currents are amplified and made to drive a loudspeaker.

Before a tape reaches the recording head it passes over another electro-magnet called the *erasing head*. A high-frequency current (that is, one vibrating at a supersonic frequency) is passed through the erasing head and causes the tape to be demagnetized, thus wiping out any

Courtesy, Grundig Ltd.
A magnetic tape recorder with its microphone.

previous recording. Sometimes the recording and playback heads are combined in one. The speed at which the tape travels varies in different recorders from $1\frac{7}{8}$ i.p.s. (inches per second) to 30 i.p.s. The higher speeds give better sound quality but of course they use up more tape.

Cassette Tapes

The usual recording tapes are 6·3 mm wide and are supplied on ciné-type spools; the loose end has to be threaded past the heads and on to a second spool before the tape can be used. A cassette is merely pushed into a slot and the machine does the rest. The cassette fits easily into a pocket, and the tape is only 3·8 mm wide. It runs at $1\frac{7}{8}$ i.p.s. (4·75 cm/sec) to give playing times of 30, 45 or 60 minutes each side.

Cassettes are ideal for pre-recorded music as well as for home recording, and record companies now issue cassettes as well as gramophone records. Small cassette players can be battery-powered and can also be fitted to cars, in the same way as a car radio.

A rival to the cassette, particularly in cars, is the 8-track cartridge system, which has a larger container and uses standard 6·3 mm tape wound in an endless loop. This gives continuous playing without turning over the tape.

Stereophonic Recording

Stereophonic recording gives a more faithful reproduction of the sounds from a number of performers, such as an orchestra. A microphone picking up these sounds listens, as it were, with one ear. When the sounds are reproduced, they come from the small area of the loudspeaker instead of from instruments spread over the whole width of the platform. The result does not sound quite the same. One early way of overcoming the difficulty was to use two microphones mounted like ears on a dummy head. They were connected to telephone earpieces on the listener's head.

In 1931 the effect was tried of making two separate recordings of a performance, using two microphones specially spaced, two amplifiers and two separate recorders. Then the two recordings were played back together through independent channels to two loudspeakers about 7 feet apart. This was called *stereosonic* reproduction. However, modern methods of recording music may use as many as 20 microphones, each connected to a separate amplifier on a control desk. There the sounds are either mixed or recorded separately on magnetic tape. The general name *stereophony* has been given to these arrangements, which faithfully reproduce the differences caused by distance, breadth, height and movement.

Magnetic tape recording makes it easy to record and reproduce two or more channels together and in 1955 stereosonic tape records were put on sale. They need a special instrument for reproduction. This has its playback head in two parts, one of which picks up from the top half of the tape and the other from the bottom half. Each has its own amplifier and loudspeaker.

Stereophonic discs are now usual for classical and "pop" music, and have replaced the old "mono" dics. The two independent channels are both recorded in one groove and picked up by one stylus, which is a specially shaped sapphire or diamond—the latter lasts about 40 times as long.

The method first tried used hill-and-dale recording for one channel and lateral for the other. In 1957 this was dropped in favour of recording one channel on the left-hand wall of a V-shaped groove and the other on the right-hand wall. The pickup tracks both recordings with a single stylus, separates them and passes them to the amplifiers and loudspeakers.

Quadraphonic Recording

The twin speakers of a stereo system cover an arc of about 60°. The aim of quadraphonic recording is to extend the spread of sound around the listener to a full circle (360°). When we sit listening to a concert, the sound reaches our ears by reflection from the walls, floor and ceiling, as well as from the orchestra. To simulate this, engineers have developed a four-channel system known as quadraphony.

Recording four signals on magnetic tape or photographic film is simple, as separate tracks are possible. But records, cassettes and radio present problems when four separate or "discrete" channels are needed. Nevertheless, progress is being made towards a universal system of "surround sound", and it will eventually be possible to sit at home and hear music in just the same way as if we were in the concert hall.

Record Players

There have been many changes in the record player, or gramophone, since it was invented in 1877. In that year the first machine for recording and reproducing sound was made by Thomas Edison. A needle was attached to a membrane (skin) stretched across the narrow end of a horn. When he spoke into the horn, his voice made the membrane vibrate. The vibrations caused the needle to make tiny indentations in a piece of tin-foil which he had stretched round a revolving cylinder. The needle was arranged so that it traced a spiral around the cylinder as well as being vibrated to and fro

against the tin-foil surface. When the process was reversed and the needle was allowed to move along in the spiral groove, the indentations vibrated the needle and the membrane, and sound was produced through the horn. In a squeaky but distinct voice, the machine repeated the rhyme "Mary had a little lamb".

In 1886 Bell and Tainter substituted a wax cylinder for the tin-foil and a chisel-shaped cutter for the needle that had made the indentations. They also invented methods of duplicating the records.

In 1887 Emile Berliner substituted a revolving flat disc for the cylinder (although this idea had previously been thought of by Edison) and arranged for the cutter to make a wavy groove from side to side on the surface instead of indentations up and down into the surface like hills and valleys. In this way the machine was made to reproduce more accurately the sounds and notes at the bass end of the scale. Berliner's discs could be stamped on both faces in one movement of a press, so they were easier to copy than cylinders. His form of groove was known as the "lateral-cut" in contrast with Edison's "hill-and-dale" groove.

Edison called his machine a "phonograph" (the name still used in the United States). Bell and Tainter called their instrument a "graphophone". It was Berliner who invented the name "gramophone" for the instrument which played his duplicated records.

During the 40 years after 1887 there were many improvements in the design of the gramophone : clockwork motors (and later electric

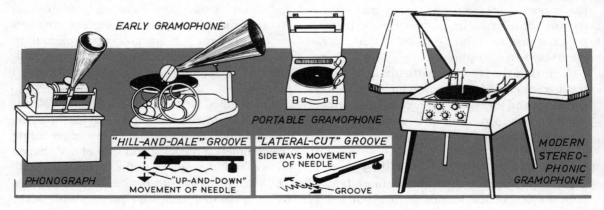

EARLY GRAMOPHONE

PORTABLE GRAMOPHONE

PHONOGRAPH

"HILL-AND-DALE" GROOVE
"UP-AND-DOWN" MOVEMENT OF NEEDLE

"LATERAL-CUT" GROOVE
SIDEWAYS MOVEMENT OF NEEDLE
GROOVE

MODERN STEREO-PHONIC GRAMOPHONE

motors) to turn the disc records at a steady speed; "sound-boxes" to make the membrane and needle more sensitive; different materials for the membrane, which came to be known as the "diaphragm"; a "tone-arm" inserted between the sound-box and the horn and arranged so as to carry the sound-box across the record so that the horn could remain stationary; and improved shapes for the horn.

The next important alteration was made between 1923 and 1927, when elecrical recording using a pickup took the place of mechanical recording with a sound-box. Electrical recording not only yields a more faithful reproduction of the original sounds but also allows the volume given out by the record player to be controlled.

It is important to keep discs and the stylus clean. The disc as it rotates attracts particles of dust, which get into the grooves and cause crackling sounds. They also get on the stylus, altering its shape so that it no longer traces the groove accurately.

RECREATION. Many public parks and open spaces have a special area called a recreation ground where games can be played. There were few recreation grounds before the 20th century, although the local authorities in Great Britain have had the power to provide for "means of exercise or amusement to the middle or humbler classes" since 1848. After World War I they became much more common, partly because organized games were more popular and partly because people began to realize that it was important for children and adults, particularly those who lived in towns, to have open spaces in which to play.

Five important developments then took place. First, the National Playing Fields Association, one of whose main objects is the provision of playing fields and recreation grounds, was founded in 1925. Second, the Carnegie United Kingdom Trust spent nearly £250,000 on playing fields, mainly between 1925 and 1940. (See CARNEGIE, ANDREW.) Third, the Central Council of Physical Recreation, a voluntary body responsible for developing sport and recreation in Britain, was founded in 1935. Next, the Physical Training and Recreation Act, which

set aside a considerable sum of money for physical recreation, intended mainly for making playing fields and swimming-pools, became law in 1937. It was restarted on a smaller scale after World War II, but was really replaced by the Education Act of 1944, which was the fifth development. This act made it a duty of all local councils to provide for physical recreation and games for people of all ages—not merely for schools.

A recreation ground may consist of little more than swings and a seesaw, or it may be equipped with quite elaborate gymnastic apparatus such as parallel bars. Play-leaders help to organize activities in the school holidays, and adventure playgrounds provide a lot of fun with the minimum of apparatus. The larger recreation grounds provide football and cricket pitches and tennis courts. The Sports Council, which since 1965 has advised the British government, encourages a wide range of sports and leisure activities, and tries to make the best use of available recreation facilities.

See also under GAMES AND SPORTS.

RED CROSS. The Red Cross takes its name from its emblem or badge, a red cross on a white background, which is the design of the Swiss flag with its colours reversed. The organization was established by international agreement in 1863 to care for soldiers who were sick or wounded in war. Since then it has greatly increased in size and activities and now has more than 100 million members who work for the relief of human suffering all over the world, in peace as well as war. The Society recognizes no distinction between race, colour or creed; in Moslem countries the name and emblem is a Red Crescent on a white background; in Iran it is a Red Lion and Sun. These national societies are united in one international organization with a common purpose—to bring help in time of human need. They are proof of man's concern for man.

In the middle ages there were no proper arrangements for nursing sick and wounded soldiers. Often monasteries were the only places where they were properly looked after, and many died before anything could be done to help them. Even when primitive medical services were sent with the armies, military hospitals were not safe from enemy attacks, and patients as well as doctors were often mercilessly killed.

The first British wartime nursing services were organized in the Crimea when Florence Nightingale and a group of nurses were sent to care for British soldiers wounded in the war. (See CRIMEAN WAR; NIGHTINGALE, FLORENCE.) The hygiene, cleanliness and comfort insisted upon by Miss Nightingale made the authorities accept higher standards and principles which have been followed ever since and which have been the basis of much Red Cross work.

How the Red Cross Began

The idea of the Red Cross suggested itself five years later to Henri Dunant, a young banker from Geneva, Switzerland. In 1859 he was travelling in northern Italy, where the French and Sardinians were fighting the Austrians. On June 24 the Battle of Solferino raged for 15 hours in sweltering heat, and Dunant, who was in the nearby town of Castiglione, saw the sufferings of the wounded. About 40,000 men lay dead or dying on the battlefield. The next day the French worked from early morning to late at night, collecting those who had survived, but it soon became obvious that their medical services were unable to deal with such huge numbers. Castiglione was turned into a vast hospital. Churches, monasteries, barracks and private houses were all filled with wounded soldiers, who had nothing but straw to lie on.

Dunant decided to organize some kind of help. He got together women and girls from the town as well as a few foreign travellers like himself. They had neither medical equipment nor expert knowledge of nursing, but they did what they could. Perhaps the most important point about their work was that they showed the same kindness to the wounded of all nationalities. *"Siamo tutti fratelli"*—"all men are brothers"—said the women of Castiglione, following Dunant's example.

Dunant came to be known as the Samaritan of Solferino, but he knew that in spite of his efforts thousands of men had died who could have been saved if they had been cared for earlier. This inspired him to write a book called

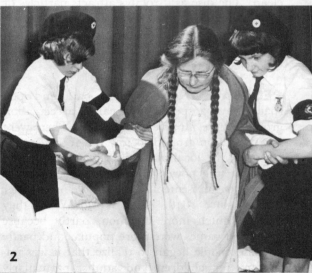

(1) Berrows Newspapers; (2) Courtesy, British Red Cross Society; (3) Keystone

(1) Red Cross members on a first-aid training exercise in Worcestershire. (2) Junior Red Cross members in Hertfordshire learning home nursing. (3) A Red Cross member escorting a baby boy brought to England by air.

A Memory of Solferino, in which he tried to bring home to people the terrible fate of soldiers wounded in battle, and pleaded for organized aid. His book came out in 1862 and before long it was being read all over Europe. Dunant described the horrors of Solferino, and went on to suggest that societies to help wounded soldiers should be set up in every country with trained volunteers and equipment prepared in peace-time; for, he wrote, "no man can say with certainty that he is for ever safe from the possibilities of war".

A young lawyer in Geneva, Gustave Moynier, chairman of the Society of Public Welfare, put Dunant's idea into practice. He formed a "Committee of Five" which called an international meeting in Geneva in 1863, as a result of which the first national societies came into being. The meeting also recommended that a diplomatic conference should be held to discuss Dunant's idea that neutral status (see NEUTRAL) on the battlefield should be granted to the wounded and to those who went to their help. This conference was held in Geneva in 1864, and on August 22 the first Convention of Geneva was signed by 12 governments. Its principle was that sick and wounded combatants in war, whatever their nationality, should be respected and cared for; that the people looking after them, the buildings sheltering them, the equipment needed for them and the transport conveying them should be protected, and that the red cross on a white ground should be the symbol of this.

The international committee in Geneva soon became known officially as the International Committee of the Red Cross. It is limited to 25 members all of whom must be Swiss, for Switzerland never takes part in war and its citizens are therefore most suitable for dealing with both sides in a war. Its main duties are to recognize new national Red Cross societies after it has checked that they are properly organized; to see that the Red Cross remains an impartial, non-political body (one that does not take sides in war or politics); to organize help for victims of war; and to arrange Red Cross services for prisoners-of-war.

As more and more governments signed the Geneva Convention, the number of national Red Cross societies increased. The British Red Cross Society was started in 1870 during the Franco-Prussian War, as the result of a letter to *The Times* by Colonel Robert Loyd-Lindsay, V.C., a veteran of the Crimea. The Lord Mayor of London opened a fund which raised £250,000 in two months to equip field hospitals and ambulances. French and German prisoners and wounded alike received attention from surgeons and nurses sent from England who numbered 200 by the end of the war. In 1898 special recognition was given by the War Office, and in 1908 a Royal Charter was granted by King Edward VII.

Meanwhile a further convention was signed at The Hague giving protection to victims of war at sea, and in 1907 regulations were made concerning the rights of prisoners of war. As war threatened, the Territorial and Reserve Forces Act was passed in Britain calling on the Red Cross to set up Voluntary Aid Detachments to be trained in case of war.

The Red Cross in War and Peace

This Act was fortunate, for World War I broke out in 1914. Thousands of volunteers staffed hospitals and sanatoria, and ran ambulances to transport wounded and disabled men. Parcels were packed for prisoners and search was made for wounded and missing men. The International Committee established a central organization in Geneva to deal with the affairs of prisoners of war which forwarded letters and parcels between prisoners and their families.

War brings an upsurge of humanitarian ideals, and in 1919 the League of Red Cross Societies was established with the task of re-building the devastation of war and helping national societies to follow a peacetime programme for the betterment of mankind. Starting with five founder members of which Britain was one, it now has 111 national societies. The League is the body which acts in times of national disaster such as flood, famine, earthquake or hurricane, and helps newly established societies with workers, material and money.

Between the wars a third Geneva Convention was signed concerned with prisoners' rights and the obligations of their captors, and in 1934 a draft convention for civilians was prepared in Tokyo. Five years later, when World War II broke out, the Red Cross again took over all the tasks it had undertaken in World War I to reduce suffering among the armed forces and to trace and care for prisoners of war. This time the work was extended to care for civilians injured in air raids and refugees (see REFUGEES). After the war the British Red Cross Society sent volunteers to the concentration camp at Belsen in Germany (see HITLER) to help look after the 60,000 inmates, and organized extra food and vitamins for the $1\frac{1}{2}$ million displaced persons in Europe. The sufferings of these people remained so alive in the conscience of the world that in 1949 the draft convention of Tokyo became the fourth Geneva Convention for the protection of civilians during war.

The British Red Cross Society has 63 branches in England and Wales, 37 in Scotland, 7 in Northern Ireland and one each in the Isle of Man and Guernsey. Jersey has a committee. In 1945 the Society extended its work to include civilian welfare. Its tasks can be grouped under the three main headings of first aid, auxiliary nursing and welfare. When there is a disaster or a serious accident these activities are combined to bring relief to the victims.

Trained V.A.D.s do first aid duty on highways, at exhibition centres, public gatherings and places of entertainment, street processions and sports events. They hold certificates in First Aid and Nursing, although men V.A.D.s do not have to take the Nursing Course. They man ambulances, help in major accidents by supplementing the work of the mobile hospital teams and give service in local hospitals, old people's and convalescent homes and under the direction of the district nurse.

The Society's welfare activities help sick persons, disabled children and adults and the aged and infirm. Clubs are run for old people and handicapped children; there is a Meals on Wheels service for those tied to their homes; while in hospital the volunteer helps to create a friendly atmosphere which speeds recovery.

The richer countries of the world feel a sense of responsibility towards the societies in the developing countries with poor resources, few technical staff and limited means. The British Red Cross Society first helped its overseas territories to form branches and then helped the branches to form independent societies. Aid is given to these societies with staff, advice and material assistance. Field officers, training officers, nurses and young volunteers are sent overseas; there is a gift scheme in operation, and in some areas the British Red Cross runs milk and feeding schemes, ambulance services and nurses' training schools.

The Junior Red Cross

The Junior Red Cross helps to bring new ideas, energy and trained volunteers into the adult Society. The first Junior Red Cross groups were formed in Australia, Canada and the United States during World War I; the British Junior Red Cross started in 1924 and soon the idea spread all over the world so that by 1968 there were 95 junior sections with 75 million young people. The ideals of the Red Cross appeal just as much to the younger volunteers as to the older ones. Members train to help in accidents and emergencies, man first-aid posts under a trained member, work in hospitals and old people's homes, visit the elderly and the handicapped and do their shopping for them. In the field of international goodwill juniors pack Disaster Relief kits for child victims of earthquakes and floods. They also prepare parcels of training equipment for juniors in overseas branches and newly formed societies.

The principles of the International Red Cross are humanity, impartiality, neutrality, independence, voluntary service, unity and universality. Perhaps these are best summed up in the motto of the Junior Red Cross: "Serve one Another".

RED INDIANS. The Redskins or Red Indians are a group of people found in America. You can read about them in the article INDIANS, AMERICAN.

RED SEA. Between Africa and Asia lies the Red Sea, almost separating the two continents. It is long and narrow, being about 1,900 kilometres from end to end and between 200 and

400 kilometres broad. Along much of its shores there are narrow coastal plains behind which rise rocky mountains or barren tablelands. At its northern end the Red Sea forks like a Y into two long narrow arms. The western arm is the Gulf of Suez and from it the Suez Canal leads to the Mediterranean Sea. (See SUEZ CANAL.) The eastern arm is the Gulf of Aqaba.

Little fresh water reaches the Red Sea so its waters are very salty. They are also very warm,

Keystone
The port of Eilat lies on the Gulf of Aquaba at the northern end of the Red Sea. The sea fills a deep trough between mountains.

the surface temperature reaching 29°C towards the southern end. The numerous coral reefs and banks are mostly near the coast but include the dangerous Daedalus Reef, which is just below the surface and right in the middle. These reefs and the irregular currents make navigation in the Red Sea difficult. As the lands on both shores are neither very fertile nor thickly populated, there is not much coastal trade. The chief ports are Suez in Egypt, Port Sudan in Sudan, Massawa in Ethiopia, Hódeida in Yemen, the port of Jedda for Moslem pilgrims journeying to Mecca in Saudi Arabia, Aqaba in Jordan and Elath in Israel.

Big ships carrying passengers and goods from Europe pass through the Suez Canal and Red Sea on their way to East Africa, India, Indonesia, the Far East and Australia. The voyage is often unpleasant because of the great heat.

It is not known for certain how the Red Sea got its name. It may have been from the reddish tint of some of the surrounding hills or of the coral reefs. The Hebrew name for southern Palestine is Edom, meaning "red", and the sea may owe its name to this. The crossing of the Red Sea by the Israelites, which is described in the Bible, probably took place near the head of the Gulf of Suez.

REDSHANK. Its long red legs ("shank" means leg) have given the redshank its name. It is a wading bird about 28 centimetres long, mainly greyish-brown with a white rump and white on the wings. This shows very plainly when the bird is flying. The bill is pinkish, with orange at the base of the lower half.

The call of the redshank consists of musical, whistling notes which it often utters as it flies. If it is disturbed when its young are small it will fly round and round calling angrily at the intruder with sharp, short notes. Its food includes insects, worms, small snails and sometimes grass and seeds.

In winter the redshank is generally seen on tidal estuaries (where the rivers enter the sea) and on mudflats. In the spring it haunts marshes, meadows, pastureland and moors. Here it lays its eggs in a hollow lined with dry grasses and usually well hidden in a tuft of grass. There are four eggs and they are blotched with dark brown on a background varying from buff to greenish.

The redshank is found in most countries of Europe where there are suitable places for it, and also in Africa and Asia. A larger bird, the spotted redshank, nests in the far north and spends the winter in the Mediterranean countries and southern Asia. It has often visited the British Isles on its journeys from one place to another, especially in the autumn. In the breeding season the spotted redshank has black

Two redshanks, one showing the white on its wings.

plumage spotted with white on the back and crimson legs. In winter it is very similar in appearance to the common redshank, but it has no white on its wings.

Greenshank. Another visiting bird is the redshank's relative the greenshank, so called from its green legs. It is larger than the common redshank and has a slightly upturned beak. Some greenshanks breed in the highlands of Scotland, where they nest on bare moorland. In winter the greenshank goes very far south, sometimes even to Australia.

REDSTART. The birds called redstarts have the very noticeable habit of flicking their orange-red tails up and down when they perch. The male common redstart, found in many parts of Great Britain in the summer, has orange red underparts also, but its back is grey, its face and throat black and its forehead white. The female

Redstarts are lively, insect-eating birds. As can be seen from this drawing, the male and female have different plumage. The female (left) is brown with a reddish tail. The male has a grey back and a black face and throat.

is the same size (about six inches) but is generally brown, except for the tail. Redstarts move about constantly, feeding by fluttering into the air after flies and small moths, or by picking insects and caterpillars off leaves; they do not feed much on the ground. Their call note is a sad "weet", which, when they are alarmed, becomes a loud "wee-tuk-tuk". The male has a short jangling song but may also imitate other birds. The nest may be built from the end of April until June, for there are sometimes two broods in a season. It is usually built in a hole in a tree or in a wall or other stonework. It is made of moss and grass with a soft lining of hair and feathers. About six bright blue eggs are laid.

The black redstart is also a European bird, which has been moving northward in recent years. A few pairs now nest regularly in south-eastern England. The male is mostly black or blackish except for the red tail; old males have white bars on their wings. The female, too, is darker than the common redstart. They nest in holes in buildings, even in cities such as London, and feed more on the ground than the common redstart.

The American redstart, found from Canada as far south as Bolivia, belongs to a different family. The male has salmon-coloured breast, wings and tail, but these are yellow in the female.

REED. The common reed is often found growing along the margins of lakes and dykes, in wet ditches, marshes and shallow waters. It grows almost all over the world from the tropics to the Arctic Circle and often forms reed swamps. It belongs to Gramineae, the grass family, and its leaves are tough and grass-like.

The flowers are purplish-brown and hang like long plumes from the height of summer to the end of autumn. Before they are fully out they are a deep colour, but as they open the plumes become looser and lighter and droop to one side. Later on they become greyish-mauve as long silky hairs grow out of them. These hairs turn into a mass of down which carries the seeds as they are blown away by the wind.

The rootstock of the common reed is long and stout, because it has to support the tall, stiff stems—sometimes ten feet high—and the broad, bright green leaves.

Besides being graceful and beautiful, the common reed is also useful. In country places in England it is often called windlestraw, and in Cornwall its name is goss. It is used for thatching, fencing and sometimes for making furniture. Reed thatching is common in parts of Norfolk, Suffolk and other counties where reeds grow abundantly. Reeds also provide food and nesting-places for some marsh birds.

The reed-maces look like reeds but belong to a different family. They grow on the shores of lakes and ponds and on river banks, and flower in July and August. The great reed-mace, or cat's tail, is often wrongly called the bulrush, but

Left: The common reed. Right: The great reed-mace.

the real bulrush is one of the sedges. The great reed-mace grows six or seven feet high, and gets its name from the way in which the tiny flowers are packed together in a velvety cushion round the stem, like the head of the mace, a heavy club, often of gold or other metal, carried on some ceremonial occasions.

Perhaps it was the sound of the wind sighing through reeds that suggested the Greek legend of Pan and Syrinx. Pan, the woodland god with the hooves of a goat, fell in love with a nymph called Syrinx, who escaped from him and was changed into a reed. From this reed Pan made a pipe, also called syrinx, and played upon it in memory of the nymph.

REED ORGAN FAMILY. Although very unlike one another, the members of the reed organ family nearly all work on the principle of the "free reed". This consists of a strip of springy metal held in a slit. The reed vibrates and produces a musical note when air is blown or sucked past it. Instruments of this family contain a whole series of reeds each of which produces a different note.

One of the simplest reed organs is the mouth-organ or harmonica (see HARMONICA), which is moved along the player's mouth, according to the notes required. The harmonium is a key-board instrument with a range of five octaves, and obtains the air for blowing on to the reeds from bellows worked by the player's feet. The

American organ, or cabinet organ, is a similar instrument but has a softer tone, and depends on air being sucked past the reeds. Harmoniums and American organs are often used in small churches and chapels.

The accordion is a hand-held instrument with bellows worked by squeezing and pulling. By pressing buttons with his fingers, the player admits air to the various reeds. His right hand plays the melody and his left hand works the bellows and at the same time presses buttons that provide the harmony. The piano accordion has a small keyboard like that of a piano instead of buttons. The concertina is a smaller form of accordion with the bellows between two six-sided ends.

The earliest form of reed organ had reeds fixed in pipes, producing notes in the manner described in the article ORGAN. These small pipe organs could be carried about, and were called regals. It is believed that the name comes from the Latin word *regula* and that the instrument was used for regulating the chanting of the monks. Regals were popular from the 15th to the 17th centuries.

REELS are Scottish folk dances arranged for groups of two or more couples. Wherever Scottish people gather for a big social occasion a reel is almost sure to be danced, for the reel means as much to the Scots as the jig means to the Irish. Reels are intended to express joy and pleasure. They are vigorous and extremely graceful dances and are particularly suited to performance by young dancers.

Although their exact history is uncertain, reels as they are danced today are believed to have taken shape towards the end of the 17th century. The earliest one known is probably the Reel of Tulloch, which started at Tulloch on Deeside (Aberdeenshire), where a congregation was waiting in a snowstorm for the preacher to arrive. To keep themselves warm they began swinging each other by the arms and dancing reel steps, accompanying themselves by their voices, and thus the Reel of Tulloch was founded.

The exact steps used in dancing these early reels are unknown, but those used at the present day seem to have been introduced by dancing masters from the European mainland who were fashionable at that time.

There are two kinds of reels—country-dance and Highland. More difficult steps are generally used in Highland reels. In country-dance reels the usual steps are the *pas de Basque*, or setting step, and the skip-change step, which is used for

Radio Times Hulton Picture Library
Scots girls dancing a strathspey and reel. They are wearing kilts and "kiltie jackets" with lace cuffs.

travelling forwards and backwards. In Highland reels the country-dance steps are elaborately developed and varied, and are more lively.

The Reel of Tulloch is danced by two couples who face each other, but the most popular reel is the Eightsome Reel, which is performed by four couples who face one another on opposite sides of a square. This reel has many figures, or set movements, and is beautiful to watch when properly danced. Variations of it are known as the Sixteensome and the Thirtytwosome, the names indicating the number of dancers taking part. The Threesome and Foursome are Highland reels.

In Scottish country-dance reels the women always hold their skirts and the men's arms hang by their sides. Men always give their right hands to their partners to lead them, and turn them with both hands, using the *pas-de-Basque* step. In Highland dancing, the dancer raises the opposite arm to the foot that is pointing. This is supposed to suggest the antlers of a deer.

Reels are best danced to the music of the bagpipes (see BAGPIPE), but nowadays they are usually danced to violin and piano. In distant parts of the Highlands where instrumental music is not obtainable, *Puirt-a-Beul* (Gaelic for "mouth music") is sung by those watching or by a chosen person. Many composers have written reel tunes for bagpipe and violin, among the better known being Niel Gow and Scott Skinner.

For Highland reels the men should wear traditional costume. This consists of kilt, tartan hose, doublet or tunic with silver or metal buttons, collar and tie, leather sporran or, for special occasions, the plaid with shoulder brooch, and seal sporran. By day the women usually wear a tartan skirt and plain white blouse, and for special occasions a white or light dress with tartan sash passed over the left shoulder and kept in place by a Highland brooch. Dancers who have a claim to a tartan should wear it. (See TARTAN.) Women and men wear light heel-less shoes or what they find most comfortable.

Highland reels may be seen at the Highland Games at Braemar, Aboyne, Inverness and Oban (see HIGHLAND GAMES). Both Highland and country-dance reels are danced at all the Highland balls in Scotland and at Caledonian balls all over the world. Books with dances have been published by the Royal Scottish Country Dance Society, which was founded in 1923 and has branches in many parts of Great Britain and the Commonwealth.

The Eightsome Reel

The following is a short description of the Eightsome Reel.

The eight dancers take their places in couples, side by side, each couple forming one side of a square. They all face inwards, with the woman on the man's right. Joining hands at shoulder level, the dancers slip-step in a circle to the left for eight steps, and back again to the right for eight steps.

The women, still with their left hands held by their partners, give their right hands to the women opposite them in the form of a right-angled cross, they being in the centre. All dancers then take four skip-change steps forwards. Next, all partners face each other and take four *pas-de-Basque* steps, turning each other with the same number of steps while giving both hands at shoulder level. Then, using 16 skip-change steps, they form a circular grand chain, giving right and left hands alternately and the women going in the opposite direction to the men, until all are back in their places.

The first woman then stands in the centre and dances any reel steps while the remaining dancers, facing inwards, join hands, and slip-step eight steps to the left and then eight to the right. The woman in the middle now dances to her partner with two *pas-de-Basque* steps, and is turned by him, giving both hands at shoulder level, in two *pas-de-Basque* steps. The man returns to his place, while the woman sets to the opposite man and is turned by him in the same way. She finishes facing her partner, ready to pass by the left shoulder for a "reel of three", or figure-of-eight, danced with her partner and the opposite man. The whole figure is then repeated, the woman in the centre setting to and dancing with the men of the other two couples.

Then the figures are repeated by the men, after which the eight dancers join hands, facing inwards, and slip-step in a circle first to the left and then to the right, then repeating the figures of the cross and the grand chain.

REFLECTION is a word which comes from Latin and means "bending back". Objects that do not give off light by themselves can be seen because they reflect, or bend back, the light which falls on them. It is this reflected light which, when received by the eye, makes the object visible. Heat, sound and radio waves can also be reflected. Waves in water can be reflected from cliffs or even by the sides of a bath.

The general rule is that regular reflection does not happen unless the irregularities in the surface of the reflector are fairly small compared with the wave-length being reflected. (The wave-length is the distance between the crest of one wave and the next.) Sea waves are not reflected by jagged and broken cliffs. In the same way, light waves—whose wave-length is only about one-fifty-thousandth of an inch—are not reflected regularly except by very smooth polished surfaces. Rougher surfaces scatter the light because their surface particles are inclined to one another at various angles, forming large numbers of tiny reflectors which reflect light in all directions. The page on which this article is printed is an example; it looks white from any direction because the many little reflectors on its surface reflect white light in all directions.

When light or any other kind of wave motion (sound, heat, radio) strikes a regular reflector, it bounces off at the same angle as that at which it met the reflecting surface. On looking into a plain (flat) mirror a person sees a full-size image, or picture, of himself, but his left eye is opposite the right eye of the image and his right eye opposite the left eye of the image. Also, the image

DRIVING MIRROR

SHAVING MIRROR

MIRROR

PATH OF LIGHT IN CONVEX MIRROR

PATH OF LIGHT IN CONCAVE MIRROR

A convex mirror reflects many objects in miniature. A concave mirror gives an enlarged reflection of an object.

appears to be as far "behind" the mirror as the person is in front of it. These effects are caused by the laws of reflection, which state that the angle of reflection is equal to the angle of incidence and is in the same plane. (The *incident* ray is the one between the object being reflected and the mirror.)

Curved mirrors may be convex or concave. A convex mirror bulges out in the middle and a concave one has a hollow (cave) in the middle. When the object is close to a concave mirror it gives an enlarged image and this type of mirror is therefore used for shaving and by dentists and doctors for examining their patients' teeth, throats and so forth. A concave mirror shaped in a special curve called a parabola reflects a parallel beam from a source of light held at a point called the *focus* of the mirror. Parabolic mirrors are therefore used for searchlights, motor-car headlights and long-beam electric torches. Convex mirrors give an image smaller than the object and are therefore used as rear-view mirrors by motorists, as they show the driver a view of the whole width of the road behind him.

Heat waves have a wave-length somewhat greater than that of light waves. They can also be reflected by smooth surfaces, and it is common to have a curved or bowl-shaped reflector in an electric fire. The reflection of sound causes echoes (see ECHO). Use is made of the reflection of radio waves for finding the direction and distance of objects out of sight, such as distant aircraft. This is explained in the article RADAR.

REFORMATION.
This is the name given to the religious movement started by Martin Luther (1483–1546) which resulted in the form of Christianity called Protestantism. Luther was a German friar who came to think that the explanation given by most men in his day of how God saves man was wrong. He held that man himself is too weak to do anything at all towards achieving his own salvation; God alone can save him. All that man can do is to make use of God's gift of faith, by which he is convinced that Christ's death on the Cross has forgiven his sins. Luther thought that men had wrongly come to believe that they could win salvation

from God by prayers and good acts and he rejected the teaching of the Catholic Church that grace, the power which God gives man to enable him to live the Christian life, really changes man's inner nature. He believed that man remained inwardly just as sinful as ever, but that grace prevented his sinful nature from getting the upper hand.

It was in 1517 that Luther first came into conflict with the Church, by protesting against the sale of indulgences. An indulgence was not (as some people imagine) either a licence to commit sin or a forgiveness of sin, but a pardon of the punishment due for past sin. It was held by the Catholic Church that even when a man had repented and been forgiven by God he still had to make amends to God for his wrongdoing by suffering, either in this world or in Purgatory. It was believed, too, that the Pope had been given by God the power to lessen this punishment because of the good deeds done by Christ and the saints. To gain an indulgence a man was required to perform a good act himself and, as this often took the form of giving money for church purposes, it seemed as if the church were selling these pardons. Luther protested, not only against this, but also against the whole idea of indulgences which did not fit in with his belief that man is saved by faith.

He had thought that the church would agree with what he said, but soon found that he was regarded as a heretic. Sure that he was right, he refused to alter his mind and was excommunicated by the Pope. Many people in Germany supported him, for the church was in a corrupt state and they were ready to revolt against it. Many of the important church offices were held by priests who thought more of making money than of carrying out their duties; many held more than one post and got their work done by others; some were men of bad life. The Pope took much money from Germany in taxes and among the laity there was much ignorance of religion and much superstition.

Everyone who thought at all knew that reform was needed, although many saw no need of any alteration in teaching. With so much support behind him Luther went on to attack other Catholic beliefs, teaching that all men were priests and that the clergy were no more than men set apart to do what any Christian could do. He denied that the Eucharist (see SACRAMENTS) was a sacrifice in which Christ's death was represented before God and taught a different doctrine of the sacraments, saying that they did not give men grace but only strengthened their faith, and he changed church services in accordance with his ideas. He held, too, that all men could find the Christian faith in the Bible directly, without any need for Popes and bishops to explain Scripture. He said that the church had hidden the true gospel for centuries, and therefore it was right to separate from a church which had gone astray, to recover the teaching of the Apostles and the early church and to form new Christian communities in which the truth, as he saw it, could be taught.

Catholics of course thought that Luther entirely misunderstood the Bible and so there grew up a division in Germany between them and the Protestants, as Luther's followers came to be called after 1529. This split in Germany was accompanied by others elsewhere, for in Switzerland Huldrych Zwingli (1481–1531) at Zürich and John Calvin (1509–1564) at Geneva preached a Reformation very much like Luther's in its main points but different in detail. They denied the doctrine that Christ is really present in the bread and wine of the Eucharist (a belief that Luther kept) and their ideas of the organization of the church were different from his. These differences weakened Protestantism, for there were fierce arguments between Lutherans, Zwinglians and Calvinists. Partly for this reason, and also because at the Council of Trent (1545–1563) Catholicism made its beliefs clearer and reformed abuses, Protestantism did not make such rapid progress after the middle of the century as it had done earlier. Lutheranism only won half of Germany and, although Calvinism spread greatly in France, Holland, Scotland and elsewhere, nearly all south Europe and much of the north remained Catholic.

In England the Reformation took a special form. King Henry VIII (1509–1547) quarrelled with the Pope about his marriage, rejected papal authority and claimed to be Head of the English Church. But he made few other changes. Under Edward VI, his son (1547–1553), Protestantism was established, but his sister Mary I (1553–1558) brought back Catholicism and the authority of the Pope and burnt many Protestants alive. Elizabeth, her younger sister (1558–1603), again turned against the Pope and tried to keep both Catholics and Protestants in one Church of England controlled by bishops in the same way as before the Reformation. She did not entirely succeed ; both the supporters of the Papacy and the extreme Protestants rejected her settlement, but nevertheless the Church of England to this day is not exactly like the other Christian bodies which developed out of the disputes of the 16th century.

Practically nobody at this time believed that there could be more than one religion in a country and most thought it their duty to persecute those Christians with whom they disagreed. So all over Europe people were put to death, imprisoned or deprived of rights or property for their religion. Catholics persecuted Protestants where they had the upper hand and Protestants persecuted Catholics in countries where the Reformation was supported by the government. Wars of religion occurred in Germany when the Emperor Charles V (1519–1556) tried to put down Protestantism. The Thirty Years' War (1618–1648) was also the result of the rivalry between the two religions. Neither Protestantism nor Catholicism won and Germany has remained divided in religion down to our own day. In France the Catholics and Protestants fought each other from 1562 to 1598, when King Henri IV, who had been a Calvinist, but had become a Catholic, guaranteed toleration to the Huguenots, as the French Calvinists were called.

Nearly all European countries now allow freedom of religion but this has not of course healed the division in Christendom caused by the Reformation and the opposition to it. Although much more friendly to each other than they used to be, Catholics and Protestants still understand Christianity in very different ways and both naturally think the others' beliefs mistaken. Many who want Christian unity restored are doing their best to see whether the differences, when looked at closely, are as great as they seem, but it will need many years of patient work by scholars before any result can be expected. Meanwhile western Europe and other parts of the world contain large numbers of both Protestants and Catholics with some countries, such as Spain, Italy and Belgium, almost entirely Catholic, others, such as Sweden, Norway and Denmark, almost entirely Protestant and others in which both religions are to be found in different proportions. From this can be seen the importance of the Reformation in Christian history: in the Middle Ages the Eastern and Western Churches had broken apart; in the 16th century Western Christianity was even more deeply divided by the differences arising from the Reformation.

REFRACTION is the name given to the bending of rays of light when they pass from one transparent substance to another. Transparent substances are those such as air, water, glass and clear plastics which allow light to pass through them. If, however, a ruler is dipped slantwise into water or a house is viewed through an empty bottle, it may be observed that something happens when the light passes from one transparent substance to the other. The ruler appears to be

THE PENNY CANNOT BE SEEN

UNTIL WATER IS ADDED

An experiment with refraction. The bending of the ray of light as it enters the water brings the penny into view.

bent and the house looks distorted, or misshapen. These effects are caused by refraction.

If a ray of light falls on a transparent substance at right angles to the surface it continues in the same straight line. (This direction at right angles to the surface is called the normal.) Rays that make an angle with the normal, however, are bent. The Dutch scientist Willebrord Snell discovered the laws of refraction in 1621. When a ray of light passes from air into glass or water it is bent *towards* the normal. When the ray travels from glass or water into air it is bent *away from* the normal. This explains why the ruler dipped slantwise in water appears bent and why a fish in a clear stream looks nearer the surface than it is. In the same way, a swimming bath looks shallower than it really is because light from the bottom is bent away from the normal on leaving the surface of the water, and thus seems to come from a point nearer the surface.

Here is quite a good trick depending on refraction. Put a coin at the bottom of an empty pudding basin and then place yourself so that by peering over the rim of the basin you can just *not* see the coin. If someone now fills the basin with water you will see the coin appear.

The property of refraction is used by shaping pieces of glass in special curves so that all the rays of light passing through them are refracted in such a way as to form an image, or picture. This happens because the rays are caused to converge (come together) or diverge (spread out) according to the shape of the curve. You can read more about this in the article LENS. Another effect of refraction is explained in the article MIRAGE.

White light consists of all the colours of the rainbow (see COLOUR) and the angle through which each colour is refracted differs. The violet rays are refracted most and the red ones least. Therefore white light is split into bands of light of different colours when passed through a triangular-shaped piece of glass called a prism. The same thing happens when the sun's rays are refracted by raindrops (see RAINBOW).

REFRIGERATOR. The refrigerator is a machine used for making and keeping things cold. It takes its name from the Latin word *frigidus*, meaning "cold". A refrigerator may be a small domestic one for keeping milk and foods fresh, or a "deep freeze" for keeping quick-frozen foods, or a large machine, such as those for making ice cream or for cooling the holds (cargo spaces) of chilled-meat ships.

The reason why cold helps meat, fish and other perishable foods to keep fresh is that the tiny creatures called bacteria (see BACTERIA) become less active as the temperature falls. Above a temperature of 10°C, bacteria grow rapidly and cause food to decay.

Long before refrigerators were invented, people used to collect snow and ice for making cool drinks and for keeping food fresh. The ice was normally stored in pits or special underground ice-houses. Sometimes the ice was used in the old-fashioned ice-boxes. These were boxes whose thick walls were insulated (padded) to keep out the heat, and they were arranged with a top compartment for the ice and a bottom compartment for the food. Heat from the food warmed the air, causing it to rise and give up its heat to the ice, some of which therefore melted. The cooled air, being heavier than warm air, then sank into the food compartment and took more heat from the food. This process went on until all the ice had melted.

Courtesy, Electrolux Ltd.
A domestic absorption refrigerator with seven-and-a-quarter cubic feet of space, including shelves behind the door.

Most refrigerators depend on the fact that when a liquid is evaporated, or turned into vapour (gas), it takes heat from its surroundings. If a little methylated spirit is poured into the palm of the hand it feels cold because it takes heat from the hand as it evaporates. Wet your finger and blow on it; it feels colder for the same reason.

In refrigerators, the cooling is done by evaporating some chemical substance that changes from a gas to a liquid and back again at a convenient temperature. One such substance is ammonia, a gas which makes this change at a temperature of $-33.5°C$. The English scientist Michael Faraday in 1823 changed ammonia gas to ammonia liquid by compressing (squeezing) it, and thus laid the foundations of refrigeration without knowing it.

Compression Refrigerators

Ammonia is sometimes used as a refrigerant (a substance which refrigerates) in large cold-storage plants. The simplest form of refrigerator is that making use of a compressor. This type of machine is often used in household refrigerators and it is the easiest to understand. It is also the oldest, having been developed in the 1870s by the German scientist Karl von Linde.

A small compression refrigerator has outside the storage compartment an electric motor which takes current from the mains and drives a compressor. The compressor draws in gas and compresses it just as a bicycle pump draws in air and compresses it. The compressor grows hot by compressing the gas in exactly the same way as the bicycle pump does when pumped hard. The heated gas is passed through coils of pipe called condensing coils. These coils are exposed to the outside air and give up their heat to it. They are helped to do this by having fins which give out heat as a radiator does. The air is kept moving through the coils by a fan driven by the motor.

The effect of cooling the compressed gas is to liquefy it. It is then led through a small nozzle into a much larger pipe called the evaporator pipe, which is coiled round the frost-box inside the storage compartment. The pressure in this pipe is much less, so the liquid gas squirted into it expands and evaporates, or changes into gas again. To do this, however, it must obtain heat from somewhere. The only place it can obtain it from is the frost-box and the contents of the storage compartment, so these are forced to grow

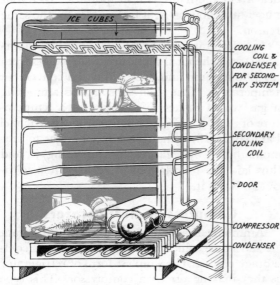

A compression refrigerator, showing the cooling mechanism.

colder. The gas from the evaporator pipe is then led back to the compressor, which sends it round on another journey in the same manner.

The refrigerator is usually fitted with a thermostat in the frost-box. The thermostat is a switch that can be set to work at any particular temperature, thus regulating the temperature inside the refrigerator between cool and very cold. When the temperature inside the frost-box rises to the temperature to which the thermostat is set, the switch closes and the compressor-motor starts to work. When the inside temperature is reduced below the set temperature once more, the thermostat opens the switch and the motor stops.

Besides ammonia, other gases used in refrigerators are sulphur dioxide, methyl chloride, carbon dioxide and a rather complicated chemical called freon. In large machines, such as those used at skating rinks and meat-freezing works, the evaporator pipes containing cold liquid gas are generally used for cooling brine (salt water) which is circulated round the rink or storage compartment to cool it in its turn.

Absorption Refrigerators

The working parts of an absorption-type machine look very different from those of a compression refrigerator. The absorption type is common for household refrigerators. It makes use of ammonia, which it heats, condenses into liquid and evaporates, but it has no mechanical pump for compressing the gas.

In the absorption-type machine, liquid ammonia is heated in a boiler or generator by means of an electric heating coil like that in an electric iron, or even by a flame burning gas or paraffin (kerosene). The liquid ammonia is made of a strong solution (mixture) of ammonia in water. The heating drives off the ammonia as gas which is led away to a condenser which cools it so that it liquefies. The liquid ammonia then flows to an evaporator where it is able to expand, thus changing into gas again and absorbing heat from the frost-box. The evaporator also contains hydrogen gas, which mingles with the ammonia, forming a heavy mixed gas that sinks to the bottom of the evaporator. The mixed gas passes through pipes to a container called the absorber. The absorber in turn is connected with the boiler. Some of the water from which the ammonia was driven off trickles back from the boiler to the absorber and combines with the ammonia in the mixed gas. This ammonia solution returns to the boiler to be heated again. The hydrogen from the mixed gas, being light, rises to the top of the absorber and returns to the evaporator.

Although more difficult to understand, the absorption refrigerator has some advantages over the compression type. It has no moving parts to wear out or make a noise and will work without electricity or gas from the mains. Also, its gas and liquid system can be joined up as a "sealed unit" which cannot leak. On the other hand, the compression refrigerator, being much more efficient, costs less to run.

Dry Ice

A substance called "dry ice" is much used in modern refrigeration. It is actually solid carbon dioxide, which is obtained as a by-product, or extra product, from the artificial manufacture of ammonia. The great advantages of dry ice over ordinary ice are that it is much colder $(-78\frac{1}{2}$ degrees Centigrade instead of 0 degrees Centigrade) and that it does not melt to a liquid but *sublimes*, or changes directly from a solid to a gaseous state, without leaving behind a wet mess.

The first important use of dry ice was for packing ice cream. Nowadays meat, fish and other perishable foods are sent thousands of miles and kept in perfect condition with dry ice. The carbon dioxide gas given off surrounds the food in the lorry or railway van and helps to protect it against the bacteria in the air.

In the same way, eggs preserved with dry ice remain fresh for a very long time. In the ordinary way, eggs grow stale because carbon dioxide leaks out of them through the pores (tiny holes) in the shell. This does not occur when the eggs are refrigerated with dry ice as they are surrounded by carbon dioxide gas. Florists can delay the opening of rosebuds for three days in the carbon dioxide atmosphere given off by dry ice.

Chilled meat is carried from countries like New Zealand, Australia and Argentina in ships whose holds are cooled by compression-type refrigerators. The ships that carry meat may also carry butter or cheese but not fruit, as if the three kinds of produce are carried together they spoil one another.

REFUGEES are people who have been driven from their homes. Usually the cause is war or some political upheaval, but sometimes people have been forced to flee for religious reasons. For example, the Huguenots, or French Protestants, took refuge in England, Germany and the Netherlands after 1685, when King Louis XIV made Protestantism illegal in France. (See HUGUENOTS.) The Israelites when they were led by Moses out of bondage in Egypt were really refugees, and so were Jesus Christ and Mary His mother and Joseph when they fled to escape King Herod's slaughter of male babies.

There is a clear difference between refugees and emigrants. Emigrants are people who settle in other countries because they want to (see EMIGRATION); but refugees have no choice.

Great Britain has since 1914 given refuge to people from many countries: from Belgium in World War I; from Russia after the revolution

Keystone
A refugee and her child seek shelter in a concrete pipe.

of 1917; from Spain in the Spanish Civil War of 1936–1939; and from Germany and Austria in the years when the Nazis were persecuting Jews and others who would not accept Nazi ideas. (See NAZISM.) Later there came refugees from Poland and in 1956–1957 from Hungary. Some of the biggest refugee movements in history took place when India was divided into the two independent countries of India and Pakistan in 1947. Soon afterwards about 5,000,000 Hindus and Sikhs moved out of West Pakistan into India, and about the same number of Moslems left India for West Pakistan.

It is hard to be a refugee. It means finding a new home, new friends, and a new school, and often having to learn a new language and a new way of life. Fortunately there are kind people in all civilized countries, who are willing to befriend refugees and help them to find homes and work. Refugees often become valuable citizens of their new country, for they bring new blood and new ideas, and most governments recognize the importance of helping them to become contented and useful people.

Nearly every refugee problem is connected with more than one nation and therefore the best organization for helping refugees and for giving them a new start is an international one. In 1921 the League of Nations appointed the Norwegian explorer and statesman, Dr. Fridtjof Nansen, as High Commissioner for Refugees. (See NANSEN, FRIDTJOF.) This did a great deal to help the refugees of World War I and the Russian revolution, and the idea has been continued by the United Nations since World War II. Some of the countries which have received large numbers of refugees in recent years, such as Canada and Australia, call them "new citizens" instead of refugees. This helps the newcomers to forget the terrors of the past and to think of a settled and hopeful future.

REFUSE DISPOSAL.

What happens to the rubbish produced daily in every household? Some hundreds of years ago some of it would have been left lying on the floors of people's houses and some would have been thrown into the streets. Since then there has been a considerable increase in our population and a greater herding together of people into large towns and, more important still, a general desire to improve living conditions. Therefore more attention has been paid to the proper disposal of waste matter.

It is estimated that household refuse contains the following :

Material	Percentage by weight
Fine dust	15
Cinders	3
Vegetable and other matter liable to decay	20
Paper	37
Metal, including metal containers	9
Rags	2
Glass	9
Plastics	2
Other matter such as wood, pottery, stones etc.	3
	100

The amount of refuse produced daily in England is about 805 kilograms per 1,000 population, or nearly a kilogram for each person, in one day.

Apart from looking very untidy, it would be dangerous for refuse containing broken bottles, pieces of metal and so on to lie about the streets and houses. Also much of the refuse consists of vegetable and other matter which may go bad. When damp, this sort of refuse rots very quickly and it may give off an unpleasant smell. In order to safeguard health and to keep streets and the surroundings of houses tidy there must be an organized system of refuse storage and disposal.

For this three things are necessary. The first is that all refuse shall be properly stored, the second is that the refuse shall be collected as frequently as possible in order to remove it before it rots, and the third is that the refuse shall be disposed of in a sanitary manner.

It is necessary to store refuse in such a way that flies and other pests cannot get at it. The most suitable container is the dustbin, made of metal or plastic, which can be cleaned and has handles by which it can be carried, or a non-returnable paper or plastic sack, fitted into a protected holder, which is easily collected. Refuse should be removed as speedily as possible. Most sanitary authorities employ special staff and covered vehicles for the purpose. Everybody knows the dustmen who call once or twice a week with their big dustcart. They may call at large blocks of flats more frequently and at restaurants—which produce a lot of refuse but have little storage space for it—once a day.

Refuse is usually collected in one of the following ways : (1) The dustman takes an empty bin to the house, tips the contents of the householder's bin into it and carries it back to the dustcart. This means that the dustman has to make only one journey, but it is not a satisfactory method as the tipping of contents from one bin to the other gives a chance for dust and paper to be blown about. (2) The dustman takes the householder's bin to the dustcart, empties it and returns the empty bin. This needs two journeys. (3) The dustman takes an empty sack to each house and removes the full one, this procedure being followed throughout the collection. This system is hygienic as a fresh container is left each week, there is no dust when the contents are discharged into the vehicle and the system is much quieter and cleaner than handling metal bins.

To get some idea of the quantity of refuse to be disposed of let us take Greater London. The total population is about 7,400,000 and the

A compressor dustcart automatically lifts a bin, empties it and crushes the rubbish.

quantity of refuse disposed of annually is about 2,858,000 tonnes. This includes refuse from businesses, shops and civic amenities. The amount of refuse produced in Greater London is higher than the average for Britain because of the additional number of people working in London, the number of tourists and the large number of hotels and restaurants.

Destroying and Saving Refuse

The methods of disposal most generally used are controlled tipping and incineration (burning). Controlled tipping is the tipping of refuse into disused gravel pits, quarries and other holes in the ground. It is necessary to control this tipping if fly-breeding and insanitary conditions are to be avoided. This is done by putting the refuse down in layers and covering each layer with earth, by preventing papers or other debris from being blown away, and by seeing that no refuse is left uncovered. Many authorities have used this method to fill in unsightly pits and have afterwards levelled the site, planted trees, sown grass seed and so transformed useless and ugly areas into parks and recreation grounds.

By incineration most of the combustible (burnable) material found in the refuse is burned in a specially designed furnace or incinerator. One very important advantage of this method is that all offensive matter is made harmless, and substances that might breed flies and disease-carrying organisms are destroyed. The heat produced by incineration is often used to drive machinery and to provide hot water for the staff at the disposal station. The Turkish baths of Cairo (Egypt) have been heated for many centuries by the heat produced by burning the city's refuse. Refuse from several towns in the Ruhr District of Germany is burnt in a special power station near Essen. The refuse is passed over a magnetic separator to remove tins and pieces of iron, and then burnt with the aid of fuel oil and powdered coal to provide electric power. Refuse from an area in north London is taken to a large incinerator. The refuse is burnt and the heat generated is converted into electricity, the surplus being supplied to the National Grid.

With all methods of refuse disposal some form of salvage, or saving of usable materials, should be undertaken. Many local authorities have plants to recover from refuse such materials as metals, bottles and jars, paper and cardboard. (See SALVAGING.)

The Garchey System

A new method of disposing of refuse, called the Garchey system, was invented in France about 1930. This uses water to carry off refuse direct from the dwelling, much like the method employed in a water-closet. It was introduced in Leeds in 1934, London in 1949, Birmingham and Newcastle upon Tyne in 1954 and in Sheffield in 1959. So far it has been used only in blocks of flats.

The whole of the apparatus to be used with the Garchey system may be installed within the housing estate to be served. Each flat has a special sink with an outlet at the bottom and a plug. Fitted underneath the sink is a large metal container looking like a water-closet. A branch pipe is taken from the container to a vertical pipe which runs the height of the building.

When household refuse of any sort is to be disposed of, the sink plug is lifted and the refuse and water are discharged into the container beneath. Then the housewife operates a valve in the container and the refuse is carried by water down the vertical pipe into a chamber at the bottom, outside the building. At regular intervals the refuse is withdrawn from the chamber through underground pipes to the incinerating plant, where the water is driven off and the refuse is dried and finally burnt, leaving behind a small residue known as clinker.

With this system dustbins are not required and much of the unpleasant work associated with refuse collection and disposal is abolished. However, this system is expensive to install and it makes salvage very difficult, so it may not be widely used until the need to salvage certain valuable materials has passed.

(The disposal of waste water from domestic drains is explained in SEWER.)

REGIMENTS are army units, but the word regiment has several meanings. For instance, the whole of the British Army's artillery is known as the Royal Regiment of Artillery, but this is divided into several artillery regiments, which are fighting units each consisting of a regimental headquarters and (usually) three batteries. Besides artillery, there are also regiments of cavalry, tanks and infantry. Cavalrymen were mounted on horseback until shortly before World War II when they received light tanks and motor vehicles instead. A regiment of cavalry or of tanks is one unit of about 700 men and 100 vehicles under the command of a lieutenant-colonel. A regiment of infantry, however, consists of one *or more* battalions, each of about 800 men and 60 vehicles under a lieutenant-colonel.

As a regiment of cavalry or tanks consists of a single unit it requires no further explanation. The infantry is more complicated. Most infantry regiments are connected with some particular part of the country and have county names, such as the Cheshire Regiment.

Until the 1960s most infantry regiments consisted of one regular battalion and one or two territorial battalions. In 1966, however, the territorial Army was disbanded and replaced by the Territorial and Army Volunteer Reserve (TAVR), which was much smaller and was organized in small formations such as companies. As a result, infantry regiments were reduced to one regular battalion. Some were allowed to remain as separate regiments under their old names, but others were amalgamated (joined) with regiments of the same kind to form what are called "large regiments" and have more than one battalion. For example, the Royal Greenjackets were formed by amalgamating older infantry regiments, including the Rifle Brigade and the King's Royal Rifle Corps. The riflemen were the first British soldiers to wear camouflage green instead of red coats—hence the regiment's name. All the battalions of a large regiment carry on the traditions of the old regiments forming it, so if one battalion is later disbanded its traditions are maintained. The "large regiment" is now the standard infantry unit.

All British regiments have a "Colonel of the Regiment" who, strange though it may seem, is often a field marshal or a general. He looks after the interests of the regiment as a whole. Several regiments have the Queen or some other member of the royal family as their Colonel-in-Chief. A few have a foreign sovereign—the queens of the Netherlands and Belgium are Allied Colonels-in-Chief of the Queen's Regiment.

Over the years many changes have been made in British regiments and their titles. In 1881 Edward Cardwell, the War Minister, introduced reforms which resulted in the amalgamation, or combining, of infantry regiments to form about half the previous number. Each of the new regiments consisted of two battalions, one of which was to serve at home and the other abroad. Under this system the regiments were given names in place of their old numbers.

The next big change came in 1908 when R. B. Haldane (later Lord Haldane) changed the old "volunteer infantry battalions" into territorial units which were brought into the infantry regiments. Thus until 1966 regiments had both regular and territorial battalions. In World Wars I and II all infantry regiments raised extra battalions. Some had as many as 20 battalions.

After World War I several cavalry regiments were amalgamated and given new titles which combined their old numbers, such as "13th/18th Royal Hussars" and "17th/21st Lancers". After World War II most infantry regiments were reduced to one regular battalion and in many cases the number of territorial battalions was reduced.

In 1957 it was decided to reduce the size of the regular army and this resulted in the amalgamation of 12 regiments of the Royal Armoured Corps (6 cavalry and 6 tank regiments) and 30 infantry regiments. The infantry regiments were grouped into brigades. Each brigade contained three or four regiments. Most of the brigades were given geographical names such as Lowland, Highland, Home Counties, Midland, Lancastrian, Yorkshire and Welsh.

Among several famous regiments which disappeared as a result of this change were the Queen's Bays (2nd Dragoon Guards) and the Buffs (Royal East Kent Regiment).

Today, brigades and the "battle groups" which will succeed them in the 1980s, are grouped into larger formations called divisions. These are described in the article ARMIES.

Traditions and Customs

Every British regiment has its battle honours, consisting of a list of the campaigns and battles in which it has fought. Most regiments have colours, which are flags beautifully embroidered with the regiment's badge and chief battle honours and are always treated with the greatest respect. Rifle regiments do not have colours, as in earlier times they acted as scouts in advance of the rest of the army where large flags would have shown up too much.

The first battle honour was that of Tangier, which is a town in North Africa. The honour was awarded to the Royal Dragoons, the Grenadier and Coldstream Guards, the Royal Scots and the Queen's Royal Regiment, which had been sent to protect Tangier when it came to Charles II in 1662 as part of the dowry of his wife, Catherine of Braganza.

The Minden battle honour was won by six regiments. They were the 12th, 20th, 23rd, 25th, 37th and 51st Foot, later known as the Suffolk Regiment, the Lancashire Fusiliers, the Royal Welch Fusiliers, the King's Own Scottish Borderers, the Royal Hampshire Regiment and the Yorkshire Light Infantry. At the Battle of Minden, Germany, which was fought on August 1, 1759, during the course of the Seven Years' War, these regiments defeated the whole French army of 50,000 men. As they advanced the soldiers plucked roses from the hedgerows and put them in their hats. Ever since then, all six regiments have worn roses on the anniversary of the battle.

Another honour was that gained by Bland's Dragoons, now part of the Queen's Own Hussars. At the Battle of Dettingen in 1743 they captured a pair of silver kettle-drums and afterwards were allowed to have an extra drummer and drum-horse for them. The regiment's battle honours are inscribed on the drums.

The wars against Napoleon gave rise to many of the traditions that distinguish regiments from one another, such as the winning of a new hat-badge or a nickname. For instance, at the Battle of Alexandria in 1801, the 28th Foot (later Gloucestershire Regiment) was attacked both in front and from the rear. Therefore the rear rank turned about and beat off the attack. In memory of this the regiment was given the "back number" to be worn at the back of the head-dress. At first this was the number 28, later changed to a badge of a sphinx (see SPHINX). At the Battle of Albuera in 1811, the 57th Foot (now part of the Queen's Regiment) won the name of "The Die-Hards" from the last words of their colonel, who was killed at their head urging them to take careful aim and die hard.

Some customs and traditions commemorate things other than victories or gallant actions. The East Yorkshire Regiment continued to wear mourning for General Wolfe, who was killed in 1759 in the battle for Quebec. Sir John Moore, who was killed at the battle of Corunna (Spain) in 1809, was remembered by the mourning lace worn by the 9th Foot (now part of the Royal Anglian Regiment) who buried him at dead of night. Silver wreaths of immortelles (the everlasting flowers) were borne on the colour spike of the South Wales Borderers (now the Royal Regiment of Wales) to commemorate the tragic fate of the regiment when massacred by the Zulus at Isandhlwana in 1879. The "flash" of black ribbons worn on the coat collar by the Royal Welch Fusiliers is a reminder of the days when men wore their hair in a short tail tied with a ribbon bow.

There are also some musical customs with varied origins. For instance, the Royal Lincolnshire and the Worcestershire Regiments served together in India in the 19th century. After that each of them played the other's regimental march before its own in order to seal the friendship. The march of the 34th Foot (later the Border Regiment) commemorated the Battle of Arroyo Molinos in 1811 during the Peninsular War, when they captured the whole of the 34th French regiment. The march of the Gordon Highlanders is "The Cock of the North", with which the wounded Piper G. Findlater, V.C., played the regiment into battle in the Tirah campaign, an Indian frontier war of 1897.

Many regiments have special days on which they commemorate a battle or other great event in their history. For example the Gloucestershire Regiment kept April 23 to mark the magnificent stand of their 21st Battalion in 1951 during the Korean War.

Each regiment has its place in the book known as the Army List, so that it is always possible if two or more are on parade together, to know which is the senior and should therefore take up its position on the right of the line.

REINDEER.

REINDEER. Everyone has seen pictures of reindeer, for they are the animals that are said to draw the sledge of Father Christmas. Reindeer are a kind of large deer, today found only in the far north, including the group of arctic islands known as Spitsbergen. In prehistoric times, however, they roamed over much of Europe and were even found in the far north of Scotland until about the 12th century. In 1952 reindeer from Sweden were let loose in Rothiemurchus forest in Inverness, Scotland.

Reindeer, which are the domesticated form of the caribou (see CARIBOU), are the only deer in

M. N. P. Utsi

There have been reindeer in Scotland since 1952. This photograph, taken in the Cairngorms, shows a reindeer bull, cow and ox (a male that cannot breed).

which both the males and females have antlers. These are wide-spreading and branched. Reindeer are heavily built animals, more than 1 metre high at the shoulder. They are protected from the cold by a thick skin and two coats of hair, a long coarse outer one and a fine, woolly inner one. The colour of the outer coat changes from dark brown in summer to a lighter brown in winter, and a whitish collar of long hair round the neck hangs down like a mane.

Reindeer have short, stocky legs and very broad hoofs which spread out, making it easier for them to travel over snowy or swampy ground. They have a shuffling, sidling way of moving, but can travel fast and go for a long way without becoming tired.

During the summer reindeer feed in large herds in grassy inland valleys. In autumn some herds set off towards the coast, where they feed on seaweed. When winter comes reindeer return inland, this time to hilly country where the snow does not lie as deep as in the valleys. There they eat reindeer moss (a lichen, not a moss), scraping away the snow with their hoofs to get at it.

The reindeer is the only deer to be domesticated. The Lapps of Lapland—the northernmost parts of Norway, Sweden and Finland—and the people of northern Siberia have tamed it, as it is more suited to their cold regions than horses and cows would be. They milk it, eat its meat and make tents, harness, boots and other articles of clothing from its hide, as well as tools from its antlers and bones. They have also taught it to draw sledges and to carry loads.

RELATIONSHIPS.

Every child knows that his mother and father and his aunts, uncles and cousins are his relations. However, even among these people he is likely to have relations of different *kinds*, and this group certainly does not include *all* the kinds of relations that it is possible to have.

People who are related by blood are called *consanguineous* relations. People who are related only because a blood relative of one has married a blood relative of the other are called *affined* relations. There are also what may be called "legal" relations : in these cases the relationship is fixed by law as, for example, in the case of an adopted child. In addition there are "spiritual" relations : in this case the relationship is between a godchild and the godparents, and it is created by the vows the godparents have made at the child's christening ceremony.

Consanguineous relations are relations of the same blood, such as an aunt who is a parent's sister (and not merely the wife of a parent's brother); an uncle who is a parent's brother (and not merely the husband of a parent's sister); a nephew or niece—the child of a brother or sister; and a cousin. A first cousin is the child of a parent's brother or sister, a second cousin is the grandchild of a grandparent's brother or sister and a third cousin is the great grandchild of a great grandparent's brother or sister. A first cousin once removed is a child of a first cousin or a first cousin of a parent, and a first cousin twice removed is a grandchild of a first cousin or a first cousin of a grandparent. A second cousin once removed is a child of a second cousin or a second cousin of a parent. Other degrees of relationship can be worked out in a similar way.

Affined relations include all relations by marriage. A brother-in-law is the husband of a sister or the brother of a husband or wife, and a sister-in-law is the wife of a brother or the sister of a husband or wife. Similarly aunts, uncles and cousins by marriage are people married to consanguineous aunts, uncles and cousins.

When a man marries for a second time the children of his first marriage become stepchildren to his second wife and are stepbrothers and stepsisters to any children his second wife may already have. When, however, he and his second wife have children those children become the half-brothers or half-sisters to the children of his first marriage and of his wife's first marriage. This is an example of a relation of the half-blood as distinct from a relation of the whole blood. Thus if a grandparent were to marry three times, having a child of each marriage, the children of those children would be grandchildren of the whole blood to the grandfather, but they would be cousins of the half blood to each other.

The relationship of guardian and ward is created by law if, when a child's parents are dead or unfit to look after it, some other person is legally given charge of the child. (Generally the person is appointed either by the will of the parent or by an order of a court.) The person appointed becomes the guardian, and the child becomes his or her ward. A guardian's powers and authority are not as great as those of parents, for a guardian is responsible only for the education and protection of his ward. A guardian's duties come to an end either when his ward reaches the age of 18 or when the ward marries if under that age.

If, however, a child is adopted, the adopting parents have the same rights and duties as though the child had been born to them.

Godfathers and godmothers have no legal responsibility for their godchildren, but a godparent often becomes the guardian of a child whose parents die or are unable to look after it.

The word kinship generally refers to all the consanguineous relations of a person. Next-of-kin means either the nearest blood relation (the father or mother) if a person is unmarried or divorced, or, if the person is married, a husband or wife. The phrase kith and kin is sometimes used, and although the two words are linked together, kith does not mean any sort of relation at all, but merely one's acquaintances.

RELATIVITY. When we say that one object is moving *relatively to* another we mean that it is moving when viewed from the other object or compared with it. Only relative movement can be detected and measured because there is no object in the universe that can be said to be absolutely at rest. Starting from this simple truth, the great scientific thinker Albert Einstein worked out his Theory of Relativity. This theory caused important changes in scientific thought and progress. You can read more about it in the article EINSTEIN, ALBERT.

RELIGION. Although modern men know far more about the universe than their primitive ancestors knew, they still have to admit that there are forces in the universe which they do not understand and which they cannot control. Through the ages men have asked questions about the universe, about the meaning of their life on earth and about their own nature. Their lack of knowledge makes them feel insecure. They know that there are things which they ought to do and things which they ought not to do. All men go through such experiences, but some are more disturbed by them than others. It is from such experiences that religion, in its many forms, has sprung.

In primitive times men knew little or nothing about the world outside the area where they lived, and they had no scientific knowledge about natural events such as rain and sunshine, thunderstorms and earthquakes, eclipses of the sun and moon. In their ignorance they believed that these things were controlled by spirits who dwelt in the rivers and trees and mountains. Believing, also, that the spirits were pleased or angry at what men did, our primitive ancestors carried out many strange ceremonies in order to secure the help and goodwill of the spirits—asking them to send rain or good hunting.

Many primitive tribes regarded some animal, plant or even a lifeless object as especially important for the safety and well-being of the tribe. This *totem*, as it is called, was treated with great reverence. It was often believed that the tribe was descended from its totem animal, plant or object and that the totem and the tribe owed

SOME OTHER ARTICLES TO READ ON RELIGION

ANGLICAN
   COMMUNION
APOSTLES, THE
ASSUMPTION
BAPTISTS
BIBLE
BRAHMA AND
   BRAHMANISM
BUDDHA AND
   BUDDHISM
CHRISTIANITY
CHURCH OF ENGLAND
CHURCH OF
   SCOTLAND
CONGREGATIONALISTS
CROSS
DEVIL, THE
EASTER
FLOOD, THE
FREE CHURCHES

GOD
GOSPELS
HEAVEN AND HELL
HERMIT
HINDUS AND
   HINDUISM
ISLAM
JESUITS
JESUS CHRIST
JEWS AND JUDAISM
KORAN
LENT
METHODISTS
MIRACLE
MISSIONARY
MOHAMMED
MONKS AND FRIARS
MORMONS
MYSTICS
NUNS

ORTHODOX EASTERN
   CHURCH
PARABLE
PILGRIMAGES
POPE, THE
PRAYER
PRESBYTERIANS
PRIEST
QUAKERS
ROMAN CATHOLIC
   CHURCH
SACRAMENTS
SAINT
SALVATION ARMY
SHINTOISM
TAOISM
THEOLOGY
UNITARIANS
UNITED REFORMED
   CHURCH

each other help and protection. It was also be-lieved that certain objects and certain actions were *taboo* (this word comes from a Polynesian word, *tapu*, meaning set apart) and must be avoided at all costs. (See MAGIC; TOTEM; SPELLS AND CHARMS; WITCHCRAFT.) Such beliefs and customs still linger in many parts of the world, but as scientific knowledge spreads they are being destroyed.

More advanced forms of religion developed when men began to live a more settled life in villages and towns. This happened first where water was plentiful and other conditions were good, as in the great river valleys of Egypt and Mesopotamia. In such areas men began to farm properly and left behind the haphazard methods of less settled peoples. They kept sheep and cattle and grew crops regularly year by year. The warmth of the sun, the light of the moon and the events of sowing-time and harvest played an important part in their lives. They knew that sowing-time and harvest were depend-ent on the changes of season, and they began to hold religious festivals to celebrate those changes. Their priests—the more learned men—realized that the seasonal changes were accompanied by changes in the position of the sun and other heavenly bodies and these, too, became import-ant in their religion. Shrines and temples were built, complicated ceremonies of worship and sacrifice grew up and priests became some of the most important members of society. Religious writings began to appear. The influence of seasonal festivals and the ideas and stories attached to them can be seen in the religious festivals described in the Old Testament. The creation stories of the Book of Genesis also have their origin in those early days.

The higher religions which still play an im-portant part in the modern world began with, or were influenced by, great teachers who lived round about 500 B.C. The 6th century B.C. was the period of the great teachers Confucius and Lao Tse in China, and of Gautama Buddha in India. At about the same time, two of the great Hebrew prophets—Ezekiel and Deutero-Isaiah (who wrote Chapters 40 to 55 of the Book of Isaiah)—were at work in Palestine. (See the article PROPHETS.)

About 955,000,000 people in the world are Christians; about 216,000,000 are Confucian-ists and Taoists (followers of Confucius and Lao Tse); over 524,000,000 are Hindus; about 250,000,000 are Buddhists; about 538,000,000 are Moslems, followers of the religion called Islam; and about 14,500,000 are Jews. Nobody knows *exactly* how many people follow each religion, or what effect Communism has had on religion—for the Communists do not believe that people should have any religion, yet many people in the U.S.S.R. and other Communist countries do still manage to follow their own religion. However, the figures given above are good enough to give a general impression of the numbers of people who belong to the various religions. Let us now look at the main religions a little more closely.

Far Eastern Religions

China has been influenced mainly by three systems of religion and morals—Confucianism, Taoism and Buddhism. The first two started in China but Buddhism was carried there from India in the 1st or 2nd century A.D. Confucian-ism was usually regarded as the official religion of China until the revolution of 1911. Islam entered China in the 7th century A.D., although its real influence was not felt for another 600 years. It had some 20,000,000 Chinese followers. Christianity also reached China in the 7th cen-tury and flourished for a time. It died out in about A.D. 900 and was revived by missions from the West, first in the 13th century, and later in the 16th century, under St. Francis Xavier.

Confucius, who was born in the 6th century B.C., lived in troubled times. He taught that human happiness comes from the relationships between people; that is, the way in which people treat one another. Five of these relationships were very important—that between the ruler and his subjects, between husband and wife, father and son, elder brother and younger brother, friend and friend. If the relations be-tween these sets of people were not right there would be no happiness. The worship of ancestors —an old Chinese custom—was warmly recom-mended by him because it helped to keep the old ways unchanged. God was to be honoured, but man could not know much about Him and should not try to find out about supernatural things.

Confucius gathered together the writings of earlier teachers and called himself "a transmitter and not a creator" (that is, he did not claim to have created new ideas himself but did claim to have passed on the teaching and ideas of earlier thinkers). However, he and his followers left a deep mark on Chinese life. His famous saying "Do not do to others what you would not have them do to you" sums up his moral teaching.

Taoism was founded by Lao Tse, who was born about 50 years before Confucius. Very little is known about him and it is not even certain that he wrote the little book on which Taoism is based. However, it seems likely that his teaching is contained in it. The word *Tao* is often translated as "the Way", but its full meaning cannot be given in one single English word. Lao Tse taught that men should train themselves to be unselfish and that they should practise gentleness, humility and mercy. Both Confucianism and Taoism were difficult for ordinary people to follow and as time went by they became mixed with superstitious and magical ideas because such ideas were easier to understand and to follow.

Buddhism began in India, where Gautama Buddha lived. Many legends are told of him and some of them may not be true, but it seems clear that he was a very great moral and religious teacher who had a deep sympathy for all the sufferings of men. He believed that men brought about their own suffering because they were full of worldly desires. They could escape from suffering—and enjoy the blessed peace known as Nirvana—by training themselves to get rid of all desires. To do this they would have to follow the Eightfold Path, which consists of right beliefs, right aims, right speech, right conduct, right occupation, right effort, right thinking and right meditation.

Buddhism spread quickly through central India during Buddha's lifetime. Later, in the middle of the 3rd century B.C., the Indian emperor Asoka became a Buddhist and spread the Buddhist faith over a much wider area. Now it has almost disappeared from India but it is still the main religion of Tibet, Sri Lanka, Burma, Thailand (Siam), Laos and Cambodia, and there are Buddhists in China and Japan. However, Buddhism in China became mixed with some of the ideas of Confucianism and in Japan with those of Shintoism.

Hinduism has no single founder and is a very complicated religion. When the Arya (a people who invaded India from the northwest about 1500 B.C.) entered India they brought with them a number of songs and hymns called the *Vedas*. These spoke of many nature gods and during the following centuries two of them became particularly important—Vishnu and Shiva. Elaborate forms of worship grew up, with many sacrifices, and the priests had an important part to play.

About 500 B.C. another collection of sacred writings, called the *Upanishads,* came into existence. These tried to bring out the deeper meaning of the Vedas and spoke of one supreme being, called Brahma, from whom all things came. Many people came to regard Brahma as the supreme ruler and Vishnu and Shiva as two of the forms in which he might appear. Vishnu is looked upon as the god who preserves life and Shiva as both the creator and the destroyer of life. The doctrine of Karma (a Sanskrit word meaning "fate") is widely held. This doctrine teaches that until a man finds God his soul keeps on being born again and again, and that in each life he is rewarded or punished for what he has done in the previous life. When he has found God his soul is merged in God and when he dies it is not born any more.

The Religion of Judaism

The most important religious writings of the Jews are the first five books of the Old Testament and the writings of the ancient prophets. They tell of the beginnings of the Jewish nation and the Jewish religion. Jews believe that their God Jahweh (in English this is often translated as "Lord" but sometimes as "Jehovah") made himself known to them. He rescued them from slavery in Egypt and had a great future in store for them. When more suffering and disaster came to them, prophets like Amos, Isaiah, Jeremiah and others gave deeper meaning to the promises that

Jahweh had made to them. The prophets interpreted all the disasters that happened to the Jews as God's punishment upon them for their disobedience, and all blessings as God's rewards for obedience. In 586 B.C. the Babylonians captured Jerusalem, their capital city, destroyed the Temple of Jahweh there and carried off many Jews and all the Jewish leaders into exile.

However, in the following century the Babylonians were defeated by the Persians, and the Jewish exiles were allowed to return to Jerusalem. The Temple, which was the only place where sacrifices could be offered, was rebuilt and synagogues were built for the teaching of the Law and the Prophets. Later centuries brought further sufferings, however, and the Jews began to pin all their hopes on the coming of a Messiah (see MESSIAH) through whom God would save them. Then Jesus Christ was born among them, and when He grew up began His teaching. Those Jews who believed that He was the expected Messiah followed Him and became known as Christians. However, most Jews did not believe that He was the Messiah, and the Jewish community as a whole refused to have anything to do with the Christians. Jerusalem and its Temple were again destroyed in A.D. 70 —when the Jews rebelled against the Romans who had become the masters of Palestine. From that time until 1948 the Jews had no country of their own. (See ISRAEL.)

The Religion of Islam

Islam, the religion of the Moslems, was founded in Arabia in the early years of the 7th century A.D. Mohammed, the founder, wanted to lead his people to the worship of one God. His religious beliefs seem to have been gained largely from Jewish and Christian teaching. According to tradition he received messages from God, telling him to go out and teach that there was only one God and that he, Mohammed, was his prophet. He continued to receive messages, which were written down and collected together to make the Koran, and this became the holy book of the new faith. Mohammed was a military leader as well as a prophet, and his religion was spread largely by military conquest. In the 100 years after his death his followers carried their religion into Syria, Persia, Egypt, North Africa, Spain and India.

Islam teaches people to believe in one Supreme God, Allah, whose will men must always obey. It also teaches that Mohammed was the last and greatest of his prophets. Moslems have the story of Jesus Christ in their holy book, but they believe that He was merely one of the prophets.

Christianity

Christianity is based on the belief that Jesus was the Son of God, that He was God Almighty in human form. Thus in the first chapter of St. John's Gospel it is written, "In the beginning was the Word . . . and the Word was God . . . and the Word was made flesh, and dwelt among us, (and we beheld his glory, the glory as of the only begotten of the Father,) full of grace and truth". In the Creed, also, Christians state their belief in ". . . Jesus Christ . . . who for us men and for our salvation came down from heaven . . . and was made man".

Christianity is the only great religion which claims that its founder was more than just a prophet and that He is God Himself (see TRINITY, THE), who made the universe and the world in which we live.

The Jews expected the Messiah to be a great leader who would deliver them from the Romans —but Jesus turned out to be quite a different kind of deliverer. He offered people deliverance from their sins : they were to repent of their past wickedness, put their trust in Him and be baptized into His church. Those who accepted these three requirements found that He was really their deliverer.

However, Christianity offers people more than deliverance from sin : it invites them to live the new life, which is life under the guidance of the Holy Spirit and within the fellowship of the Christian Church. By living the new life, Christians become co-workers with God, helping to build His Kingdom on earth. They invite men to accept Christ as King and to let Him influence their homes, their work-places, their governments and every part of their lives.

Christianity proclaims that God enabled people to overcome sin and to live the new life by what He did for us in the life of Christ and by what He is still doing through His church. Four of His acts are of especial importance—His coming from heaven to earth at Bethlehem, His death on the Cross, His resurrection and His gift of the Holy Spirit which is renewed at Pentecost, or Whitsunday (see WHITSUN). Christians believe that the church is, as St. Paul called it, the Body of Christ. They believe that He feeds His church through the Word of God revealed in the Bible and through the Sacraments, especially those of Holy Baptism and Holy Communion. (See SACRAMENTS.)

Christians believe therefore that God has a plan for the remaking of this world, and that He calls upon each of His children to work with Him on his plan. At the same time they believe that God is not only concerned with remaking this world, but with preparing His children for life in His other world. They believe that Christ, by His resurrection from the dead, showed that death is not the end but rather the gateway to a newer and fuller life in which His children continue to serve Him for ever and ever.

REMBRANDT, REMBRANDT HARMENS VAN RIJN (1606–1669). The Dutch artist Rembrandt, one of the most famous in the world, was

Courtesy, Metropolitan Museum of Art, New York
Detail from "Lady with a Pink" by Rembrandt.

also one of the busiest and hardest working. His works include at least 600 paintings, several thousand drawings and very many of the kind of pictures called etchings. (Etchings are printed from a design cut into a sheet of metal. The method of making them is described in a separate article ETCHING.) Many of the portraits Rembrandt painted were of himself, showing his powerful face with its determined chin, heavy eyebrows and keen, steady gaze. In all his pictures, whether they were of an interesting face, a happening in everyday life or a scene from the Bible, Rembrandt was especially fascinated by light and shade. Often it was not so much the shape of a figure or an object, nor its colour, that he concentrated on but the gleams of light and the dark patches of shadow which made the scene living and interesting.

Rembrandt was born at Leyden in Holland in 1606. His father wanted him to enter a learned profession but the boy soon determined to be a painter and studied as a pupil of two well known painters of the day. By the time he was 20 he was painting on his own and beginning to make a name for himself.

He drew and painted everything that he possibly could. He saw beauty and interest in the most ordinary things that went on around him, and in his sketch books there are pictures of a dog searching for fleas, a tramp sunning himself, a grandfather teaching his grandson to walk, the village gossips—all drawn with quick definite strokes of Rembrandt's quill pen. Among his pictures during these first years of his career were religious paintings, landscapes and portraits.

By 1632 Rembrandt's fame was growing so fast that he moved to the city of Amsterdam. Immediately he became the favourite portrait painter of the city, and requests for portraits began to pour in. His first great picture there was called "The Anatomy Lesson". An *anatomist* studies the way in which the human body is constructed, and in the picture Rembrandt showed his friend Dr. Tulp, who was famous as an anatomist, lecturing to doctors who are gathered eagerly around him. In 1634 Rembrandt married a beautiful fair-haired girl named Saskia van Uylenborch, and the years that followed until she died in 1642 were the happiest of his

"Portrait of the Painter in Old Age", one of Rembrandt's many self-portraits.

life. He had many pictures to paint, and a number of pupils and assistants. With the money he earned he was able to buy a large house and fill it with all kinds of works of art, including armour from the East, rich fabrics and fine Italian paintings and sculpture.

Triumphs and Sorrows

In 1641 the civic guards of Amsterdam asked Rembrandt to paint a portrait of their company going on parade. They expected, of course, a straightforward group rather like a team photograph of today, but Rembrandt was determined to give them something better. He pictured them coming out of their clubhouse, making the scene natural and lively and bringing out the light and shade of their richly coloured uniforms. Their faces, however, were half hidden or indistinct, and this did not please them. Rembrandt refused to alter what he felt was his finest picture, and his popularity as a painter grew less.

In the same year that this wonderful picture was finished, Saskia died, and with that Rembrandt's life was changed. The paintings and etchings of his later years were even greater than the earlier ones, but they were painted in hardship and loneliness. Money troubles followed Saskia's death until in 1656 Rembrandt had nothing left, and his house and all its treasures had to be sold to pay his debts. His servant Hendrickje Stoffels, who had looked after him since his wife died, managed to set up an art dealer's business with his son Titus, and they were thus able to help Rembrandt to continue painting.

He now gave all his thoughts and time to his art. A picture of himself which he painted about this time (now in the National Gallery in London) shows his face changed by suffering, but not bitter. By 1661 his sight was failing and he had to give up etching, but he went on painting in spite of illness right up to his death in 1669.

Until modern methods were used to clean Rembrandt's pictures, many people thought they were drab and gloomy, but now that the old varnish and soot have been cleaned off the rich colours can again be seen. Some of his finest paintings are in the National Gallery and the Wallace Collection, and there are others, also in London, at the Victoria and Albert Museum and the British Museum. There is a reproduction of one of them in PAINTERS AND PAINTINGS.

RENAISSANCE is a French word that means "rebirth", and it is used to describe the period of European history that stretched from about 1340 to 1600. During that time enormous changes took place in ways of thought, in what men wrote, in their painting, sculpture and architecture and, indeed, in every aspect of life. It seemed as though man's spirit was being reborn : hence the name Renaissance.

The Renaissance was the period when the middle ages (see MIDDLE AGES) came to an end and the modern world began. The middle ages had achieved great things—nothing is more beautiful than its Gothic cathedrals (see ARCHITECTURE)—but the Renaissance opened up completely new possibilities. Until that time man's chief concern in this world was to save his soul in the next : God was the centre of all things. The men of the Renaissance, however, saw *themselves* in the middle of the stage. They thought less of death and more of life, and this made them eager to find out all they could.

As a background to this excitement of the mind, the political and religious structure of Europe was also changing. The Holy Roman Empire (see HOLY ROMAN EMPIRE), which had been a symbol of the political unity of Europe, no longer counted for very much. The Papacy (see POPE, THE), which had stood for the religious unity of Europe, was disgraced when two popes fought over the right to be pope. People were becoming less attached to the idea of belonging to Christendom and were becoming far more conscious of belonging to one particular part of it—their own country. This was particularly strong in England and France. At this time, too, the Portuguese and Spaniards were discovering the New World, sailing round Africa and penetrating to India. In the 16th century in Switzerland, Germany and northern Europe there was the spiritual and religious crisis of the Reformation (see REFORMATION). This must not be confused with the Renaissance, although the new knowledge that the Renaissance released was useful to the religious reformers. The artistic and literary movement of the Renaissance, with its love of life and respect for the freedom of the human mind, was separate from the intense religious concerns of the Reformation.

New ideas were speeded by new inventions. Printing took the scholars' writings cheaply to all who could read; greater use of the mariner's compass enabled the voyages of discovery to be made (see EXPLORERS); gunpowder made nations stronger and war more terrible. There was a growing use of money in Europe and with it grew trade and the wealth of bankers and merchants. These people, together with the princes, used their wealth to buy the work of artists and writers, and to help them.

The intellectual excitement of the Renaissance started in Italy, where a few people had become greatly interested in the works of the ancient Greek and Roman writers (see GREECE: ANCIENT; ROMANS). The poet Francesco Petrarch (1304–1374) was the first to delve into the ancient writings. We know him today as a great poet, but he himself was far more interested in going through the old Latin writings than in composing Italian poetry. Unlike Giovanni Boccaccio (1313–1375), however, he knew no Greek. These two men and their followers were fascinated by what they found out about the ancient world from the writings of men who had lived in it so many hundreds of years ago. The enthusiasm of Petrarch and Boccaccio spread to other scholars, and more and more people became aware of the achievements of the ancient Greeks and Romans and of how they had lived. Many Greek scholars from Constantinople began to settle in Italy, for Constantinople was threatened by the Ottoman Turks (see OTTOMAN EMPIRE) for many years before they captured it in 1453. As it was a great centre of learning it had many manuscripts of Greek and Latin authors, and the scholars who fled to Italy took some of those manuscripts with them. All Italy welcomed these scholars, eager for what they had to say.

The painters of the Renaissance were influenced by the atmosphere of the Greek and Roman myths. Although they continued to paint mainly religious pictures, the way in which they painted them was different: unlike the earlier painters, they were not content with painting the human body—they tried to bring out its beauty. So did the sculptors. (See PAINTERS AND PAINTINGS.)

Florence was the chief centre of the renaissance of art in Italy, and its rulers, the Medici family, spent great amounts of money on pictures, buildings and statues. (See MEDICI FAMILY.) Among the great painters, sculptors and architects who worked in Florence either for most or part of their lives were Michelangelo, Donatello, Botticelli and Leonardo. (See BOTTICELLI, SANDRO; DONATELLO; LEONARDO DA VINCI; MICHELANGELO BUONARROTI.) They were many-sided men. Michelangelo is remembered not only for his statues and the famous frescoes (wall-paintings) in the Sistine chapel of the Vatican, but also as a military architect and as the author of some famous sonnets—which he wrote when he was 70. Leonardo painted the "Mona Lisa" and the "Last Supper", but he was also an architect, an engineer and a scientist. The architect Filippo Brunelleschi was a Florentine, too. Other great architects of the time—who were not Florentines—were Donato Bramante and Andrea Palladio.

Spread of the Renaissance Spirit

In their admiration for the ancient Greeks and Romans, some of these scholars and artists turned their minds away from Christianity, and some people in other European countries followed their example. However, others found that far from turning them against Christianity, the new ideas of the Renaissance actually strengthened their Christian belief. At the same time it broadened their minds. The great Dutch scholar Erasmus remained true to his religious beliefs but was one of the most broad-minded men of his time. (See ERASMUS, DESIDERIUS.)

In Germany most people's energy was taken up with the religious problems of the Reformation. However, some of the chief reformers, like Philip Melanchthon, were typical scholars of the new learning and the Renaissance spirit came out clearly in the work of the artist Albrecht Dürer (see DÜRER, ALBRECHT). In France the essays of Michel de Montaigne and the lively humour of Francois Rabelais showed the

Left: "The Creation of Man" by Michelangelo. This is a detail from the great painted ceiling of the Sistine Chapel of the Vatican in Rome, which Michelangelo completed between 1508 and 1512. Bottom left: Portrait painters in the Renaissance sought not only to show what a man looked like, but also to show the qualities he represented. Piero della Francesca's portrait, "Federigo da Montefeltro, Duke of Urbino", painted about 1472, shows not only the Duke as a man, but also the painter's idea of the great power wielded by an important Italian prince. Below: Religious subjects were often painted amid a contemporary setting; an example is "Madonna and Child" by the Venetian painter Giovanni Bellini (c. 1430–1516).

Courtesy, (left, bottom left) Scala; (below) Metropolitan Museum of Art, New York

Top: "Disputation on the Holy Sacrament" by Raphael, in the Vatican in Rome. Left: Artists in many European countries were influenced by Italian Renaissance artists. This French painted dish, made about 1575, in Lyons, was inspired by Italian pottery. Right: "Virgin and Child" by Andrea del Verrocchio (1435–88), a terra-cotta relief completed about 1475.

Courtesy, (top) Scala; (left) Victoria and Albert Museum; (right) Metropolitan Museum of Art, New York

Books during the Renaissance. Above: "The Printing of Books", an engraving based on a drawing by Johannes Stradanus (1536–1605). Printing took the writing of the Renaissance scholars cheaply to all who could read. Bottom left: A page from a Florentine manuscript dedicated to Lorenzo the Magnificent. Bottom centre: Erasmus, from a woodcut made by Hans Holbein in 1535. One of the greatest scholars of the time, Erasmus spent some years in England. Bottom right: A portrait of the Italian poet Petrarch, within an illuminated initial in a manuscript of one of his works.

Courtesy, (top) Trustees of the British Museum; (bottom left) Biblioteca Medicea-Laurenziana; (bottom centre) Öffentliche Kunstsammlung, Basle; (right) Biblioteca Nazionale S. Marco

268

Que ofeleur ne font menus ofiaus a glu. ton fus tous en quí ot fon efpoir

These are copies from drawings in a French manuscript of the 1300s—at the beginning of the Renaissance. They show everyday life, children playing bowls and walking on stilts. The writing is in mediaeval French.

inquisitive mind of the Renaissance. These writers observed their fellow men honestly, reporting both their goodness and their faults.

In the Renaissance the human spirit freed itself from many ideas that had prevented people from developing what was in them. Instead of being burdened with the idea of his sinfulness, man became aware of his vast powers. Therefore perhaps it is not surprising that there was an undercurrent of cruelty and heartlessness—this comes out clearly in Machiavelli's book *The Prince* (see MACHIAVELLI, NICCOLO). What he said about politics shocked many people of his own time—and still shocks people—for its praise of force and the idea that might is right.

Modern science grew out of the Renaissance. In the middle ages, except for a few people like Roger Bacon (see BACON, ROGER), scholars took their scientific knowledge from books. They seldom carried out experiments to find things out for themselves. However, this would not do for

the men of the Renaissance and it was when men like Copernicus and Galileo began to experiment and observe for themselves that modern science began. Until the time of Copernicus men believed that the Earth was the centre of the universe and that the sun revolved round it. (See COPERNICUS, NICOLAUS; GALILEO GALILEI.) Andreas Vesalius, the father of modern anatomy (see ANATOMY), first dissected the human body in a scientific way—and the knowledge he gained was useful for sculptors and painters as well as for doctors. The Englishman Francis Bacon set out the new attitude to science in his great book *The Advancement of Learning* (see BACON, FRANCIS). He argued that men could not depend for their knowledge of the world on ideas they merely *thought* to be true. It was necessary to be *certain* of their truth—and the only way of being certain was by observation and testing. In his argument we can see the foundations of modern science.

The Renaissance was a time of looking forward, as well as backward. Leonardo da Vinci dreamed of the day when people would fly. He made drawings of flying machines—a mechanical bird's wing (left) and a "flapping wing" craft—but never succeeded in building one. His dreams were ahead of their time.

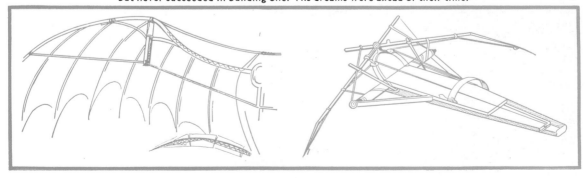

Paisley pattern

east window Paisley Abbey

wild pansy

industries at Renfrew

cargo ship at Greenock
Abbotsinch airport

Highland Mary, Dunoon

RENFREWSHIRE was formerly a small county in the west of Scotland. Since 1975 it has been part of the larger Strathclyde region (see STRATHCLYDE), and is divided into the local government districts of Eastwood, Renfrew and Inverclyde.

The town of Renfrew is a royal burgh and used to be the county town of Renfrewshire. It stands on the south bank of the River Clyde, about nine kilometres west of Glasgow, Scotland's most important industrial city. In fact, the whole of this area is a busy industrial region whose activities include shipbuilding, marine engineering, sugar refining, textiles, whisky distilling and textiles. There is farming, too, mainly dairy cattle with some orchards, market gardens and smallholdings.

The largest town of Renfrew district is Paisley, which is famous for its shawls (copied from Indian designs in the 1800s) and for its thread-making industry. West of the town of Renfrew is Glasgow's airport.

In Roman times this area was part of the kingdom of Strathclyde. It was later the home

of the first members of the House of Stuart, and today Baron Renfrew is one of the titles of the Prince of Wales. Renfrewshire was the birthplace of Sir William Wallace, James Watt and Captain William Kidd (see the articles on them).

RENNIE, John (1761–1821), was an engineer who became famous for his bridges, canals and harbour works. He was a farmer's son and was born at Phantassie in Scotland. While a boy he spent much time in the workshop of Andrew Meikle, a man who made mill and farm machinery. After leaving school he studied at Edinburgh University and in 1784 he was put in charge of the design and construction of one of the first steam-driven flour mills. In 1791 he set up his own business as an engineer in London. Work was his passion. He rarely took a holiday, usually starting work at 5 a.m. and going on until late at night.

His first important work in England was the Kennet and Avon Canal. Other canals constructed by Rennie were the Rochdale Canal, the Lancaster Canal, and the canal linking Dublin with the River Shannon. He is better known, however, for his bridges. In Scotland he built bridges at Kelso and Musselburgh and in London he was responsible for Southwark Bridge (replaced in 1921), Waterloo Bridge (replaced in 1942) and London Bridge with its five stone arches. This was removed to the United States in 1971 and a new bridge replaced it. In Rennie's day there was little to serve as a guide to the engineer, and new constructions were quite liable to fall down because they were wrongly designed. The earlier stone bridges had mostly been built with such tall arches that the roadway sloped steeply upwards towards the middle, but Rennie's work showed that good bridges could be built with an almost level roadway. When Waterloo Bridge was opened in 1817 he was offered a knighthood, but he preferred to remain plain John Rennie.

Rennie was responsible for a number of docks and harbours, including the East India and London docks in London, and those at Hull, Grimsby, Leith and Holyhead. He also designed the great breakwater which shuts off Plymouth Sound from the open sea. While constructing Hull docks he was the first to make use of the bucket dredger for raising mud and clay from the bottom (see DREDGING). He also did much to develop the diving bell for use in underwater work on foundations (see DIVERS AND DIVING EQUIPMENT).

Rennie's work was continued by his sons George and John (later Sir John Rennie), both of whom became well-known engineers.

Radio Times Hulton Picture Library

The London Bridge, designed by John Rennie, was completed by his son John and opened in 1831. Traffic jams were a problem then as now.

RENOIR, Pierre-Auguste (1841–1919).

The French painter Pierre Renoir, whose pictures are full of joy and gaiety, had to struggle against difficulties all his life. As a young man he was very poor; people did not understand or like his pictures; and as he grew older he suffered from arthritis which made it painful for him to move his hands and arms. Yet in spite of everything he kept on painting.

Renoir was the son of a poor tailor of Limoges, a town famous for the porcelain, or fine china, made there. Renoir's first job was painting the designs on the porcelain, and this taught him to enjoy painting with pure clean colours and careful delicate strokes of the brush. Later he managed to save enough of the money he earned to go to an art school.

It was then that his career as a painter really began, for there he became friendly with the artist Claude Monet. (See MONET, CLAUDE.) Later on, the two friends were among the artists who experimented with a new kind of painting that people called *Impressionism*. The first ex-

hibition of paintings that the "Impressionists" held was in 1874, and some of Renoir's pictures were shown in it.

In 1880 he travelled to Italy, and came back feeling dissatisfied with his own skill; although he was 40 years old, he went back to art school in Paris to learn how to plan his pictures more carefully. He was by now less of an "impressionist". Fame and success came to him, however, and by 1907 he had enough money to retire to a village called Cagnes in the south of France. His last years were marred by pain; arthritis affected his hands so badly that he had to paint with the brush tied to his fingers. Renoir died in 1919. His son, Jean (1894–1979), became a well-known film director.

All Renoir's pictures are fresh and full of life. (See also IMPRESSIONISTS and PAINTERS AND PAINTINGS.)

Renoir painted people as well as landscapes; this nude is in the National Gallery, London.

RENT

is money that one person pays to another for the right to use that person's property. The word is probably most often heard in connection with houses and flats, but many people pay rent for shops, offices and factories, or television sets. Farmers who farm somebody else's land may also pay rent.

Rents are usually paid weekly, monthly or quarterly (see QUARTER DAYS), according to the agreement that has been made between the owner of the property and the tenant (the person renting it). Usually they also have an agreement about the period of notice (warning) that has to be given—either if the owner wishes to have the property back or if the tenant wishes to stop renting it.

The laws about the rights of landlord and tenant and about rent control are complicated. Fair rents and housing are subjects on which political parties often have sharply differing views, so when there is a change of government, the rent laws often change too.

REPRODUCTION.

Every kind of living thing, whether plant or animal, is able to produce other living things like itself. Oak trees produce acorns which grow into new oak trees. Butterflies lay eggs which grow, by way of caterpillar and chrysalis, into new butterflies. Human

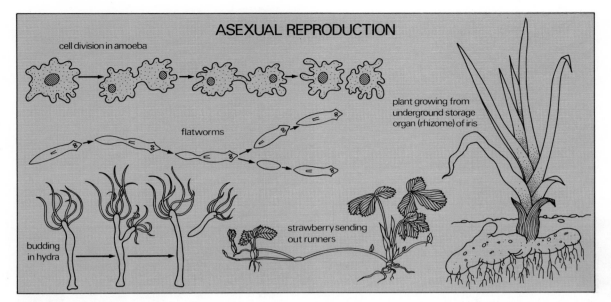

ASEXUAL REPRODUCTION

cell division in amoeba

flatworms

budding in hydra

strawberry sending out runners

plant growing from underground storage organ (rhizome) of iris

beings give birth to babies. This is what is known as reproduction, and it is the means by which life goes on. (A few living things, like the mule, cannot reproduce themselves.)

Although living things reproduce, they do so by different methods. The simplest method of all is by division. For example, the tiny, invisible germs which cause disease reproduce by dividing into two. Each of these parts grows until it is full size and then divides again. In this way germs can multiply at a tremendous rate. Such a simple method of reproduction is possible because the germ consists of one cell only. (See CELL.)

Some other living things, although made up of many cells, are nevertheless able to reproduce by breaking off parts of themselves. Strawberry plants send out growths called runners which in time develop roots and shoots of their own and become detached from the parent plant. Some fairly simple animals can reproduce in the same way. The little freshwater polyp called *Hydra* forms buds which break off and grow into new polyps.

These are all forms of *asexual* or vegetative reproduction. The new organisms are formed by separating off some of the body cells of the existing organism. Since all the body cells of an organism contain identical *chromosomes* (see HEREDITY), the resulting new individuals are genetically identical to each other and to the parent from which they came.

Sexual reproduction produces variation in the offspring, as there is "recombination" of the genetic material. Generally there are two kinds of reproductive cells, male and female. The female cell is usually larger than the male one, for it contains some food which is needed at first by the new growing plant or animal. The small male cell is able to move to meet and join with the female cell. A male and a female cell then, from the same kind of living thing, join together to form one cell. This cell then divides again and again until it becomes a mass of cells which develops into an animal or plant of the same kind as the parents.

Flowering plants produce male and female cells. The female cells are contained in the part of the flower known as the ovary. This contains tiny round ovules, and the ovules, in their turn, contain the female cells. The male cells are contained in the pollen, which comes from the anthers, another part of the flower.

The pollen is so light that it is easily carried by insects or the wind from flower to flower. Above the ovary of a flower there is a kind of stalk called the style, the top of which, the stigma, is often sticky. Some of the pollen grains come to rest on the stigma. A pollen grain sends out a tube which grows down the style until it reaches

273

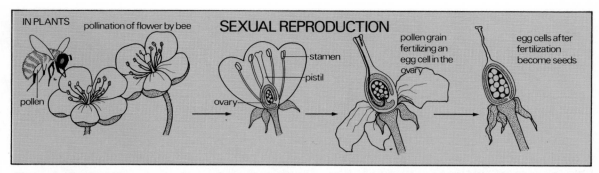

SEXUAL REPRODUCTION

IN PLANTS — pollination of flower by bee

pollen

stamen

pistil

ovary

pollen grain fertilizing an egg cell in the ovary

egg cells after fertilization become seeds

These two diagrams illustrate two forms of sexual reproduction. Flowering plants produce both male and female cells. In animals, including human beings, the male and female cells are brought together in a sexual act during which the male's sperm enters the female's body to fertilize her egg. The fertilized egg grows into an embryo which eventually emerges as a new individual.

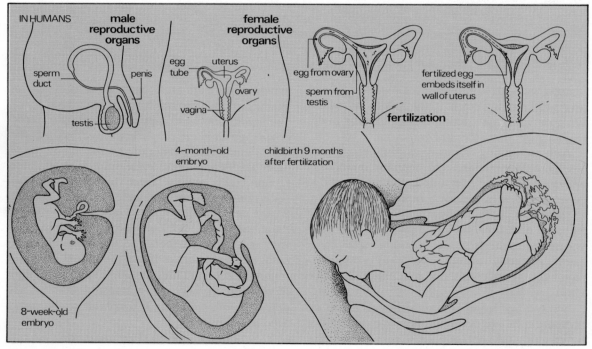

IN HUMANS

male reproductive organs

sperm duct

penis

testis

female reproductive organs

egg tube

uterus

ovary

vagina

egg from ovary

sperm from testis

fertilization

fertilized egg embeds itself in wall of uterus

4-month-old embryo

childbirth 9 months after fertilization

8-week-old embryo

the ovule. The male cell travels down the pollen tube to the female cell inside the ovule and the two cells meet and join. The ovules become seeds which grow into new plants. (See FLOWER.)

Most flowering plants are therefore what are known as hermaphrodites, which means that each plant produces both male and female cells. Nevertheless, in most cases the male cells from one flower join with the female cells of other flowers on the plant. (Snails, earthworms and some other animals are also hermaphrodite, and reproduce in this way; in most cases the male cells from one animal are transferred to meet the female cells of another animal.)

Some holly trees produce only male cells, and others only female cells. Some other flowering plants do the same, and so do many animals, including mammals. Each individual of these kinds of plants and animals is therefore either male or female.

Sperms and Eggs

In animals, including human beings, the female cell is called the egg and contains a store of yolky food. The male cell is called the sperm and is very tiny. Usually it has a long tail with which it can swim in search of the egg. Egg and sperms contain *genes*, which cause the new young creature to look like its parents. This is more fully explained in HEREDITY.

The sperms and eggs of most animals that live in the water are discharged into the water and meet almost by chance. An example is the sea-urchin, a prickly relative of the starfish. Male sea-urchins produce millions of sperms and females produce millions of eggs. There have to be so many because in the sea, although some happen to meet, most are certain to be lost.

If a drop of sea water containing sperms of the sea-urchin is mixed with a drop containing eggs, and the mixed drop is put under a microscope, it can be seen what happens when the sperms and eggs meet. Swarming round each egg are hundreds of sperms. They look like long, thin tadpoles, lashing their way towards the egg with their tails. At last one sperm wins the race and its head enters the egg, leaving the tail outside. A thin wall separates from the surface of the egg and keeps all the other sperms away. The egg is now said to be fertilized and it begins to divide into cells, into two, then four, then eight and so on over and over again until the little sea-urchin becomes fully developed.

Most fishes reproduce in the same way. The female lays millions of eggs and perhaps only one or two are fertilized by one or two of the enormous numbers of sperms which the male fish sheds into the water. Frogs and toads lay fewer eggs. The male lies on top of the female and sheds his sperms over the eggs as they are laid. This makes sure that most of them are fertilized.

Some fishes, including rays and skates, fertilize their eggs inside the female. This means that the sperms pass out of the male's body but the eggs remain inside the female. For the sperms to reach the eggs, it is therefore necessary for them to be placed inside the body of the female, and this is the most certain method of fertilization.

Birds and mammals fertilize their eggs in the same way. The placing of the sperm inside the female occurs during what is known as mating, and the method of mating is not quite the same for birds and mammals. The male bird has an opening in its body, through which the sperms pass out. It stands on the back of the female

and presses this opening against a corresponding opening in the body of the female. Some liquid, known as semen and containing millions of sperms, passes through the female's opening and along the egg-laying passage inside her body. One of the sperms fertilizes an egg that is on its way down.

The egg cell is enormously swollen with food, forming the yolk, and after the fertilization the white and shell are formed round it. The egg then continues its journey down the egg-laying passage and is then laid, but it still needs care or else the young bird inside will die. The eggshell acts as a protection and the whole egg is kept warm, usually by the mother's body, until the young bird breaks out of the shell. (See EGG.)

How Mammals Reproduce

Mammals (with the exception of the duck-billed platypus and the echidna) do not lay eggs. Instead, the fertilized egg develops inside the mother and the young creature remains there for a length of time which varies according to the kind of mammal. At the end of that time it is born. Some young mammals are fairly well able to look after themselves when they are first born, though they depend on their mothers for food. Others, including human babies, are quite helpless. (See BABY.)

The baby mammal develops in a special hollow muscular organ inside the female called the uterus or womb. Because the egg is going to develop inside the mother, it must be fertilized inside her. So male mammals have an organ called the penis through which the sperms made in the testes can be passed into the passage of the female called the vagina, which leads to the lower end of the uterus. (Urine from the bladder is also passed out through the penis in the male, but that cannot happen in mating.)

The eggs leave the ovaries where they are made and enter two tubes called oviducts which lead to the upper end of the uterus. If mating has taken place and sperms have been released into the vagina, they travel rapidly up it and through the uterus. They then enter one or both of the oviducts, and if they meet an egg travelling down there one sperm fertilizes it, in the same way that the sea-urchins' eggs are fertilized.

Male mammals release an enormous number of sperms when they mate, but only one is needed for fertilizing an egg.

When the egg has been fertilized, it continues its journey down the oviduct and enters the uterus. The lining of the uterus has already been prepare to receive it. It has grown thicker and is well supplied with blood vessels, for the developing young one receives its food materials and oxygen from its mother's blood.

For more about how the human baby develops, see BABY.

REPTILE. Reptiles living today are divided into four groups, or orders : (1) the alligators and crocodiles; (2) the tuatara, a strange, lizard-like reptile found only in New Zealand; (3) the turtles and tortoises; and (4) the snakes and lizards. Reptiles live all over the world except in the polar regions and they are commonest in hot countries. Some live on land, some in water.

Reptiles are higher forms of life than amphibians and lower than birds. The article EVOLUTION explains how, millions of years ago, some fishes began to develop limbs and to live on land for a time, and so they became amphibians. In their turn, some of the amphibians developed

further. Their skins grew thick, dry and covered with horny scales, like those of reptiles today, and they became able to live altogether on land.

For a long stretch of time the reptiles were the only land animals. Among them were the dinosaurs, some enormously large and like dragons in appearance but with tiny brains. All the dinosaurs died out, however, and the reptiles living today are comparatively small, although some crocodiles and snakes grow to 10 metres in length.

It is believed that birds and mammals, as well as the reptiles of today, developed from the early reptiles. Birds lay the same kind of eggs as many reptiles—eggs covered with hard shells to protect them. Some reptiles, however, lays eggs with soft shells like parchment, and others give birth to living young, in the way that mammals do. Some reptiles, such as the alligator and the British grass snake, lay their eggs in rotting vegetation, which generates, or causes, heat that helps the eggs to hatch. Other reptiles lay eggs in the sand and leave them to hatch out in the sun. The pythons brood (hatch) their eggs by wrapping the body around them.

Young reptiles, such as tortoises and crocodiles, that hatch out from hard-shelled eggs have a horny growth on the end of their snouts which

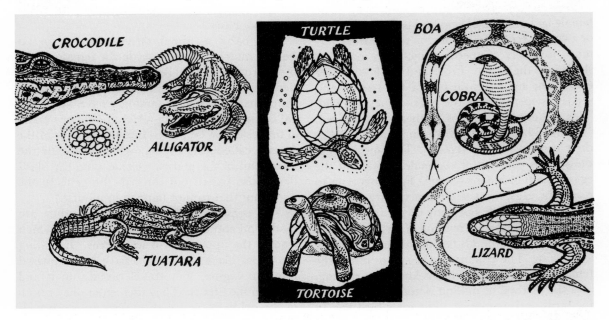

There are four groups of reptiles, shown here. The alligators and crocodiles; the tuatara (which is by itself and is probably the oldest); the turtles and tortoises; and the snakes and lizards (which make up the largest of the four groups).

they use to cut their way out of the shell. Young reptiles are exactly like their parents when they are born, except that in many cases they are a different colour. The parents either take no notice of them or do so for a short while only, and they can look after themselves from the first.

Although some reptiles, such as the marine turtle of tropical seas and the terrapins of fresh water, live in water, they, like land reptiles, breathe through lungs all their lives. Like amphibians, they are cold-blooded, and their bodies are usually about the same temperature as the air around them. In mild climates reptiles sleep during cold weather.

The word reptile comes from a Latin word meaning "to crawl". Some reptiles have short limbs on which they crawl slowly along; others, such as some kinds of lizards, can move quite fast. Some lizards, among them the European slow-worm and the so-called glass snakes, have no visible limbs and move as snakes do, by wriggling along the ground. On the other hand some

snakes, such as the boas and their relatives the pythons, have traces of back legs which look like claws. The marine turtles have paddle-like limbs with which they swim.

Most reptiles, except snakes, have upper and lower eyelids, and many have a transparent

Top: Zoological Society of London; Above: Alan Beaumont

Top: The chameleon is a reptile with a grasping tail, a long tongue with which it catches insects, and the ability to change colour. Above: A Nile crocodile. Crocodiles, unlike many reptiles, are watchful parents, sometimes carrying their young gently in their enormous jaws.

membrane, or film of skin, across the front of the eye. Others have small "windows" in their eyelids. Snakes have no eyelids at all, and so their eyes are always open.

Orders of Reptiles

Alligators and crocodiles are long, four-limbed animals with scales or plates covering their bodies. They are very much alike, and it takes an expert to tell them apart. In both, the fourth tooth in the lower jaw is larger than the others. This is clearly seen in the crocodile when its mouth is closed, but the alligator's fourth tooth cannot be seen when the mouth is closed.

Both alligators and crocodiles have their eyes, ear-slits and nostrils on the top of their long flat heads so that they can see, hear and breathe in the water with only the top of the head showing. They swim by means of their strong tails and use their legs only for walking or running. They eat only animal food, chiefly fish. All lay oval, hard-shelled eggs which are hatched out by the heat of the sun or by rotting vegetable matter.

Turtles and tortoises can be at once distinguished from other reptiles by their bony shells, which are covered with horny shields. Usually they can draw the head, legs and tail under this covering. They have toothless jaws covered with a sharp, horny substance, and all lay eggs.

In Britain the word tortoise generally means the land animal, which is often kept as a pet, and freshwater tortoises are called terrapins. The word turtle generally means the ones that live in the sea. In the United States, however, all are usually known as turtles.

The order that includes the lizards and snakes is by far the largest order of reptiles, for there are more than 2,500 species (kinds) of lizards and about 3,000 species of snakes. Lizards are generally harmless, only one kind, the Gila monster, being poisonous. However, many snakes have poison fangs.

Lizards have visible ear openings, but the ears of snakes are hidden under the skin. The lower jaw of a lizard is formed in one piece, but the two halves of a snake's lower jaw are joined together by a piece of an elastic-like substance. The lower jaw can be stretched very wide, so that a snake can swallow prey larger than its head.

REPUBLIC. The word republic comes from two Latin words, *res publica,* meaning "public affair". At first it was used to mean simply the state, but by degrees it was used to mean the kind of state that was governed by elected rulers, instead of by kings or emperors. The Roman Republic, often regarded as the greatest period in Rome's history, lasted from the 6th century B.C. until 30 B.C. There were also republics in ancient Greece, one of them being Athens.

Today the general meaning of republic is a state which has no king. Generally republics come into existence after a revolution in which the people overthrow the king. This happens for various reasons. The French overthrew their king, Louis XVI, during the Revolution of 1793 because the monarchy had been greedy and extravagant while the poor people starved. (See FRENCH REVOLUTION.) The only time that England was a republic was between 1649 and 1660. In that case there was a civil war before the king, Charles I, was executed, for many people supported him against parliament. His enemies, however, were the stronger, and Oliver Cromwell, known as the Lord Protector, became ruler in his place. (This is more fully explained in the articles CHARLES I; CIVIL WAR; CROMWELL, OLIVER.)

The United States came about as a result of a rebellion when it consisted of English colonies ruled by the English King George III. (See AMERICAN WAR OF INDEPENDENCE.) The constitution, or set of rules by which the state is governed, of the United States later became the model for the countries of South America when they broke away from the rule of Spain and Portugal and became separate republics.

These South American republics, however, often became dictatorships, which means that one man, although not crowned king, becomes so powerful that he is able to put down all opposition to him. (See DICTATOR.) This has also happened in several European republics, particularly Spain after the Civil War of 1936 to 1939, when General Franco came to power, and Germany under Adolf Hitler. Few kings have become dictators. In most countries which are still ruled by monarchs the monarchs have become "constitutional"; that is to say, they rule as their parliaments and ministers advise them. Thus, although Britain and the Scandinavian countries of Norway, Sweden and Denmark still have monarchs, their people are freer to choose the people who really govern them than are those of many republics.

France has had five republics since the first one of 1792, and has returned to monarchies on two occasions. (See FRANCE.) The Fifth Republic began in 1958 under General Charles de Gaulle, after a series of weak governments and because of the danger of civil war.

The heads of republics are generally known as presidents, but the power of the presidents of different countries varies considerably. The president of West Germany, for example, does little more than take part in ceremonies, the real power being held by the chancellor or prime minister. On the other hand, the president of the United States, although elected for only four years at a time, is as powerful as a king and prime minister combined.

RESEARCH is a word used to describe a thorough search for facts. Research may be carried out in any subject but its methods can be most clearly seen in science. Scientific research is never-ending, because even the simplest object is much more complicated than the most vivid imagination could suppose. A stone looks simple enough, yet a geologist could give a long and learned lecture about its past history and how it was formed. A physicist could say at least as much about its properties. Several chemists, each an expert in a particular branch, would be needed to describe the exact composition of the stone and the fantastic structure of the molecules and atoms of which it is composed. Each of these scientists would have to admit that he or she knew only a limited amount about the subject and that much more lay beyond, which he or she might never know.

From the beginning of civilization people have tried to find out more about the world in which they lived. By very early times they had already made some great discoveries, such as how to make fire and pottery, how to obtain metals from rocks and earth, how to weave cloth and make paints. No one knows who first discovered these things. The ancient Greeks about 2,500 years ago, however, wanted to go much further. They wanted to find out the *reasons* for what they saw, and this meant careful thought. Their method, which is well shown in Plato's *Republic*, was to try to arrive at the truth through discussion. Unfortunately this method does not carry the searcher very far, and for centuries little progress was made. (See PLATO.)

The Experimental Method

In the days of Queen Elizabeth I the great thinker Francis Bacon suggested a much better method, which was later widely adopted. (See BACON, FRANCIS.) His idea was to begin by making experiments, then to observe the results and finally to draw conclusions. Where experiments cannot be made, as for example with the stars or—in some cases—with rocks and animals, then observations are made and their probable meaning is thought out. According to the conclusions thus reached, an attempt is made to form a picture of what has happened and why.

The experiment is really a question put to nature and the observation is what appears to us to be nature's answer. However, the conclusion we draw from the observation is our own idea entirely. Still more so is the attempt to picture

Courtesy, I.C.I. Plastics Division
Scientific research is carried out by making experiments. Here two chemists await the result of an experiment.

how the process works. The picture formed is called a *hypothesis*, which was the Greek word for "foundation." When a number of these pictures has been collected it is possible to put them together and obtain a kind of general view called a *theory*. (The word theory comes from the Greek *theoreo*, "to behold or contemplate".)

The process is very like solving a jig-saw puzzle. Each little piece may be likened to a hypothesis or an observation and the completed puzzle to a theory. However, just as the solver of a jig-saw puzzle knows he is wrong if at the end he is left with a piece that cannot be fitted in, so in making a theory the scientist must be able to fit in *all* his observations. If he cannot do this he must repeat his experiments to check that the observations are correct. If they *are* correct, then he must abandon that theory and try another.

The pioneers in science often began by making experiments in a haphazard way on a sort of hit-and-miss principle. Joseph Priestley, on whom there is a separate article, did this at the end of the 18th century. He knew that melted metals formed a scum, or dross, on the surface when exposed to air. He collected the scum off mercury, now known as mercuric oxide, and on heating it in a glass jar found that it gave off a gas which until then had been unknown, but which is now called oxygen.

Priestley likened this way of going about things to the old style of hunting, when a sportsman went out to shoot *something* but never knew beforehand what—it might be a hare, a pigeon or a rabbit. Many of the underlying facts of science were discovered in this way. Much better methods, however, are used nowadays.

Great advances in research have resulted from improvements in weighing and measuring. Lord Rayleigh in 1894 found the exact density (heaviness) of the gas nitrogen, using methods far more accurate than ever before. He prepared the gas in two ways: by removing the oxygen and carbon dioxide from the air and by heating the substance ammonium nitrite. The nitrogen obtained from the air appeared to be a little heavier than that obtained from ammonium nitrite. This at first was not surprising, for there are always small errors in every

observation. However, the size of the probable error can be calculated, and in this case it worked out at much less than the actual difference observed.

The chemist William Ramsay saw a way in which this could be accounted for. Instead of having two samples of the same gas, Rayleigh must have prepared two gases which in some way differed. The difference must be due to the presence in the nitrogen obtained from air of some heavier gas or gases, which hitherto had escaped detection. Ramsay looked for them and found four. (See NEON.)

The discovery of the planet Neptune in 1846 was due to a theory based on accurate observation. In the 1820s it was noticed that the planet Uranus was not travelling quite along the orbit, or path, that it should have followed according to Newton's law of gravitation (see ASTRONOMY). In 1834 an amateur astronomer, the Reverend T. J. Hussey, suggested that this was because some undiscovered planet beyond Uranus must be affecting its behaviour. The French astronomer Urbain Leverrier and the Cambridge student John Couch Adams calculated where the unknown planet must be in order to cause the observed difference in the orbit of Uranus. They then indicated whereabouts in the sky the telescopes should be pointed to find the new planet. A search was made of that part of the sky and there Neptune was found.

The increasing accuracy of scientific instruments has given rise to many valuable researches by revealing something quite unexpected or some small difference not shown by the older and cruder instruments. When the scientists studying plant life first began to examine the nutrition (nourishment) of plants, they grew the plants in solutions made by dissolving in water the salts of the various chemical elements. They found that the salts of six elements—nitrogen, phosphorus, potassium, calcium, magnesium and iron—were needed by the plants in measurable quantities. This appeared to be the complete list. It was known that the salts were impure, but that was not considered important.

Later, when pure salts were available and very sensitive chemical tests were developed, it was found that five other elements were equally necessary—boron, copper, manganese, zinc and molybdenum. The amounts of these needed are tiny and can be represented by diluting a bathful of water with a few drops of liquid chemical. Animals, too, need tiny quantities of cobalt and iodine. The detection of these "trace elements", as they are called, has been made possible only by the development of very sensitive methods of analysis and measurement. (To analyse a substance is to make a detailed examination of its composition.) Some startling agricultural developments have resulted. Wide areas of land have grown better crops and many plants and animals have been saved from disease.

Following up a Clue

Sometimes a discovery is the result of a little accident which most people would ignore. For example, in 1896 the French scientist Henri Becquerel noticed fogging (blackening) of some photographic plates that had been kept in a drawer, although they were properly wrapped to protect them against light. For most people this would have been just a nuisance. Becquerel, however, recognized that the fogging must be caused by some kind of rays with the same effect as light. In the drawer was a chemical containing the element uranium. He tried this and found that it fogged plates in complete darkness; it therefore was the source of the rays.

Later, a Polish woman who afterwards became Madame Curie studied uranium minerals to discover which of the substances was the cause of the rays. None of the substances making up the bulk of the minerals gave off the rays, so the source was evidently something present only in tiny quantities. With great patience, she isolated this particular substance, or obtained it by itself, and called it radium. (See CURIE, PIERRE AND MARIE; RADIOACTIVITY; RADIUM.) Wonderful developments, which you can read about in the article NUCLEAR POWER.), followed the discovery of the radioactive elements.

The discovery of the germ-killing substance called penicillin was also the result of a trifling accident seen by a careful observer. In 1928 Professor Alexander Fleming of St. Mary's Hospital, London, was growing the germs called

staphylococci on some jelly in a plate. This was quite an ordinary task in hospitals and laboratories, for the staphylococcus is important. (It causes boils and some skin complaints.) The plates are usually kept covered, but in order to examine them the lids are taken off for a few moments every now and then. This short exposure is long enough to admit the spores (seeds) of bacteria, fungi and other organisms. On this occasion a fungus spore got in and, as had often happened before, it began to multiply.

Fleming, however, noticed what many others would have missed: that the colonies of staphylococci close to the fungus colony began to dissolve. The change was very small, and Fleming afterwards admitted that if he had not been wearing spectacles he would not have noticed it. However, he realized its possibilities. He made a solution containing the food needed by the fungus, grew the fungus on it and found that this solution was able to destroy staphylococci, and also to check the growth of other harmful microbes. Evidently it contained a powerful poison, which he called penicillin, but he could not separate this out.

Then Professor Howard Florey of Oxford and some other chemists succeeded after much patient work in isolating what they thought was the penicillin. They tried it on mice, and found that it worked. Then they wanted to try it on a man, but the methods of preparation were so slow that it took months for one test, for a man is 3,000 times the weight of a mouse and therefore needs very much more penicillin.

At last they prepared the material and made the test. To their dismay, the patient started shivering and his temperature rose. This effect was found to be due to an impurity in the penicillin, and when it was removed the penicillin behaved properly. Then other chemists worked out methods of preparation suitable for large-scale manufacture and now penicillin is available to all hospitals and doctors for use in curing disease. (See ANTIBIOTICS; FLEMING, SIR ALEXANDER; PENICILLIN.)

In most cases the sequence is the same. First, a shrewd observer notices something that the ordinary unobservant person would miss. Then this observation is followed up and its meaning examined. Next, other workers in a different branch of science, using different methods, develop the original discovery and make it useful for purposes quite unsuspected by the first discoverer.

Modern Research Work

The more usual method of research is to draw conclusions from the observed facts and to test these conclusions by new experiments. The observations can often be expressed mathematically, and the procedure may then become very complicated. Equations or formulae (mathematical expressions) can be developed so as to lead to something new and entirely unexpected. It was in this way that the great scientist Albert Einstein developed the theory of relativity. (See EINSTEIN, ALBERT.)

Einstein's little book called *Relativity* is remarkable. Each chapter is short and begins with a simple and easily understood proposition. Then it proceeds step by step to a wholly unexpected conclusion. One of Einstein's conclusions was that light is bent in the neighbourhood of a very heavy object like the Sun. The bending is so slight that only very delicate instruments could detect it, but nevertheless it was found to occur and Einstein's conclusion was proved correct.

Modern research work is based on these methods but has become very complicated. As in the search for gold, a few of the pioneers may hope to pick up nuggets, but that is largely a matter of luck. In the later stages of research, much more elaborate work is needed and the individual scientist has to give place to the large company using complicated machinery and employing a big staff of experts. The work becomes far more systematic and more certain to yield results.

In research the path has often been opened up by a person keener-sighted and sharper-witted than most. Development of the subject, however, calls for men and women trained in several different branches of science who can approach it from different points of view. Working together, they can often observe something that each individually would have missed. This is called team work and is now widely used. Its success depends on the spirit in which the members of the team work together, and also on good leadership and a clear aim.

As there is no end to the marvels and mysteries of nature, so there can be no end to research. The Rothamsted Experimental Station in Hertfordshire studies the growth of crops and started in 1843 with two men, J. B. Lawes and J. H. Gilbert. It continues the same work but now has a staff of more than 200 scientists of many different interests. There are many other research stations throughout the world, carrying out research in many different subjects. Some may be trying to find new cures for diseases, others a more advanced design of computer, a completely new form of transport, or new strains of plant able to grow in deserts or mountain lands. Their work may prove to be of great scientific value, but it may take years before it affects our everyday lives.

RESERVOIR. A structure for storing a reserve supply of water is called a reservoir. It may be built to store water for irrigation, or watering the land; for supply to houses and factories; or for use in driving turbines to provide electric power. (See IRRIGATION; WATER POWER; WATER SUPPLY.) A large reservoir made by building a

Aerofilms

The Pen y Gareg dam in the Elan Valley, Wales.

dam across a valley is called an impounding reservoir. Sometimes the level of an existing lake may be raised and the amount of water in it increased by damming the outflow. An example of this is the Owen Falls dam in Uganda, which raises the level of Lake Victoria. Several cities in Great Britain obtain their water from reservoirs which are built in the high parts of Wales, the Pennines, the Lake District and Scotland, where there is a heavy rainfall.

During the rainy season, the water level in a reservoir rises. When the dry season comes, the level falls as water continues to be drawn off.

One of the ways of purifying water is to let it stand so that any solid matter in it sinks and germs have time to die. Storage reservoirs are built for this by water-supply authorities. After purification, the water is pumped through mains (large pipes) to service reservoirs near the town or village and holding about two days' supply. These are built on high ground if possible, so that the water can run down to the buildings, but they may have to be built in the form of a large tank at the top of a tower. They ensure that there is a steady supply of water at all times.

RESINS. Natural resins are the sticky substances obtained as gums from trees. The best known is rosin, which is a product of pine trees. It looks like yellow crystal, softens when heated and dissolves easily in turpentine and many other solvents, or dissolving liquids. Rosin is widely used in the manufacture of paints, paper, soap and adhesives.

Most of the rosin comes from the southern states of the United States, where forests of young pine trees in what is called the "gum belt" are chipped and scraped by hand to yield the sticky gum. This is collected in metal cups attached to the trees. The purification of rosin is carried out in large steam distilleries which produce turpentine and pine oil as by-products (see By-Products). A good deal of rosin is also extracted from pulpwood and old stumps of pine trees. Other natural resins, such as damar, mastic, sandarac, lac and elemi, are used in the manufacture of paints and varnishes. Some of the tree gums or resins contain fragrant oils which are of great value in perfumery.

Synthetic Resins

By examining the structure of natural resins, scientists have discovered how to manufacture a wide range of synthetic (artificial) resins. In many cases these synthetic resins have replaced the natural ones. In some cases it is possible to combine the qualities of natural and synthetic resins. Today synthetic resins are very widely used, particularly in the plastics industry. (See Plastics.) Many synthetic resins are made from phenol and other chemicals obtained from coal tar and petroleum.

Synthetic resins are often used in paints and other forms of coating, because they are tough, long-lasting and give a gloss finish. Polyester and polyethylene resins are widely used in plastics and fibre glass, and polyurethane is used in paints, adhesives and insulating material. Epoxy resins are used as textile finishes, melamine-formaldehyde resins give a porcelain-like appearance and silicone resins are used as lubricants, varnishes and insulator coatings. Resin adhesives are used in making plywood and for treating wood. One of the most common uses of synthetic resins is on textiles, which can be made non-shrink, crease-proof and drip-dry.

RESTAURANTS AND CAFÉS. Many of the words in the catering industry, which is responsible for the preparation of food and wines in public places, are French. This is because France has always been the leading country in cookery. The words "restaurant", "café" and "hotel" are all French. Restaurants provide elaborate and therefore expensive meals while cafés offer simpler, cheaper meals or merely drinks like tea and lemonade.

The three main groups of workers in a large and typical catering concern can be classified very simply as the kitchen staff, the serving staff and the office staff.

Chefs and Cooks

The word *chef*, which means head, or chief, is used for male cooks, and there are many different chefs, named according to the kind of cooking they do. The cook in charge of the kitchens in a large establishment is known as the

Courtesy, Forté's and Company Limited

Top: Chefs at work in the kitchen of a large restaurant. Above: A quick-service café.

chef de cuisine, and he is assisted by *chefs de partie*. Besides chefs, there are also kitchen porters, who prepare vegetables and keep the kitchens and all the equipment clean.

Youngsters learning to become chefs do some of their training in each part of the kitchen. A learner will probably work first in the *garde-manger* (larder). The work in this section is very varied and gives the learner an excellent knowledge of the different foods that make up the different dishes.

The learner will also work under the *chef entremetier*, preparing vegetables and egg dishes and perhaps making soups. Next he may work for the *chef rôtissier*, cooking joints, poultry and game, and for the *chef poissonier*, preparing and cooking fish.

Later he will work under the *chef pâtissier*, where he learns to make and decorate cakes, pastries, sweets, icings and similar delicacies, elaborate and painstaking work. Under the *chef saucier* the learner will be taught how to make hot sauces and *entrées*, which are special dishes served between courses at a large meal. In some restaurants he may grill and fry meat and fish. Further experience may be gained as *chef tournant* or relief cook, taking charge of a section when its *chef de partie* is off duty.

During his training the young chef is also taught to carve and to dish up and serve portions. He learns about costing (pricing food) and kitchen control, sometimes working for a time as a kitchen clerk—passing the quality of the food; checking the weight and price, and the size of portions served to customers.

The training usually lasts five years and boys and girls can enter at normal school-leaving age. There are also full and part-time courses provided by technical colleges in cities and large towns and organized by the Hotel and Catering Institute. Since food and the restaurant business is international, many students travel abroad to gain experience.

Serving Staff and Office Workers

The second most important group in a catering organization is the serving staff. In a large restaurant there is always a manager (perhaps with an assistant as relief) in charge of each room where the guests take their meals. In each room there is also a *maître d'hôtel* or head waiter, with a staff of *chefs de rang* or station waiters. In smaller restaurants and cafés there is often a head waiter or manager in charge.

Each station waiter looks after a group of tables, receiving orders from the guests and serving the food. He is assisted by a *commis* or assistant waiter, who fetches and carries dishes, cutlery, glass and linen. There is also a wine waiter or waitress who takes orders for both alcoholic and other drinks. A good wine waiter is polite and knowledgeable. He must know wines, where they come from, the vintage, the temperature at which they should be served and the most suitable wine to serve with the various dishes or courses. (See WINE.)

The work of a first-class waiter is both interesting and varied and can include a period of training abroad. A learner should have training in a kitchen in his own country first and become acquainted with kitchen French. He will then go into the restaurant as *commis* waiter and so through the whole range of waiting duties.

There are many possibilities for both boys and girls on waiting staffs as head and station waiters, wine butlers, waitresses, bar staff and cellar staff. Both boys and girls can also work as counter-hands in cafés.

The third main group is the office staff. This includes the buying and storekeeping departments, book-keeping and accounts departments and departments that look after the catering staff themselves.

A Typical Catering Day

A brief description of a catering day will give some idea of how varied is the work the keeper of a small London restaurant has to do. Usually he has progressed from *commis* waiter to waiter and had some kitchen experience; then he has become a head waiter, manager and eventually, by saving and hard work, a proprietor (the owner of a restaurant).

At early dawn he will be at the markets, buying meat, fish, and fruit and vegetables. He returns to the restaurant about breakfast time

and gives instructions to his chef. Then he inspects the restaurant, gives orders to the waiters and makes sure that everything is spick and span before the first lunch-time customers arrive. He tries to welcome every customer who comes into the restaurant and to attend to their comfort.

When lunch is over the proprietor checks the amount of business that has been done, finding how many customers have been served, how much money has been taken and whether his kitchen control agrees with the money taken. Then he inspects the kitchen again, giving particular attention to wastage, talks to the chef about the result and general progress of the lunch session and gives plans and instructions for the dinners that evening. The restaurant has to be tidied up, the tables relaid and preparations begun for the evening trade.

The lunch time process is repeated during the evening. At the end of it the proprietor checks his takings, prepares his cash for the bank and closes for the night.

REVERE, Paul (1735–1818), was an American patriot. He was a Boston man who was

Paul Revere riding to rouse people against the British.

among the leaders of the revolution against British rule, and in 1773 took part in one of the earliest acts of revolt. This was the Boston "Tea Party", which is described in the article AMERICAN WAR OF INDEPENDENCE. When the Americans began their war for independence they had some military stores at Concord, Massachusetts. Revere learned that the British planned to seize the stores and he undertook to spread the alarm. His comrades agreed to hang one lantern in the church tower if the British moved by land and two if they went by sea. The signal came on the night of April 18, 1775—two lights! Revere sprang on a borrowed horse and rode through the country waking the people, so that when the British approached Concord next day there were armed men to meet them. The story was told in verse by the American poet H. W. Longfellow as "Paul Revere's Ride".

Revere rose to the rank of lieutenant-colonel and after the war became active in public affairs. The house in which he lived at Boston can still be seen.

REVOLUTION.

We speak of revolutions happening whenever very great changes take place in the way states are governed, or in the way people make their living or in the way they think. The changes need not come about through the use of force, but usually a great revolution brings with it so much upheaval that it leads to violence or bloodshed in the end.

In modern times the three most important revolutions that have brought changes in government have been the American Revolution (or War of Independence), which began in 1774 when the 13 North American colonies rebelled against the British government and soon afterwards claimed their independence; the French Revolution, which began in 1789 and within a few years overthrew the king, the nobles and the clergy; and the Russian Revolution of 1917, which led to the making of the U.S.S.R. (Union of Soviet Socialist Republics)—the first Communist state in the world. (See AMERICAN WAR OF INDEPENDENCE; FRENCH REVOLUTION; RUSSIAN REVOLUTION; UNION OF SOVIET SOCIALIST REPUBLICS.) There have been many other revolutions in modern times which have overthrown one system of government and replaced it by a very different one. Thus we speak of the Fascist Revolution of 1922 in Italy and of the National Socialist Revolution of 1933 in Germany. In Italy the existing system of government was overthrown by the Fascists under Benito Mussolini and in Germany it was overthrown by the Nationalist Socialists led by Adolf Hitler. (See GERMANY; ITALY.) However, both these dictators were overthrown in World War II and these revolutions did not bring about such deep and lasting changes in social life and ways of thinking as did the three mentioned earlier.

Great changes in the way that people make a living are called economic revolutions. It is quite right to call them revolutions, for such changes lead to lasting alterations in how people live and behave. Two examples of economic revolutions that have taken place in Britain are the agricultural revolution of the 18th century and the industrial revolution which started in the 18th century and, some people think, is still continuing. During the agricultural revolution great amounts of land were enclosed (see ENCLOSURES) and new ways of cultivating it were found. New crops and new breeds of sheep and cattle were introduced. The result of all this was a complete change in the lives of all who were concerned with agriculture—and in the lives of all British people, for it meant that far more food, and more varied food, became available.

The industrial revolution, with its new machines, its new steam power and its new factory towns made enormous changes in the lives of all who earned their living by making things —and again, in the lives of all British people, for it gave them vast amounts of factory-made goods at cheap prices. (See INDUSTRIAL REVOLUTION.) The full effect of these changes was felt when railways were introduced during the first half of the 19th century. Britain sold to other countries many of the things it made and so became "the workshop of the world".

When people change their way of life, their way of thinking also changes. Naturally, therefore, the agricultural and industrial revolutions produced revolutions of thought. However, ways of thinking have sometimes been revolutionized by ideas themselves, and not as a result

REVOLUTIONS

Below are listed some of the most important revolutions in recent history—since 1600.

1642–52	ENGLISH CIVIL WAR fought between Parliament and King.
1688	THE "GLORIOUS REVOLUTION" in England; King James II is forced to flee the throne and is succeeded by William and Mary.
1775–83	AMERICAN WAR OF INDEPENDENCE results in American colonies breaking away from Britain.
1789	FRENCH REVOLUTION begins; in 1793 the French executed their king and queen.
1810–25	SOUTH AMERICAN REVOLUTION. Led by José de San Martin and Simon Bolivar, the countries of South America fight off Spanish and Portuguese rule to become independent.
1821–30	GREECE wins its independence from Turkey.
1848	EUROPE IN REVOLT. Revolutions in France, Germany, Austria and Italy against harsh and unfair rule. (In this year Karl Marx published the Communist Manifesto.)
1857	INDIAN MUTINY (or War of Independence) against British rule in India —unsuccessful.
1859–61	ITALY freed from foreign rule by Garibaldi and Cavour.
1912	CHINESE REPUBLIC replaces the old empire, with Sun Yat-sen as first President.
1917	RUSSIAN REVOLUTION. Communists led by Lenin and Trotsky seize power in Russia. The Tsar is overthrown and later shot.
1918	FOLLOWING WORLD WAR I emperors of Germany and Austria overthrown and republics set up.
1922	MUSSOLINI'S FASCISTS seize power in Italy.
1933	NAZIS led by Hitler take command of Germany.
1949	CHINESE COMMUNISTS led by Mao Tse-tung win the civil war in China, which becomes a Communist country and for years goes through violent changes.
1956	HUNGARY. Unsuccessful revolt against Communist government put down by U.S.S.R. which sends troops into Hungary.
1959	FIDEL CASTRO leads Communist revolution in Cuba; Cuban revolutionaries later active in revolutionary movements in other parts of Central and South America, as well as in Africa.
1979	ISLAMIC REVOLUTION in Iran. The Shah (emperor) is overthrown by extreme Islamic leaders demanding a return to old ways.

of something else that was going on at the same time. Thus in the 16th century new ideas about religion produced a religious revolution, and new forms of Christianity—which we now call Protestantism—were born. (These changes are explained in the article REFORMATION.) In the 17th century the new ideas of Sir Isaac Newton and a few other scientists brought about vastly different ways of thought in scientific affairs— a scientific revolution—and later men like Charles Darwin and Albert Einstein produced equally startling changes. (See DARWIN; EINSTEIN; NEWTON.)

The greatest revolution of recent times is the Chinese Revolution. It began in 1949 when the Communist Party, led by Mao Tse-tung, seized control of this vast nation and undertook to change its whole way of life. (There is more about this in CHINA.) Later revolutions have included those in Cuba, Cambodia, Portugal, Libya and Ethiopia.

REYKJAVIK is the capital and largest city of the republic of Iceland. It lies in the southwest of the island on the spot where the first Norseman settled in 874. The name Reykjavik means "smoking bay" and the city is so called because of the steaming hot springs near by. The water comes out of these springs at a temperature of about 87°C and is led through pipes to supply

ZEFA

Reykjavik's busy harbour through which passes most of Iceland's trade.

hot water to the public buildings and houses. The springs also heat a swimming bath and make hothouse gardening possible.

Fishing is one of Iceland's main industries and most of the cod is landed at Reykjavik. Most of the country's trade passes through the port, where a stone breakwater completed in 1917 protects a harbour which can be used by medium-sized ships. Other industries in the capital are shipbuilding and the manufacture of rope, oilskins, fishmeal and margarine. Power is supplied by hydroelectric plants at Sog outside the city. There are regular steamship services to the United Kingdom, Denmark and Norway, and Keflavik airport is just outside the city.

At the beginning of the 20th century Reykjavik was only a small town with a population of about 6,000. The streets were unpaved and many of the houses were built of wood with corrugated iron roofs. Now it is a spacious city with a parliament house, a large modern university, a national theatre, a national library, a national museum, two cathedrals and fine public buildings, and many charming villas with a beautiful view of the bay.

The population of Reykjavik is about 86,000.

REYNOLDS, Sir Joshua (1723–1792). Sir Joshua Reynolds, one of the most famous of English artists, could not only paint many kinds of pictures equally well, but could also write books that were as good as his paintings. He was one of the cleverest and most popular men of his time, and his name is remembered today not only for his pictures but because he helped to found the Royal Academy, the chief society of artists in Britain, and was its first President. (See ROYAL ACADEMY.)

Joshua Reynolds was born in Devon, but when he was 17 he was sent to London to be a pupil of the portrait painter Thomas Hudson. The young man had such pleasant manners and talked so wittily and entertainingly that it was not long before he was a welcome visitor wherever he went, particularly at the house of a wealthy and generous nobleman, Lord Edgcumbe. There Reynolds met Captain Keppel, who invited him to go to Italy in his ship "Centurion". Reynolds accepted the invitation, and was able to spend three years studying the paintings of the great Italian artists.

In 1752 he came back to England, and thanks partly to Lord Edgcumbe's help, he quickly became the most fashionable portrait painter in London—in one year he had 677 clients who wanted their portraits painted by him. Even the gruff Dr. Samuel Johnson enjoyed his friendship and praised his learning. In December 1768 the Royal Academy was founded, with King George III as its patron, and a few months later Joshua

National Portrait Gallery
A picture of Sir Joshua Reynolds painted by himself.

Reynolds was knighted. One of the duties he performed as President was to give lectures to the students of the Royal Academy School, and these *Discourses,* in which he wrote of great artists and of his own ideas about art, were then published.

As Reynolds grew older the deafness which had troubled him for years grew worse and his sight failed, and he gradually withdrew from public life. He died peacefully in 1792, and was buried in St. Paul's Cathedral.

Some of his delightful pictures are in art galleries in London such as the National Gallery, the National Portrait Gallery and the Wallace Collection. They include "The Age of Innocence", a picture of his young grandniece (in the Tate Gallery), and the portraits of "Captain Robert Orme", in fine uniform (in the National Gallery), "Nelly O'Brien" (Wallace Collection) and "Lady Cockburn", who is shown with her three eldest sons (National Gallery). Pictures

like this one, of women and children, are perhaps the most graceful and perfect of his works.

RHAPSODY is the name of a piece of music, generally exciting, that is based on the popular music of a country. Liszt's *Hungarian Rhapsodies,* based on Hungarian gipsy music, and Dvorak's *Slavonic Rhapsodies* are early examples. In modern music the title is used by Ravel for his *Rhapsodie Espagnole* ("Spanish Rhapsody") and by Vaughan Williams for his *Norfolk Rhapsodies.* The American composer George Gershwin wrote a work inspired by jazz music called *Rhapsody in Blue.*

Brahms used the name in a slightly different way. He wrote three rhapsodies for piano, which are stirring pieces, though they are not based on any national music. He also wrote a rhapsody for contralto, men's chorus and orchestra.

RHEA. According to ancient Greek legends, Rhea was the mother of many of the gods, including Zeus who eventually became their king. The Greeks thought of Rhea as being the same as Cybele, about whom you can read more in the article GREAT MOTHER GODDESS.

RHEA. Rheas are large birds related to the ostrich, emu and cassowary, and they live in South America. There are two kinds, one of which is found from Brazil to Argentina, the other in countries more to the west and south.

The rhea is like the ostrich in general appearance but smaller. The plumage of the head and neck is dingy white, that of the body is mostly

The rhea lives in South America. The male, not the female, brings up the young and even hatches the eggs.

brown and ash-coloured and the under parts and thighs are white. The rhea has no beautiful wing plumes like those of the ostrich, nor has it a tail. It has three toes on each foot, instead of only two as the ostrich has.

Although it cannot fly, the rhea is able to run extremely fast over the plains where it lives. Its breeding habits are unusual. Each cock bird mates with several hens who lay their large, yellowish-white eggs in one nest on the ground. The cock bird hatches these eggs—sometimes there are as many as 20—and also looks after the chicks, which have striped feathers. The rhea is a devoted father and takes great care of the chicks. Sometimes he will even try to steal the chicks belonging to another rhea. The hens, on the other hand, take not the slightest interest in their families.

RHEUMATISM is the general name for any disease which causes pain in the muscles or joints. Among illnesses that cause this pain are rheumatic fever, muscular rheumatism, lumbago, sciatica, rheumatoid arthritis, osteo-arthritis and gout.

Rheumatic fever, which used to be very common among children and young people, is serious, not because of the pain in the joints but because heart disease sometimes occurs as well and the heart may be damaged for life. When rheumatic fever comes on, there are pains in the limbs, first in one joint and then in another. The patient sweats a good deal and has a high temperature and a sore throat.

Muscular rheumatism, which is also known as fibrositis, includes pain, aching and stiffness, and is usually brought on by cold and damp. Older people are more likely to have it than young ones. Poultices and hot baths are a help.

With lumbago, patients suffer from severe pain low down in the back. This often comes on when they stand up and also seems to be brought on by cold and damp. Sciatica is pain in the great sciatic nerve which runs down the back of the thigh.

In rheumatoid arthritis, the joints become inflamed and eventually stiffen and grow deformed (out of shape). Usually small joints, such as those in the fingers and toes, are affected. Rheumatoid arthritis attacks older people and especially women. Osteo-arthritis is a disease of the larger joints (hip and knee) caused mostly by a wearing out of the surfaces of the bones at the joint.

Gout was a disease from which many people suffered in the 18th century. Young people seldom get it. It is a hereditary disorder, which inflames the joints and causes a violent pain which often comes on suddenly, and is usually in the foot. Chalk often appears round the joints, looking like stones under the skin.

Unfortunately almost any vague pain in any part of the body, but especially in the back and limbs, is called rheumatism and this may be dangerous if people treat themselves without getting medical advice. Equally unfortunately, the exact causes of the different types of rheumatism described in this article are not fully understood. Treatment has to be largely a matter of relieving the pain and other symptoms and there is no simple and certain cure.

RHINE RIVER. The most important waterway in Europe is the Rhine. For centuries nations have fought for control of its banks and main crossings. It rises in the central part of the Swiss Alps and flows into the North Sea in the Netherlands after a course of 1,320 kilometres. In Switzerland the two chief headstreams of the Rhine meet near Chur and flow northeast as a rapid torrent through a deep narrow valley into Lake Constance. Westwards from Lake Constance the Rhine drops fairly steeply to Basle, plunging 25 metres over the Rhine Falls at Schaffhausen and being joined from the south by its first great tributary, the Aar. This part of the river forms the boundary between Germany and Switzerland. (See BASLE.)

At Basle the Rhine turns northwards and flows through a broad fertile valley where wheat, hops, sugar beet and tobacco are grown. On the west rise the Vosges Mountains in France and to the east are the fir-clad slopes and valleys of the Black Forest in Germany. Below Strasbourg the Rhine is joined from the east by the Ill. Two further tributaries are the Neckar flowing in at Mannheim and the Main at Mainz, both coming from the eastward.

At Mainz the Rhine begins the most beautiful

section of its course. Here it flows for about 130 kilometres through the Rhine Gorge, a very narrow valley shut in by high cliffs or steep hills. On rocky crests stand the ruins of ancient castles. Some of the villages and towns are walled round and contain many old buildings. The slopes facing west and south have been cut into terraces (flat stretches arranged like steps) on whose stony

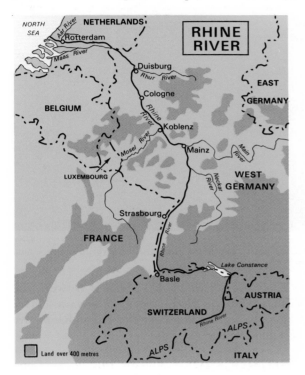

soil grow the vines from which the famous Rhine wines are made. At Lorelei the east bank rises in an almost vertical cliff 133 metres above the river, which is here at its deepest and takes up the whole 115 metre width of the gorge. It is said that a beautiful golden-haired maiden once lived on the cliff and by her singing tempted the men in ships and boats passing by to come nearer and nearer until their vessels crashed. (See LORE-LEI.) At Koblenz the Rhine is joined by its beautiful tributary the Mosel (or Moselle), whose valley is also famous for its wines. The name Koblenz comes from the Latin *confluentes*, meaning a "confluence", or joining of two rivers.

The gorge ends at Bonn (see BONN) and at Cologne, where the Lower Rhine begins, the river enters the plains. Cologne was originally

built by the ancient Romans and became the great crossing-point for traffic between Paris and Brussels on the west and Berlin, Warsaw and Moscow on the east. (See COLOGNE.) At Düsseldorf, which is also an important city, the Rhine enters one of the greatest industrial districts in the world. This is the Ruhr, a collection of mining and manufacturing towns on the east bank which form a region named after the River Ruhr, whose valley contains a rich coalfield. It joins the Rhine at Duisburg-Ruhrort (see RUHR).

As the river, here about 1 kilometre wide, crosses the Dutch frontier near Emmerich the land changes in character. For thousands of years the Rhine has brought down huge quantities of fine mud. Its current here is so slow that it can carry this load no farther. The mud sinks to the river bed as silt, and over the years has raised the level so that the river is now flowing above the level of the surrounding land. In the old days this was dangerous, as in the spring floods the Rhine often broke free and flooded the country. Also, it often changed its course and reached the sea through several channels.

Practically the whole of the Netherlands drains into the Lower Rhine. The Dutch people have learned to manage this difficult river and have made their land into one of the most fertile regions in the world. Their first task was to keep the river to one or two channels. They blocked up many of the minor channels so that most of the Rhine waters reach the sea through the Waal, only a little flowing through the Lek and scarcely any through the Ijssel. The banks of the river channels were raised and strengthened and their courses were straightened so that the water flowed more directly and deposited less silt. Then the low marshy lands were drained by cutting canals from which pumps lifted the water into the rivers so that it flowed away to the sea.

Near the mouth of the Lek is Rotterdam, the greatest port in Europe (see ROTTERDAM). The channel called the Waal mingles with the River Maas coming from the south (see MEUSE RIVER) and the great river enters the sea at last through the Hollandschdiep.

The Rhine is a very important trade route and its chief port, Duisburg-Ruhrort, is the largest inland harbour in Europe. Iron ore (from which

The Rhine River at Lorelei, where the river flows between high cliffs. The Rhine is a beautiful river, but also a busy industrial and trade route.

ZEFA

iron and steel are made) is unloaded here, together with grain and oil, while coal and manufactured goods are sent both upstream and downstream. Seagoing ships call regularly at Cologne. Trains of big barges carry goods to and from Mannheim-Ludwigshafen, the second largest port on the river. The large barges can reach Strasbourg and smaller ones can reach Basle. Winter freezing sometimes stops the Rhine traffic for as much as a month.

Canals have greatly increased the importance of the Rhine. The Marne-Rhine canal links the Rhine at Strasbourg with Paris and with the iron-ore fields of Lorraine. Another canal connects the Rhine with the Rhône River and thus with southern France and the Mediterranean. From Duisburg-Ruhrort the Rhine-Herne canal links the Rhine with other waterways leading to north and east Germany. The old Ludwigs Canal between the Main at Bamberg and the River Danube at Kelheim is no longer used. It has been replaced by a new route up the Main and then by canal to Regensburg on the Danube.

The busiest part of the Rhine is between the Ruhr and the Netherlands waterways. More than half the barges on the River Rhine are Dutch-owned.

RHINOCEROS.
Among the largest land animals alive today is the rhinoceros. It is a distant relative of the horse and is found in Africa, India, Malaya and Indonesia, including Borneo. In prehistoric times the woolly rhinoceros lived in Europe.

Rhinoceroses are now rare in the wild. Their natural habitat has been reduced by the encroachment of humans, and poachers kill them for the sake of their horns. These horns are made of hair, unlike the horns of all other animals, and are falsely believed by some people in Asia to have magical powers. (See HORN.) The word rhinoceros, often shortened to rhino, means "nose horn".

Today there are five species, or kinds, of rhinos. All are ungainly animals with short thick legs and three hoofed toes on each foot.

Courtesy, Satour

White rhinos in a reserve in South Africa. After the elephant, these are the largest land animals found on Earth.

Their heads are large and heavy and their tails are short with a tuft at the end. The different species of rhinos, however, vary in their skins and horns. The largest rhinos, those of Africa, may be up to 2.5 metres long and weigh as much as five tonnes.

Paul Popper

An African black rhinoceros on the move. A charging rhino can match a truck for speed, but only over a short distance.

Rhinos are short-sighted animals. They are usually found alone or in family groups, wandering in open grassland, scrub or marsh. Only in Asia do rhinos live in thick forest. Although their eyesight is poor, their senses of smell and hearing are excellent. Most rhinos will avoid people if they meet by accident, but sometimes a bad-tempered male rhino will charge blindly as soon as it catches any unfamiliar smell or sound. Rushing towards you at a speed of some 45 kilometres an hour, a five-tonne rhino is an awesome sight, and despite its bulk it can change direction with surprising agility.

Usually, however, rhinos are peaceful animals. They have no real natural enemies, since their size and thick armoured skin make them safe from predators—although a lion may attack a young or sickly rhino. Rhinos are found only in the tropics. They enjoy wallowing in deep mud, for this is the only way in which they can get rid of the flies that torment them. Sometimes little birds called oxpeckers ride on their heads or shoulders and pick off the ticks that cling to their skins. Rhinos usually sleep through the middle of the day and feed for the rest of the time. The female rhino has only one young at a time.

Asian and African Rhinos

The Indian rhinoceros, which is just under 2 metres high at the shoulder, is dark grey in colour. Its ears are long and erect and its small eyes are placed far forward on its head. Near the end of its nose is one horn, which may be 30 centimetres or more in length. With its upper lip the Indian rhino can seize leaves, twigs and grass. Its skin is arranged in heavy folds which cover its body like armour.

The Indian rhinoceros was once common throughout much of India. Now only a few are left in Assam, Bengal and Nepal in the northeast. They live among dense grass and are never far from water. The Asian rhinos are now protected in reserves in India and Indonesia.

The Javanese rhinoceros, which lives in the Malay peninsula, Borneo and the Indonesian islands of Java and Sumatra, is smaller and lighter in build than the Indian rhino. The male has a horn but the female is frequently hornless. This rhino's skin is also in folds.

The Sumatra rhinoceros is the smallest, being only about 1.3 metres high at the shoulder. It has two horns and a hairy skin.

The black rhinoceros is the commoner and smaller of the two African species, and there are more of this kind than all the others together. It has smoother, more close-fitting skin than that of the Indian rhino, a pointed upper lip and usually two horns, the front one sometimes very long. The black rhino lives south of Ethiopia.

The white or square-lipped rhinoceros, which is also smooth-skinned, is the largest of the rhino family. In colour it is similar to the black rhino; it was probably called the white rhino because it often bathed in pools of light coloured mud

Indian rhinos. Notice the way the skin lies in heavy folds, unlike that of the African rhinos. The ears and top lip of the Indian rhino are also larger than those of its African relatives. The birds on the backs of the rhinos are egrets, which feed on ticks and other parasites living in the rhino's skin.

Aquila Photographics

and so appeared white. Today it lives only in one small region of South Africa and in part of the Sudan, along the White Nile River.

RHODES, Cecil John (1853–1902).

The great aim of Cecil Rhodes was to promote the growth of the British Empire, especially in southern Africa. He founded Rhodesia (now Zimbabwe) and he wanted to see as much of Africa become British as possible. He was a man of great strength of will, but was often crude and unscrupulous in his methods.

Rhodes was the fifth son of a clergyman and went to Bishop's Stortford Grammar School in Hertfordshire. When he was 16 his health broke down and he was sent to southern Africa. Diamonds had recently been discovered at Kimberley, so Rhodes went to the diamond diggings and made money. Then he returned to England to study at Oxford University, but his health again broke down and in 1873 he returned to Africa. His doctor thought Rhodes had "not six months to live", but he recovered.

Rhodes was a clever business man. By buying up the claims of the other diamond diggers he was able to control the supply of diamonds, and therefore their price. Later he combined all the Kimberley mines in one company, called De Beers Consolidated Mines. He became very rich.

Rhodes became a member of the Cape Colony parliament and in 1885 persuaded the Cape to take over the southern part of Bechuanaland and the British government to take the northern part under its protection. To the north of Bechuanaland was a country ruled by Lobenguela, chief of the Matabele. Rhodes sent agents to Lobenguela who granted them rights of mining and promised not to grant land to others. Rhodes formed the British South Africa Company, which in 1889 received a charter from the British government to govern land. Soon this land became known as Rhodesia, in honour of Rhodes.

In 1890 Rhodes became Prime Minister of the Cape Colony. His great aim was still to unite all South Africa under British rule. The main obstacle in the way of this was the existence of the republics in the interior—the Transvaal Republic under Paul Kruger, and the

Orange Free State. (See SOUTH AFRICA.) Rhodes joined in a plot to overthrow Kruger's republic and at the end of 1895 an armed force from Rhodesia, commanded by Dr. L. S. Jameson, invaded the Transvaal Republic. Rhodes realized that this action would be a failure and tried to stop it, but too late (see JAMESON RAID). In consequence Rhodes had to resign as Prime Minister of Cape Colony.

Mansell Collection

Rhodes (right) greeting General French, who commanded the British cavalry against the Boers.

Then he turned his attention to the development of Rhodesia. He no longer held any public office, but when the Matabele rebelled in 1896 Rhodes played a brave part in persuading them to submit, riding unarmed into their camp to talk things over. When the Boer War broke out in 1899, Rhodes went to Kimberley. It was besieged by the Boers for four months. Rhodes played a strenuous part in organizing the defence but his health was broken by his exertions. After a last visit to Europe he returned to the Cape and (before the Boer War was over) he died at Muizenberg. He was buried in a grave cut in the solid rock of the Matopo Hills in Rhodesia.

Rhodes' dream of making the whole of southern Africa part of the British Empire was not to be realised. For the later history of the land named after him, see the separate article RHODESIA. In 1910 the Union of South Africa was formed as a self-governing country in which British and Boers had equal rights. It is now the Republic of South Africa. In his will, Rhodes left his beautiful old Dutch house on the slopes of Table Mountain, Groote Schuur, as a residence for the Prime Minister of South Africa. Today, he is remembered not for his empire-building but for the money he left to provide scholarships at Oxford University for students from the Commonwealth, the United States and South Africa. These students are still known as "Rhodes scholars".

RHODES. The Greek island of Rhodes in the Mediterranean Sea is the most easterly of the Dodecanese Islands (see DODECANESE). Rhodes, which is somewhat larger than the English county of Bedfordshire, is separated from the Turkish mainland by a strait 15 kilometres wide.

The island is hilly and its central mountain range rises to 1,215 metres at Mount Attavyros. The hills are clad with forests of pine trees. The climate is pleasant and the fertile soil is cultivated to grow grain, fruits such as oranges and figs, and vines, potatoes and tomatoes. There are rich pasture lands in the valleys.

The only large town is the capital, also called Rhodes, which is at the northern tip of the island. It is one of the finest remaining examples of a medieval city, being surrounded by walls and towers and defended by a moated castle. Even the harbour is fortified. The picturesque Street of the Knights, perfectly straight, is lined with old houses showing the arms (see HERALDRY) of noblemen belonging to the Knights of St. John of Jerusalem, who captured the island in 1309.

Rhodes was settled at a very early date by the Greeks who in 408 B.C. founded the city. In about 280 B.C. a huge bronze statue of the sun god, about 30 metres high, was set up near the harbour. This was the Colossus of Rhodes, one of the seven wonders of the world. (See SEVEN WONDERS OF THE WORLD.) It was overthrown by an earthquake in 224 B.C. and nothing of it now remains.

Rhodes was attacked by the Romans in 43 B.C. and later became part of the Byzantine Empire. It was surrendered to the Turks by the Knights of St. John in 1522 and remained Turkish until 1912 when it was handed over to Italy. Under Italian rule, much work was done in uncovering and restoring ancient ruins. After World War II, Rhodes and the other Dodecanese islands became Greek, and since then tourism has developed as an important all-year-round industry.

About 66,000 people live on the island, nearly half of them in the town of Rhodes itself.

ZEFA

Rhodes is the only town on the island, at its northern tip. Even the harbour is fortified, as this picture shows.

Mary Evans Picture Library

Raising the flag at Fort Salisbury in 1890 after the march from Bechuanaland.

RHODESIA was the old name for the central African country now known as Zimbabwe. It was named after the millionaire empire-builder Cecil Rhodes (on whom there is a separate article). Rhodesia was founded in 1890. Long before then, the land had been ruled by an ancient African empire of which today only the ruins of Great Zimbabwe remain. Later a tribe of cattle-herding warriors, the Ndebele or Matabele, carved out a kingdom here, enslaving the more peaceful Shona tribe.

Europeans (mostly from the Cape) began arriving in central Africa during the 1800s. They were hunters, traders, gold-seekers, and Christian missionaries. Later in the century, the European powers were rivalling one another in a scramble to grab land in Africa. One man determined that Britain should have colonies in Africa was Cecil Rhodes. By 1885 he had already brought Bechuanaland (modern Botswana) under Britain's control. He persuaded the missionary J. S. Moffat to visit the Ndebele king, Lobenguela, and in 1888 Lobenguela agreed to let Rhodes' men seek for gold and diamonds in his lands. Rhodes then persuaded the British government that it would be a good idea for the British South Africa Company to take control of central Africa. In 1890 a column of settlers guided by the famous hunter F. C. Selous set out from Bechuanaland and reached the site of Rhodesia's future capital. They named their camp Fort Salisbury (after the British prime minister). Today, it is the city of Harare.

The Ndebele rebelled in 1893, but were defeated. Rhodesia grew into a rich colony, largely looking after its own affairs. The railway reached the Victoria Falls in 1904, by which date there were about 12,000 white settlers in Rhodesia.

After World War I the settlers sought self-government, and in 1923 they became a British colony, but with control of their own affairs. They were also given a new name for the country: Southern Rhodesia. Northern Rhodesia (now Zambia) and Nyasaland (now Malawi) were neighbours of Rhodesia and for a time (1953–63) all three colonies were united into a Federation. It brought economic progress, but was not really a success. In all three colonies, the black African people wanted complete independence and more say in government.

Southern Rhodesia remained under white rule after the rest of Britain's African colonies had gained their independence. When the Federation was broken up in 1963, Southern Rhodesia went back to being a colony, called simply Rhodesia.

Most white Rhodesians wanted to keep control of the government, and few were willing to share power with the black people. In 1965 the Rhodesian prime minister, Ian Smith, declared an illegal independence. A long dispute followed. Black nationalist guerrillas formed armies and fought a war against the white Rhodesians. Rhodesia was cut off from trade with the rest of the world. At last in 1979 peace was agreed. Elections were held and in 1980 Rhodesia became independent, under its first black leader, Robert Mugabe. Its name was changed to Zimbabwe, and you can read more about the country in the article ZIMBABWE.

RHODODENDRON is the name of a very large genus, or group, of shrubs and big trees in the heather family, and the name comes from two Greek words meaning "rose tree". The name was originally given by the great Swedish botanist Linnaeus to the small, shrubby Alpine rose which covers large areas in the Alps.

Rhododendrons have beautiful flowers, generally growing in clusters. The leaves are often evergreen. They vary from being small and heather-like to thick and leathery, up to 60 centimetres long and 30 centimetres wide. Some rhododendrons are as much as 25 metres in height, others are small shrubs creeping over the rocks of high mountains. High up in the Himalayas rhododendrons have taken the place of heather and cover very large areas.

Other rhododendrons grow in the Arctic regions, the Caucasus Mountains, Tibet, China, Japan and North America. Species, or kinds, which are found growing on other trees live on mountains in Borneo, Java, Malaya and New Guinea. A single species with scarlet flowers is found in north Australia.

Rhododendrons do not like lime in the soil and they do best in a peaty, acid soil that is not too dry. Some gardens, for example the Royal Horticultural Society's gardens at Wisley in Surrey, Kew Gardens and many private gardens have special areas given up to rhododendrons and azaleas (close relatives).

Maurice Nimmo

Rhododendrons are a common sight in parks and gardens. Yet their wild home is often on high mountain slopes.

A quiet stretch of the Rhône at Avignon. Here for a time during the 14th century, popes lived (instead of at Rome). The popes' palace was a formidable fortress. At this point in its course, the Rhône is changing from a rapid mountain river to a wider, slower-moving stream, before entering a broad delta plain and flowing into the Mediterranean Sea.

Courtesy, French Government Tourist Office

RHODOPE MOUNTAINS.

These mountains lie in the Balkans. They are mainly in Bulgaria but also reach into Turkey, Yugoslavia and Greece. The country is wild and difficult to travel across, with steep valleys, thick forests and fast-flowing rivers. The highest mountains include Golyam Perelik (2,191 metres) and further west, Musala (2,925 metres).

The main rivers are the Maritsa and the Arda, and water power is used to generate hydro-electricity. Tourism is important, and there is also some lead and zinc mining. In these remote mountains, the Bulgars and other Slav peoples took refuge during the time when the Balkans were ruled by Turkey. (See BALKANS.)

RHONE RIVER.

This rapid river has its source in a glacier, or river of ice, in the Swiss Alps, and after a course of about 800 kilometres flows into the Mediterranean Sea. The upper stretch of the Rhône valley carries the railway and road that enter Switzerland through the Simplon Tunnel and Simplon Pass from Italy. Before entering France the river flows through the Lake of Geneva. Then it winds in a series of deep valleys through the ranges linking the Alps with the Jura Mountains. One of these valleys is spanned by the Génissiat hydro-electric dam.

At Lyons the Rhône is joined by its largest tributary, the Saône, and turns southwards towards the sea. It is still a swiftly flowing river and therefore is not much used by vessels. Work is going on to make it easier for vessels to use it and a canal has been made to by-pass the difficult stretch at Donzère. In this part of its course the Rhône flows between the Alps on the east and the high central tableland of France on the west. Its valley forms a great corridor through which the main roads and railways carry goods between northern and central France and the great port of Marseilles. In ancient times the Romans marched this way to conquer Gaul.

At Arles the delta begins (see DELTA) and the river divides into two main branches, the Petit Rhône going southwest and the Grand Rhône southeast. Between the two lie the salt marshes and pastures of the Camargue.

RHUBARB.

The thick, fleshy leaf-stalks of the rhubarb plant are cooked, made into jam or canned. Rhubarb is a hardy plant that comes up every year. Its roots are thick and the leaves, which can be 60 centimetres across, are not fit to eat. The skin and flesh of the leaf-stalks may be either green or red and the large flower-stalks bear many small, pinkish flowers. These, however, make the crop smaller, and so varieties which do not flower much have been bred.

The cultivated varieties of rhubarb eaten to-day probably come from two Asiatic kinds.

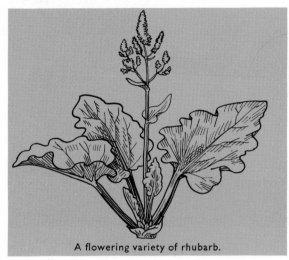

A flowering variety of rhubarb.

Many varieties were bred in England during the first half of the 19th century, but cultivated rhubarb was grown in China in 2700 B.C.

Rhubarb grows best on deep, moisture-holding soils that have been heavily manured. The high ground round Leeds in Yorkshire is the best rhubarb-producing area in Great Britain. The crop is often "forced" by digging up three-year-old roots, leaving them exposed to frost and then growing them in the dark in heated sheds. Rhubarb is also forced in gardens by covering it with straw, bracken or big earthenware jars.

RHYME. Words which *rhyme* with each other are those that have the same sound or combination of sounds at the end of them—*hair* and *pair*, *growl* and *prowl*, *star* and *far*, *sorrow* and *to-morrow*. Rhyming words are used especially in poetry, where they usually come at the ends of the lines. Because of this poems are sometimes simply called "rhymes", like the first poems we know when we are little—nursery rhymes. Poets like using rhyming words for several reasons. Probably the most important is that rhymes make a pleasant pattern of sounds and echoes in a poem, that satisfies people as they read it or hear it. Rhymes also make a poem much easier to remember, which is why many proverbs and sayings are in rhyme, like "Birds of a *feather* flock *together*", or

> A woman, a dog and a walnut-*tree*,
> The more you beat 'em, the better they *be*.

Different names are given to the various kinds of rhymes. For instance, words that rhyme with just one syllable that has the "stress", or strong beat, on it, are called masculine rhymes :

> A voice so thrilling ne'er was heard
> In spring-time from the Cuckoo-bird.

Words that have two syllables rhyming, when the second one is pronounced with less emphasis than the first, are called feminine rhymes :

> Where the mowers mow the cleanest,
> Where the hay lies thick and greenest . . .

Words that do not in fact sound alike but only look alike—words like *loved* and *proved*, for instance—are called "eye-rhymes".

There are also many different ways of arranging the rhyming lines in poetry. One of the easiest, in poems that have verses of four lines, is to make the second and fourth lines rhyme and have no rhyme at all in the first and third. Old ballads often had this kind of rhyme scheme. In this verse, on the other hand, the first and third lines rhyme as well as the second and fourth (*fall* and *shall* are eye-rhymes) :

> He that is down needs fear no fall,
> He that is low no pride;
> He that is humble ever shall
> Have God to be his guide.

Pairs of rhyming lines are called couplets :

> Thou shalt see the field-mouse peep
> Meagre from its celled sleep;
> And the snake all winter-thin
> Cast on sunny bank its skin.

There are many more complicated rhyme schemes than these, as in the kind of poem called a sonnet (see SONNET).

PONY TREKKING

by J. Kerr Hunter

If you go on a pony-trekking holiday you will be given your own pony. You will be expected to care for it and to feed and water it. It will become your friend and look after you even though you have no experience as a rider. By the end of your holiday you will have become so fond of your pony that you will be sorry to say good-bye to it.

Pony trekking does not allow fast riding. It is not safe to gallop or canter on the type of ground on which it is most enjoyed. In its simplest form the sport offers a means of exploring wild country, with other adventure-loving people, on sure-footed native ponies that are trained for the job. Their pace is steady and they can cover many miles a day over moorland, mountainsides, through rivers and up and down steep glens and forest rides. The ponies know when they must walk and when the ground is good enough for trotting.

Many pony trekking centres are recognized by one of the national associations which sponsor the sport and you should choose one of these centres for your holiday. If sponsorship is given by the Scottish Council of Physical Recreation, the Central Council of Physical Recreation or the Ponies of Britain Club, you can be fairly certain that the ponies are in good condition, trained for the job, and that the equipment will be well kept.

On a trekking holiday, you can dress quite simply. Jodhpurs or riding-breeches are most comfortable but you can wear a pair of old slacks (corduroys if possible). Jeans are not suitable for riding. You must have strong flat-heeled boots or shoes because at times you will have to lead your pony over rough country. You can wear an anorak or windcheater but a hacking jacket looks better, although you will need a waterproof coat over it in cold or wet weather. Take plenty of sweaters, gloves and string or woollen underclothing to wear when it is cold. You will also need old gumboots for stable work.

Your instructors know the countryside and will tell you not to do certain things because they are dangerous. Some people try to canter when it would not be safe even to trot, or try to make their ponies jump when they have not been trained to do so. Rather than go pony trekking, these people should go to riding schools which teach show jumping and arrange day rides across country.

Pony trekking is still reasonably cheap. The average charge for the use of a pony for six days is about £5 to £8. Add to this the cost of the type of residence you choose and it is possible to go trekking from a youth hostel for £10 or from a good hotel for under £20. Farmhouse trekking costs about £15.

Soon after arriving at a pony-trekking centre you will be told your pony's name. Your pony is chosen to suit you. It should be the right size and weight for you and of the right temperament. This means that if you are nervous you should be given a quiet pony. If you do not feel happy with your pony you should tell the groom.

At some centres you are asked to go down to the paddock before breakfast on the morning after you arrive. There you are helped to catch your pony and lead it back into its stall. You will not find much difficulty in catching it as it knows you are taking it in to breakfast. When it hears a bucket rattle, it comes up to the gate and your instructor introduces you to it. You then lead it into the stable and tie it up by a rope to its stall where you give it its breakfast : a bucketful of crushed oats, chopped straw and bran. While the pony eats you groom it with a dandy-brush to remove grit or mud from its coat. It may have been rolling in the paddock and grit under the saddle would soon produce nasty sores.

Having attended to your pony you go and have your own breakfast. Afterwards you get ready for your trek or your first riding lessons, and collect your packed lunch. Around ten o'clock you will be back in the stable ready to saddle and bridle your pony.

The equipment you use when riding a pony is called tack. This consists of a bridle, reins and bit, saddle complete with girths, stirrup leathers and stirrups. It is kept hanging in the tack room, marked with your pony's name. You are taught

Mounting the pony.

how to fit the headstall, or halter, on to the pony's head and then shown how to fit the bit.

At most trekking centres snaffle bits are used and leather bridles serve as reins. In addition there is a strong rope attached to the pony's neck with a non-slip knot. This is made up in a special coil so that it does not annoy the pony when it is grazing or trekking. This rope is always used to tie the pony up in the stable or to a post or tree when resting during a trek—never use the reins.

Saddling and Mounting

To saddle your pony, pick up the saddle with the stirrups right up against the frame so that they do not dangle. Place it gently on the pony's back, well forward towards the shoulders. Now slide the saddle into the centre of the pony's back. The saddle is held in position by girths which are taken under the pony's belly and fastened on the other side of the saddle. It is important to make the girths as tight as you can without hurting the pony, because it may be a little blown up after its breakfast so that its girth will get smaller once it starts to move. You may have to stop after about a mile to tighten up, as a slipping saddle gives a feeling of insecurity.

The next move is to pull down the stirrups, which will be adjusted to suit the length of your legs. They can be altered once you are in the saddle but you can check quickly by seeing that the length from the stirrup to the saddle attachment is the same as the length between your knuckles and your elbow.

The pony trekker's knot

302

You will be taught how to mount and dismount. To mount, stand with you left shoulder by your pony's shoulder and face the tail. Hold your reins in your left hand and use this hand to take a firm grip of the mane. Then put your left foot in the stirrup iron. A small hop with your right foot lifts you off the ground, and if you hold the back of the saddle with your right hand you will find it easy to swing the right leg up and over your pony until you are facing forward. Then ease yourself into the saddle and place your right foot into the stirrup iron. To dismount, simply take both feet out of your stirrups, lean forward on to your arms and at the same time swing the right leg backwards across the pony. Then slide to the ground but make sure you hold on to the reins.

On the Trek

At all sponsored pony-trekking centres trekkers are tested on the first morning to make sure that they know what they are supposed to be doing. There is, therefore, no need to learn to ride before going trekking, although many people do find that lessons in a riding school tone up their muscles and give them confidence. Riding a trekking pony is as simple as riding a bicycle; and moreover the pony is keeping balance for you while you concentrate on staying in the saddle.

It is not even necessary to know how to make your pony go and stop, and how to make it turn. While you are getting the feel of things it is better to leave the pony to look after you. As it knows the treks and the tricky bits it is often safer to let it lead the way. All the same, you must be firm with your pony. It must learn that it cannot play tricks with you.

At the end of a day's trekking when you start back to the stables your pony may try to go faster because it wants to get home, but you must keep it under control. Some instructors ask the trekkers to walk the last half-mile as this stops the ponies from sweating and catching cold after their saddles have been taken off. The trekkers also find that walking helps to loosen up muscles which may have become stiff during the ride.

Once the stable yard has been reached the ponies are led, one by one, to the drinking trough where they are allowed to drink their fill before being taken into their stalls for unsaddling. When the saddles and bridles have been removed and returned to the tack room, the ponies are fed and while they are eating they are brushed down to remove all sweat, which can be irritating if it dries on them. Then the trekkers return to their hotel for tea. Before getting ready for dinner they take their ponies out to the fields for the night. .

There are articles HORSE; PONY and RIDING.

MAKING A SILK-SCREEN POSTER

by Dennis Hawkins

An enormous demand exists for posters. The success of meetings, dances, fêtes, sales of work and school or church functions very often depends on them. The more copies of a poster you can make, the more likely it is that people will see and read them. By far the easiest way of making many copies of your own design is the silk-screen printing process. The basic equipment is so simple that it can be made by anyone who likes carpentry. No special skill is needed in the printing itself and with care the results can be very fine indeed.

First decide on the length and width of the poster. A small one suitable for notice-boards

(which will be read at close range) might be 15 inches by 11 inches. A medium size for display inside buildings could be 22 inches by 15 inches, but for shop windows, or display outside a building, a poster 30 inches by 22 inches would be better. This measurement (30″ × 22″) is known as Imperial and it is the size in which sheets of cartridge paper are sold. The smaller sizes can be got by cutting an Imperial sheet into halves or quarters. Decide on the number of sheets you want and then add a few extra for experiments and mishaps.

Suppose you want a poster 22 inches by 15 inches in size. Make a rigid frame of wood two inches by one-and-a-half inches thick and add angle irons at the corners to give it more strength. The joints can be simply butted, glued and screwed, as in the illustration. The size of the frame must be greater than the size of the paper you are going to use by half an inch at the sides and three-and-a-half inches at the top and bottom. Sandpaper all the edges until they are smooth. Stretch over the underside of the frame a piece of silk which should be at least one inch larger all round than the frame. This allows you to double over the extra silk when pinning it to the outside of the frame. Stretch the silk as tightly as possible across the frame, and fasten it with drawing pins or large-headed tintacks using a light hammer. The silk can be bought through an art shop or the assistants there will give you the name of a manufacturer. Medium grades of silk are No. 8 and No. 10 which are suitable to start with; finer or coarser grades can be used later if you wish. When the pinning is complete, wash the screen thoroughly in warm soapy water, which will make it shrink. It is very important that the silk should be as tight as a drum.

When the screen has dried, stick strips of Scotch tape around the edges on the underside of the silk. It should be one inch wide at the

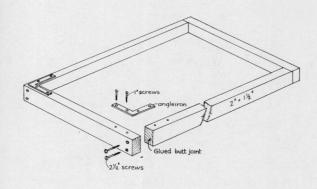

1" screws

angleiron

2" x 1½"

Glued butt joint

2½" screws

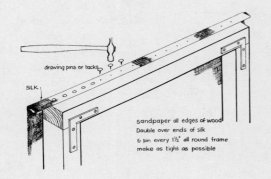

drawing pins or tacks

SILK

sandpaper all edges of wood
Double over ends of silk
& pin every 1½" all round frame
make as tight as possible

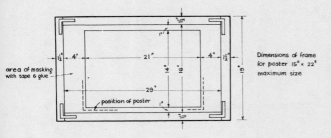

1½" 4" 21" 4" 1½"

area of masking
with tape & glue

29"

position of poster

Dimensions of frame
for poster 15" x 22"
maximum size

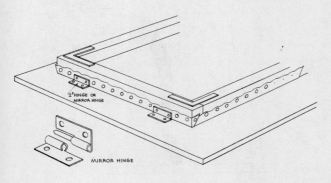

2" HINGE OR
MIRROR HINGE

MIRROR HINGE

sides and four inches deep at the top and bottom, so that it overlaps the paper by half an inch when it is put under the screen. This keeps the ink on the paper and within a border about half an inch wide all round the poster. Turn the frame over and with a brush and a piece of stiff card spread a layer of glue over the area of silk which has been blocked out by Scotch tape and allow this to dry thoroughly. (Small posters can be printed with the same screen simply by making this border larger.) This process of blocking out parts of the screen is called masking. Masking can be done in this way with tape or by a piece of newspaper which will stick to the silk as soon as you make the first print.

Fasten the frame to a sheet of plywood, preferably five-ply or even thicker, by means of two 2-inch hinges. Mirror hinges (as in the diagram) which allow you to remove the frame from the board for cleaning are very useful but they are not essential. The plywood board should be completely smooth and flat and at least four to six inches wider all round than the frame. The frame and the board must be placed on a firm table while the screen is being used. A free-swinging stick about eight inches long, screwed to one side of the frame is a great help in acting as a leg to hold the frame up while changing the paper during the printing process.

A squeegee is the tool used to push or pull the paint or ink across the screen. It consists of a rubber blade encased in a wooden handle which can be made easily by screwing three suitable pieces of thin wood together. The rubber is sold by the inch and should be a quarter of an inch narrower than the full width of the inside of the screen, so that it runs freely.

In order to make sure that each piece of paper you are going to print is in the correct position on the board under the screen, you can glue four or five thicknesses of paper three inches by one inch square on to the baseboard to act as stops or guides. Then you must make certain that the paper is properly cushioned against these guides while you are printing.

Printing

When you are ready to make the first trial printing, use a knife to spread a fair amount of the ink across the four-inch-deep masked area at the top of the screen. Hold the squeegee firmly with both hands as shown in the diagram, at an angle of about 30 degrees from the vertical. Move the squeegee up and down in the ink in order to get it to run smoothly and then, with a steady continuous pull, draw it slowly towards you until the excess ink reaches the masked area at the bottom of the screen. The ink sinks through the screen (where it has not been masked) and covers the paper with colour. The squeegee can then be rested on the bottom edge of the screen while you lift the screen up to remove your first print. If the print sticks to the screen the ink is too stiff, so that you should add more thinning liquid or turpentine to it, but remember that it should never become runny. The proper consistency (thickness) for the ink is that of thick cream.

Special inks and thinning mediums are supplied in tins by manufacturers and if you are going to print several posters you should buy the inks in 2 lb. tins. You will also need two or three pounds of transparent base if you wish to get the maximum effects from printing one colour over another. The colours require mixing with thinning medium or turpentine substitute; oil paints can also be used.

Other equipment you will need is old tin cans or jam jars in which to mix and store the inks and an old kitchen knife for mixing and stirring. To make ten posters you will need to mix enough ink to fill about half a 1 lb. jam jar or tin.

Poster Design

The design must be bold and clear, giving *all* the information as simply and briefly as possible. Avoid small detail and too many words and remember that a poster has to be seen and understood at a glance. Most people are far too busy —or lazy—to puzzle out a complicated poster.

To make an attractive poster it is advisable to use the two simple methods next described. The first is to use large shapes with sharp edges like the spiral or the star, and large lettering, all of which can be cut out of newspaper with scissors. These shapes are then laid in position upon the first sheet of paper to be printed, once it is correctly placed for printing. The shapes are held

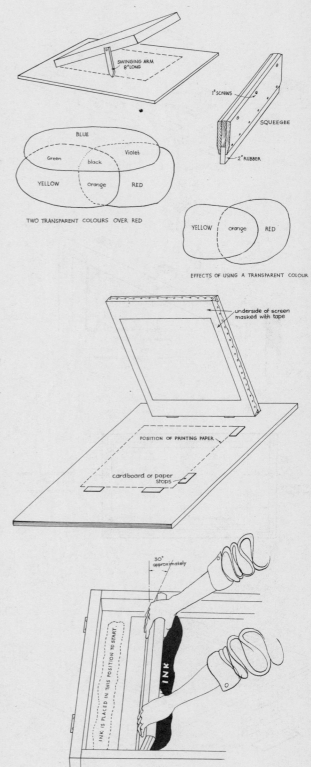

SWINGING ARM 8" LONG

1" screws

SQUEEGEE

2" RUBBER

BLUE

Green   Violet

black

YELLOW   Orange   RED

TWO TRANSPARENT COLOURS OVER RED

YELLOW   Orange   RED

EFFECTS OF USING A TRANSPARENT COLOUR

underside of screen masked with tape

POSITION OF PRINTING PAPER

cardboard or paper stops

30° approximately

INK IS PLACED IN THIS POSITION TO START

INK

TAUT WIRE   PAPER CLIPS

in place on the screen by the ink after the first printing. They must be removed at the end of the printing session when you clean the screen. If you are careful not to tear them they can be used again later. It would be possible and quite effective to do everything in this way, using only one colour as shown on the right. It is important to vary the size and type of lettering. A poster of this sort depends on variety and contrast of shape for its effect. Torn newspaper gives an interesting effect in combination with cut shapes.

The second method is to use a glue which can be dissolved in water to paint parts of the screen. This also has the effect of masking the screen and gives you soft or broken edges, rather like rapid brush strokes in a painting. A mixture of equal parts of glue and water is excellent for this, and you can try spattering (scrubbing through a wire mesh to give lots of spots and splashes) or smearing the glue on with your fingers. These effects will contrast well with the hard edges of cut out shapes. Allow the glue to dry completely. Later it can be removed easily by cold water, after cleaning all paint off the screen.

You will also need plenty of turpentine substitute, petrol or paraffin for cleaning the screen after use. This must be done very thoroughly, otherwise the screen will be completely ruined and can never be used again. Lots of clean rags and old newspapers are needed for this.

Place a thick layer of sheets of newspaper under the screen and scrape off any ink that is left with a piece of stiff cardboard. Then wash and wipe the screen over several times with rags soaked in turpentine and when it is clean, give the screen a final wipe over with a clean, dry rag. While doing this keep removing the top sheet of the newspapers as it becomes stained. In the end both sides of the screen should be spotlessly clean.

Using Several Colours

While it is possible to make a striking poster using only one colour, such as black or magenta (a reddish-purple) on white paper, it is easier to get contrast and variety by using two or three colours, but do not attempt to use more than

EQUIPMENT FOR PRINTING A POSTER NOT LARGER THAN 22 in. × 15 in.

SQUEEGEE: rubber (2 in. × $\frac{3}{8}$ in. × $15\frac{3}{4}$ in.); wood—3 pieces (3 in. × $\frac{1}{2}$ in. × $15\frac{3}{4}$ in.)

FRAME: wood—2 pieces (2 in. × $1\frac{1}{2}$ in. × 29 in.); 2 pieces (2 in. × $1\frac{1}{2}$ in. × 19 in.); leg (1 in. × $\frac{1}{4}$ in. × 8 in.)

BASEBOARD: wood (40 in. × 30 in.)

ANGLE IRONS: 4 (3 in. long)

HINGES: 2 (2 in. long)

SCREWS: 16 (1 in.); 4 ($\frac{1}{2}$ in.); 8 ($2\frac{1}{2}$ in.); 4 ($1\frac{1}{4}$ in.)

SILK: 1 piece (35 in. × 22 in.)

DRAWING PINS (74)   SCOTCH TAPE: (1 in. to 2 in. wide)   GLUE: 1 pint

BRUSHES: 1 (1 in. wide); Nos. 3 and 8 watercolour brushes

MIXING KNIFE   SPATULA

TURPENTINE SUBSTITUTE: 2 pints

THINNING MEDIUM: 1 pint

TRANSPARENT BASE: 2 lb.

COLOURS: red, yellow, blue, crimson (1 pint each)

three colours. You can get a wide range of colours by using three skilfully. With a transparent ink you can print over a previous colour and in this way obtain three colours from two printings as shown in the diagram. For example, if your first printing was yellow on white paper, a transparent red printed partly over the yellow and partly over the white paper would result in orange, pure yellow and pure red. There is a great fascination in experimenting with colour in this way.

A golden rule to keep in mind when using colours is to allow one colour to predominate. Never have equal quantities of colour; contrast a lot of one colour with a little of another. In this way you will get a bold and striking effect. Similarly you can get seven colours out of three printings. In order to print a second colour your first printing must be quite dry. This can be done by hanging the prints on stout paper clips

on a wire stretched taut across the room. It saves space and keeps the prints free from dust. You can leave the prints to dry overnight in this way. Another method is to hang the prints from a rod in which hooks have been screwed. This has the advantage that the prints will not slide and run against one another or stick together.

Once you have mastered the basic methods of printing with the screen you can produce sets of Christmas cards, invitation cards and birthday cards, or you can follow the example of many present-day artists who use this method to make editions (sets) of prints as original works of art.

You will probably gain help and encouragement if you go along to your local art school. Even if they do not have a printing department, there is bound to be someone on the staff who will help with information and tips. Printmakers are friendly people and you will find that they are delighted to talk about their craft.

JAZZ

MONDAY 5th MAY 7-10 p.m.
OLD HALL HOUSE · HIGHTOWN

NEWTOWN BATHS

JOIN OUR SWIMMING CLUB

MON · 7 TO 9 P.M.
WED · 8 TO 10 P.M.

PUTTING ON
A PUPPET PLAY

with a play for four puppets

SIR RICHARD'S TREASURE

by Colin Davies

EVEN IF you have not seen a puppet play on television, where they are very popular, then you must have seen one at a party or fair or at the seaside—where you have probably enjoyed watching a Punch and Judy show. Have you noticed that there are several kinds of puppet? They can be made out of almost anything—rags, lamp bulbs or vegetables—but the important thing is that a puppet is really a doll which is made to move, apparently on its own. The two most common types are glove puppets and string puppets (often called marionettes).

If you have enjoyed seeing puppets act, then you will have even more fun making your own play. Before beginning, you must decide which type of puppet you are going to make, for it is difficult and unwise to mix glove puppets with string puppets. However, this booklet will show you how to make both, and the short puppet play at the end can be done equally well with either type.

Glove puppets are easier to make and so perhaps better for beginners. All you need to do is make a head and hands. The rest is really a glove, disguised as the puppet's body, which fits over the hand of someone hiding under the stage. The thumb fits into one arm, the first finger fits into the neck and the middle finger or the little finger fits into the other arm. These puppets can pick things up quite easily in their hands, the stage is simple to make, and the puppets are easy to put away or store, because there are no strings to get tangled up.

Marionettes are more difficult to make but they are more exciting to use. Because you see all the puppet, not just the top half, it looks more like a real person on the stage. The surprise is all the greater when it starts to fly, jump over houses or come to pieces—all things that glove puppets cannot do without showing too much of a rather large human arm coming up from under the stage. Making marionettes walk properly is quite difficult at first—they have a habit of floating in the air or dragging along the ground—but a little experience in working them soon gets over this problem. The puppets are moved by pulling the strings which join the limbs of the puppet to the controller (the wooden bar held in the hands of the person working the puppet). The puppeteer stands behind and above the stage and is hidden by the scenery. A really complicated puppet can have many moving parts and some have mouths that open, or hands that move from the wrists, but the string puppets described here are made as simply as possible. When you become an expert you can begin to do more complicated things.

The play *Sir Richard's Treasure* is a simple one for four characters, so that the puppets can be made and worked by two people. There is nothing to stop you from adding more characters if your friends want to join in, and you will then have to give the new puppets something to say and do. It would not be difficult to add a policeman, a servant or another ghost.

Do remember that when you are making puppets it is far better to exaggerate everything—faces, actions and even the story. At the same time do not forget what puppets can and cannot do. It is far better to be too simple than too complicated, with the danger of running into serious difficulties in the middle of a performance. Follow the example of the Punch and Judy show by having a simple story and exaggerated faces and characters for the puppets.

THE CHARACTERS

JASPER is the villain of the play. He is Mary's father and the uncle of Simon. He is trying to find a chest of money which has been hidden in Mallows Castle for many years. Both the castle and the treasure really belong to Simon, but because his parents are dead Simon has been brought up by his uncle. Jasper has discovered in an old book a piece of paper that gives a clue to where the treasure is. He is a thoroughly evil man, but he is also cunning and quite intelligent. By taking the children to the castle "on holiday" (telling them that it belongs to some friends of his) he hopes to find the treasure and also get rid of Simon. Nasty accidents can happen in old ruins. Jasper has one weakness—he is frightened by ghosts.

MARY, Jasper's daughter, is fortunately very unlike her father. She is young, pretty and honest, and she is also very much in love with Simon. Of course her father does not want her to marry Simon but has a rich and rather unattractive young man in mind for her future husband. Mary has no idea why her father wants to come to the castle, but she is a dutiful daughter. She is just 18 years old, and has no idea why her father is so unpleasant to Simon. For most of her life she has lived at home and has seen little of the world and so is quite content that her father is strict and spends all his money on himself and none on her.

SIMON is 20 years old and is the hero of the play. Until his 21st birthday his uncle is his guardian, and he has been living a miserable life for the past 15 years since the death of his parents. He does not know that he is the heir to a title, lands, Mallows Castle and a great deal of money. He certainly knows nothing about the hidden treasure and is really surprised that his uncle should suddenly decide to take him on holiday. He is very much in love with his cousin Mary, but is rather frightened by his uncle, though not, apparently by anything else. Because of this he soon makes friends with the . . .

GHOST. This is the ghost of Sir Richard Mallows, who lived in an age when rich men could do almost anything they liked. He decided to become a highwayman just for the fun of it. As highwaymen go, he was quite pleasant and spent his time holding up the coaches of his very rich and rather unpleasant neighbours. In this way he made a great fortune which he hid in the castle. Ever since, his ghost has been flitting about the draughty ruins hoping that the right person will find the treasure. If the treasure is found by an evil man, then Sir Richard's ghost will have to haunt the castle for ever. If it is found by a good man, then the ghost can rest in peace.

MAKING THE HEADS

In the puppet world the head has to express as much of the puppet's character as possible, and this is especially true of glove puppets where only a small part of the body is visible. This is why most puppets' faces are what is known as caricatures (that is, extreme exaggerations) so that the audience knows something about the puppet as soon as it comes on to the stage and before it says anything at all. It is impossible to make a puppet's head look too absurd, so long as it is in character with what the puppet has to say and do. An ugly head for a young hero would look strange unless the story was one like *Beauty and the Beast*. Remember that the size of head will decide the size of the whole puppet and the size of the stage as well. A convenient size is somewhere between that of an egg and a tennis ball.

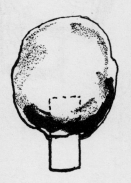

The article PUPPETS in *Children's Britannica* suggests several ways of making heads. If you like carving, you can make a head out of wood, or it can be made out of plaster modelled round a stick. The most common way to make a head is to model it in plasticine and then cover the plasticine with papier mâché—fine pieces of torn paper pasted down in layers. Start with a round stick, perhaps a piece a foot long (to give you a good handle to hold) and about an inch in diameter (the thickness of the neck). Put a large lump of plasticine on one end and model it into the shape of the head you want. A long egg-shaped head is commonly used for an evil or an intelligent person and a more rounded shape for a kind or merry person. Do not try to copy a real face. Make Jasper's face really long and thin, with a high forehead and a long, tapering chin.

When you have a rough shape, add the features slowly and carefully. Scoop out the hollows for the eyes, pull out the shape of the eyebrows, add a really prominent nose, and then use a knife to carve the finer lines of the mouth and the lines at the side of the nose which define the cheeks, and to add any wrinkles you want. Make sure that the eyes are large and are really bulging, and do not forget to add the ears. Detail is easily lost under layers of papier mâché, so exaggerate as much as possible. If you like, you can model the hair and the beards in plasticine now, or you can add wool or artificial hair later.

For the ghost's head, have a look at the article SKELETON and you will get a very good idea of what a skull is like. It can be made in the same way as the other heads. Of course, ghosts are strange things and there is no reason why you should not give the one you are making whatever type of head you wish.

Now you can begin with the papier mâché. The materials you will need for this are some flour-and-water paste, a fairly small camel hair

brush and plenty of paper. The best paper to use is crêpe paper which you can buy in different colours. You may even have some left over from the Christmas decorations. Tissue paper can also be used for the final layer to give a smooth finish. It is useful to have paper of several different colours, because it takes some time to give each head about six to eight coatings and it always helps to be able to see where you left off last time.

Tear the paper into small pieces. Do not cut it, for the rough edges of the torn paper help to bind the whole layer together. Then start pasting the paper on, with the pieces overlapping one another. The smaller the pieces of paper you use the better, and you can push them into the corners with the handle of the brush. You are bound to lose a little of the modelling, but try to make it as small a loss as possible. This is especially important for the area round the eyes and nose.

Leave the final layer to dry thoroughly. Then with a very sharp knife or a razor blade, cut the head open as shown in the picture above. Scoop out the plasticine carefully. Hold each part of the head up to the light and strengthen any weak parts you can see, by pasting papier mâché on the inside of the head. Then stick the two halves together with some strong glue and cover the join with more papier mâché—or better still, if you have used tissue paper use it again to cover the join. If you are making glove puppets, strengthen the neck by glueing some rolled paper into the inside. If you are making marionettes, cut the original modelling stick to proper neck length and glue it back so that the top end strengthens the top of the head and the bottom end can be jointed to the body.

PAINTING THE HEADS

Once the head is dry again you can paint it. You can use oil paints, but it is easier and quicker to use poster colours (powder paints). The colours needed are white, black, yellow ochre, crimson lake, ultramarine and perhaps some burnt sienna. Before you begin, have a close look at a real person's face. Notice where the shadows are and where the highlights come, and that a real flesh colour is far more yellow than pink. Mix the paint by adding small quantities of colour to the white. Remember that the colour will be somewhat lighter when it dries and do not make the paint transparent by adding too much water. A flesh colour is mostly white, with a dash of yellow ochre, crimson and black.

Simon and Mary should be healthy in colour, with a slightly darker pinkish-brown under the eyebrows and jaw. Add a slightly rosier colour to the cheeks, and paint the eyebrows, nostrils, eyes and mouth. Jasper should be a more sickly yellowish colour, with deep-sunken eyes, heavy dark eyebrows and an unhealthy greyish shadow round the eyes and under the jaw. You can also give him greyish-pink lines for wrinkles. The ghost should be a nasty, pale greenish-grey colour, with very dark holes for eyes and nose. Make the teeth prominent by painting highlights and shadows on them. You could also add a few cracks to the skull and give it glittering eyes with sequins or metal foil.

The hair and beards come last. If you have modelled them in papier mâché, paint them the correct colour. Otherwise, you can add the hair now. You can cut lengths of knitting wool and stick it on, or use cotton wool, or else buy crêpe hair, which is the hair used in the real theatre. Crêpe hair looks far the best but it is slightly more difficult to use since it needs to be straightened out and thinned before being stuck on.

JASPER and SIMON

BODIES AND LIMBS

If you are making glove puppets, you need not read these two pages. All you need for glove puppets are hands, which should be rather large, and should be made with plasticine and papier mâché like the heads: the sticks they are made on are taken out when they have been completed and painted.

The size of a marionette's body will depend on the size of its head, and that should be about one-sixth of the height of the whole puppet. (If you were making a child puppet, however, its head would be perhaps one-fifth of its total height.) First of all cut out the upper and lower parts of the body. The shape is shown in the illustration. Make sure that the wood is about the right thickness for your puppet's body, although you can shape it a little with a knife or add some padding later. The ghost does not need a body and Mary will need only the top half, since she wears a long dress. Simon should be shorter than Jasper.

The upper and lower halves can now be joined by screw-eyes. Partly open two screw-eyes with pliers, before screwing them in one half. Then screw two more in the other half and hook them on to the open screw-eyes, which should be closed up again to make a permanent linkage. The body is now jointed and can bend at the waist. All the other joints, except the elbows and knees, will be made in the same way. Next, the stick holding the head is trimmed to the right length and fastened with screw-eyes to the square gap cut in the upper part of the body. You now have a half-completed puppet.

The limbs come next. For these you need dowelling—round wooden rods. Buy them the right diameter for the widest part of the arms and

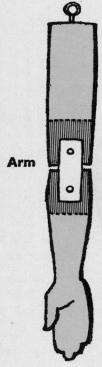

Arm

Arm

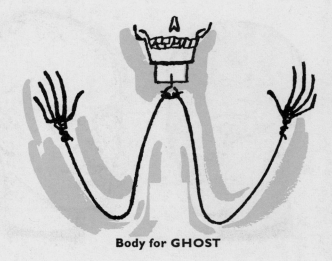

Body for GHOST

legs. Whittle away one end slightly, model a hand on it in plasticine and then cover it with papier mâché. It is not worth while trying to remove the plasticine; it makes the hand stronger. Paint the hand and then cut off the dowel at the correct elbow length. Cut another length for the upper arm. Both the pieces of dowelling which meet for the elbow joint must then be carefully trimmed as shown in the pictures. By leaving some of the flat surface at the end of each piece, the arm is prevented from swinging in any but the right direction when it is joined. Hold the two limbs together and stick or nail a piece of leather or strong cloth across the V-shaped groove. Then join the upper arm to the shoulder with screw-eyes. Do the same for the other arm and for the legs and feet, which you make in the same way. Be careful when you are doing all this that the finished arms and legs move the right way—arms forwards and legs backwards. The finished arm should hang down loosely with the thumbs facing forward.

A rather different method is used for making the ghost. Apart from his head, his most important features are his hands. These should be very long and bony, like the hands of a skeleton. The best way to achieve this is to use a fairly thin copper wire and bend it until you have a long, tapering hand with the thumb and four fingers. Cover it with a few layers of papier mâché and then paint it the same colour as the ghost's head. When you have finished both hands you join them by a length of wire which passes through a screw-eye under the neck. You thus have a head and two hands, joined by a piece of thin and not too springy wire. It is best to wind the wire round the screw-eye in the neck so that the arms remain the same length and do not slither about.

Now you are ready to dress the puppets.

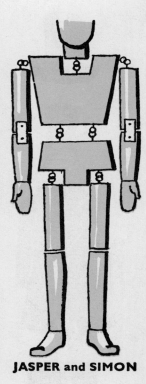

JASPER and SIMON

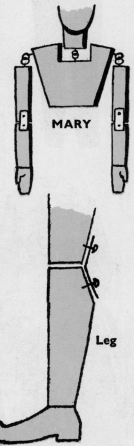

MARY

Leg

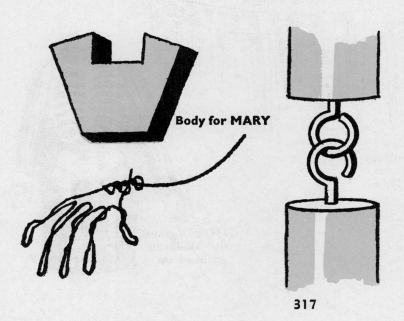

Body for MARY

317

DRESSING THE PUPPETS

It does not really matter how you decide to dress the puppets so long as they are all done in the same style. You can dress them in modern clothes (in which case Mary will need to have legs) or you can give them the more interesting clothes of another age. Before you begin, have a look at the article DRESS to see what clothes were like at different times. The drawings in this booklet show them dressed in 19th-century clothes, which may help to add 'atmosphere' to the play.

If you want to see the basic shape of any glove puppet's clothes, look at the illustration in the article PUPPETS. Cut out two pieces of cloth, the same shape front and back, sew them together and then turn the glove inside out. Then you can glue on the head and hands and add any further decoration that you want to have. A ghost puppet should be made in this way out of some pale-coloured material and then have a skeleton painted on. The other characters in glove puppets can roughly follow the styles suggested for marionettes. Over the glove you can sew a jacket, a collar and tie, or give the puppet a hat. As with the faces, you cannot exaggerate the clothes too much. Hats can be enormous and the clothes can be any colour.

With marionettes the ghost is the easiest to dress. All he needs is some torn ribbons of some half-transparent material stuck over the wire joining the head and hands. To make the ghost glitter you can stick on a few sequins to the material, but take care not to use too many.

Jasper will look splendid in a tall Victorian top hat, which can be made out of black paper. On the other hand, if you have taken a

GHOST—string puppet

MARY—dress suitable for either type

GHOST—glove with skeleton painted on

lot of trouble with putting on his hair, and do not want to waste your work, then leave the hat off. The next stage is the collar and tie. The collar can be made out of paper or card with a small piece of cloth glued in place for the tie. If you give him a really large tie or cravat there is no need to bother about a shirt, since it will not show at all. If the shirt is going to show, a ring of cloth ought to be sewn round the neck. He will need trousers and a jacket and perhaps a waistcoat. Since Jasper is an unpleasant character his clothes should be dark and expensive in appearance.

Simon's clothes are made in much the same way as his uncle's but he is a younger man and can be dressed in brighter colours. His clothes are old, and you can add patches or even tear them in places. All clothes have to say something about the puppet's character and they have to cover up all traces of the wooden body underneath. Trousers and sleeves must not fit so well that the arms and legs cannot be moved easily, or only at the risk of ripping something. Although the shapes are quite complicated and need careful cutting out and sewing together, the task is not too hard. The clothes do not have to fit perfectly and you can probably get advice and help from your mother. Only a very little material is needed for dressing these puppets and you will find almost all you need somewhere at home.

Mary will need some sort of collar, preferably white, and a long full dress which is pulled in at the waist and then falls to the floor. The sleeves reach to the wrists and you could give her cuffs of the same colour as her collar. If you are going to use material with a pattern on it, be careful that the pattern is not too large. You can add any extra ornaments you wish and you might even give her a hat.

String

Glove

String

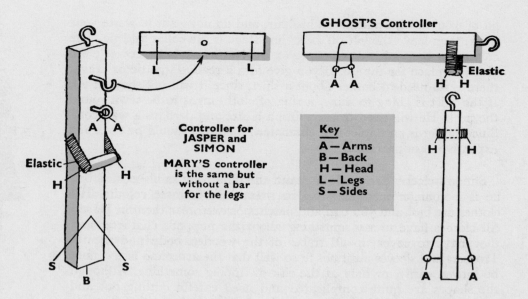

GHOST'S Controller

L — L

A A — H H

Elastic

Elastic

H H

H H

A — A

A A

Controller for
JASPER and
SIMON

MARY'S controller
is the same but
without a bar
for the legs

Elastic

H

A A

H

S

B

S

Key
A — Arms
B — Back
H — Head
L — Legs
S — Sides

HOW TO MAKE THE CONTROLLER

Here is another section which you can pass over if you are making glove puppets. In the article PUPPETS there is an illustration of several different kinds of controller for string puppets. The controllers you need for Jasper and Simon are slightly simpler than the one on the left in that picture.

The controller is a straight bar of wood, about a foot long, and wide enough and thick enough to be really firm. At the top is a large hook or screw-eye for hanging the puppet up on the wall when it is not performing. Below this there is a hook for a separate bar about eight inches long, controlling the legs. This bar has a hole bored in its exact centre so that it can be hooked to the control when not in use. When the puppet is strung it is made to walk by twisting this bar up and down. Below this on the controller you need a central screw-eye for the arms—or you can make a looped wire attachment of the kind shown in the ghost's controller, which has the advantage that it is easier to raise both the arms of the puppet at once. Below that again is the control for the head. It is a short bar which hangs down under the controller, to which it is attached by strong elastic. By pulling the bar down the puppet's head is made to nod as both head strings are loosened and the head falls forward. The shoulder strings are attached to a point below this bar, and last of all comes the single string from the bottom of the controller to the middle of the puppet's back.

Mary's control will not need a long bar; she is made to walk by gently moving the whole control up and down slightly. The ghost's control is simpler still and only has attachments for the head and arms.

STRINGING THE PUPPETS

Now you can start on the job of stringing the puppets, and it is a task that needs great care. First you need some small tintacks and some fine, strong, black or grey nylon thread. Nail the tacks into the fully dressed puppet (you may have to use longer ones in the padded or well-dressed parts), leaving just a little sticking out so that the thread can be tied on. You need tacks on each shoulder, in the middle of the back and just above each knee. Strings to the hands and head can be fixed by boring through the hands and the ears; but if you are very careful and if it will not show, you can have tintacks at the wrists. The ghost's head will probably have to have two tacks, one on each side, or even a piece of wire passing right through the head and looped at each end.

The shoulder strings are tied first and they should be judged by the height your stage is going to be. After you have made certain that the puppet hangs quite level, you can add the other strings. Tie all your strings with reef knots, not grannie knots, and make them really secure by adding a dab of glue. If any of your characters is going to have a large hat then the head strings should pass through the brim. All your strings must hang in an absolutely straight line between their place on the controller and where they join the puppet. Of course, the strings will not be always parallel to one another, because they go to different parts of the control and body. You must also take care that the strings do not cross or become twisted round one another. If you have made a wire hook or bar for the arm control, only one thread is needed, passing from the left arm up to the two loops on the wire hook and then down to the other arm. While stringing the puppet you must make constant tests to ensure that everything is working.

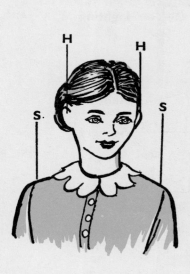

Lighting

SETTING UP THE STAGE

From the rough sketches on these pages you will see at a glance the difference between the stages needed for the two types of puppet. A glove puppet theatre is like a wardrobe with an opening near the top. There is of course no floor to the puppet stage because the puppeteer hiding underneath has to be able to move the puppets about freely. A string puppet stage is more like a real theatre in miniature. There must, however, be plenty of room above the stage for the puppeteers to remain hidden while working the puppets.

Even a table could be used in setting up a stage, though of course you would need curtains to hide the puppeteers. With glove puppets a curtain over the front of the table is enough, but you must let some light come in at the sides so that you can see what you are doing when working the puppets. The narrower the table is the better, because the puppets have to appear over the back of it. The scenery has to be set some way back behind the table so that the puppets can bob up and act in the gap. With string puppets you will need scenery along the front of the table and curtains above and slightly in front, to hide the puppeteer standing on the table.

If you are good at carpentry you can make your own stage. First you need a fairly strong wooden framework which can then be covered with curtains, canvas or hardboard. A lot can even be done with old curtains strung up across one corner of the room. String puppets, of course, will need a solid floor on which they can walk. For this part of the stage you may find that old boxes are quite useful. If you want a trapdoor for puppets to disappear into or emerge from, then leave

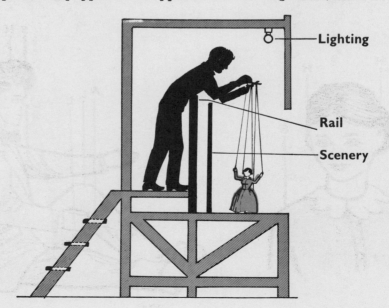

Lighting

Rail

Scenery

a hole in one part of the stage—somewhere near the back where it is less obvious to the audience. Make sure that any structure holding the stage up will not foul the puppet's strings. A marionette stage must have some sort of framework on which to hook the scenery, and above the top of the scenery you will need a rail for people to lean on while they work the puppets. Behind the stage you need a platform for the puppeteers to stand on, preferably one that is wide enough for two people working puppets to pass each other. Some sort of covering is needed on either side of the front of the stage, to hide the puppeteers moving about backstage.

Once the stage is up, try your hand at fixing up some lighting. It is not essential, but a well-lit stage always looks much better. Even a single lamp bulb, hidden above the stage, helps a great deal, but if you can manage it try to arrange special lighting for the play. There should be several bulbs just behind and above the top of the stage front, carefully arranged so that there is no risk of anything catching fire. These provide the main lighting. Then, at each side of the stage at the level of the puppets, another bulb can be placed. These prevent the puppets' faces from being in shadow. You could even add an extra blue bulb there to give an eerie effect when the ghost appears. By switching all the lights off and on very quickly, you get an effect of lightning—and someone rattling a sheet of metal or banging a drum can give the effect of thunder.

If all these ideas about making the stage and adding lighting seem far too difficult for you, then do not worry. You can manage perfectly well with the most simple means. If you do go in for lighting, then get advice from someone who knows about electricity and can tell you what to do.

THE SCENERY

The scenery is made in three pieces: a backcloth which goes right across the back of the stage and two wings which are placed, one on each side, near the front of the stage. The reason for having wings is to stop the audience seeing round the corner and catching sight of what goes on behind stage. When planning your scenery you must always bear this in mind—do not cut it off just because it cannot be seen from directly in front. The audience sitting on the extreme left and right can see much more of the sides of the stage.

The scenery is made of hardboard or canvas mounted on a wooden frame to keep it rigid and in place. You can even use paper and pin it into place. Nothing is more distracting or looks more unlike a solid building than scenery which waves gently in a draught or wobbles because it is knocked. The backcloth should be nailed or hooked to the back of the stage once it is painted. Each wing is attached to the front of the stage by a wooden bar (not to the back, or the puppets will not be able to move on or off the stage).

First draw a sketch of the scenery and paint it. Copy it on to the backcloth and paint it in powder paint (the same type of paint you used for the puppets' faces). Use large brushes and fairly thin paint and put the colour on boldly. Paint a general background wall colour (a brownish-grey) and make it darker in the corners. Then paint in doors, windows, furniture, cobwebs and anything else you fancy. The scenery should be a free invention of your own, so give your impression of the inside of a gloomy tumbledown castle. When the scenery is finished the play can begin.

SIR RICHARD'S TREASURE

The Great Hall of Mallows Castle, one of the few parts of the castle that are not in ruins. The whole place is gloomy, with one or two pieces of furniture scattered about (these can be painted on the scenery itself). It is late on a summer afternoon. The scene opens with the GHOST *slumped miserably on the floor.*

GHOST: Atchoo! I wouldn't really mind having to haunt this castle if only it weren't so cold and draughty. I spend all my time shivering and freezing. Nowadays no one comes here, because they all know the castle is haunted. [*Noises off.* JASPER's *voice is heard in the distance.* GHOST *flits over to the door to have a look outside.*]

JASPER: Come along! Come along! We want to get there tonight.

GHOST: I expect that was just people passing along the road. If only some good person would come and find the treasure . . . then I could rest in peace. [*He wanders about the stage.*] Atchoo! Of course, he must be a descendant of mine—it wouldn't do for the money to go out of the family. And he mustn't be afraid of me. I'm not really frightening, I'm just cold. Atchoo! Atchoo! [JASPER's *voice is heard again off stage.*]

JASPER: Come on—we're nearly there.

GHOST: Someone is coming. I'd better hide or they'll run away when they see me. [*He disappears slowly. Enter* JASPER, *followed by* SIMON.]

JASPER: At last. The speed *you* walk we should have started yesterday.

SIMON [*wearily*]: Well, uncle, it has been a long walk from the village.

JASPER: It's good for you. Where's Mary? What have you done with her?

SIMON: She stopped by the river bank to pick some flowers.

JASPER [*disgustedly*]: Flowers!

SIMON: Yes, by that old bridge we came across. It really was a tumble-down old bridge—I nearly fell into the water.

JASPER [*aside*]: Perhaps next time you will. [*To* SIMON] You'd better go and find her. [SIMON *goes out*.] Now I'm here at last. A pity I had to bring the children but I could not think of any other excuse. I told them I was taking them on holiday [*laughs*]. Holiday! Of course, it *is* Mary's 18th birthday, but catch me spending money on them! The sooner I can marry Mary off to my rich neighbour Jeremiah Mountebank, the better. And the sooner my nephew Simon meets with a nasty accident the better. [*The* GHOST *reappears and listens but* JASPER *does not see it*.] Next year when Simon is 21 I shall no longer be his guardian. He will then want his money. Well, I've spent it. [SIMON *reappears*.]

SIMON [*breathlessly*]: She's just coming, uncle.

JASPER: About time too. Now make yourself useful. Take the bags upstairs.

SIMON: Yes, uncle. [*He goes out*.]

JASPER: According to a scrap of paper I found in an old book there is treasure hidden in this castle. Long ago Sir Richard Mallows hid the money he had made from being a highwayman. If I can find it and get rid of Simon, I shall be richer than ever, inherit the castle and become Sir Jasper Mallows. I must make certain that Simon has a *very* nasty accident. [*Walks around the room, thinking. The* GHOST *reappears but remains hidden from Jasper*.] Now what did that piece of paper say . . .

My treasure's hidden in a chest
Until it's found I cannot rest.
It guards my house and in reverse
My castle guards a wealthy purse.

I certainly won't rest until it is found. [*The* GHOST *nods and then disappears*.] Ah, here comes Mary. [*Enter* MARY.]

MARY: Sorry, father. I forgot the time—I was picking flowers.

JASPER: What have you done with them?

MARY: I gave them to Simon.

JASPER [*aside*]: That girl is getting too fond of Simon—but I have plans to deal with *that*. [*To* MARY] Flowers indeed! A waste of time.

MARY: Father, why did we have to come here? It's so cold and gloomy, and I'm sure it's haunted.

JASPER [*nervously*]: Haunted? Why do you say that? Of course it's not. [*A sneeze is heard*.] What was that? Did you hear anything?

MARY: I thought you sneezed, father.

JASPER: No, I did not. It must have been Simon. It's no use being worried by strange sounds, there will be plenty of them here. [*He laughs but stops suddenly when the sneeze is heard again*.] Well, go and make some tea. [*She goes out*.] Now I must look for the money—an old chest, the poem says. [*As he goes out the* GHOST *reappears*.]

GHOST: So that's it, is it? He's after my money. Only if a good man finds it can I rest in peace, so the curse says. We shall have to do something about Uncle Jasper. [GHOST *goes out as* MARY *enters*.]

326

MARY: Where are they? I've put the kettle on for tea. I do wish my father liked Simon more. If only we could get married! [*The* GHOST *reappears and sneezes.* MARY *turns and sees it*] Goodness me—who are you?

GHOST: I am Sir Richard Mallows—or at least I was. Atchoo!

MARY: Oh dear! You've got a cold. Let me get you a nice cup of tea.

GHOST: You're very kind, but I cannot drink tea. I'm a ghost, you see.

MARY: Oh!

GHOST: You're not frightened?

MARY: Not by *you*, but I always thought I would be frightened by ghosts.

GHOST: There's nothing to be afraid of about me. I have to warn you and Simon—Atchoo!—I'm sorry to tell you that your father is not a very nice man. He has brought you here so that he can hunt for the treasure I hid here a hundred years ago. Your father hopes to find the treasure and make Simon disappear—for *ever*. [*He shivers and gives an almighty sneeze.*]

MARY: Oh! I didn't think he could be so evil. I know he has always been unkind to me and cruel to Simon, but . . .

GHOST: Well, I shall help you find the treasure. I'm not allowed to tell you where it is—Atchoo!—but I can lead you to it. You must do the actual finding. [*Thoughtfully*] Your father is afraid of ghosts, isn't he?

MARY: Yes.

GHOST: Come with me. This is what we must do. [*They go to the back of the stage, whispering. Then the* GHOST *disappears.* MARY *is left alone and* JASPER *enters.*]

JASPER: Well, is tea ready? Find that boy and give him his food. He's expensive enough to keep and I won't have him wasting it.

MARY: Yes, father. [*She goes out. The* GHOST *reappears in the background and listens.*]

JASPER [*alone*]: Ha! I have put poison in the sugar. Mary doesn't take sugar—so Simon will have it all. Now, while they are busy, I will search the cellars. The money must be hidden in an old chest or box somewhere. [*He goes out.*]

GHOST: Poison! I must stop that. [*He goes out and* SIMON *enters.*]

SIMON: Oh dear. I have been exploring the castle and I'm late for tea. [*He goes out. Immediately a crash is heard.* SIMON *and* MARY *are heard to say* "Oh dear" *offstage. They come in.*]

MARY: Well, it can't be helped. I'll go and clear up the mess.

SIMON: All we've missed was a cup of tea. How did you upset the tray?

MARY: You knocked my arm.

SIMON: No I didn't, I was a long way from you. I couldn't possibly have knocked your arm.

MARY: Well, something did.

SIMON: It was probably something on the wall; it's so dark there, you can't see a thing. [*A sneeze is heard.*] Has Uncle caught a cold?

MARY: No. That was probably Sir Richard.

SIMON: *Who* is Sir Richard?

MARY: Who *was* Sir Richard, you mean. He was one of your ancestors. His name was Sir Richard Mallows and he used to own this castle. He made a lot of money as a highwayman and when he died he was condemned to haunt this castle until the right person finds the treasure. It's hidden here somewhere, and both it and the castle belong to you.

SIMON: Who told you all this? I can't believe it.

MARY: Sir Richard himself.

SIMON: I'm sure you're imagining things, Mary dear. Ghosts aren't real. [*The* GHOST *reappears.*]

GHOST: Forgive me for correcting you, but they are.

SIMON [*in surprise*]: Who are you?

GHOST: I'm the ghost of Sir Richard Mallows and everything Mary has told you is quite true.

SIMON: Why were you a highwayman?

GHOST: I was very rich and very bored, so I took to it for fun. I robbed only my very unpleasant neighbours and—Atchoo!—the pleasure I had in seeing their frightened faces was much greater than the pleasure I had from their money.

SIMON: A dangerous life, though.

GHOST: But amusing. Anyway, I was in no more danger than you are now. I have just saved your life.

SIMON: My life? You've just saved it? How?

GHOST: I made Mary upset the tea tray. Your uncle had put poison in the sugar. He knows that the castle and the treasure belong to you. As your guardian he has been cheating you for years. He is worried about what will happen when you are 21 and he has to account for all the money your parents left. He has spent it all.

SIMON: Oh dear. I never knew I had any money—and now I haven't.

GHOST: He hopes to kill you, but to make it look like an accident. [SIMON *is stunned by this and collapses on the floor, scratching his forehead.*]

MARY [*in horror*]: My father tried to poison Simon? How could he?

GHOST: I have just told you how. I'm afraid you must realize that your father is a very wicked man. He also plans to marry you off to Jeremiah Mountebank.

MARY: Oh *no!* Not to Jeremiah. I love Simon and if I cannot marry him I shall marry no one. I hate Jeremiah—he is ugly, rich and thoroughly mean. Oh dear. [*She sits down and thinks while the* GHOST *flits over to rouse* SIMON.]

GHOST: Come on. Don't get depressed. At least you know the worst now. We can do something about it.

SIMON: It is far too far to go to the village for the policeman, and I don't want to leave Mary in the dark. In any case we have no proof. Where is Uncle Jasper now?

GHOST: He is searching for the treasure in the cellars. But he's wasting his time there—I was far too clever to put my treasure in such an obvious place. Very soon, Simon, your uncle will ask you to go down to the cellars and help him. On no account must you go. If he is going to murder you, the cellar is the obvious place. Unless of course he pushes you off the battlements into the moat.

SIMON: That wouldn't matter—I can swim.

GHOST: There isn't any water in the moat. Now, Simon—to work. Come with me and I shall explain to you what you must do. [SIMON *and the* GHOST *go out, talking together.*]

MARY [*left alone*]: I still cannot believe that my own father can be wicked. I will go and sweep up the broken tea things. [*She goes off.* JASPER *is heard complaining as he comes up the cellar stairs.*]

JASPER: It must be there . . . I need more light . . . Oh, bother these slippery stairs! [*He comes in.*] It is so dark down there I could not see what I was doing. My lantern kept going out—almost as if someone was blowing it out. I'll have a look upstairs. If the treasure is not there then I'll search the cellars again and get that boy to help me—and leave him there. [MARY *enters.*] Hello! What's the matter with you?

MARY: I don't feel very well. I was in the kitchen eating an apple, but it was so sour I had to put some sugar with it.

JASPER: *Sugar?*

MARY [*groaning*]: Yes. The apple has given me the most awful pain.

JASPER [*aside*]: Oh no! She has taken some of the sugar I poisoned for Simon's tea.

MARY [*aside*]: I think I'm acting this part rather well. [*She groans and collapses.* JASPER *runs across to her in alarm.*]

JASPER: Quick, come with me and I will give you something to cure the pain. Luckily I have plenty of medicines with me. [*Aside*] I brought some in case *I* took the poison by mistake. Come along! [*He rushes off to get the medicine.* MARY *revives immediately.*]

MARY: So the trick worked. My father *did* put poison in the sugar. Guilt was written all over his face. Now I shall no longer have to choose between Simon and my father. [*She goes out, groaning, and the* GHOST *reappears.*]

GHOST: Some people need a great deal to convince them—now she knows how wicked her father is. [*The* GHOST *goes out.*]

SIMON [*off stage*]: Mary! Mary!

MARY [*off stage*]: Yes? [*They both come on—one from each side.*]

BOTH TOGETHER: Ah! There you are.

MARY: Simon! Sir Richard was right—there *was* poison in the sugar.

SIMON: I never doubted it for a moment. Come here. [*They go into a corner.*] Where's your father?

MARY: He poured me out some medicine, because he thought I'd taken the poison, then he went off upstairs to look for the treasure. What have you been doing?

SIMON: Following Sir Richard's instructions. I have made it look as if I have been searching the rooms upstairs. That will make Uncle Jasper curious. I have also left a copy of that poem on the floor.

MARY: Which poem?

SIMON: The one that started Uncle Jasper on the hunt. The ghost told it to me.

> My treasure's hidden in a chest
> Until it's found I cannot rest.
> It guards my house and in reverse
> My castle guards a wealthy purse.

We must hurry. As soon as Uncle finds that in my handwriting, he'll know that I know, and he'll try to catch me. So I have left another note in the passage, saying that I am going for the police.

MARY: Oh dear, oh dear. What shall we do?

SIMON: You must hide. The ghost and I will do the rest. There's on old suit of armour in the hall. [JASPER's *voice is heard calling* SIMON.] You must hide in it. Quick, he's coming. [MARY *goes off.*]

SIMON [*loudly*]: Yes, Uncle Jasper?

JASPER [*off stage*]: Where are you?

SIMON: Down here. [*He runs out as* JASPER *runs in, breathless.*]

JASPER: Where is that awful boy? He knows all. I must get rid of him before he can get to the police. [*Searches.*] Simon! Simon!

SIMON [*off stage*]: Yes, uncle?

JASPER: Come here, dear boy.

SIMON [*off stage*]: No—you come and catch me. [*The* GHOST *appears and, unobserved by* JASPER, *stands quietly in a corner.*]

JASPER: Right, you nasty, loathsome, evil, wicked boy—I'm coming. [*He runs out.* SIMON *appears at the other side of the stage.*]

SIMON: Uncle Jasper! [JASPER *roars in the distance and* SIMON *makes off. Then* JASPER *comes in on the other side.*]

JASPER: Where are you? He can't be far away. It's so dark here and it's getting darker—there's a storm coming. All the better, it will drown the screams! I'll see if he's in the cellars. [*He goes out.* SIMON *comes in on the other side.*]

SIMON: Uncle Jasper! Cooee! [*The stage is very dark and the race round begins.* SIMON, *chased by* JASPER, *rushes across the stage and disappears off the other side.* SIMON *reappears on the opposite side, and they continue like this for some time. The direction is varied sometimes and the chase is enlivened by flashes of lightning, by* SIMON *calling to his uncle, by the* GHOST *sneezing and* JASPER *bellowing. Finally* JASPER *enters alone and does not see the* GHOST.]

JASPER: Now if I creep along quietly I will catch up with him. [*The* GHOST *follows just behind him and then taps him on the shoulder.* JASPER *turns and screams. The* GHOST *hovers over him.*]

JASPER [*hoarsely*]: Help! [*The* GHOST *laughs*] Who are you?

GHOST: I'm your ghost.

JASPER [*weakly*]: But . . . but . . . I'm not dead.

GHOST: Not yet. [JASPER *shrieks.*] You have tried to kill your nephew and have poisoned your daughter. But then—she is not your daughter, is she?

JASPER [*in a panic*]: How did you know that?

GHOST: I know everything. You married Mary's mother after Mary's father died. Not only have you spent all the money that belongs to Simon, but also all the money that was left to Mary as well. You are too wicked to live. [*He threatens* JASPER.]

JASPER: Help! Oh spare me! I will give all the money back. I haven't spent it. It's hidden in the cellar at home.

GHOST: You're a liar. You must give yourself up to the police.

JASPER: Anything so long as you spare my life. [*A pause.*]

GHOST: Very well. Wait here. I will send Simon for the policeman. Wait here. [*The* GHOST *goes out. The storm meanwhile has passed and the stage is lighter.*]

JASPER: Is there no way out for me? Years and years in prison—no, I can't bear it. I must escape. [*He rushes out and his footsteps are heard disappearing into the distance. The* GHOST *returns.*]

GHOST: He's fled, has he? Well, I gave him a chance to make amends for all his evil. Now it's too late. His fate has overtaken him. [SIMON *and* MARY *come in.*]

MARY: Has he gone?

GHOST: Yes. I gave him the chance to face his punishment—Atchoo!—but he fled. He couldn't face a life in prison and he ran off, mad with fear. As he ran across the rickety bridge across the river, it gave way and he fell into the water.

SIMON: But Uncle Jasper can't swim.

GHOST: No—Atchoo!—he couldn't swim. Mary, you know he was not your real father, but your stepfather? So you need not feel so sorry. In any case, he would have had to spend a very long time in prison. [*The* GHOST *goes off.*]

SIMON: Now our troubles are over and we can settle down to look for the treasure. Now let me think about that poem . . .

MARY: Simon . . .

SIMON: Don't interrupt me, my dear, I'm thinking. "My treasure's hidden in a chest". Well, any old box would do . . .

MARY: But, Simon . . .

SIMON [*not hearing her*]: It guards my house. What can that mean?

MARY: But, Simon, I think I know where the treasure is.

SIMON [*suddenly coming out of his dream*]: *What* did you say?

MARY: I think I know where the treasure is. You know I was hiding in that old suit of armour? Well, it's all rusty outside, but when you get inside, it is different. There are lots of things stuck to the inside of the armour. I pulled one off and it was a *coin*. The poem did not mean a treasure chest but the chest part of the armour. And Simon, the armour was for the soldiers who guarded the castle. That explains "guards my house".

SIMON: Mary, how marvellous. You've found the treasure! There are at least six suits of armour in the castle—I've noticed them. Let's go and look. [*They move to the back of the stage.*] And now, Mary, we *can* get married. [*They kiss and go out. The* GHOST *reappears.*]

GHOST: The treasure's found, the happy pair
Can now get married without fear.
Evil is conquered, virtue blessed
And I at last can go to rest.

THE END

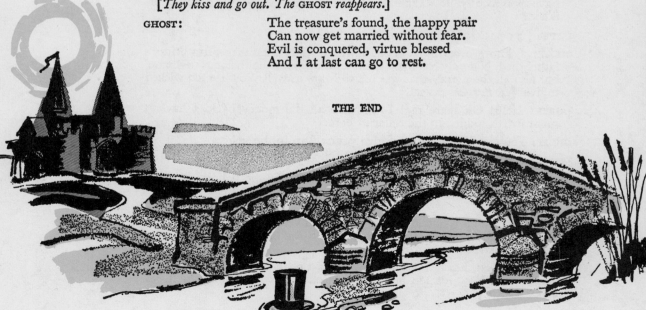